D1529288

Rev. Stephen H. Fritchman
(1902–1981)

FOR THE
SAKE
OF
CLARITY

FOR THE SAKE OF CLARITY

▼

Selected Sermons
and Addresses

STEPHEN H. FRITCHMAN

Compiled by the Fritchman Publication Committee
and edited by Betty Rottger and John Schaffer

PROMETHEUS BOOKS
Buffalo, New York

Material quoted from "The Luminous Promise" by Martin Luther King, Jr., in the *Progressive*, December 1962, found in Fritchman's essay "All Men Held as Slaves: The Centenary of the Emancipation Proclamation," pages 166–75, is reprinted by permission of the *Progressive*. Quotations from John Gerassi cited in Fritchman's essay "The Colossus of the North: The United States in Latin America Today," pages 260–68, are from *The Great Fear: The Reconquest of Latin America by Latin Americans*, published by Macmillan, 1963.

Published December 1992 by Prometheus Books

97 96 95 94 93   5 4 3 2 1

Library of Congress Cataloging-in-Publication Data

Fritchman, Stephen H. (Stephen Hole), 1902–81
  For the sake of clarity : selected sermons and addresses by Stephen H. Fritchman ; compiled and assembled by the Fritchman Publication Committee and edited by Betty Rottger and John Schaffer.
      p.   cm.
  Includes bibliographical references.
  ISBN 0-87975-784-1 (alk. paper)
    1. Unitarian Universalist churches—Sermons. 2. Sermons, American.
I. Rottger, Betty. II. Schaffer, John. III. Fritchman Publication Committee.
IV. Title.
BX9843.F758F67   1993
252'.09132—dc20   92-34551
                                                        CIP

Printed in the United States of America on acid-free paper.

Grateful thanks to the following for publication donations:

Dr. Elaine Allen
James and Pat Allen
Hugh and Emalena
Anderson
Jerry Atinsky
Dr. and Mrs. S. W.
Balkin
Elizabeth Baskerville
Jane Benedict
Darrell Berger
Ruth A. Bishop
Harriet and Paul Blue
Dr. Richard F. Boeke
Blase Bonpane
Carl V. Bretz
Jackson Browne
Rev. R. W. Brownlie
Miriam Camp
Nick Cardell, Jr.
Norene M. Charnofsky
Karlak Chew
Mrs. Katharine Cole
Bessie Cooper
Jeff and Hope Corey
Edward and Marilyn
Couture
Sylvia E. Crane
Richard L. Criley
Rev. Robert T. Dich
Roger Dittman
Mark Drake
William B. Elconin
Rob Eller-Isaacs
Carol Bernstein Ferry
Dr. John Fordan
Ruth Forrest
Frances Fritchman
Harvey Furgatch
Augustine Gunn Gaims
Dr. Aron S. Gilmartin
William M. and Paula
Gordon
Jerry Hall
Mari S. Hata
Agnese N. Haury
Peter Hawley
Alfred J. N. Henriksen
Rev. David Herndon

Anne Hines
Jaco B. ten Hove
Joan W. Howarth
Dr. Morris Hudgins
Kenneth and Pearl
Hutchinson
Peter and Luisa Hyun
Ellen Johnson-Fay
Rev. Elizabeth S. Jones
Robert Koller
Rev. Violet A.
Kochendoerfer
Corliss Lamont
Rev. Marjorie N.
Leaming
Sandra Lee
Leah London
Mark and Susannah
Lustica
Muriel Lustica
Shirley Magidson
Rev. William Main
Rev. John Marsh
Charles N. Mason, Jr.
Dr. and Mrs. Howard
Matson
John T. McTernan
Alexander Meek, Jr.
Melbourne Unitarian
Peace Memorial
Church
Rev. Ralph Mero
W. Richard Meyers
Ronald A. Myers
David and Gladys
Nielsen
Jeannette Orel
Carol and Thomas
Owen-Towle
Edgar and Phyllis Peara
Dr. and Mrs. Robert
Peck
Sylvia Pepper
Martin Pimsler
Paul and Phyllis Prickett
John Randolph
Rev. Peter T.
Richardson

Ramona Ripston
Samuel and Sylvia
Rosenwein
Betty Rottger
Nancy E. Ruhl
John B. Rusch
Ethel M. Sanjines
Rev. Paul Sawyer
John Schaffer
Jerome Schnitzer
Pete and Toshi Seeger
Stanley K. Sheinbaum
Miriam Sherman
Rev. Steve Shick
Frieda Canrel Siegel
Florence M. Sloat
Laura Wooley Smith
Elaine Smitham
Dr. Dorothy T. Spoerl
Ronald Spriesterback
Max Stern
Mary Stoddard
Eugene R. Stone
Jane and Marvin Sure
Carol Anne Tavris
Sally Alice Thompson
Harry A. Thor
Adele Towbin
Helen Travis
Cleo Trumbo
Unitarian Assoc. of
Tacoma
Rev. David Usher
Elna Vandergoot
Richard F. incent
Eleanor and Murry
Wagner
Lowell and Martha
Wayne
Rev. Alice Blair Wesley
Dr. Farley W.
Wheelwright
Rev. Bets Wienecke
Ned Wight
Frank Wilkinson
Katherine H. Winthrop

Acknowledgments

We acknowledge with deep gratitude those who assisted in the tedious job of reading the galleys. Thank you Kenneth Brown, Bessie Cooper, Alice and Mike Dudish, Patricia Ingalls, Pauline and Malita Johnson, Thompson O'Sullivan, Georgia Petrie, and Gene Stone.

Contents

Unless otherwise noted, talks included in this volume were given at the First Unitarian Church of Los Angeles, where Rev. Fritchman served as minister from 1948 to 1969 and was then minister emeritus until his death in 1981.

The material in this book is in chronological order within the five chapters, except for the first address, "For the Sake of Clarity," and the addresses on Thomas Jefferson. In certain cases records do not reveal complete dates.

Part I: Religion

Part II: Our Society

Part III: Government

Part IV: The Human Condition

Part V: Biographical Sketches

Introduction
Norman Corwin

It is time to reject the oft-repeated canard that nobody reads sermons any more. It depends on who wrote them.

—Stephen H. Fritchman

Steve Fritchman was descended in a straight line from incontestable giants of letters and ministry—Ralph Waldo Emerson and his neighbor Thoreau, and the great Unitarian heavyweights William Ellery Channing and Theodore Parker, and before them, generous cross-fertilizations of Daniel, Jeremiah, Jesus, Socrates, Voltaire, Tom Paine, Jefferson, and after them, Schweitzer and Gandhi.

He had a keen mind and he spoke it. And lived it. Few of us either in and out of religion are as widely read. The collected sermons and statements in this volume, representing only part of his output, amount to an informal seminar in history, ethics, politics, secular humanism, labor relations, national and world affairs, and, from top to bottom, just plain common sense, mostly expressed with clarity, vigor, bite, charm, and humor.

He was much more than a person speaking from a pulpit in a comfortable church. In a bitter East Boston winter he walked a picket line to support underpaid workers whose job was making Christmas tree lights. ("Wages are still, as in Paul's day, a religious matter, because they involve human rights and happiness.") He was fired as editor of a religious house organ "for staying anti-fascist too long after the war and attacking the Truman Doctrine in Greece and Turkey.") He raised funds for anti-Franco Spanish refugees in southern France. He stood up against the House Un-American Activities Committee, telling them to their faces, "We in the church have no tradition of docile conformity to other men's statements of loyalty and sound patriotism. If this committee should succeed in subpoenaing the ministers of this country and intimidating them, both American democracy and unfettered religion will vanish. I wish to have no part in such a disaster and I shall do all I can to prevent it." No matter how inconvenient, unpopular, or risk-taking it was for him to seek the truth in anything bearing on freedom of thought or conscience, or affecting the human condition, Steve believed, as the Talmud does (and as he quoted in one of his sermons) that the search for truth is itself a religious quest. He acted consistently and persistently on that belief. "There can be no veneration for spiritual dignity, for private insight of mind and conscience, that is indifferent to the accompanying problem of sharing discovered truth or moral judgment. Today a book publisher can be a greater servant of truth than a cardinal. . . . All truth, from the prophet's tongue in the sanctuary of religion, or from the laboratory of the scientist, waits on communication."

Although he never assumed the mantle of a prophet, it turns out that he was one. Thirty years ahead, he foreshadowed the Rodney King phenomenon: ". . . all-white juries exonerating policemen are no answer to a community's need for security against sadism in uniform." In 1955 he foresaw a cult of antirationalism, of the idealization of lawbreakers, of the spreading influence of television violence and films of the Rambo type: "It is not sufficient today that we admit the existence of an increasing amount of violence of all kinds in our daily lives. . . . It is necessary to see behind this prairie fire of violence the effort to capture *consent* (his italics) for violence to give it status to domesticate it. . . . Shakespeare somewhere suggests that the dyer's arm becomes the color of his vat. Walt Whitman speaks of a child that goes forth each day becoming what it sees."

In 1962 he warned against abuses in commerce and industry that have steadily compounded since then: ". . . we are poisoned in our supermarkets by preservatives and adulterants in our half-filled boxes of food, and imperiled on the highways by motorcars far from adequate in design to withstand the stress of modern traffic."

In 1962, speaking on "Our Bad Conscience About Panama," he warned, "There is danger of an American-engineered coup . . . a bloodbath that could result from a mood of desperation." In 1967, eight years before we pulled out of Vietnam, he wrote, "The political fact (is) that we cannot win the war militarily in Vietnam; that massive power alone cannot bring victory. It can kill—it cannot win." He proposed immediate unilateral withdrawal of U.S. forces because "our wholesale destructiveness . . . is supported by no persuasive reasons for remaining." Had Steve and others of like mind been listened to, the lives of thousands of Americans and tens of thousands of Vietnamese would have been spared.

In 1976, well before the so-called Year of the Woman, in a passage concerning "compassion and concern of man for man," he added parenthetically, "I use the term *man* generically, meanwhile genuflecting reverently toward Susan B. Anthony and Gloria Steinem!"

He was ahead of his time also in awareness of the problems of older people. In 1973 he wrote, "I am weary indeed, after nearly half a century in the ministry and teaching professions, of older Americans being treated as nonpersons, as sort of plastic people. . . . I do not accept the official government figure of age sixty-five as proof positive that one must retire. That is one of the most absurd and arbitrary numbers ever drawn out of a bag. . . . I rejoiced when the eighteen-year-olds got the right to vote. Now I am equally concerned that eighty-year-olds *use the vote.*"

But Rev. Stephen H. Fritchman was more than a prophet. He did not go around warning and preaching doom, for there was much too much to keep busy with in his own here and now. High on the agenda for him was what he perceived to be the day-to-day obligation of religion: "The church or temple must assume some responsibility for cleansing our culture of its most deforming sins, or become an accomplice in their perpetuation." By deforming sins he did not mean bingo, or X-rated movies, or the ordinary run of petty or grand crime, but ethical apathy, ecclesiastical fascism, political eunuchism, and what he called "museum guards of artifacts and tribal sacerdotal gear."

In a speech delivered as he was nearing the end of his service in the ministry, he said, "Whatever my misdemeanors, I never slipped on the absurdity that politics, economics, and religion must never mix. I wish to make it clear that I am still doing my homework as I stagger into retirement." But he never staggered. He walked as he preached, steady and firm. He had time for pleasures and amenities, time to laugh, time to enjoy music, time to see movies and watch the tube and listen to radio. In a letter commenting on his credentials as a fan of S. J. Perelman, whom he read in the *New Yorker*, he wrote, "I have taken the *New Yorker* since it first began, when I was a theological student, and have never missed a year since."

What this remarkable minister once wrote of Dr. Linus Pauling, whom he honored, and who several times was a guest in Fritchman's pulpit in Los Angeles, could without alteration be said of Steve himself: "There is so much to understand about (him): his immense courage, his willingness to join in necessary confrontations, his decades of teaching students how to study and think for themselves in and out of the college classroom, his sense of social responsibility to his fellowmen and women."

The ministry is not famous for producing heroes, but in my book —and certainly in this one—I believe Steve Fritchman ranks with the very best to be found in the Pantheon.

On the Consolidation of the Unitarian and Universalist Association

During his ministry at First Church Rev. Fritchman attended the Organizing Convention of the Unitarian-Universalist Association [UUA] in Boston, where on May 11, 1961 at 11:00 A.M. the formal consolidation of the American Unitarian Association and the Universalist Church of America was achieved. Almost 2,000 delegates voted, and followed the consolidation action with the election of Dr. Dana McLean Greeley as president of the new denomination. Parish plebiscites held in 1959 and 1960 throughout the United States and Canada indicated that 91 percent of the Unitarians wanted this action and 79 percent of the Universalists felt likewise. There were not more than a dozen dissenting voices at the hour of final action.

The consolidated organization numbered 189,000, of which 118,000 were Unitarians and 71,000 Universalists. In addition, 86,000 children were attending church schools in the merged body.

The above statement is excerpted from the introduction to Rev. Fritchman's report to his Los Angeles congregation on May 28, 1961, in which he expressed extreme displeasure and disappointment at "the apathy of religious liberals in large numbers at a conference dedicated to magnificent principles and ideals."

He concluded his report with a suggestion and prophet-like warning: "The Unitarian-Universalist Association has made a good start, for all the handicaps of the merger process and the first convention. We can become a great and strong liberal movement, but we will achieve this end only by exercising, by taking off the ecclesiastical fat in our local churches and fellowships. I recommend some parish calisthenics for the next twelve months, starting on West Eighth Street. There is not all the time in the world. The historic process has been known to lose its temper at slothful churchmen. Popes have learned it; so should Unitarian-Universalists!"

Reply to Doctoral Degree Award
Presented by the Starr King School for the Ministry in San Rafael, California
May 21, 1967

President Bartlett, members of the board, faculty and student body of Starr King School, and friends:

It is a profoundly satisfying psychic experience to have the handle used by Unitarian congregations toward me for over thirty-seven years made legitimate. I feel I am a far more educated man than I was this morning in Los Angeles. The traumatic effect upon our members will come next Sunday when I appear in this resplendent plumage. But that is their problem to handle with maturity, not yours.

President Bartlett indicated clearly that all three of us were to discuss our plans for the future, not the past. None of the agendas, no retreads, no rebuilt engines of faith or good works, none of Marshall McLuhan's rear-view mirror interpretations of the world. In speaking of the new academic wings I would receive today, he indicated that he expected more sustained flight and higher altitudes than I had previously attained. But I am no Icarus, no Leonardo, not even good apple-pie-American Orville Wright. I am a prop-flight man in the jet age and know it. He indicated on the telephone that the honored candidates should omit all apostrophes to their admitted merits of yesterday and get on to projects pending.

The implication was far from subtle: What, man, do you propose to do now, in this age of medicare, social security, and fat-free diets, to rebuild the Garden of Eden?

What new enterprises beckon me this afternoon? There are many. I never shared the Frothingham syndrome. He, you may recall, was the eminent minister of Dr. Channing's Church in Boston over a century

17

ago, who found the agitational sermons of Theodore Parker exceedingly disturbing, and, on occasion, complained to one of his fellow clergymen: "What on earth bothers Theodore so much in a world so nearly perfect?"

I will suggest four concerns which will occupy my attention:

First, in the personal area of human relations. I speak of the enormous misery of multiple divorce, the consecutive polygamy we try to rationalize as the death of male chauvinism and the birth of freedom. We are faced with a sexual pluralism which may bring more satisfaction than the present marital conventions, which are honored as much in the breach as in the performance.

Second, there is the utterly unsolved problem of the aging men and women who live longer, but at the end of their lives are faced with the terror of a medieval ethic toward the senile, the cruelly forgotten who endure mortal diseases from which no physician dares release them. If we Unitarians truly cherish and reverence life, we are sadly delinquent in finding some form of controlled euthanasia that can avoid both the perils of genocide and the murder of the innocent in the name of social welfare and eugenics. One thing I know, that the coming generation of ministers must exhibit more compassion and intelligence toward aiding those who truly wish to die than my colleagues and myself have yet been able to show.

But there are two other sources of greater scope than these two matters I have just mentioned. As Dr. Robert McAffe Brown courageously said last week in Oregon: "The beats and the hippies have surpassed the last several generations of Christians in practicing the love ethic . . . which the church has preached but left to die on the vine." I am certain my task, from here on in, is to make *agape* far more a fact of experience and not just something relegated to pulpit rhetoric. The ethic of love in personal relationships is so revolutionary to the older generation that they are certain something strangely un-American is going on. Young men and women, without the use of a Christian myth, and more times than not, using no psychedelic chemicals, advocate the end of wars, the sharing of personal property, the abolition of capital punishment, the pinning of flowers on policemen's jackets, and above all else, the exhibition of affection toward one another. I am not being frivolous. In a world of fantastic hate and pathological fear, I want to associate myself with every boy and girl, every man and woman who has taken tenderness and love to heart, and chosen to bypass the adoration of the Golden Calf and all its genuflecting worshippers. They do not reject capitalism's cornucopia of plenty as Marxists cursing Wall Street, but as human beings unimpressed with a world drowning in consumer's goods—and bereft of joy.

I rejoice that my friend, Joan Baez, can, with her magic of integrity, inflame millions of her fellow mortals to practice charity and to love peace, wholesale and retail, without denaturing the product or poisoning it with built-in obsolescence. She is worth more than a house of bishops or a college of cardinals.

My final and most urgent project is to make social justice and equality prevail in spite of everything that the sons of Belial undertake. Arnold Toynbee fears that America is becoming the new Roman Imperium— more fearful than that of the ancient Caesars. There is a new American generation, fortunately, who reject this lust for empire even with the fringe benefits and pensions at fifty-five. Half of our population is under twenty-five years of age and they are not terrorized by the painted Herods of communism. More important, these young people are not impressed by the compromises of aging revolutionaries or the tardy half-measures of the liberals. I stand before you ashamed of the crimes committed in these latter years by those who use the word "liberal" with such pride. I remember, for example, the betrayal of Mossadegh, Arbenz, and Vargas. I am losing faith with the liberal who surrenders when the noonday sun grows hot over the battleground. Neither Arthur Schlesinger, Jr., nor Hubert Humphrey can save us from fifty years of liberal compromises.

I propose, in my remaining years, by grace of a humanistic providence and a so-far rugged metabolism, to be a radical. I want to catch up with the secular revolutionaries, at home and abroad, who are captive neither to liberal illusions nor to payroll of the CIA. There is room in our ministry, and in our growing laity for men and women stripped clean of rhetoric and nonsense.

I do believe the age of the chameleon liberal is fading fast. Organized justice, an occasional impeachment, parliamentary flexibility, recognition of the new power groups of the disinherited, a militant church—these are what I find on the agenda for tomorrow, and I rejoice.

Like many of you, I grow weary of the eternal dialogue, the Unitarian Decathlon, the words without end or substance. I look to those in the ghettos and the mountains, the Asian rice paddies and the Austrian mines to teach me the radical disciplines. I am persuaded that promises are overripe from repetition; that only deeds, swift and thorough and born of love, can save us. May I be spared participation in the treasons of the intellectuals.

Presentation of the Holmes-Weatherly
Award to Dr. Fritchman
1969

On July 18, 1969, at the closing plenary session of the Eighth Annual Assembly of the UUA in Boston, Rev. Brooks Walker read the following as he presented Dr. Fritchman with the Holmes-Weatherly Award given each year for outstanding service in the field of socially responsible religious involvement.

*　　*　　*

Stephen Hole Fritchman, in making the John Haynes Holmes-Arthur L. Weatherly Award for 1969, we have no intention of providing you with an epitaph for a gravestone or even the material for another honorary D.D. We want rather to recognize you for the man that you are: humanitarian, spokesman for the oppressed, and minister to a congregation of the militantly concerned. You have stood firm when showered with epithets. Now, we beg of you, stand still while we tell you what you mean to us, your fellow liberals.

You, Stephen Fritchman, have consistently offered moral sustenance to your friends and parishioners even when beleaguered by detractors and besieged by opponents. When other men have retreated into craven silences, you have spoken with a clear, courageous voice, happily free from the clichés of sodden rhetoric, eloquent in the strength of tested convictions, and secure in the sense of your own identity. Even those who may have considered your politics disturbing have admired the clear character of your conscience. You have never equivocated. You have refused always to temporize. And you have habitually stated your convictions with candor.

To some this has been infuriating, to others frustrating, to many liberating, but no man can claim to have encountered you with indifference. Your deep and driving passion for economic, social, and political justice for the chained and the unchained, the black, the red, the yellow, the white, and the brown men of this broken and splintered planet has been repeatedly translated into concrete, specific action. You have seen men as potentially one, bound up in a universalism of brotherhood unbroken by prejudice, exploitation, or oppression.

Stephen Hole Fritchman, it is for that vision and your willingness to act on it that we honor you today. May the blessings and the spirits of John Haynes Holmes and Arthur L. Weatherly be on your head and in your heart!

Dr. Fritchman's Message to Friends Attending His Tribute Dinner
(at the Sheraton West Hotel)
September 20, 1969

As I anticipate being moved next January 1st in the First Unitarian Church hierarchy from minister to minister-emeritus, my deepest desire is that the shared venture of our church and community may continue with accelerated effort. Some of you may be Essenes or Ebionites (without knowing it) laboring to end the oppression of mankind in this present time. May your tribe increase as you seek to stem the pillage of the earth and the dehumanization of men and women!

The struggle for justice and peace, for freedom of mind and inviolability of conscience must not cease if we care for ourselves and others. The threat of a police state is no chimera of paranoid minds. Violence replaces reason, and many (not you!) retreat from the essential involvement required for doing what needs to be done.

Tonight I want to thank all of you who allowed me to be a part of your collective efforts these past twenty-one-and-a-half years. This dinner really is a salute to several thousand members and friends who have shared in a host of battles against apathy and mindlessness . . . and worse. It has been a magnificent experience to be a part of many victories, as well as some defeats. It has been a privilege, beyond words to express, to have shared in those struggles. No minister in our land ever had more supportive members and friends at his side. House Committees with pink subpoenas vastly underestimated Los Angeles Unitarians in the fifties. I am a very fortunate man—and I know it. Tonight I am uninhibited in expressing my profound gratitude that so many of you nudged me on those occasions when I seemed not to see the target. Praise be for friends with tough agendas, uncompromisingly presented when most needed. Even Amos of Tekoa had no such luck.

We must continue to share a vision of a world where we shall live at peace with one another and with nature. I feel that all of us must, from now on, abandon any world of fantasy and become a part of the world of reverberating fact. We must replace syndromes of hate with syndromes of love, even as we decide "which side we are on." You may be sure that as long as I am ambulatory and conscious, I shall share with you in attending to the unfinished business of the world. Peace!

Part One

Religion

For the Sake of Clarity:
An Address on What Unitarians
Are *Not*—and What They Are
April 22, 1951

The Unitarian Church is one of America's smallest religious denominations. Any religious society of 78,000 members in a nation of 150 million people is perpetually faced with the need for definition. Older members in this church may feel it is a reiteration of the commonplace, but as minister I must say over and over what Unitarians are *not*, because there are few non-Unitarian sources today that give a fair, objective, just report on the Unitarians—certainly not the publications that reach the masses of Americans, certainly not the orthodox pulpit spokesmen who still find us a useful scapegoat to send sin-laden into the wilderness.

The *Encyclopedia Britannica* has a fair and just description of us. The National Council of Churches, in its January Information Bulletin that goes to readers of all Protestant denominations, had a very objective review of my book of radio talks, *Unitarianism Today*, as a counterstatement to a review of recent books on Christian orthodoxy in America today. But the examples are few. You and I must still be our own interpreters. We would gladly, as Unitarians, prefer to let our deeds be our best public relations—such deeds as a Unitarian Service Committee's medical mission to Asia, now in process of formation; an Ormsby Village for Youth, now shaping up in the Topanga Canyon area; a support of peaceful negotiations in Korea as sent to President Truman by a unanimous vote of Unitarian and Universalist ministers meeting in Phoenix last Wednesday; a modernization of public worship as seen in our own services under Mr. Maury and Mr. Robinson each week, or in our churches in Madison, Wisconsin, or at the Charles Street Meet-

27

ing House in Boston—because these examples say what Unitarians are and are *not.*

Before I turn to a positive statement of Unitarianism—a message I shared in Phoenix and Palo Alto this past week—let me say briefly what Unitarianism is *not.*

First, I would begin by saying for the benefit of our visitors and our more recent members that, contrary to irresponsible and even malicious sources, the charge that the Unitarian Church is a "Communist Church" is too absurd to call for comment, were these not days of fantastic beliefs about almost everybody. In Phoenix this past week presumably adult school officials exhorted some of their teachers not to attend the dedication services of the new Unitarian Church because it was a "Communist Church." There is hardly a minister in our fellowship who does not almost daily find this careless slander voiced in his presence. In more normal times it would be passed over. I wish to make one or two comments, and I hope and feel the matter may then be dismissed for a long time to come. Those of us who find charges of communism in almost every news story, almost every radio broadcast, and in hundreds of private conversations should be able to enjoy one place of meeting where this obsession need not be raised at the end of every other sentence.

The Unitarian Church, now as always, belongs to no one political party and has no political test for membership or association. The number of Communist Unitarians in the United States is probably no more than the fingers and toes of one man, though this is a matter of wild speculation even at that. In my twenty-two years as a Unitarian minister exactly two Unitarian laymen have told me (I might say, with dignity and pride) that they were members of the Communist party. There are doubtless others, and if they are as mature, un-neurotic, and devoted workers as these two, I would say that they are an asset to any church they choose to adorn.

But this census taking that goes on today, as a major occupation of so many people, is not the point. Senator Jack Tenney knows this is not the point! His objection, and that of many who share his outlook, is the fact that Unitarians, like many liberal Baptists and Episcopalians and other church people, have a highly serious concern about social progress and attempt to put their ideals into practice whenever it seems possible. One way to diminish this moral dedication, Senator Tenney and his friends believe, is to impute that all who work for these reforms are members of the party of Stalin and Mao Tse-Tung; enough people will believe this charge if it is said often enough and in the right places. Unitarians have long agitated for an end to lynching, either in cotton fields or in courtrooms. Unitarians have long labored for civil rights and the end of slums, and have rejoiced in the fellowship of all who shared in these campaigns, be they Republicans or Communists. (To the credit of both of these parties, there have been members of both groups in most of these American struggles.) This the slanderers know well, but their hope is to detach and immobilize the Republican and the Unitarian by the repeated charge of association with the left-wing members of the campaign for new legislation, and thereby defeat it.

While the Unitarian is not a Communist in any but the rarest of cases, it is to his everlasting glory that he has not retreated in many of these battles for a finer America and a more united world when this brutal device of "guilt by association" has been employed. I thank whatever gods there be, and even more thank the men and women themselves that there are ministers and laymen in our Unitarian churches in scores of cities who are not put to flight by the shrill cry of the investigator and the editor, in their search for scalps. The long five-year moratorium on social advance, noted by Carey McWilliams here in this pulpit three weeks ago, would become permanent if all of us with liberal ideals fled under these unrelenting efforts of those so frankly opposed to the doctrine of progress, that doctrine which stiffens our faith like a spinal column.

If current administrations in city, state, or federal government never felt the critical word from pulpit or pew, we might as well never have won the struggle to disestablish the church from the state in the days of Thomas Jefferson. There is nothing more American than a church free to speak its mind, knowing that no archbishop appointed by a prime minister can discipline its minister. We are not lovers of a state church, formal or informal.

Since I do not intend to reiterate these sentiments every Sunday (you will be happy to hear), I should add what would not be necessary in less choleric times, namely the statement that we will have no peace or security in the world until we realize that Communists are no more monsters than ourselves. They are not griffins, or manticores, or unicorns. They are men and women with our virtues and frailties. The caricature of the Communist in Mr. Hearst's *Examiner* is no more just than the Soviet cartoons of capitalists in their magazine *Crocodile*. I learned at Union Seminary twenty-four years ago that there is such a reality as the moral, adult Communist who thinks there is much wisdom in the analysis of a Marx or a Lenin, and who believes his theory would solve many of the problems of distribution of goods and culture that confront people in every land. I have read English Marxists like Bernal and French Marxists like Joliot-Curie, and would report that we cannot solve the issues of war and peace by simply refusing these men visas, or pressing for their removal from office, as has been done. We must meet their minds and reasoning head on and come up with better answers. This calls for far more than frenetic invective—and it is the business of a liberal church to say so, even though it may not be thanked for doing so until a better day dawns.

While practically all Unitarians are not Communists, they refuse to make a gospel of anticommunism because they recognize that however different the answers, Communists and Unitarians are both working on the same problems of aiding man in his quest for a better life—which in both cases is a better thing than dismissing the issue and feathering one's own nest—and the devil take the hindmost.

Secondly, Unitarians are not mystics, in the usual definition of the term. To be sure, James Martineau of England and William Ellery Channing of America, and their spiritual heirs and successors would use some of the vocabulary of the mystic, but it is a fair statement that even among the most theistic believers, even among those who militantly describe themselves as "Unitarian Christians," today there is a healthy pragmatism, an insistence that the spiritual life is measured more by its fruits than by its blossoms, more by its reconstructed personalities than by its evocation of states of supernatural illumination. The value of reflection, of concentration of mind, of openness to the unconscious, of unpredictable intuition is not denied by theist or humanist Unitarian, for these are all methods of growth and progress for us as persons, sentient and sensitive. But we are not mystics of the kind so often found, who prefer prayer to practice, rituals to reform, apathy to action.

If we are mystics, we are the rare kind, that kind Emerson preferred when he said, "The open secret of the universe calls for heroism." It was Emerson who wrote somewhat bitterly in 1845, "After this generation one would say mysticism should go out of fashion for a long time."

We Unitarians are suspicious of people who find their mystic inspirations only in ancient seers, who see no new saints, who prefer the trance and ecstasy to the urgent act of mercy at one's own doorstep. We Unitarians find Jesus' parable of the Good Samaritan more convincing than the words ascribed to Jesus by the Gospel of John, so spiritualized and philosophical, so remote from the publicans and sinners, the fishermen and the tax gatherers who heard him gladly.

Let me repeat: Unitarians are not mystics, as a rule, but they are not necessarily extroverts, always hammering and pounding the timbers of a new world order—or a new city administration. They believe also in privacy, quiet, rest, the influx of suggestion and stimulation. One of the most repeated slanders is that Unitarians are coldly intellectual—given to books and polysyllabic sermons. But even these guilty ones, overrun with words and talk, are shy about communion and candles. Republican or socialist, Harvard-taught or grade-school taught, Unitarians bend the knee with difficulty, tell beads poorly, find the pontificating clergyman a bore.

We have seen mysticism used as a retreat from cooperative living, as a blind to rational judgment and criticism, and the supernatural illumination be proved a psychic delusion. Mysticism has been too often an ivory tower for the neurotic and the maladjusted, whose recovery was not improved but aggravated by the promises of vision and revelation. Let me put it this way: We do not dismiss the mystic with condescension; rather, we say we prefer other methods of religious living. We prefer the discussion to the expected influx of power through prayer; we prefer history and biography and science to the reported findings of the mystics, who report words are impossible to find to describe the satisfactions of the soul found in the beatific vision.

It is the sober conviction of most Unitarians that what is richest and finest in a mature religion, free of magic and superstition, can be communicated from person to person, and whether we use traditional words or new ones, we Unitarians in Boston or Los Angeles expect man to be larger, not smaller, because of his religion. The image of man groveling before a cosmic potentate and confessing his impotence and asking for heavenly insight seems a grotesque contradiction to us.

William Sullivan was a devoted Unitarian mystic, a refugee from Roman Catholicism, who honored our New York church for several years. But he was a rarity and few followed his mystical conclusions, though they cherished him as a man and a leader. He never quite detached himself from the two worlds of the orthodox Christian. It takes great courage for a son of Rome to decide to walk henceforth entirely on the firm earth unaided.

Thirdly, Unitarians are not twentieth-century hedonists. We are not willing to say that our ultimate goal is personal gratification of one's appetites, with one's neighbor a poor second in one's plans. In fact, we deny that the calculated effort to make us envious of the sybarite is acceptable to the thoughtful American. It is my private view that an overwhelming number of church members in this country follow their various creeds and preachers not because they agree with their Apostles' Creeds or Westminster Confessions or Lessons from Science and Health, but because they blunderingly and gropingly resent the seven-day-a-week campaign, fabulously financed, to make them comfortable at any price—gentlemen and ladies of dubious distinction—cradled in Cadillacs, gowned and garmented by Adrian and Kuppenheimer. The instinctive feeling of being our brother's keeper irresistibly comes out. Man is too good to be damned as a mere consumer. For all of our paradise of plumbing and the deep freeze, we still want our minds to be more than gadget-managers. We want the pleasure of ideas, shared by men and women, secure but also equal.

While we Unitarians are a materialist people—that is, not disembodied spirits—we try to practice a holy materialism where things are not in the saddle to ride mankind, but subordinate, the servants of man.

The Unitarian knows that in a comfort-loving America the idealist, the thinker, and the artist is only suffered, not encouraged, and he insists upon rejecting the mad passion for the latest fashion and the newest trinket as the deception it is—a substitution of the second best for the best—the best thing, as it always has been, the life of the spirit and the mind. In spite of his boasted thirteen million dollar profit in 1950, we Unitarians are not persuaded of the wisdom of Mr. Earl Puckett, the department store king quoted in *Time* magazine this week as saying to his store managers: "It is our job to make women unhappy with what they have." This slogan leads not to the peace of mind that passes all understanding, but to the psychiatrist's couch and the insane asylum. Until every child has a pair of shoes a year and a quart of milk a day, I'm for no talk against materialism, but when the Pucketts substitute saturating a few women with too much merchandise for giving all people the basic essentials, I say let the church speak out. We reach back two thousand years and remember one man who had no more property than he could carry on his back, saying "Beware of the mammon of unrighteousness. Life is more than bread and the body than raiment." Dives and the rich young man are examples of the horror of the accumulative instinct gone out of bounds; Mary, the woman at the well, Nathaniel, and Nicodemus, examples of those who preferred the riches of the mind and the satisfactions of fraternity to the acquisitiveness of the hedonist, bent on the endless quest of things.

These are a few things Unitarians are not, but often are said to be by different critics of our movement. I might list a few more:

- We are not Unity with its complete detour around the social needs of man.

- We are not Christian Scientists with their subjectivism and contempt for science.

- We are not Theosophists, Rosicrucians, or Vedantists—and I say this without prejudice. They may be right and we wrong, but we are not the same.

But let us proceed to a more positive statement of the Unitarian task today.

Remember Walt Whitman:

Underneath all, individuals,
I swear nothing is good to me now, that ignores individuals.
The American compact is altogether with individuals, . . .

The whole theory of the universe is directed unerringly to one
single individual—namely to you.

(*By Blue Ontario's Shore*)

Here is a creed fit to girdle the universe without exception. Today
we are coming to grips with the invulnerable integrity of the individual
in our concept of religion. We reject the idea of the "Mass Man." We
believe the Christian, Jewish, American dream has been rooted and has
grown to its present power in the freedom of the unfettered man, whose
mind has liberty, whose conscience is unbound.

The basic concept of religious liberty that began with Roger Williams, Tom Paine, and Thomas Jefferson is today under hammer blows
of attack. The Prophet Ezekiel refers to the Valley of Decision—we are
in that valley now! Either we build on the foundations laid by valiant
pioneers who honored religious toleration as fundamental to America,
or we succumb to ancient tyranny of prince and priest, dictating the
deadly uniformity of the docile believer, afraid to say "no," afraid to
say "I dissent."

We are today in a world which sets terms for any religious institution to meet, and the Unitarian is not exempt. We Unitarians will not
remain in this world unless we meet these terms, whatever our numbers
or our wealth or our prestige or our traditions. This is true for Catholic,
Jew, Unitarian, or any other organized religious society. We will be suffered only if we pull our weight. This is as inescapable as tides or the
law of gravity. Certain questions are being asked by history and by living millions. We all must answer them and nothing will prevent them
being asked and answered, by direction or by default. No test oaths,
nor loyalty pledges, nor resorts to witch hunts, nor reaffirmations of
orthodoxy will prevent them being faced. There is no escape; we are
in a Valley of Decision.

We Unitarians have a long and honorable tradition of religious liberty from before the Reformation with John Hus, with Servetus and
Socinus. We have declared the primacy of the searching mind, the priority of the sensitive conscience. Today we Unitarians stand with John
Biddle in England, with Francis David in Hungary, with Channing and
Parker in America, breaking centuries of orthodoxy, opening the Bible
to independent interpretations honoring no authority but that of human reason, defying the gospel of fear taught by popes and Protestants
alike, which terrified men with the threat of hellfire and excommunication.

For four centuries the Unitarian has built his altar to truth-seeking,
made his holy of holies the pursuit of brotherhood, and made his communion of saints the building of a city of love and justice. This is faith
enough—and to spare!

These are the questions the religious liberal—Unitarian or otherwise —in Los Angeles or Phoenix or London or Prague or Manila must answer if he expects to be allowed to preach and practice in the new world being born:

1. Do you accept the world Science presents to you, no matter what its variance with Revelation? Do you rejoice at each new frontier extended by Pasteur, Steinmetz, or Einstein? Do you stand up to cardinal or president or any others who bless science turned diabolical—the evil work of gasoline jelly, atomic bombs, and bacteriological warfare? Do you see the scientist as the friend of the church, the school, the service committee, the minister in his counseling? The church that cannot welcome our modern Galileos and Tycho Brahes is doomed; the scientist is here to stay.

2. Do you welcome, not resist, the demand of the peoples of the earth that master and slave theories of society be ended and full democracy be practiced here and now? No other issue so commands the attention of the earth's millions in this century. The Asian peoples, the African peoples, the forgotten men and women of the planet are coming into their own; the words of Israel's prophets are being fulfilled and no power or combination of powers on earth can hold back those who have discovered they are individual, human beings with rights and privileges—not only the right to eat, but the right to think; not only the right to work, but the right to rest; without fear of death or old age.

   Ralph Waldo Emerson in 1872 wrote: "One thing is certain—religions are obsolete when reforms do not proceed from them." I would add that the church that thinks of itself as a bulwark against change instead of a reforming force against established privilege ceases to have a future. The palace religions of Assyria and Babylon, Egypt and Cathay are one with Ninevah and Tyre—obscure subjects for scholarly research, while the creative and explosive ethics of Jesus and Socrates, Channing and Gandhi break social orders on the anvil of history. This church is part and parcel of an earthwide emancipation. No syllable from this pulpit should contradict this mighty movement.

3. Do you recognize the impact of the new knowledge on philosophy, the impact of naturalism on the ancient theologies, the passing of the tribal gods, national deities, the kings of heaven, and the mysteries of priestcraft that have kept men bound?

   A greater world dawns—where man leaves his craven fear behind, assumes his cosmic manhood, and rejoices in the talents of maturity. John Dewey and [Alfred North] Whitehead, Howard Salsam and Thomas Mann plow this ground of philosophy first turned by our elder Unitarian prophets—Emerson and Thoreau, Frothingham and Parker—men who loved the creative faculty, who saw new systems replacing Plato and Aquinas.

This church deals with our daily derelictions, our terrible betrayal of our better selves, our vulgar contempt for personality by gossip and careless morals by the shifting of responsibility to other shoulders, by the degradation of culture. But always above and behind such rebuking of our lower selves is the prime task, the archetypal obligation to give men a framework for their lives that reaches to the distant stars—a religious reference far beyond the cosmic guesses of our forefathers, so timid and restrained. We want the amphitheater of the myriad universes for our homes. Any theology that offers less is a contradiction of our faith in man. This pulpit, like the lens at Palomar, should reach to the celestial corners of all space.

4. Do you accept the new knowledge of man about himself—the end of the vulgar canard about "human nature being what it is"? This is the heresy of our time. In this church we provide a center for honest and courageous men and women where they may meet together and proclaim their faith that there is nothing wrong with human nature that a wider sharing of the earth's resources cannot repair. Children nurtured in homes where affection flourishes have no repressions to explode in adult life. Youths given education and needful employment do not turn to crime. Women given equality and love and work of significance do not slay their children, murder their husbands, or plunge over cliffs. Men devoting themselves to the creative work of building a good society as teachers, doctors, mechanics, or statesmen do not devote themselves or their nation's wealth to the destruction of cities and the death of thousands through atomic blasts.

Human nature, we Unitarians believe, when given half a chance does very well. The physical endowment of man is not an evil but a neutral instrument that can be used for the devil's own work or to prove man is but a little lower than the angels. Fear can transform us into beasts. Unleashed avarice can make us into magpies, gathering merchandise with an insane passion for accumulation—and missing out on the possibilities of a rich and fertile humanity. We know more about the nature of the child, more of the pitfalls in its nurture, more of the manmade obstacles to its happy maturity than ever before in the history of the race. The tragic and bitter cynicism of St. Paul and St. Augustine, of Niebuhr and Horton—about man's seeing the good and doing the evil—

is continued today because it permits a corrupted and decayed theory of power to remain unchallenged, while the bracing truth that man can perform the good he dreams of calls for a change of personnel in the throne rooms of our unfinished democracy. The day of the predatory cynic is ending!

We have a long tradition of trust in man of advocating progress onward and upward, by fits and starts, reversals and victories. The Unitarian remembers the interracial Church of the Strangers in England in 1630, remembers Theodore Parker's Brook Farm in 1845, the formation of the Unitarian Service Committee in 1939, and says, "Compassion and good will are stronger than hate and cringing fear."

We suffer no illusions about the task before us, we hold no false confidence that the summer soldiers will join our cause. But be the times stormy or benign, the liberal faith is rooted on principle and not whim, not on values that are traded in for social approbation of those in high authority. Let me recapitulate that there be no misunderstanding.

Unitarians are men and women of the free spirit. No party has us in its pocket, no dictator writes our creed, no monolithic power robs us of our native strength to say, "The King is wrong." We are a people braced by centuries of freedom, who love maturity and despise, as men despise the plague, all meek surrender to those in search of witches, or a world bereft of change. We cry with a Galilean revolutionary twenty centuries dead: "I came that ye might have life and have it more abundantly." This is our faith, our banner's strange device, our call to battle, and our hope. We are resolved to settle for nothing less than brotherhood itself.

How do Unitarians Think of Jesus?
"Unitarian Time"
Sunday, December 25, 1949

Yes, friends, this is "Unitarian Time." How do Unitarians think of Jesus? Do they think of him as God or as a man? Have liberals a right to celebrate Christmas with sincerity? This is Stephen Fritchman, minister of the First Unitarian Church of Los Angeles, giving the fourth talk in a series of thirteen on our Unitarian principles and program as a liberal church.

It is a special privilege on this Christmas morning to try to answer these questions, which so many people ask. Happily, Christmas for Christians and non-Christians alike is no time for theological disputation. It is an occasion for a celebration of a birthday—the birthday of Jesus—and by implication the birthday of all children. It is a day of sharing and friendship, good will, and the outstretched hand of understanding. We must admit it has been used by theologians and merchants for their own ends. For centuries, careless and sometimes even malicious men have used this great festival as an occasion to make liberal religion their whipping boy and say, "Unitarians don't believe in Jesus." They mean, of course, that Unitarians do not share many of the doctrines that have been built around the simple figure of the Jewish lad who was born in Palestine nineteen centuries ago, and who came to such a tragic end at the hand of Roman power twenty-seven years later. And they are right! But such an absurd statement—that Unitarians don't believe in Jesus—calls for a word or two of comment, especially on a day when several hundred thousands of Unitarians around the earth rejoice at his advent, along with millions of orthodox Christians and many of no religious faith at all.

Program aired on KABC Radio, Los Angeles.

So let me take a moment to say what Unitarians *do* believe about Jesus.

Unitarians believe profoundly in the historic Jesus, the son of Mary and Joseph, who became the leader of a group of bold disciples. We revere his teachings, known to us by fragments in the gospels of the New Testament.

We think of Jesus as a great teacher and prophet, steeped in the ethical traditions of Judaism and its penetrating insights regarding the primacy of human personality and its worth. We revere his memory and we seek to employ his teachings, which at so many points still seem shockingly advanced and radical.

And I might add, Unitarians and the pre-Unitarians, who were known by other names, have held this respect and admiration for Jesus for a long, long time. For example, we were in agreement with Pelagius, a saintly Irish monk, since the fifth century, who stood courageously before St. Augustine, the spokesman of orthodox Christianity, and said, "If I ought, I can." This took valor in a day when Augustine taught that man is a moral cripple and cannot act for himself freely. Pelagius denied the ancient idea of original sin, and his words, "If I ought, I can," echoed down the centuries and inspired a later Unitarian, Ralph Waldo Emerson, to write a line every American schoolboy learns: "When duty whispers lo, thou must, the youth replies, 'I can.' "

But this is Christmas day, and possibly the clearest thought of how Unitarians consider Jesus is to look at Christmas and its origin for a minute or two. For many years before the Christian church selected December 25 as the time to celebrate the birthday of [its] founder, other religious sects observed the winter solstice with feasting and ceremonies. The Jews had long observed the season of the winter solstice in nature as a time to commemorate Hanukkah, the Feast of Lights in honor of the Maccabean victory over the Greeks and Syrians when Jerusalem was recaptured and the lamps of the Temple lighted once more. But for all of the great traditions, for Unitarians the heavens and the gods of our forefathers cannot be our heavens and our gods. We have entered a new world, and we are helping to fashion a new religion, a more universal and inclusive faith for free minds. Unitarians find different meanings in holy days and festivals than did their forefathers.

The folklore of Christianity is but a part of the heritage we treasure and interpret to our children. The meanings we give to the Christmas legend are often at variance with many taught at this season of the year. Even at Christmas it would be a seven days' wonder if our churches throughout Los Angeles began to practice the ideals of Jesus, found in the episodes of the Good Samaritan, the Syrophoenician woman, and the woman taken in adultery. It is important to remember that it is the birthday of this man who consorted with publicans and sinners that occasions the decoration of our boulevards into regal highways fit for the triumphal entry of a Roman conqueror.

Christmas is a day when we remember a child obscurely born, Renaissance painters and Christmas card art notwithstanding—a child born in a dingy and malodorous stable, without benefit of physicians or medicine, but a child all the world today knows for his later significance as teacher and prophet. One thing I hope: that this child, so encumbered with fantasy and swaddled in fiction, will remind us of the value of every living child today, everywhere. Today, at this very hour, newborn children are crying in their mothers' arms, certain to suffer hardship and needless disaster because of our failure to place children high on our priorities as a people.

There is a cruel contradiction about the Christmas season. We honor a Bethlehem child none of us ever saw or knew—a Semitic youngster in a far-off land. Yet we fail, as a people richly able, to provide for the necessities of children born within our own city limits. No Herod pursues them; just poverty, hunger, and, in the case of many Jewish children, the curse of being Jewish in a non-Jewish world.

I am sure that it is not bad taste on Christmas Sunday to say, "Behold the child, be he yellow or brown or black or white, rich or poor— behold his promise and his unspent years." We can, by the lifting of our collective fingers, give him strong bones, clear eyes, a lighted mind, a buoyant hope. The impersonal god of history will show no sentiment; he will hold us accountable if we do less than our best to give these living children a chance to live out their lives to old age, without the madness of another world war or the deliberate baptism of superstition and manmade fears. Every child must be free to sing his carol without a contradiction, without fear in his heart. I love the Christmas season. I am addicted to pine cones and gay wrappings, yule logs, and caroling. I love to see children receiving and giving presents. I am no Scrooge or even a third cousin to Scrooge, but I abhor the church or the preacher or the layman who preaches eloquently about the Christ child of Bethlehem and forgets the Christ child of East Los Angeles.

This brings us face to face with the unspoken first principle of Christmas. It is not just a holy birthday; it is the birthday of Jesus, the birthday of a prophet. A prophet is a certain kind of saint, a man who presents to us, by precept and example, the infinite possibilities of human existence for all living people. He turns our world upside down. He shows no veneration for our sanctified shibboleths of selfishness. He does not make a god of property, of things. He salutes the man of goodwill wherever he finds him. Jesus was not great by virtue of a miraculous birth, but because he proved himself the prince of prophets, the boldest teacher of the commonplace of brotherhood.

We Unitarians try to do all we can to recover the clear voice of

Jesus, the preacher to the common people who, the Bible reports, heard him gladly. We cherish his few hundred reported words in the Sermon on the Mount and to his disciples as we do the wisdom of Socrates and the insights of Gautama Buddha. What greater reverence can there be than to welcome with willing ears a teacher's burden of conscience? On Christmas morning the Unitarians ask their friends everywhere to take Jesus with the greatest possible seriousness. We object to doctrines of his supernatural origin or his later transfiguration, obscuring the challenge of his life and teaching.

Unitarians remember that Jesus was given no halos by the first-century artists. Those came later, when his lips were still. We remember this is the birthday of a prophet, not simply the advent of a carpenter's son in Galilee, even less just a miracle of nature. We light our candles and festoon our trees and greet our friends with mistletoe and holly not because Jesus was born, but because he lived long enough to set a mighty thought in motion, with sufficient force to split kingdoms into fragments, to unseat monarchs, and to disturb the ordered teachings of a millennium.

The Christmas insight is many-sided, but it is not obscure nor difficult. Jesus, the prophet of the plain shepherds and publicans of Galilee and Tyre and Sidon, gave men a sense of their own dignity and promise, the kernel of truth that later blossomed as the democratic faith. "The Kingdom of God is within you." "Beware that the light that is within you be not darkness." "You are sons of God, and it doth not yet appear what you shall be." "Suffer the little children to come unto me and forbid them not, for such is the Kingdom of Heaven." "Cast not your pearls before swine." "If your right hand offend you, cut it off; it is better that you go through life maimed than that your whole body be filled with darkness." These are seeds brought to flower by Jefferson and Thomas Paine and Lincoln. This is a prophet, not a child, that we honor.

Man has not only immortal longings; he realizes them in time and space. Life is no delusion of freedom. We must not be confused by Renaissance painters or theologians. For the twentieth-century man it is the prophet's birthday that we celebrate. Unitarians, you see, take Jesus with tremendous earnestness. We resent his removal from the simple contact with publicans and sinners and his elevation to stained glass windows of great cathedrals. The windows are things of transcendent beauty. But the spirit of the man who walked over the hills of Galilee is obscured by them. Let my final word on Jesus this Christmas morning be that of a beloved American of a century ago, our Unitarian essayist, Ralph Waldo Emerson. He wrote in his Journal: "The history of Christ is the best document of the power of character which we have."

The world might well pause in its celebration and resolve to possess such character, to find its secret and multiply its power in a day when character is our greatest need.

Good morning and Merry Christmas!

Should the Church Stay Out of Politics?
"Unitarian Time"
Sunday, April 23, 1950

Good morning, friends. This is Stephen H. Fritchman, minister of the First Unitarian Church of Los Angeles, speaking on "Unitarian Time" in a series on Unitarian ideals in today's world. This morning I am suggesting a few answers to a question we hear very often: "Should the church stay out of politics?"

Of course we shall miss the issue entirely if we do not say a word or two about that word "politics." Since the answer most Unitarians in America would give is a "No, the church should not stay out," I ought to say that this morning I am not recommending that the church sponsor one particular party or stand for one particular candidate over against another candidate. Our liberal churches, on the whole, include members of several parties, and when it comes to election day, we may mark our ballot with considerable similarity or considerable diversity of opinion, as the case may be. Yet the answer to the question, "Should the church stay out of politics?" is "no," because we see politics as a moral struggle of man's corporate life, a life in which he hammers out what character he possesses. Political issues, to Unitarians, are very often ethical issues which involve the demolition or survival of our basic values: justice, equality, brotherhood, truth-seeking.

In the days of early Israel, and also of early Christianity, the issue I am discussing today would never even have arisen. It would then be a commonplace that religion affects all of life on the everyday level. When our present Unitarian minister in San Francisco, Mr. Harry Meserve,

Program aired on KGFJ Radio, Los Angeles.

said, as he did not long ago, "We have proclaimed that the whole of life is the business of religion," he was being true to a long tradition predating Unitarianism. He did not say "the whole of life excepting politics." He kenw his history of religion too well. He doubtless was remembering the words of Ecclesiastes, "The profit of the earth is for all," or the words of the prophet Amos, "Are ye not as the children of the Ethiopians unto me, O Children of Israel?" Mr. Meserve may have been thinking of the author of the Book of Acts in the New Testament saying,"God hath made of one blood all nations of men for to dwell on all the face of the earth."

One need be no scholar to see how "political" these sentiments are when seen in the context of their times. Any church that begins to preach such principles will find itself judging our entire economy critically because it so clearly does not share the profit of the earth with all inhabitants. Few churches yet act as if the Ethiopian is equal in the sight of God and man. We would not be in fearful danger of a third world war if we seriously practiced the teaching that God hath made of one blood all the nations of the earth.

It would be very easy today to remain right within the pages of the Bible to demonstrate the deep concern for political affairs which the authors of that ancient book strongly felt. And the politics they believed in was not always on lofty altitudes of racial equality and world peace. Sometimes the church of yesterday, in Biblical times, spoke of very homely political matters. In Leviticus we read, "Thou shalt have just weights and balances." The author of Proverbs stresses the point later, "A just weight and balance are the Lord's." Yet think of the overeager butchers and grocers during the centuries who have doubtless complained that such interference with prosaic business matters is political meddling by the church.

In Matthew's Gospel we find the words "Why stand ye here idle?" spoken to a group of men unemployed long after the morning hour when most work begins. They replied, you will recall, "No man has hired us." How modern it all sounds! Yet today a church that indicates a practical concern about unemployment, not only for a handful of men, but for five million Americans, is in danger of being called a meddler in politics.

One thinks of thousands of employers today with their eyes on a stockholders' report and a sales chart rather than their workers' mounting cost of living, and one remembers the words of Paul to the Colossians: "Masters, give unto your servants that which is just and equal." Yes, just wages are a political matter in our modern world, with government boards and trade unions and employers' associations all involved —but just wages are still, as in Paul's day, a religious matter too, because they involve human rights and happiness.

We Unitarians, like *many* Baptists, Methodists, Episcopalians, Jews, and Catholics, often find it necessary to say that these earthly matters of profits, wages, and unemployment are *both political and also religious concerns.* Henry Demarest Lloyd, an early social prophet in American religion, once put it very clearly when he said, "The social conscience sees that wherever man walks, there is the Holy Land." I am sure the Unitarians across the continents of the world today, and specifically in our Unitarian Church here in Los Angeles, would agree.

When Dr. Frederick May Eliot, president of the American Unitarian Association in Boston, Massachusetts, said at our national 1947 Unitarian Conference, "We propose to mobilize the full energy and resources of religious liberalism for the defense and extension of the democratic way of life in a world where the forces of tyranny are exploiting the discouragement of many," he was true to our long Unitarian heritage of religion mixing properly with politics. For Dr. Eliot, like Mr. Meserve in San Francisco whom I quoted earlier, knows that the democratic way of life is held and advanced throughout the world only by group effort—ardent, consecrated, and directed by moral principles—and that this is a political task. Group effort to alter our social life is one definition of politics. Today the word "politics" is given a shabby and often negative connotation by people who shun responsibility, who leave the reforming of man's corporate life to others. Hence we find politics being taken out of such a vacuum by racketeers, self-seeking and power-hungry persons eager to make a fast dollar and utterly indifferent to the human rights of which we have spoken this morning.

A few years ago, I noticed in a national magazine a photograph of two Catholic priests on a picket line supporting the stockyard workers of Chicago in their campaign to win a much-needed wage increase. A few short weeks later I found myself with Episcopalian and Methodist and Baptist ministers on a picket line in the cold winter atmosphere of East Boston, Massachusetts, where the Electrical Workers, mostly young Italian-American girls who made Christmas tree lights, were on strike for a wage increase. It seemed like a strange heresy to the reporters and news photographers who gathered to watch the preachers on the picket line that these preachers simply took St. Paul seriously when he told the Colossians two thousand years earlier that masters should give unto their servants that which is just and equal.

Unitarians have been interfering in politics, if one calls it that, for several centuries. It is second nature to us. The right—in fact, the duty— is quite well recognized, although any particular situation often raises the issue again, because this is an aspect of religion where there is room for strong difference of opinion and room for error of judgment.

Today we Unitarians look back and see in the perspective of history some of the issues that were then called political, which we now see were not only political, but also basically religious and ethical. The struggle in the late eighteenth century by Unitarians for religious freedom from state power in Virginia was certainly political also. The efforts of the Unitarians in Dublin, New Hampshire, in the early nineteenth century to establish the first free public library were political, though also profoundly spiritual, because the right of every child and adult to have a book in his hand was at stake. The struggle a few years later by the Unitarian Horace Mann to inaugurate a free public school system in America was likewise a moral struggle, but it was almost certainly political also, as his notebooks and writings make transparently clear.

When Theodore Parker struggled to interest his Unitarian congregation in the old Music Hall in Boston in the 1850s in the abolition of slavery, decent prisons and reformatories, in the work of the peace societies and the temperance organizations, he was up to his ears in politics, and his people with him. Yet today he is considered the nearest thing to a Hebrew prophet that we have yet produced in the Unitarian churches of America. One is tempted to speak of other Unitarians who answered "yes" to the question, "Should the church engage in politics?" One thinks proudly of Susan B. Anthony and Caroline Severance educating hundreds of thousands on the woman suffrage issue. One remembers Dorothea Dix and the hospitals for the insane she insisted be built. One thinks of Abigail Eliot in Boston giving new scope and depth to the training of teachers of little children of all classes of society. In every case the religious quality of the struggle is more important than the political steps which needed to be taken. The man who denies the legitimate work of politics usually has a very thin and mystical concept of religion, far above the earth, removed from the cruel and desperate necessities of families toiling to maintain themselves without surrendering their moral ideals or their integrity.

A modern Unitarian, Brock Chisholm of the World Health Organization in Geneva, Switzerland, is working to bring new resources of medical care to the children of all nations through the facilities of this United Nations agency. This involves political action in the United Nations, yet it is the heart of religion and ethics also. My *New York Times* tells me that our Federal Security Administrator, Oscar Ewing, recently said, "A reasonable share of the fruits of free enterprise must be devoted to solving some of our more pressing social problems." This is politics. Is it not also high and ethical religion in which a church must take a part? It is my strong feeling that no excuse of the pressure of ecclesiastical business is morally acceptable today as a reason for not acting on political issues. I know the always desperate necessity of raising a church budget, of conducting orderly services with good musicians, of providing a refuge for disturbed and harassed individuals. But these duties do not exempt any churches from helping to cure the basic evils, the vast diseases of a sick economy. Where politics comes to grips with the social needs of men and women who are suffering, no morally responsible church dare be neutral. Our fine principles mock us if we do not enter into the arena of struggle for justice. No church will lose its power by such participation, even though it may lose a member here or there who sees no relationship between religion and unsolved problems.

So I would conclude this morning by saying that we in the liberal churches recognize the necessity felt by Amos and Paul and Savonarola and John Tyndale, and so many others in history, of relating politics to religion. They cannot be separated without ending the meaning of religion. The church will become a complete vestigal organ of our society, like the vermiform appendix to our bodies, if we cease to let religion strengthen and purify our political life. The church has long sanctioned the warfare against gambling, prostitution, and the drug traffic. The other issues of human injustice and exploitation are no less in need of moral participation, which cannot avoid, nor should it seek to avoid, political involvement. The Unitarians welcome your understanding and participation in this age-long struggle for goodness and brotherhood, here upon this earth, here in this city.

Good morning.

How Do Unitarians Face Death?
"Unitarian Time"
January 28, 1951

Good morning, friends. Today on this twelfth broadcast of "Unitarian Essentials," I should like to speak to you about the question, "How do Unitarians face death?" I must confess at the start that I have long had a bias against many discussions on the subject of immortality and the nature of the afterlife. One reason I shall not discuss these matters on this broadcast is that I confess I know nothing about them. There is need by our churches to say candidly that religion has no sure answers about what happens when one dies. Science has no authoritative word. The churches have indulged in a shocking amount of credulity. Year after year there is a vast amount of charlatanism and an equal amount of self-hypnosis about things we should, with humility, admit we know nothing.

This morning I am discussing how we Unitarians as a whole look at the fact of death. What I shall say has very little to do with traditional teachings about the streets of heaven, or the last judgment, or the assurance of immortal life as found in the Fourth Gospel. After five thousand years of recorded history, the best we can honestly say is that we do not possess proof of survival beyond the grave, and we have much to confirm our skepticism.

Let me state one basic Unitarian attitude toward death: If this life be all, it should be lived the better, not the worse. If there be but one world, it should be made as fine as possible. Religion has too long been otherworldly. Our fundamental task is to be successful veterans of living here rather than claiming too eagerly that we are candidates for immortality. My own conviction in these matters is that we should make this world more of a heaven, being prepared to meet death with a more

Program aired on KGIL Radio, Los Angeles.

substantial record of goodness than is the general practice. If I be wrong in my understatement about heaven, what better visa could there be than a rich and noble life on earth? Quality, not duration, is the chief matter in a life. Many a man taken by death in his twenties has left a more glorious record for human goodness than some people achieve after a hundred years.

Unitarianism is a religion for both life and death. It is not as pre-occupied with the repeated story of the death of a savior as is the case in orthodox Christianity, yet it does not blink at the fact that our exis-tence on this earth is limited, for most men, to seventy or eighty years. Unitarians exalt man's glorious creative powers, his unmeasured enthu-siasm for adventure and friendship, his sharing and singing as a free spirit. We say man is indeed marked by intelligence, driven by generous com-pulsions and deep affections to love others, to establish families, to teach the young, to build graceful ships, to play symphonies of supernal love-liness. These things he does, knowing that he is encompassed by mor-tality, hemmed in by time, often wracked by painful disease, and baffled by undiscovered truths just beyond his grasp.

To the Unitarian there is a rare glory in the man that can find joy, happiness, and satisfaction while he, at the same time, sheds ancient props of legend and mythology as unworthy of his full humanity. We say that there is no merit in avoiding the fact of death. To turn from this sol-emn reality with averted eyes is to play the child overlong. Much in our American society seeks to blindfold us from the admission of death as one of the facts in our existence. We are encouraged to make a pag-eant of it in elegant memorial parks, to anesthetize our minds with poetry and fables instead of confessing the simple truth of nature—that all that is born must also die.

Should we not tell our children what we know, rather than what we do not know? We have no moral right, it seems to me, to pass on to our children our unconfirmed speculations as though they were indubitable facts. Let us tell our children that it is natural and good to want to live. Only a fiend would want death cherished as better than life. We honor doctors for seeking ever new ways of saving life. Every advance in the lifespan of man should be heralded as a glorious victory.

But we should also tell our children that it is not evil that men die, except as they die because of man's violence and greed. It is nec-essary that we die in our time just as there is birth into life. The cycle of nature requires both life and death. This the American Indians in their early legends told us more beautifully and honestly than many of our Sunday schools, which are so often preoccupied with the story of death found in the New Testament; a story, to be sure, that includes a resurrection, but only on a supernatural level, not as a part of the familiar seasons of the life cycle of the plants and animals about us.

We need to teach our children one of the finest statements ever made on this subject, made by a so-called pagan philosopher, not one within the circle of the church. Socrates, the man condemned to drink hemlock because of his passion for truth-telling, said, "No evil can befall a good man, either in life or in death." Many men who have faced the worst tortures of faggot or gibbet have been able to repeat these great words of Socrates without sensing a paradox, for they still possessed a loyalty to truth, and enjoyed the respect and affection of their fellow citizens. Saint Joan, Archbishop Cranmer, Servetus, and the heroes of the Warsaw ghetto in the late war all testify to this great truth.

When Unitarians talk about facing death, they talk about life and make mighty affirmations. We are not cold and intellectual Unitarians, as some have sometimes thought. That is absurd. On the subject of living within the framework of our years on earth, we Unitarians have boiling convictions, and the warmest of beliefs. Because we cherish life, knowing that it is a precious possession with limits upon it, we think of its unfulfilled possibilities. Our hope, for example, is for a world without war and penury, without ignorance and hatred. We place our confidence in the conviction that men and women can live magnificently on their merits, without fear of hell or hope of heaven; living life for life itself, rich, full, and free. This is our faith that shakes the timbers of the universe.

We believe in living as though each day were our last, not grimly thinking of the dark visage of death, but of the tremendous possibilities of these twenty-four hours for adding to the goodwill of others, of enjoying the beauty of our mountains and the glory of the sea. The power of Christianity in present living lies not in its story of the empty tomb of the resurrected Christ; it lies in the life and teaching of Jesus, who taught men how to find dignity and maturity without the accompaniment of riches, but with the strength of a lighted mind, whether one is a king or a shepherd. His precepts and personal example will long outlast the story of his ascension into the sky.

We Unitarians say there is no substitute for a sense of personal achievement—of seeing cooperation between different races and nationalities and creeds, of discovering the enthusiasm of people at work and play when freed from fear. We are often bereft by the loss of a partner, a member of the family, a lifelong companion, a noble tribune of the people; but new strength comes to the good person who sees deathless actions survive the body.

Death can leave great wounds and take from us the elevation of a companion spirit, leaving us impoverished for years to come. But there is also that remaining which defies time and makes mockery of the grave. As we see the stirring work of men and women for a better world, the discoveries by scientists, the highways built by the toil of industri-

ous men, as we watch the nursery teacher in the kindergarten, we rejoice that mankind can throw away its crutches of fantasy and myth.
We have found immortal qualities of goodness and justice and joy, which
speak eloquently for themselves. They defy the stories from the childhood of the race about reincarnation and resurrection.

We know death is real, and without morbidity we face it as a fact.
This is progress for the human race and marks an advance over the
earlier teachings built upon fear and insecurity of spirit. We rejoice at
every new gain of man in his conquest of nature, as he, through invention of new tools, lifts burdens from the shoulders of those long
familiar with toil. We rejoice at new ways of solving old problems.
We are glad that more socially responsible governments and industries
have pension plans for the aged, security plans for workers that lift
the fear of poverty from millions who formerly hated the prospect of
their closing years.

This approach to death I have suggested this morning should brace
us for the stiff years before us. It should challenge us to use our energies
with greater wisdom, to see that the madness of a competitive society
is supplanted with a cooperative society of nations, a republic for humans and not for things. Here we stand with some eighty years of life
for most of us. Let us find ourselves and play our roles as men and
women. Let us not be the shadow of someone else, nor cower before
stereotypes made by timid men for our craven imitation. Let us not
negate life, but affirm it and help to see that fewer miss its satisfactions,
as they now do with such pathetic frequency.

We have been so involved in describing the beauties of a speculative afterlife that we have failed again and again to help our neighbors
to see the radiant glory around our very feet. I would suggest that for
a season we speak less of the *deaths* of the saints and more of the *lives*
of the sages. Let us proclaim our high confidence in man's infinite possibilities here on this green and fragrant earth.

I should like to conclude this morning with the words of Edwin
Hatch:

> For me—to have made one soul
> The better for my birth;
> To have added but one flower
> To the garden of the earth;
>
> To have struck one blow for truth
> In the daily fight with lies;
> To have done one deed of right
> In the face of calumnies;

To have sown in the souls of men
One thought that will not die—
To have been a link in the chain of life
Shall be immortality.

(*Towards Fields of Light*)

The Church and Anticommunism
"Religion and Modern Life"
January 16, 1955

MR. HARTMAN: Good evening, friends. Tonight the First Unitarian Church of Los Angeles presents its radio program, "Religion and Modern Life," a quarter hour conducted by its minister, Stephen H. Fritchman, who is speaking tonight on "The Church and Anticommunism." And now, transcribed, Mr. Fritchman.

MR. FRITCHMAN: Good evening, friends. My subject tonight, "The Church and Anticommunism," grows out of a statement I made some months ago on this program when I was discussing an article in *Look* magazine by the distinguished Roman Catholic bishop, Dr. Bernard J. Sheil of Chicago. I spent my entire time in that talk supporting splendid statements by the bishop on behalf of the church working in all areas where human need called for prophetic insight, a sensitive conscience, and a call for heroic and immediate action. I took exception only to the paragraphs in the article where Bishop Sheil reported on his long campaign against communism, and I promised at a later time to explain my position on the matter. This is the occasion for that delayed commentary.

Quite a bit has happened in the months intervening to support my position, which can be simply stated tonight: Anticommunism is a very weak battle station for a clergyman working for a principled dedication to a better world. We are tonight living on a small, spinning planet where over a third of mankind, wisely or unwisely, are under socialist or communist governments. Millions of the citizens in these countries are members of the same churches and faiths as ourselves in America, and they believe, as earnestly as most of us do, that they are seeking to solve

Program aired on KABC Radio, Los Angeles.

great problems with moral integrity and practical skills. They may be wrong, as we sometimes are wrong, but we are not dealing with black and white issues, or dealing with total angels on one side or total devils on the other. My files are crowded with statements in recent days by Churchill, Eisenhower, Nehru, Chou En-lai, and others, all stating the necessity and possibility of coexistence for years to come. Churchmen, politicians, scientists, and labor leaders (among others), facing the ultimate alternatives of peace or atomic extinction for the first time in history, are taking a sober second thought about the ideological war of nerves that has kept us in a whirlpool of hostility since the end of World War II.

As a churchman, I wish tonight to call attention to the high cost of the anti-Communist mania in America. I call it mania with great deliberation, as others have done, again and again. To so denote the mania is not to dismiss or underestimate the objective failures of men, parties, and peoples in socialist and communist countries. Hundreds of books and articles pour from our presses documenting, often with much passion and prejudice, but at times with care and sincerity, the high cost of revolutionary change in countries emerging from feudalism into technology and democracy. The cost in civil liberties, in freedom of thought, in religious toleration, and other values is often high. I need not spend precious moments in a familiar rehearsal of programs and policies in European or Asian communist lands which are unacceptable to American leadership today. They are repeated constantly through all media of public information day after day. But let me make it very clear that the rejection of the programs of a communist government by a capitalist one does not mean that there is merit or value in the kind of anti-communist hysteria which has for some years gripped the American people. Here is where I feel even Bishop Sheil has failed in his usual good judgment. The church, over the centuries, has been an agency of reconciliation and understanding between peoples of differing ideas, doctrines, economies, and political systems.

A Christian minister or a Jewish rabbi or any other sectarian leader is at his worst, not his best, in anything as negative and divisive as the present anti-Communist crusade, where distinctions are not made, facts of importance are not recognized, and human needs are tragically ignored.

There must be voices today—in pulpits, on radio stations, in the press —that will say the obvious but unpopular truth that the Communists are not a supernatural breed of men, their leaders are not all diabolical men with satanic conspiracies, and their programs for legislation and reform are not directed at the enslavement of mankind. The church should be one place where it is said that Communists, like capitalists, propose industrial, agricultural, educational, medical, and cultural projects, which are made by very human creatures; projects of merit oftentimes, but carried out by men and women of human frailties, subject to the same weaknesses and strengths as men have always had. I am profoundly grateful that a Dean Pike of the Cathedral of St. John the Divine in New York City, or a Dean Francis Sayre of the Washington Cathedral, or any one of a score of prominent churchmen in our land today remind us, even if some resent the rebuke, that the only valid criticism of Communist proposals for human health and welfare anywhere is a counterproposal that will meet the problem as adequately or a lot better. If this is done with facts and figures, not mere passion and invective, it can gain far more consideration and a better chance at being tried.

I feel, and I hope Bishop Sheil would agree with me, that the ultimate logic of the anti-Communist campaign, as it has been carried on, leads to a worldwide atomic war of utter destruction, with millions dead and civilization set back to the Stone Age. If there is no room for reconciliation and coexistence on the planet, then Syngman Rhee's plea for an immediate preventive war has a terrible and unholy logic to it. Happily, saner counsels are prevailing today, as Dr. Gallup's polls and responsible high-level governmental statements make clear. Fortunately, the world is reluctant to plunge itself into a suicidal struggle out of which nothing of profit could emerge.

Anticommunism is a very feeble platform for a Christian or any other religious leader to occupy. It denies any ground for facing the common problems which the communist and capitalist of sincere motives both wish to solve, each in good conscience, and with some scientific objectivity. Any religious person, professional or layman, who knows the history of Judaism and Christianity, knows that there is an ethical imperative to face the realities of hunger, of poverty, of ignorance and disease with compassion, and with an unshakable resolve to find better than existing answers. There are hundreds of millions of living people who see the indubitable efforts of Communist governments to undertake drastic, thorough-going programs aimed at the alleviation of prevailing misery. Those millions are not interested, most of them, in the verbal assaults of anti-Communists anywhere, of whatever nationality or religious persuasion, that do not start with an acceptance of the misery and with proposals of some very practical answers. The kind of anticommunism which hurts us as Americans, for example, in the eyes of world opinion is our dilatory attitude toward Point-Four programs, toward loans and grants at least as large as our armament budgets for meeting mass poverty in vast areas of the world. I, as a clergyman in a capitalist country, cannot in good grace join an anti-Communist crusade when I know, as many of you know, that my own country has not done all it might have done toward aiding those now turning to Communist and social leadership.

Dean Griswold of the Harvard Law School recently emphasized that in past struggles of equal intensity, justice and liberty have eventually won out, and the reason was that the issues were faced, not avoided. I am convinced myself that Americans, if not stampeded into silence or undemocratic conformity in a season of fear, can indeed provide answers for themselves and for others in the world who want less vituperation and hysteria and a lot more common sense about ways and means for human welfare in this technological age. Frankly, I think much of the unacceptable repression and dictatorial policy-making of socialist and communist governments will be abated by the peoples in those nations themselves as the education they are now getting and the existence of a climate of peace begin their leavening work. Raymond Robbins, Edgar Snow, I. F. Stone, Madam Pandit, and others have borne similar testimony with far more authority than myself, an untraveled person dependent on second-hand reports. There is no system without grave imperfections, no system not administered by men open to corruption and greed and power-complexes. I doubt if these evils will for centuries be utterly extirpated from society anywhere on earth. But the testimony of history is available to thoughtful people. There have been societies in China, in India, in Mexico, in portions of Europe and Africa in centuries long past that kept these evil compulsions to a minimum and established for long years social orders marked by a high degree of responsibility, equality, and peace. These undeniable achievements of the past remind us that with our added techniques, inventions, and discoveries of the twentieth century about human behavior it can be done even better again. Acquisitive societies can be transformed into cooperative societies if men have a chance to take part in the process of change with unshackled minds. I believe that experiments are going on in East and West to see how we can avoid rewarding the aggressive man, the greedy man, giving him less prestige and power. Today there is an implacable will to feed all, clothe all, educate all before we tolerate enormous inequalities of wealth and privilege. If some of you are saying this sounds communistic, let me assure you it is something existent centuries before Karl Marx, namely, the essence of the Jewish prophets and the Sermon on the Mount. It is found in Buddha's eight-fold path and Lao-Tse's twenty-five-hundred-year-old teaching of nonaggressiveness and goodwill. And these teachings have inspired emperors and princes, administrators and builders again and again. A campaign of anticommunism obiterates these facts, it arouses passions of nationalism and sectarianism, which only add fuel to the flames of hatred and fear. That is why thousands of churchmen in the world, including America, refuse to be drawn into the anti-Communist crusade. It is no solution, it solves no basic problems, it robs people of their resources as mature and intelligent folk.

America is the richest nation on earth today, the most advanced in technology and know-how for fulfilling the prophet's dream of transforming the desert and building a highway for all to share. My task, and I hope many of you feel your task also is to promote an exchange of ideas and citizens between all nations, to melt down iron curtains and all other barriers to human commerce of mind and body. The best ideas for solving our unfinished tasks will be found only as scientists and diplomats and teachers traverse the earth. Good faith breeds good faith. Evidence of nonaggression breeds nonaggression. The good that lies in the hearts of the people under socialist and communist rule has as much right to expression as the good in your heart and mine. It is the secret and mystery of religion that such faith has proven more important than armies with banners, that such faith can remove mountains of prejudice and distrust. If such a faith is a fantasy, then mankind is indeed doomed. I do not share in such a melancholy conclusion. Rather, I believe with the Galilean carpenter that "Ye shall know the truth, and the truth shall make you free." Good evening.

That Vastly Overrated Bestseller
The Bible
February 17, 1963

There have been a number of Unitarian sermons in recent weeks on the subject of the Bible. I am happily indebted to the Reverend James Wilkes of Albuquerque, New Mexico, for his provocative title so similar to my own, and to the Reverend John Crane of Santa Barbara for his development of several ideas on the use of the Bible by religious liberals. A few direct quotations from his recent sermon will be found at the end of this address. Particularly useful was Dr. Rolland E. Wolfe's What is the Bible?, a small and very useful booklet issued by our Department of Education of the Unitarian Universalist Association, Boston. I have used several passages directly in my text and am indebted for ideas in other portions of this treatment of the subject. None of the writers mentioned, however, is in the least responsible for the conclusions presented by myself in the course of this address.—SHF

If fire from heaven were to be called down, in the manner of Moses, this is the day it would come. This may prove to be the most misunderstood sermon I ever preached!

As is suggested in the title of this address, the Bible is still the world's bestseller, always a few million copies ahead of the works of V. I. Lenin, which is the next most popular book throughout the reading world. It was Erich Fromm who said that "The Bible is the most widely sold and presumably the most widely read book in the West, and yet this same book fails to have any marked influence on the real experience of modern man, either on his feelings or his actions. In short, the Bible has become escape literature, needed to save the individual from facing the abyss of emptiness that his mode of life opens to him, yet without much effect because no connection is made between the Bible and his real life."

This is a psychologist's way of saying that the Bible is a modern totem, a magic talisman, kept on the table, or by the bed, or in the pulpit, the very presence of which gives a certain relief and support, though its covers may never be opened. And in millions of cases this is the only way the book is used. To say less would be to avoid a common-sense explanation for its fantastic sales to people who do almost no reading at all of the Bible, or fiction, or classic literature, or history, or world affairs, in hard cover or paperback.

To this congregation, after my many years of service, it will be far from breathtaking news that I can take my Bible or leave it alone. It is not habit-forming with Unitarians. To recent members and visitors I can say that there has been an epidemic of sermons on the Bible in Unitarian and Universalist pulpits in recent months—most of them, I gather, along the lines of this one. And let me state my thesis at the beginning very simply: the Bible, a library of sixty-six books of varying value, reading from 0 to 90 percent on a scale of one hundred, must be used with great discrimination. One should have no sense of guilt for never reading some parts of it, which are better left to dust and the worms, while other parts have a great contribution to make to a sensitive, searching man or woman. But like all books from the past, the context must be known and we must be able to sift gold from dross at every turning of the page. It is a vastly overrated bestseller.

My first job after finishing college was in the Department of English Bible at Ohio Wesleyan University. This early conditioning still influences my feelings, even in these later Unitarian Humanist years of my life. I frankly enjoy many chapters of many books in both the Old and New Testaments as literature, as ethical prods to conscience, as anthropology, as studies in two ancient religions—Judaism and Christianity. I would not deliberately leave a Bible off the van if I were moving to another home, nor would I run into a flaming house to rescue it. My behavior is fairly typical of the modern religionist: I find my mind and my emotions stirred by some of the highest passages of the prophets and the gospels, the psalms and Ecclesiastes, yet I find most of the Bible a dead weight, a tradition which holds me back even unconsciously from honest and nonconformist thinking on matters it speaks about. It has taken me over half a century to come to this point of view and say so.

If this is true of myself, I am sure it is true of many other Unitarians who are also people in transit intellectually. Here probably is as good a test as any other of whether you have become a religious independent: Are you able to say you read the parts of the Bible you like and find nourishing, and that you omit with a generous hand those vast areas which are of no interest to anyone but an anthropologist or religious historian?

This sermon is no daring adventure. I am just about even with Tom Paine in *The Age of Reason* (which came out about two hundred years ago) when he said: "Whenever we read the obscene stories, the voluptuous debaucheries, the cruel and tortuous executions, the unrelenting vindictiveness, with which more than half of the Bible is filled, it would be more consistent to call it the word of a demon than the word of God. It is a history of wickedness that has served to corrupt and brutalize mankind." And I would add that scores of Bible-inspired spectaculars out of Hollywood film studios have proved how right Tom Paine really was—and these are only the films that have passed the Board of Censors!

Three weeks ago I read some of Mark Twain's *Letters from the Earth*, which revealed his horror also at the sadism of much that is found in the Old Testament; at its moral perversion, its sanctifying of child-murder and fratricide. For these things do form a considerable part of a book that generations have held up as a holy book, inspired by men writing at the dictation of the Almighty. Today, with the support of the First Amendment, one can say this—in Tom Paine's words or in one's own —and not anticipate being sent to jail for it or hung by the thumbs.

One thing a Unitarian can do, modest as his influence may seem to be in our culture, is to support people who insist upon being discriminating in the disciplines of their religion, including the use of ancient literature, especially the Bible. There is still a considerable inherited irrationality about the Bible, even in our own denomination. Parents who do not read the Bible now, and possibly never did, often insist upon a thorough study of the Bible in our church schools. This is often an unconscious totem-worship and it should be so described. As a matter of fact, we do teach the Bible in our Unitarian church schools, but only in part, and then with the tools of modern scholarship at our elbows. Any less careful treatment would be irresponsible child abuse.

I am pleading today for moral honesty in all that we do in our religious life, without apology, in fact with pride. If you were asked that hoary question, "What books would you take on a year's banishment to a deserted island?" would you say the Bible, or would you choose Shakespeare or something else? I like to remember Bernard Shaw's answer, "A pile of notebooks and some pencils."

A man named Morton Enslin, in a brief article entitled "The Bible: Asset or Liability?", had the same feeings I do about the misuse of the Bible, for at one point he says,

> The book that can be a lamp to the feet has too often been a lamp post from which to hang those whose views differed from his own. Quotations are often used as celestial cashier's endorsements for arguments or contentions which are utterly irrelevant to the quotation

in its proper context. The Bible is not in essence different from every
other book. It is not the creation of a God external to this world.

Carl Sandburg once said that the American mind is not made up
by the reading of books, but from reading newspapers and the Bible.
If this is true—and I doubt it—the Bible filters into the national mind
very indirectly and unconsciously. This is a generation that does not
know the Bible, even its higher elevations or classic mountain peaks.
Certainly we Unitarian ministers of the older categories do not count
on a Biblical quotation to clinch a point, for we know that it would
not be clinched for more than a handful of those listening. Shakespeare
or Emerson is safer for such a purpose. The Bible may still be a bestseller, but it is not read, selectively or otherwise, by 1 percent of those
who lay down their money for it.

As Professor Rolland Wolfe has written so cogently in his Beacon
Press book, *What is the Bible?*

> Today all the great sciences have forged so far ahead of the ancients
> that the lore of those times is mostly an irrelevant curiosity. Religion
> is the only area of present-day knowledge where practically no progress
> has been made in the last two thousand years. Because of the shallowness
> and lack of creativeness during this long time, it seems necessary to
> many people to go back to this ancient Bible for inspiration.

It is a great rebuke to the twentieth century that, with all our education and material advancement, we have not been able to rise to higher
spiritual levels than those found in the more worthy portions of the
Bible. For sustenance contemporary man often goes back to the better
parts of the two Testaments. As you will discover at the end of my
remarks today, I think many modern writers have more genuine help
to offer the contemporary American than can be found in most of the
Bible, and I shall give two or three illustrations.

Professor Wolfe later reminds us,

> By the superficial and dogmatic it has always been assumed that in
> the Bible there is only one religion, with all its parts correlated toward
> that single end. By contrast, close examination reveals that it is a collection
> of books of many religions, some of them existing side by side at the
> same time. As each area evolves a new culture, so each age demands
> a new religion.

There are at least nine religions in the sixty-six books of the Bible,
and today I should like to refer to but four of them, the first three

the most profitable for the modern reader, and the last an example of the most decadent and useless.

After discussing the earliest religions of the Bible (the Mesopotamian religion of Genesis 1–11, the patriarchal religion of Genesis 12–50, the Mosaic religion of the Hebrews 1225 to 586 B.C.E.), Dr. Wolfe discusses the Bible's fourth religion: the prophetic religion which began in earnest with Amos at approximately 750 B.C.E. and ended for all practical purposes with Second Isaiah at 540 B.C.E. The prophetic movement was primarily concerned with developing the ethical side of religion. Hebrew religion had been like a circle, revolving around the one center, worship or ritual. The prophets turned this into an ellipse, revolving around two foci, worship (or ritual) and ethics. These prophets were the great social reformers of all time. They inaugurated the golden age of Old Testament religion as they built it up to the highest ethical dimension that religion has perhaps ever achieved.

The sixth religion, according to Dr. Wolfe, appeared during the last three centuries of the pre-Christian period. It came into being in the form of what might be called humanistic wisdom religion. Although the inspiration for this had been supplied much earlier by kings David and Solomon, its delayed flowering was postponed until just before the Christian era. This humanistic wisdom development was a practical religion that reacted against the priestly emphasis of normative Judaism, with its hair-splitting meticulousness over seemingly insignificant matters of minute religious ritual and regulations of daily life. The new humanistic wisdom religion, Dr. Wolfe reminds us, was noninstitutional, not patronizing the priesthood or even mentioning it, and doing virtually the same with the Sabbath. Sometimes, as in the Song of Songs and the Book of Esther, it became so secular that the name of God was not even mentioned. Psalms, Proverbs, Ecclesiastes, and Job were the great books of this religion.

The seventh religion of the Bible, in Dr. Wolfe's summary, is the religion of John the Baptist and Jesus. "This," he tells us, "was a religion that condemned wealth, was devoted to abolishing poverty, and strove to establish a measure of economic equality among men. Its primary emphasis was on spiritual culture. In the Sermon on the Mount, especially, the demands of ethical living were carried to such a high dimension that even the thought of evil came to be considered as bad as the act, at least potentially." The faith of Jesus thus became a "preventive" religion, not concerned with forgiving past sins, but with preventing future ones. This was an exacting religion that demanded service and sacrifice in the task of redeeming the world. It replaced anger, hate, and enmity with love. It was a wholly nonritualistic religion of the spirit. Its main goal was establishing the "kingdom of God," i.e., the rule of God in the lives of men, thus transforming this life into a heavenly existence now.

Dr. Wolfe continues,

> The ninth and final religion of the Bible is a tragic affair, a religion
> of radical anti-climax, as found in the latest books of the New Testa-
> ment. The communion was made into a matter of transubstantiation.
> In the Book of Hebrews, Jesus was transformed into a great high priest,
> with all the accompanying paraphernalia. In the Book of Revelation,
> Jesus was made into a militaristic hero, the king and conqueror of the
> world, with his tongue elongated into a two-edged sword with which
> to cut off the heads of his enemies. This religion wallows in the sadism
> connected with its concepts of the judgment day and terrors of hell,
> with its lake of fire.

The Bible is not original or unique. Today it is becoming generally
realized that even Jesus was influenced by other cultures and religions,
as I indicated in my Christmas sermon. Most Christians do not realize
the origins of Jesus' immortal summarizing of the whole of religion into
two commandments. When he designated the most important
commandment as, "Hear, O Israel, the Lord is one, and you shall love
the Lord and God with all your heart, and with all your soul, and with
all your mind, and with all your strength," (Mark 12:39-30) he was
quoting with only slight elaboration the Shema of Deuteronomy 6:4,
the most basic command of Judaism. When he said, "The second is
this: You shall love your neighbor as yourself," he was quoting Leviticus 19:18.

Since the discovery of the Dead Sea Scrolls it is becoming apparent that Jesus was influenced in many of his ideas and emphases by those
Essene sects that resided in and about the monastery of Qumran near
the northwest shore of the Dead Sea. It is also becoming clear that the
birth narratives concerning Jesus have been almost completely recast so
as to make them conform to the Buddhist cycle of birth narratives as
applied to the whole line of Buddhas. It is even likely that the eight
beatitudes of Jesus, which begin the Sermon on the Mount, were suggested
by the eight beatitudes of Buddhism, which have come to be known
as "The Eightfold Noble Path."

Perhaps the greatness of Jesus lay not so much in his originality as
in his remarkable ability to synthesize into his program for life the best
elements of those religions and cultures with which he was acquainted.
Modern scholarship is aiding us in understanding the evolution of religion. The Bible is our laboratory specimen par excellence. If we can read
it as a book preserved by courageous students of history, often at great
risk to life itself, we can use it as a document of enormous value. To
use it as a guide for present conduct can be as disastrous as a doctor's
using Galen or Servetus for an understanding of his patients' medical

problems. I am urging an intelligent reading of some of the Bible as I would encourage the reading of the Upanishads, the Analects of Confucius, the Koran, and the sutras, to learn of man's striving for wisdom over the centuries.

Scholars will tell us, if we will listen, that whole parts of the Bible have been borrowed from other cultures and peoples. Not one story in Genesis 1-11 is Hebrew or Palestinian. All that body of material was borrowed from the lands of the east, mostly Mesopotamia. Through archaeology, original cuneiform versions of most stories in Genesis 1-11 have by now been unearthed from the sands that have come to cover the remains of those ancient Sumerian, Babylonian, and Assyrian cities. Psalms 19 and 104 are basically Egyptian psalms, written by the Pharaoh Ikhnaton, learned by the Hebrews during their bondage in Egypt, carried with them when they made their Exodus to Palestine, and used by Jews and Christians ever since. The Book of Job was originally an Arabic production. Borrowed from Arabia by the Jews and translated into Hebrew, it has become the Shakespeare of the Bible. Ten of the twelve sayings in Proverbs 22:17-23:14 are clearly adaptations from a classic Egyptian document, *The Wisdom of Amen-em-ope*. The immortal Ten Commandments of Moses are basically a boiling down of the forty-two commands in the Egyptian *Book of the Dead* into the ten simple but basic laws that Moses enunciated.

The arrogance of many of our local evangelists, on radio and television, is seen in their assumption that the Old and New Testaments are totally superior. They are not. The Bible is a compendium of material from many other faiths. It ought to make us realize the universality of all great religion, East and West, ancient and modern. The idolatry of THE BOOK is one of the darkest pages in human history. I do not of course say that the answer is a bonfire of all scriptures. I only ask for a little tolerance and knowledge about the origin of the Bible and its encouraging similarities to the writings of other religions.

Of course, there are many disagreements in the Bible, for it is broad as life itself. People then had their variant views, as we have today. It is therefore impossible to speak of the "biblical view" on any subject. In one strand of the Bible man is regarded as a depraved being, a worm of the dust, a vile sinner. This is found in parts of the Garden of Eden story, in Psalm 51:5 with its "in sin did my mother conceive me," and in the writings of the apostle Paul, psychologically one of the most morbid religionists of all time. In a competing parallel strand that also runs throughout the Bible, man is a child of God, with many characteristics of deity, fundamentally good, a creature but a little lower than the angels.

Proverbs 23:29-35 forbids the use of intoxicants, and Isaiah 5:22 says, "Woe unto those who drink wine and mix strong drinks." By contrast, a writer of 1 Timothy 5:23 said, "Be no longer a drinker of water, but use a little wine for your stomach's sake." Between the two, man has to make his own decision.

With regard to the subject of war and peace, the Bible supports pacifism and disarmament in Micah 4:3 and Isaiah 2:4, where "they shall beat their swords into plowshares and their spears into pruning hooks." But those who prefer armament and militarism can find the exact reverse in Joel 3:9-10, where the command is to "Beat your plowshares into swords, and your pruning hooks into spears." When I read the Bible through in college in 1923, I could hardly believe that text. Now I call the author "Pentagon Joel."

Parts of the Bible support slavery, and other portions just as vigorously condemn it, a painful fact that many people first learned in Civil War sermons. Part of the Old Testament is violently antiforeign, while much of it has love and understanding for all peoples. Some of the Bible is devoted to human betterment, but in the closing chapter, Revelation 22:11, it leaves as Christianity's final testament, "Let the evildoer still do evil, and let the filthy still be filthy."

People who call the Bible the "word of God" apparently have never read it discerningly, for how can any person hold any god worthy of serious consideration responsible for some of the deeds and attitudes attributed to him on its pages? Can one believe in a god who called out two she-bears to mutilate or kill forty-two children just because they had called Elisha "baldhead"? Can one believe in a god who told Abraham to murder his son Isaac? During most of his days, Jacob led a life of deep deception against his father, his brother, and his father-in-law, and yet God is always represented as having blessed him in preference to others. Joshua thought that God wanted the Hebrew people to have the land of Palestine, and that God told him to kill off every man, woman, child, and animal in order to get it, leaving "nothing that breathed," and his scorched-earth policy nearly succeeded. Samuel was sure that the deity did not want Israel to have a king but that God sanctioned his renegade sons to continue the judgeship. In short, the ethics of the Old Testament at many points are too depraved to be considered by a serious mind. Mark Twain, [Robert G.] Ingersoll, and Upton Sinclair did more to tell me this than did all my teachers in seminary.

As Dr. Wolfe tells us in his *What is the Bible?*,

> For all of the beauty and grandeur of Job and Isaiah, of the Psalms and of First Corinthians, the Bible, on the whole, is a book of massive intolerance and dogmatism. It assumes the existence of One True Religion—Judaism in the Old Testament and Christianity in the New Testament. It is a book of closed doors, of issues not open to discussion. Moses and Jesus were shockingly narrow in their humanitarianism, as the Canaanites and the Samaritans could testify if the case came to trial

in any courtroom today. It may not be fair to judge them two or three millennia afterward by our standards, but, on the other hand, we do not have to accept their rules and examples in our age when more should be expected. We should have learned something from two thousand years of living.

The Bible is simply inadequate as a textbook for people living in so altered a world as our own. All things considered, it is a very limited asset, a vastly over-rated guidebook for the good life. It requires too much explanation, revision and cutting, to make it practical. Its presuppositions are not our presuppositions. We are beguiled by its poetry and overawed by its claims to authority. We have given it more credit for moral insight than it deserves. The biblical tradition has become a chain upon the ankle. To people in a new age it speaks of a world that no longer exists. It is irrelevant to our present needs. It closes debates that need to remain open.

Do you remember Ralph Waldo Emerson's query in one of his diaries, "Why do I not take up the Bible to start me on my task as I do Plutarch or Marcus Antonius? Is it because the Bible wears black cloth, because it comes with certain official claims against which the mind revolts?" Then Emerson adds, "The book has its own nobilities it might well claim if left to its own merits, but this 'you must,' 'it is your duty' repels."

Do not misunderstand me. I am not urging that Unitarians burn their Bibles. I am asking rather that they read the Bible with discrimination and knowledge, along with many other books from other religions and from the many cultural traditions not considered religious—the Greek philosophers, the Roman Stoics, the giants of the Italian Renaissance and French Enlightenment, as well as the thinkers of our own time. The disciplines of independent living are often hard and demanding of time and energy. There are no short cuts if one is truly a seeker for solutions that will help in one's present need.

More important, I believe Dr. Wolfe is correct in saying that our American habit of stressing the Bible in our churches and schools is a tragic confession that we have lost the power of creativity in religion and ethics today. Why should we now, two thousand years after the birth of Jesus and thirty-two hundred years since the days of the early Hebrews writing their songs of vengeance, lean so heavily on such a mixed tradition? We have new problems, new tools, new experiences. We ought to do much better than Joshua and David, Joseph and Paul of Tarsus. If we believe in evolution, it ought to include ethical and moral evolution also. Without carefully prepared teachers to guide them, I would prefer that the Bible be kept from the children in our homes or our schools. There are better heroes to honor than Abimelech and Jacob. Thomas Jefferson sat in the White House during his occupancy of it and cut up his Bible with scissors and made one of his own, and it is a fine one indeed. I am for doing the same thing with the Bible and the scriptures of Taoism, Buddhism, Islam, and many other ancient faiths.

Let me quote a comment made by Albert Schweitzer recently about our Unitarian Universalist Association: "Today, when a dogmatism foreign to its nature has gained such ground in Protestantism that men are beginning to regard liberalism as a thing of the past, it is particularly salutary that your institution is based on the free religious-ethical spirit."

I hope we deserve Dr. Schweitzer's compliment. Our independence of current bibliolatry is a good test for finding out. Use the Bible as one of many instruments in your intellectual and spiritual life with great selectivity. It is a book made by men for other men. It has errors and it has genius, and it is for all of us to know the one from the other.

I should like to close this address by reading three passages by three modern writers. They are men who have much to say that no Biblical author, as a prisoner of his age, could possibly have said. A modern religious man needs to read the best that is written in his own age, as well as the best that has survived the centuries. Listen then to Bertrand Russell, to E. H. Erikson, and to Herbert J. Muller.

> Religion is based, I think, primarily and mainly upon fear. It is partly the terror of the unknown, and partly, as I have said, the wish to feel that you have a kind of elder brother who will stand by you in all your troubles and disputes. Fear is the basis of the whole thing—fear of the mysterious, fear of defeat, fear of death. Fear is the parent of cruelty, and therefore, it is no wonder if cruelty and religion have gone hand-in-hand. It is because fear is the basis of those two things. In this world we can now begin a little to understand things, and a little to master them by help of science, which has forced its way step by step against the Christian religion, against the churches, and against the opposition of all the old precepts. Science can help us to get over this craven fear in which mankind has lived for so many generations. Science can teach us, and I think our own hearts can teach us, no longer to look around for imaginary supports, no longer to invent allies in the sky, but rather to look to our own efforts here below to make this world a fit place to live in, instead of the sort of place that the churches in all these centuries have made it.
>
> The whole conception of God is a conception derived from the ancient Oriental despotisms. It is a conception quite unworthy of free men. When you hear people in church debasing themselves and saying that they are miserable sinners, and all the rest of it, it seems contemptible and not worthy of self-respecting human beings. We ought to stand up and look the world frankly in the face. We ought to make the best we can of the world, and if it is not so good as we wish, after all it will still be better than what these others have made of it in all these ages. A good world needs knowledge, kindliness, and courage; it does

not need a regretful hankering after the past, or a fettering of the free intelligence by words uttered long ago by ignorant men. (Bertrand Russell, *Why I Am Not a Christian*)

Where do we stand? In our time, for the first time, one human species can be envisaged, with one common technology on one globe (and a bit of outer space). At the same time, psychological insight has made our consciousness wiser by the recognition of the body's wisdom of the power of the unconscious, and of the ego's functions and limitations. This increased margin of consciousness, in itself a major step in evolution, enables men to visualize new moral alternatives, and to strive for a perfection both abundant and adaptive which mediates more realistically between his inner and outer world than do the fatal compromises resulting from the reign of moral absolutes. (E. H. Erickson, *The Roots of Virtue*)

The most unique distinction of man, and that which we value most, is his striving to attain a higher state for himself and his fellows through his rational efforts. This, the very substance of man, will not be relinquished but will be strengthened and exalted. Why lament if the adventitious wrappings should become replaced by worthier ones, so long as the inner essence is enhanced?

Thus we see the future for man as one of his own making, if only he will have it so. And it is deep in his nature to have it so if he can. The Prometheus who once stole common fire is now taming nuclear furies, probing the brain with electrodes, and taking apart and putting together the genes. Soon he will venture into the cosmos and his jobs of external creation will have begun in earnest. (Herbert J. Muller, *The Human Future*)

*   *   *

These are the words of three writers. And there are hundreds of others —not unread bestsellers, but fresh, honest, humane, and free. Let the Bible play its part in the culture of mankind, without prejudice or special favor. Only then will it survive into man's age of liberation.

The Curia and the Bishops
A Discussion of the Second Session
of the Vatican II Council
January 19, 1964

The late George Santayana, the urbane Catholic writer and professor for many years at Harvard University, was born just one hundred years ago. It seems appropriate, as I venture into an evaluation of the Catholic church's Vatican II second session, that I quote this rare and brilliant son of the Roman tradition in religion. Since my thesis is today that Unitarians can, if they want to try a bit, understand the winds blowing in the Catholic world, it might be wise to begin by quoting a man who, by trying a bit, understood Unitarians. He wrote a witty and coruscating novel in the 1930s, *The Last Puritan*, which showed his perception about our own heretical sect. He also has a penetrating section in his classic book *The Life of Reason* regarding the impact of eighteenth-century scholasticism on religion:

> Mediocre natures continued to rehearse the old platitudes and tread the slippery middle courses of one orthodoxy or another; but distinguished minds could no longer treat such survivals as more than allegories, historical or mythical illustrations of general spiritual truths.
>
> So Lessing, Goethe, and such lay prophets as Carlyle and Emerson had for Christianity only an inessential respect. They drank their genuine inspiration directly from nature, from history, from the total apprehension they might have of life.

In those few words Santayana indicates his awareness of the mature Unitarian's cutting through much of the poetry of historic institutions and rituals (even if there be some loss attendant) to get to the firsthand sources of life's meaning and joy. I mention this today because I feel on my part a desire to be as tolerant and understanding of healthy developments within the Catholic church as he has shown toward my own liberal tradition.

As a matter of fact, I have chosen a small area of the canvass for this brief discussion today: the struggle between liberalism and reaction in Catholicism as seen in the recent second session of the Vatican II Council meeting in Rome; a power struggle seen dramatically on one side in the ancient Curia and on the other in the growing independence of the bishops all around the world who are insisting on their voice and their vote being recognized. The struggle in Rome last fall at the Vatican II Council session is but one more fascinating example of similar struggles between conservatives and liberals in many diverse religious governments and societies today. The same basic struggle we shall note today is also visible in the Protestant churches, in Unitarian Universalism, in Soviet communism, and in the economic-social-political complex called the United States of America.

Tonight, in my annual report to the members of this church, I shall discuss the vigorous emergence of the layman in American Unitarianism in the past thirty years. Ours is a religious movement long boasting of democratic and populist foundations. It is this emergence of the Catholic layman and the layman's nearest official with power—the bishop—that concerns us this morning. The sharp, hot winds of modern thought have reached into the Vatican as never before in history. I am not playing prophet and predicting what the ultimate outcome will be fifty or a hundred years from now, but I do commend to you the value of measuring this Catholic firestorm, if for no larger reason than better to understand our own Unitarian development in the year 1964. Nothing is more absurd than to dismiss the Catholic church as a great monolithic structure that has no concern with dissenting laymen who protest outmoded practices, outmoded ethics, and outmoded theology. In the last three years the world has heard the clamor and controversy in this so-called monolithic institution. Television, radio, press bureaus, and non-Catholic guests all carried the open dialogue of Roman Catholic life for hundreds of millions to witness. When else in Unitarian history, since the sixteenth century, have our laymen known the differences between a Cardinal Bea and a Cardinal Ottaviani?

I sincerely trust that by now there is no one here who fears that a sermon on Catholic thought and action is prima facie evidence that your minister has suffered senile dementia and is flirting with what our puritan clergy in a franker age of English speech called "the whore of Babylon."

When I was a boy in Ohio, the modernist movement in Roman Catholicism was having its brief day of popularity. Few of you probably remember the timid but sincere efforts of some Catholic clergy and lay-men to have the church recognize the gains of modern scholarship, to make a new assessment of the historical Jesus, to give some intellectual integrity to the research and public utterances of Catholic leaders. I remember the names of Hermann Schell in Germany, Alfred Loisy and George Tyrrell in France, and Baron Von Hugel in England.

But it was a brief period indeed. In 1907 Pope Pius X issued a de-cree "Lamentabeli" and an encyclical "Pascendi" in which he commanded his bishops to purge the clergy of the sickness of modernism. Books were banned, priests were excommunicated, and teachers dismissed. A year later this same pope required clergy serving as pastors or as teachers to take an antimodernist oath. When the Catholic magazine *Le Sillon* advocated vigorous social action in cooperation with Protestants and with unbelievers beyond Protestantism, Pope Pius issued another encyclical against "social modernism."

But today the controversy, silenced by action of a conservative pope and a supporting Curia in 1910, has broken out again, primarily because of half a century of revolt, intellectual and political, throughout the en-tire world, and because a rare and courageous pope, John XXIII, fully concerned with insuring the survival of his worldwide institution, gave aid and comfort to the new modernists.

Unitarians are not expected to be overly familiar with the term "Curia," so allow me a brief word of definition. For four hundred years an entity has intervened between the pope and his hundreds of bishops throughout the world; it is called the Roman Curia. It consists of the various administrative arms with which the pope governs the church. It has acquired superepiscopal powers. This group has often arrogated unto itself the papal function in policy making, especially as the Vatican became more and more centralized. Until very recently, bishops any-where outside of Italy found it unwise to take any important action on any continent without first clearing it with the Curia. The atmo-sphere has not been unlike that of the FBI during the worst of the McCarthy period in our own secular government. By ignoring corre-spondence from the bishops, by intolerable procrastination, by unre-mitting surveillance of all that crossed their desks, the thirty-one mem-bers of this tight body reinforced its control and authority over the church. (I hope there is no smugness arising in any Unitarian minds at this point. Even Protestants, Presbyterians, Methodists, Lutherans, yea, Unitarians and Universalists also have known their own brands of Curia behavior in our own time. I shall not distract you with docu-mentation or we might not get back on the main road of our discourse today.) During the reign of Pope Pius XII (just before John XXIII), the bishops found the pontiff ignoring their reports, making them cool their heels for days and weeks to see him. When Cardinal Montini of Milan was elected to succeed John XXIII, he, like John, listened to, welcomed, and respected the bishops from all parts of the world. This alone does not make Pope Paul VI a proven defender of the bishops in their struggle to modernize the church against the tight controls of the Curia. Only the next months and years will reveal his fundamental position. His recent trip to Palestine was dramatic, but not relevant in measuring his leadership in this battle of the Curia.

One hundred years ago a Roman Catholic archbishop attending Vatican I (the council meeting parallelling Vatican II now in recess) left these unambiguous words about the Curia:

> The experience that I have acquired during many years of the personnel of the Pontifical Curia has produced in me an unconquerable conviction that never, never until the end of the world will they consent to renounce temporal power. They will utilize every means, at one time public, at another secret, at one time more violent, at one time less so, to repossess themselves of that power.

This is not Emmett McLaughlin nor Paul Blanshard speaking, but a working archbishop speaking his mind. Amongst the young clergy and laity of Catholicism in many parts of the world today, this kind of strong speech is occurring in theology, in social and political issues, and in a demand for reform in administration. The major theme last fall at Vatican II was church reform.

To be sure, I do not wish to paint a picture of unmitigated reaction in the Curia. It does contain Cardinal Bea as well as Cardinal Ottaviani; the first a leader of the liberal forces at the Vatican II council, the second the most reactionary of the conservatives.

Time forbids a thorough report on the signs of a liberal spirit at work in the Catholic world. The demand of the bishops for a voice in the next period of Catholic life in a revolutionary world is one illustration. A few others must suffice.

A Rome-based correspondent recently asked South African Archbishop Dennis Hurley if he would baptize the correspondent's newborn child. "Certainly I will," said the archbishop. "We will take care of it at St. John Lateran." The correspondent said he had planned to have it done at St. Peter's. "St. Peter's!" boomed the Archbishop. "Never! It was built with the sale of indulgences bought by the simple faithful who were cruelly told they were buying their way out of purgatory and hell." The baby was christened in St. John Lateran and named John.

Or take another news story from my file. On October 23 the Roman Catholic bishops of the United States took a strong stand for racial equality at the Ecumenical Council (Vatican II). The bishop of Baton Rouge was the spokesman for the Americans. Bishop Robert Tracy (one of the 178 bishops from the United States) has had his own troubles with segregationists in his own diocese in the United States, but he spoke without hedging on the need for racial equality in and out of the church; and at the end of the speech, contrary to tradition and the rules, he was applauded in St. Peter's Basilica. (We Unitarians are not the only ones who have trouble about applause within the sanctuary.)

Just before the Ecumenical Council opened last October, Rev. Robert Graham in the Catholic magazine *America* appealed to the bishops on their way to Rome to set up a charter of civil rights for Roman Catholic writers and intellectuals. He urged that the Supreme Sacred Congregation of the Holy Office (a section of the Curia) cease some of its most notorious practices of censorship and repression. His list of proposed reforms sounds like a fine, fresh release from the American Civil Liberties Union. It was one more blast at the power of the Curia over the thinking and writing of Catholic writers.

Or turn to another area: human misery in South America. On August 11, 1963, from Santiago, Chile, the *New York Times* reported that the archbishop of Santiago, Cardinal Silva Enrique, issued a call for sweeping reforms affecting the welfare of the masses in Chile. In his letter to all of his churches he called for new housing programs, for more schools, and for job opportunities for the workers. Otherwise, he said, "the changes will be effected by extreme leftists or Communists." I am not today debating whether it should be done by Catholics who are for feudal or mild democratic capitalist reforms, or by Marxists who are for radical socialist change and the end of class rule. What I do note is that the church is hearing from bishops on the local scene who know what the issues are, and are insisting that the Roman Church turn its attention to immediate human remedies for intolerable conditions.

I have praised Father Hidalgo in Mexico for the past fifteen years in this pulpit, as I have praised Bishop Ambrose of the fifth century for his radical social views. In the same spirit I salute a Cardinal Enrique in Chile who insists that religion focus on the need for land reform, for curbing the wealthy industrial and agricultural barons of his own country. His pastoral letter went out in two hundred thousand copies. If there is to be a social dialogue between Catholics and Communists today in the world, let it be over who can most rapidly bring relief to the disinherited, the forgotten, and the hungry. I was interested in the final line in the *New York Times* story, "While the Cardinal has ruled out any collaboration with Communism, he said there could be specific occasions when the church would agree with the Socialist-Communist front on certain reforms." If the western powers, including the United States, could have said that in 1939 in the face of Hitler's fascist challenge, many millions of war dead would probably be alive today, and the problem of peace and survival would not be nearly so difficult.

I wish I had time to document further this challenge from the bishops and laity to the Curia now shaking the Catholic church. I must suffice with a statement by Professor Gordon Zahn of Loyola University in his article, "The Church as a Source of Dissent":

> The kind of dissent and deviance most needed today is the kind that would speak out against government policies concerning nuclear testing and nuclear war, that would encourage the faithful to stand apart from other community and national practices which fail to meet the tests of their religious value.

Could a returned Theodore Parker say it better?

I can say that in recent weeks Unitarian ministers in several cities have reported the initiative of Catholic high officials and church colleges in calling interfaith symposia and conferences on civil rights and disarmament issues. Alas, the cardinal in Los Angeles is not one of the liberals in the present dialogue.

If we Unitarians mean what we say about rejoicing at the growth potential of people, then we should rejoice at evidence such as I have been offering in the past few minutes. You may be sure that the Curia's thirty-one members, or most of them at least, do not rejoice at these signs of a new intellectual and social modernism in their church. But religious liberals, democratic advocates, should rejoice. I am not making any romantic claims today that the spirit of free inquiry and social revolution is sweeping, or will sweep, the Catholic church around the world, but I am saying that it is for the good of all mankind that a demand for more debate, more dialogue, more reform, more concern for the earth's exploited be discovered in this final third of the twentieth century.

I agree with our Unitarian minister in Ann Arbor, Rev. Erwin Gaede, when he states in a recent sermon, "The Roman Catholic Church has come to the end of the Constantinian era where the church was in close union with the state, to a situation where the church can no longer depend upon the protection or favor of the state." This Constantinian era, fifteen hundred years old, emphasized concentration of power in the hands of the pope and, for the past four centuries, shared with the Curia. The papacy had a reactionary social and political policy that abetted colonialism and class exploitation. The cross and the sword mutually abetted each other. Those of you who have been reading, as I have, the play *The Representative*, now running in London, know that it deals with the relationship of the Vatican and Hitler's fascism even as people's priests were being killed in concentration camps along with anti-Fascist lay Catholics, Jews, and Protestants. But since 1945 it has become more and more clear that the Constantinian era is really over. The crack in the dike of Catholic reaction is visible to all who choose to look. That is why a pope like John XXIII is so welcomed, even by the Kremlin and by liberal sectors of American, British, and French life.

Why the change? Because new ideas (which we Unitarians say we encourage) have been fermenting in many heads, most of which are not Unitarians. Today, as Mr. Gaede reminds us, one out of every three human beings lives under officially "atheist" regimes. Only one out of every five citizens of the world is a Christian. If governments are not hostile to institutional religion, they are at least neutral, rather than friendly, as I myself discovered in East Berlin and Warsaw and Tokyo. The rebirth of the non-Christian religions—Confucianism, Hinduism, Buddhism, Mohammedanism—has shaken the Catholic Protestant world. The Constantinian era is indeed over.

Why am I talking about the struggle between the Curia and the bishops today in my discussion of Catholicism? Because it is here that the focus is found for the dialogue between the past and the present, between the Constantinian power structure and something more democratic, more consonant with our new age. The Roman Catholic Church finds itself saddled with a medieval theology, an authoritarian administrative hierarchy, and social loyalties to the wealthy, the possessors, and what Marxists correctly call "the ruling class." Can it change or will it change? Many thoughtful critics, Catholic and non-Catholic, think that it will. It will not happen overnight.

To be sure, the session last fall in Rome was not very encouraging. Many writers have made assessments of it, but none claim that it matched the vigor, the zeal, and the vision of the first session during the reign of Pope John XXIII in 1962. Superficially, there were things that one who is liberal could applaud: the voice vote favoring authority for the bishops to share with the pope in ruling the church, referred to as the principle of "episcopal collegiality," a democratic notion. But it was not finalized, and many bishops returned home, often thousands of miles, predicting that the third session to make this reform stick officially would never be called.

The schema, or agenda item, on the evils of anti-Semitism was lightly touched upon, but not made solid with an official vote making individual freedom of belief for all men a working principle. It was agreed and later confirmed by a papal decree that liturgical changes would make possible a using of vernacular language in the mass and sacraments at some point. This is not much to cheer about.

Even so Catholic-oriented a magazine as *Time* observed that the Curia men slowed down the sessions by controlling commissions, by failing to get reports written or printed, and by constantly revising the schema—the agenda items—so that great confusion resulted. Efforts to replace road-blocking Curia officials with elected bishops were defeated. The new pope,

Paul VI, an aristocratic intellectual and a man far more popular with the Curia than was the late Pope John, seemed to be fulfilling John's description of him as a Hamlet. The new pope is either a prisoner of the Curia at present, or a diplomatic pro-Curia pontiff able to preach some of his predecessor's sermons as he allows action to be tangled up by men he could control better if he wanted to.

One can be troubled at Pope Paul's indecision, his hot and cold positions, his declaring at the end of the session, "I fear the bishops are rushing headlong toward the brink of schism." Next September 14 the third session is supposed to meet. If it does, one can only tremble at the fact that the revisions and reforms proposed will be edited and presented by Curia cardinals at Pope Paul's recent insistence. Unless this decision is reversed, there is no reason to think the third session will be much more productive than the second. The Curia will fight to the last minute of play. One dare not forget the remark of Genoa's Giuseppe Cardinal Siri on his way home, "The Pope and the bishops pass, the Curia remains."

But let us not prematurely conclude that the modernism of this era has failed or will fail in the years ahead. This would be oversimplifying a complex matter. It is probably true that the Constantinian era is over, with its Inquisition, crusades, persecutions, and control of governments by manipulation. It is quite possible that with elephantine meanderings, with a snail-like pace, with forward and backward movements, the Roman Church will, under many massive pressures upon it, come to terms with the twentieth century, not only with modern biblical scholarship and modern science and the new science of psychiatry, but also with communism and democracy. The dialogue is open. Cardinals are thinking. Bishops are contradicting the pope and the Curia in public, in print, and from the sacred halls of the basilica of St. Peter's itself.

I do not believe that Pope Paul VI has either the good intentions or the universal humanisim of spirit of the late Pope John. I do not share the excessive benedictions heaped upon him by Alice Leone Moats in the *National Review* on October 22, when she reassured the readers of that ineffable publication that the new pontiff was a dedicated supporter of free enterprise and the mortal foe of even John-like fraternizing with the Communists. She assured her readers that on the day the election of Paul as pope was proclaimed, Cardinal Ottaviani looked positively radiant as he appeared on the balcony of St. Peter's to make the announcement. She assures us that there has been a stepping up of anti-Communist declarations since the new pope came to power and refers to Radio Vatican broadcasts for evidence. She reminds us of Cardinal Wyszynski's recent sermon against the Polish government and the anathema against Marxism that came out of the episcopate of Tuscany a few weeks ago. She finally reminds us that Paul spent thirty years in the service of the Curia and that he has not lost the old school tie. She may be right; she may be whistling in the wind. I do not know. Time will tell.

As I said in my sermon after the first session of Vatican II, I am not yearning for world Christian unity and I am not trying to devise ways of saving the Catholic Church. The ambitious project of Pope Paul VI and many leaders of Protestant Christendom and many Eastern Orthodox prelates to achieve unity is an act of despair and defeat, not of strength and confidence. Like my friend, Erwin Gaede in Ann Arbor, I look on such a project with real apprehension. But like him, I rejoice at the aroused dialogue between Catholic and non-Catholic today because only in such debate—open, vigorous, and informed—can truth circulate and closed minds be opened. The Curia no more wants such dialogue than the heirs of Channing and Jefferson welcome it. The end result of free speech, social prophecy, revolutionary calls for reform will be a new order. Some of you may be sure to know how it is all coming out; I do not. But I do know that the door of truth once opened can never be locked again! The passion for freedom can never be burned out of a man, or intimidated out of a man. I do not care too much whether people want the poetry of religion presented with the grandeur of a Roman service on Easter or with the more contemporary brilliance of a Unitarian cantata with humanistic vocabularies; these can be matters of taste and temperament. Our concern should be for releasing man's power freely to say "I believe" or "I protest" without penalties, to lift burdens off the shoulders of his exploited brothers—intellectual burdens or economic burdens—any kind that now bend their backs and force them to their knees. If a Cardinal Bea or an archbishop in Santiago or an editor of *America* or the *Catholic Worker* can move a few million people a little closer to the light, I say: "Power to their tongues and their hands. May the Unitarians do as well or better, as time and opportunity permits." It is a competition of peace, not of destruction. Where there is light all errors can be discovered in spite of mischievous and evil men at work to maintain darkness. This is the testimony of a one-time Catholic, Michael Servetus, who started us on our way four hundred years ago as rebels against the Trinity and the tyranny of popes who called themselves infallible.

Let the Catholics encourage more ecumenical councils. Let the free thinkers join in the conversation, loud and clear. John Milton's ghost may bless the dialogue, and rascals will flee in disarray. And the rascals will not all be the sons of Mother Church. I have for thirty-five years been an ardent advocate of separation of church and state, but I have never called for a new crusade of extermination of my fellowmen who failed to share my own blinding vision of the truth.

Why Do Churches Panic
at the Word "Socialism"?
October 10, 1976

This is no straw man subject. It is highly possible that this address can be over in three minutes, and you can all take off for home and your favorite TV show or re-reading your Tennyson and Browning. I might, with ESP microwaves, hear you say, "We all know the answers, good or bad, and you know we know them. We have been debating socialism for years." But my reading of church history and weekly bulletins convinces me that this is mostly illusion. We have not been doing so.

One reason why so many churches panic is that they fear the dark, the unknown, or being compelled to use their brains to consider new conditions in society. They see no possible reason for "mixing religion with politics" (the most hoary of clichés on the subject). Father Drinan and Father Daniel Berrigan know better. Why don't Baptists and Presbyterians? Church people have become intoxicated with what Gore Vidal calls "the sweet sickness of the bourgeoisie." They would prefer to sit in apathy or a coma rather than to listen to Mr. Vidal's next statement that "the society of 'nice people' is dying and that we are and shall continue to sense the birth pangs of a new establishment."

A great many American church people of standard brand religions during my seventy-four years on earth have declared unambiguously that socialism is evil, against nature (especially human nature), and was brewed in a caldron by the devil himself. They prefer being twice born! "Fix up yourself and society will then be pure." If they are Unitarians or Universalists, as some of them are, they resent being reminded that much of American Unitarianism up to 1850 was socialist in its thinking and

---

Address delivered at the Community Church of Boston.

advocacy, and they prefer to forget that William Henry Channing in Boston said, "The charity we need is justice," and that James Freeman Clarke, one of the most revered of Unitarian leaders in those days, wrote,"Capital can wait. Labor cannot." Many religious liberals have never read Theodore Parker's "A Sermon on Merchants," probably the most brilliant address of his famed Boston ministry, which still sends chills down my spine.

I shall take no time defending my right to collect wages from congregations for pressing upon listeners and readers the often revolutionary words of Eugene Debs, Edward Bellamy, G. B. Shaw, Harry F. Ward, or Karl Marx, or Castro, or Mao. I am speaking today primarily of the orthodox Christian churches and the evangelical churches and fundamentalist groups. I read in *Newsweek* of the Campus Crusade for Christ, with five thousand staff members working in eighty countries, based at Arrowhead Springs near San Bernardino, California, an organization led by the candy manufacturer, William R. Bright, the master strategist for a born-again Christian gospel. He and his cohorts of thousands are right now staging campaigns in 265 American cities to mobilize twenty-five million Americans for Christ and to get a Christian president and Congress elected to office this November 2. Unless this is done, Mr. Bright asserts, "this nation will fall to Communism."

We are foolish indeed if we think such politically reactionary campaigning as the Campus Crusade is so absurd as to warrant no serious attention from free thinkers, liberals, and radicals. Let me remind you that when editor John Dart of the *Los Angeles Times* wrote a covering story on the week of the Unitarian Universalist Assembly held this past June in Claremont, California, he opened it with the statement, "The Unitarian Universalists are the only historic denomination in America that openly declares it stands for liberal religion. Unitarians do not necessarily believe in God." Over the years few Unitarian ministers have been dismissed and none defrocked for socialist views.

The Campus Crusade for Christ is but one example of this evangelical conservative Christian drive, fueled with millions of dollars, to get "Christians" into power positions with all possible dispatch. In my ears I hear the batlike screech of a slogan from twenty years ago: "Kill a Commie for Christ"; only it now is handled with more sophistication and more structured public relations guidance. We are staring American fascism in the face. That is something to panic about.

Saturday, September 18, 1976, the *Los Angeles Times* ran this story:

Johnny Carson, Hugh Hefner and Elvis Presley have something in common. They are all repeaters on a list of the "ten most wanted men for God and country" released here this week by evangelist Bob Harrington of New Orleans. The others on the current list are Muhammad

Ali, A. J. Foyt, Evel Knievel, Joe Namath, Howard Cosell, Walter Cronkite and Henry Ford II.

"In no way am I judging their faith," Mr. Harrington said, "but I'm saying if they spoke out for Christ and country they would have great influence on the nation."

Rev. Bob Harrington's first list appeared in his 1969 book, *The Chaplain of Bourbon Street*. His targets then (to whom he wrote letters) included Howard Hughes and Jimmy Hoffa. Also, ex-baseball pitcher Don Drysdale and entertainers Frank Sinatra and Dean Martin. Muhammad Ali, who heads the revised roll, speaks out about his Muslim faith. But Harrington indicated that his list was an effort in part to persuade people that Christianity and U.S. destiny are linked—a belief that is widely held in conservative Protestant circles.

"This country," he added, "is the greatest nation, the only nation that calls itself 'One nation under God.'"

He does not mention the ethical dilemmas of the death penalty, or armament sales, or 10 percent unemployment.

I have seen several anti-Communist Christian crusades in my four-and-a-half-decade career, and they are not to be taken as one more big "Laugh-in" charade. These humorless religious organizers have every intention of giving us Christian fascism. In 1917 during the Russian Revolution, the church was with the Czar; and if you remember Franco Spain or the Kuomintang years of Chiang Kai-shek in China, you know it is no fantasy we are discussing today. For the one historic denomination in America—the Unitarian Universalist that claims to be a liberal religious movement—not to resist such vast expenditures of energy, manpower, and money for a "Christian" government in this year 1976 is to betray every Jeffersonian and Justice Holmes notion we ever inherited. We have always been a small religious sect, but not known for silence or moral indifference. Thoreau supported John Brown, Emerson spoke out against the fugitive slave law, and hundreds of our members and clergy were at Selma for civil rights, and later struggled for the ending of the slaughter of Vietnamese and Americans in Asia. Can we equally protest the selling of America to extreme reaction and closing off talk on socialism in an election year?

Churches panic at the words "secular socialism" getting into sermons, discussions, and forums because—let us face it—for a thousand years in Western society Christian churches have operated on the basis that man had no business on earth except to get off it and that he was a totally unnatural creature. He was here as an alien, as a stranger. He had come from another realm, and he was to go back to another realm in the skies. There were a thousand years of persuasion, well-organized and directed to countless millions, that this was God's supernatural plan. In essence, kings and princes and prime ministers said: Leave the driving to us. You and I know that in the last century and a half an intellectual revolution has shaken the world, denying that man was an unnatural creature. Men and women discovered the real world of here and now. Heaven grew dim and misty. They discovered that they had a capacity to think for themselves, to build families and communities to create a civilization for enjoyment in their lifetime. They found the means and techniques to achieve the dreams of Isaiah, Amos, and Hosea—and many other seers and prophets—now! They learned to speak out as had bold John Lilburne in Cromwell's day, who told the farmers of seventeenth-century England that the preachers talked to heaven to keep them from asking for justice now: land, herds, wages, and rest from excessive and intolerable labor.

But the church resisted in the seventeenth century, kicking and screaming, burning and hanging the advocates of the premature proposals of Lilburne. Let us be candid. They panicked at socialism.

Most American churches at this hour, three hundred years later, if you check up with polls and computers, do not now embrace the concept of human liberation, justice, and equality. Churches panic at socialism because it challenges both the religious establishment and the economic establishment. The government—federal, state, and local—used the church as sacristan, defender of the faith, and lackey for these one thousand years, and paid well for these services. An ecumenical poll of 2,490 clergy this very month by the National Council of Churches office of research found that in the five denominations polled, the ministers regarded being outspoken on social issues as one of the least important tasks facing the church today. Sixty percent said their most important task was to help members to be Christian at work, at home, and in community life. Leading the way on social issues fell far behind supporting world missions and caring for the old. The blind leading the blind.

The churches have an enormous investment materially in the maintenance of the present capitalist order, monopoly capitalism, and the world of multinational corporations. Never forget that the churches enjoy tax advantages in property exemption many billions of dollars worth, as Madalyn O'Hair has documented so devastatingly in Freedom Under Siege—not church sanctuaries and parsonages alone, but hospitals, homes, businesses. Churches enjoy grants from state and federal tax funds for parochial schools, salaries, and transportation. The clergy enjoy a real, even if diminishing, status and prestige—fighting all the way against U.S. Supreme Court decisions to end prayers and Bible reading in public schools. We clergymen are part of the public ornamentation at commencements, political conventions, inaugurations, and the opening of Congress. How many socialist clergy get honorary degrees at Harvard, Yale, and Texas Christian College?

You may smile at the thought that millions of American Christians, some multimillionaires, many middle-class men and women of trade and commerce, as well as twice-born workers in fields and factories, profess, in the words of the old hymn, "We are but strangers here; heaven is our home." But they are reading the Dow Jones Averages all the way to the Pearly Gates. The late Kathryn Kuhlman, Oral Roberts, Billy Graham, all find personal pelf and social power no contradiction to this ancient theme of the heavenly destination. Charles Colson may have found Christ after the Senate Investigating Committee on Watergate found him a co-conspirator in Mr. Nixon's Oval Room cabal, but his months in prison studying the Scriptures did not bring forth a desire to so change the system that the ethic of Amos or Jesus might have a chance to be tried under more favorable circumstances here on earth. Colson is for saving souls, not society.

The House of Representatives has recently passed a resolution demanding that "secular humanism" be driven out of our public schools and the political establishment. And what does that mean? Secular humanism is what our Constitution is all about: the separation of church and state; the use of science, technology, and law to bring some measure of equality, justice, and a fair share of the fruits of our labor to all the citizens of our country. It is opposed to oppression. Churches panic at the word socialism because evergrowing numbers of people have not given up their commitment to solving earthly problems. They are not all disillusioned with politics.

Many church members despise the word socialism because socialism has shown, in this century, that it can vastly improve the lot of working people—the great majority of our people who are, even with strike funds and a modicum of welfare, a few short weeks from starvation and total disaster when pay envelopes cease coming and unemployment compensation stops. Socialism would give real power to workers, as it has proven again and again in the old world and the new, and churches would in most cases be irrelevant.

Church people with private resources, stock portfolios, large savings accounts, productive pieces of real estate, and other parts of the action in one or more businesses or professions find the advocacy of basic human values through socialist organization intolerably threatening, anathema to their pocketbooks. They felt the same for the 1930s during the Great Depression and the New Deal reforms. As long as I live I shall remember that President Roosevelt at an American Youth Congress dinner at the White House turned to me, present as an adviser to that young people's movement, and asked, "Mr. Fritchman, as a minister will you explain to me why the churches in America are silent or even hostile to my proposals for public housing, stronger labor laws, unemployment insurance, and social security?" What would you have said? "The churches fear socialism, with your unwitting aid. I do not agree." What would you have said!

Two months before I left the editorship of the *Christian Register* at Unitarian headquarters in 1947, I published in the journal Pierre van Paassen's address in Arlington Street Church, Boston. The war against the fascist powers was less than two years over. Truman was in the White House. I want to read two paragraphs of that magnificent address as I try to answer the question—why do the churches panic at the word socialism?—by a writer and speaker of great eloquence and influence, who did not panic. These are his words:

> Look! The rudiments of fascism are dinned and hammered into our people's head night and day. But they do not even notice it because their minds have been anesthetized, numbed and dulled to such an extent that the significance of events does not penetrate. The lessons of history are not allowed, are not given time to connect with anything in the people's consciousness. The narrowing and starving of our apprehension goes on at such a pace that we have not noticed that it is fascist doctrine which is being inculcated in America's soul by means of the selfsame slogans and tactics as those which the Nazis used to foist their philosophy of death on Europe.
>
> Didn't Hitler deify the state and declare its acts and deeds sacrosanct, inviolable, above criticism? Didn't he, too, declare war inevitable and necessary? Did he not denounce every forward-looking person or liberal as a starry-eyed dreamer or a potential Bolshevik? Did he not brand every man who looked beyond the borders of his own country and who recognized those living on the other side as brothers, did he not brand every such man as a criminal internationalist, as a traitor to the national ideal?
>
> It is these crude slogans of fascism that are being forced down our throats in this country. The minds of men are poisoned against and made afraid of the splendid and glorious new era, the era of the common man, the new dispensation of peace and well-being for all.

That was Pierre van Paassen in 1947, this is 1976!

Socialism, let me say clearly, insists upon putting human values first and making an end of the exploitation of the fear of tomorrow or the hereafter. This stock-in-trade whip used by the churches must be flung onto the junk heap of history.

Church people who are physically comfortable and believe they are secure in their jobs bitterly resent ministers, rabbis, or priests who remind them that America has twenty-three million poor, most of them silent, inarticulate, cynical, and alienated. Many of these poor see no point in voting, sensing correctly that the electoral process is made complicated and distant with infinite deliberation. Sixty million potential voters will not vote this November 2, we are told. Trust in the moral responsibility of Congress and the White House, even the Supreme Court—now a hanging court—has sunk to a new low in this century. This is not due alone to the vast corruption withn government and business—Lockheed Aircraft's bribes to Prince Bernhart and, now jailed in Japan, ex-Premier Tanaka—nor is it due alone to Howard Hughes and Robert Vesco and Richard Nixon's gameplaying with other people's millions to bleed us white before Doomsday comes. It is also due to the fact that we have churches, temples, and cathedrals (with all too few exceptions) that prefer to keep things as they are, claiming that man is hopelessly greedy and selfish, incapable of taking the general welfare clause or the Ten Commandments or the words of Gandhi or Martin Luther King seriously. The wish is father to the thought. The church establishments and those who still chiefly support them despise democracy, cannot abide the thought of a classless society, and the sharing of work, service, and the fruits of the earth with anything remotely resembling evenhanded justice. Henry James, Senior, conservative writer that he was, said it plainly: "Democracy is a resolution of government into the hands of the people, a taking down of that which has before existed, and a recommitment of it to its original sources." And today I am saying, to church and unchurched persons before me, that no decent, sincere liberal or radical should fear or oppose this restructuring of our society—which Henry James advocated—as rapidly as possible. If the churches continue to ignore the ethics of democracy and refuse to truly serve the people, we must doubt whether they can, or should, survive. No wonder so many youth look on churches as tongue-tied eunuchs—museum guards of artifacts and tribal sacerdotal gear.

This is not an academic economics lecture tonight, though I never apologize for discussing economic theory in a church, having learned some of my professional duties in religion from Dr. Harry F. Ward at Union Seminary and Rabbi Stephen A. Wise at the Free Synagogue in New York. Whatever my misdemeanors, I never slipped on the absurdity that politics, economics, and religion must never mix. I wish to make clear that I am still doing my homework as I stagger into retirement. I am reading Robert Heilbroner and G. William Domhoff, and many others, about the complex business of transforming America into a socialist democracy, and the uncertainty of the future before us in the twenty-first century. I commend to you Professor Heilbroner's third book in the last two years, *Business Civilization in Decline.* Our capitalist civilization is doomed, he feels, because of such manifest factors as runaway population, nuclear and other types of advanced weaponry hanging over our heads, and the increasing toxicity of the global environment. We are fouling our own nest to the point of its uninhabitability. Our only hope, he believes, is some variant of socialism; a disciplined society in which morality and the public interest would form the fabric of collective living. He foresees the end of capitalism within the next hundred years, describing the stages of that demise—an analysis which every ethically concerned citizen should read and judge for himself. In the postindustrial society, he envisions men and women will learn that they can control their own lives, and that planning is a necessity and not an option. They can regulate their communities and abandon the type of social fatalism of today's alienated citizens who cry in mock or real concern: "You can't change the system."

"Without an explicit pattern of social values the world cannot survive," says Heilbroner. Living collectively calls for a viable morality we in America have not known for over two hundred years, and even then but partially. What Thorstein Veblen sixty years ago called "pecuniary canons" will have to be superseded by compassion and concern of man for man. (I use the term *man* generically, meanwhile genuflecting reverently toward Susan B. Anthony and Gloria Steinem!)

The churches of America panic at the word socialism because it would demand a drastic 180 degree turn for a vast majority of them, middle-class as they are, on the attitude to be taken toward workers, people with sweat on their hands, less food on their plates. You know well that factory and service workers have been long dismissed as nonpersons by our government and finance elites, their academic and media mandarins.

I know that there are men and women in our liberal churches, our ethical societies, our nonsectarian community churches, who feel the despair and cynicism of believing that Doomsday is inevitable, that we cannot roll back our avalanche of social crimes at this date, that socialism cannot get a hearing. Neither does some nameless wight in the Vatican in Rome who edits an official magazine under the papal eye. I am convinced that there are some Catholic Marxists in there, working three shifts a day, because I read one essay recently about the People's Republic of China, which I had visited just thirty-six months ago, and this Catholic scrivener on the holy turf wrote, regarding the land of Mao Tse-tung, as follows: "One cannot deny that human values are being affirmed. The civilization of China is forging ahead. Even if it is materialistic philosophically, it has not turned toward the worship of the golden calf. Far from it. It makes its appeal to authentic human values; it even speaks of the spirit of poverty, of sacrifice, of self-denial." The Marxism of Mao, he concludes, "is indeed atheistic, but present-day China is tending toward a mystique of unselfish work in service of others, towards an aspiration for justice and exaltation of the simple classes." Not bad for a papal editorial minion!

Now that is not my vocabulary, dear friends, but I would say that the Chinese are using the operative teaching of the Christian ethic, as they have simultaneously sent the foreign missionaries home where they might be needed more. By way of contrast, the editor of that often perceptive the *New Yorker* spelled out the mind-boggling contempt a recent American church-going president had for the brotherhood of man, the ancient ethical teachings of the Old and New Testaments, as Richard Nixon spoke to the Seafarers Union International in December 1973. He said:

> There are only seven percent of the people of the world living in the USA—and we use 35 percent of all the energy. That isn't bad. That's good. That means that we are the richest, strongest people in the world, and that we have the highest standard of living in the world. That is why we need so much energy, and may it always be that way.

The *New Yorker* editor comments: "As we turn our thermostats down and drive at 55 miles an hour on our highways, we can warm ourselves with the thoughts of how much colder it's going to be for those people in other parts of the world who have to make do with the fuel that's left over."

This is an obscene vignette of so-called "Christian" thinking in high places that causes me to panic at the thought of churches which tolerate such concepts without organized outrage surviving another hundred years. Who needs Christianity like that and lay members like Mr. Nixon or his survivors in and out of office? Can we help turn our churches around?

Comfortable pacifists in many secular groups as well as the historical Protestant and Catholic churches often say, "But Mao declared that socialism comes out of the barrel of a gun" (which he did say). So does capitalism! The Chairman could have added that the Christians in the West who so deplore the need for a people's revolutionary army in a land of eight hundred million people, so savagely and so long occupied by foreign powers, should ask themselves, as they deplore violence, why they accept such good dividends on stocks in armament firms, airplane companies, chemical defoliant manufacturers whose products lay bare the earth and all that moves or grows upon it. As I hear people deplore Mao Tse-tung's remarks about guns, I recall the words of beloved and gentle Dr. William Ellery Channing in Boston over a century ago: "So far is any existing government from being clothed with an inviolable sanctity, that the citizen, in particular circumstances, acquires the right, not only of remonstrating, but of employing force for its destruction."

This is a tragic reality that church people must understand as the World Council of Churches has recognized. Americans whose ancestors fought in our war for independence in 1776 and/or in the Civil War in 1860–65 should not have to be told how cruel, violent, and bloody revolutions are. Friends in other lands of all continents know what freedom from domestic or foreign tyrannies costs in treasure, homes, jobs, and lives; irreplaceable, cherished, and forever missed.

Having put down on paper over the last three years a personal history about to be published, which includes a report on my emergence into a socialist from a Republican cocoon in 1924, I shall not do more now than say that sound Methodist Ohio Wesleyan University, which I attended, had two full professors, both in the sciences, who voted for Debs in 1920, and that its Gray Chapel forum presented Philip LaFollette in 1924, the year I cast my first vote for president for Philip's father, Senator Robert LaFollette. I was nourished intellectually and emotionally over the years in my heresy by such monitors as George Bernard Shaw, W. T. Tawney, Thorstein Veblen, Leo Huberman, Harry F. Ward, and G. William Domhoff, as well as by tracts slipped under my bed—unmentionable polemics by Lenin, Marx, and Mao. Far from making me panic as I faced a career in the church, such provender gave me hope that the gulf between ethical precepts and practical programs of change might be greatly narrowed. It still amazes me to find so few sons and daughters of the middle class (from which I came) who want to take the same route: sing in the church choir, preach in the pulpit, and also build socialism. I have long contended that I knew personally enough bishops—Methodist, Episcopalian, and Roman Catholic—to be aware that they were not all "running dogs of imperialism," to borrow a phrase from the faithful on the left. In the sear and yellow leaf, I can now testify that I have never played either role—bishop or running dog—for which my anticlerical Quaker ancestors are doubtless very grateful.

As I close, let me recapitulate. The churches of America panic at the word socialism because they do not wish to respond to its assertions about the power and strength of the common people when released from their many prisons of ignorance, misery, and fantasy. The churches panic because they tremble at the possibility of a new order of society where the shark and the tiger are not elevated into gods, and where the current possessors will inevitably lose power, privilege, and luxury. As one Unitarian in one of my New England parishes said in the thirties, "Steve, I agree with you, socialism is the only hope for the future; but I don't want to live to see it." And I remember a young socialist organizer in New England who said to me, given as I was at times to discouragement and fatigue, "All the battles of the working class are defeats, except the last." I understand those words far better forty years later as I travel the globe meeting friends who confirm that dictum from the experience of their own people—millions of them. So I take fresh hope for the next century coming up. I feel Professor Heilbroner is correct: American capitalism will be dead in one hunderd years. I want to believe that many men and women in the churches will learn the lesson in time. We do not need to panic: We need to organize for a world of peace and human service, where the profit motive is rejected and class walls topple, and where no man rides on the shoulders of his brother—none master and none slave.

Part Two

Our Society

America's Unconscious Giant
The Men and Women of Labor
May 1, 1949

The great majority of Unitarian churches in the United States are closed on Labor Day Sunday in September. Most of us in the pulpits must find another occasion to speak on the theme of labor, and I find no time more appropriate than the first of May, the annual festival of workers around the earth.

Governor Warren has asked that May Day, a day traditionally a revolutionary celebration, be christened Loyalty Day. Might not we in the churches help bridge these two concepts by suggesting that the highest loyalty in America today would be a rededication of all citizens to the welfare of the people of this nation, especially that overwhelming majority who are workers, skilled and unskilled, in city and country, who now feel almost no sense of responsibility or involvement in our government and its work?

May Day was first observed in Chicago by American workers demonstrating for the eight-hour day. A workers' worldwide proclamation of solidarity will continue for years to come until in every land, advanced or retarded, the masses of people are conscious of their own leadership, until they exercise their leadership so that there will no longer be a gulf fixed between toiler and statesman. In our own land there will be a traditional emphasis upon May Day as a day of struggle for labor's demands *until* our Congress consists primarily of men and women from the ranks of labor. You and I will continue the frustrating business of writing and wiring Congressmen on issue after issue until they, as representatives of factory workers as well as attorneys and industrialists, vote in the interests of all workers, all citizens, without such costly prompting.

Address given in celebration of International Labor Day.

May Day belongs to all workers and their families in every land; and we of the churches should, in the names of a carpenter, a tentmaker, and a fisherman, who founded the Christian religion, feel a sense of participation.

Surely the churches of all creeds and faiths should be the first to encourage a sense of unity and goodwill among all who toil, with hand or brain, on all the continents and the islands of the sea. Solidarity is a religious word as well as a cherished word of the working man. This is by all odds our greatest hope for peace and the carrying ahead of the work of building a better house for the children of the earth. No nation, no party, no sect should divide those who unite at this task.

It is my own conviction that for a score of reasons the workers of America are almost totally unconscious of the power to reshape our land nearer to their dreams. It is my conviction that organized and unorganized labor in the rank and file is unaware of its potential for a far richer and more secure civilization, at peace with other nations, led by those of its own choosing: men and women devoted to the common interest rather than to private interest. The working people (and I mean all who work at any task of social value in home, office, mart, mill, or field), the working people are divided, asleep, uninformed, and, therefore, unconscious of their tremendous power. This is a peril to our future as a people, a costly failure of democracy which can be our undoing. If the sleeping giant of labor is not awakened, he may be tied and trussed to the earth as was Gulliver by the Lilliputians.

I am sure some of you may have come today saying, "The minister will probably press for a new social order where the workers are in control, and I will hear nothing of the greed, the irresponsibility, and the incompetence of the trade union members." If there be any who thought thus, if this be not an invention of my own mind, then let me reply: Thousands of Unitarians do indeed look forward to a brotherly society here on earth, undivided by nationality or race or creed, where the workers shall directly govern through their parliaments and agencies, because all shall be workers and none drones, all shall share in the making of the culture and social policies through the use of the ballot, through the contribution of their unions to critical thought and suggestion, through the teaching of their schools and universities open to every youth in the land. Only when this occurs will there be an end to what is called the greed and selfishness of labor. As long as labor feels itself shut outside the halls of government or commerce or industry, it will fight for its share of money and reward. When the gulf between worker and nonworker is ended, then this warfare will cease. And we in the church can do much to end that warfare, far more than in the past.

Labor sermons are so rare in churches that any such address is apt to be interpreted as an uncritical encomium on behalf of the workers. I cannot more than mention in passing the tragedy of labor's own betrayers from within, as well as its enemies outside its ranks. The Kefauver and Fulbright investigations have surely demonstrated that greed is not only characteristic of corrupt business men and racketeers in the ranks of management, but is also to be found in the unions. A sick society without a sense of public responsibility diseases its entire body. We are all tainted, even if our hands do not deliberately reach into the public purse. Yes, indeed, there are labor leaders who are more interested in their jobs, their pie cards, if you prefer as I do the vivid metaphor of the unions, then they are interested in the rank and file members. There are too many union officials who succumb to the blandishments of management, or the possible rewards of compromise, and who therefore sedulously surrender the struggle for the man behind the lathe or tractor. Thus labor remains impotent when it should be strong, remains outside of the halls where policy is made, standing hat in hand hoping for a few cents more an hour but dependent on the charity of those not familiar with the devastating race against poverty and fear.

There is much that could be said about the betrayers of labor, the mistakes of labor, but it is not becoming that it be said, in or out of churches, by those who in their hearts do not *want* labor sitting in the seats of highest authority, who do not believe that in tomorrow's world all should be laborers and none idlers, and whose instant reminders of labor's sins are a thinly disguised effort to keep people under the illusion that labor is in general untrustworthy, selfish, and incompetent. If people who read Mr. F. E. Dunmire's lecture, "What the Liberal Church Can Offer Organized Labor," can say "I'm for that," then the legitimate criticism of unions and union leaders can be discussed in good faith. So far, the churches have not come into the discussion with clean hands and pure hearts. They have reflected the interests and desires of employers, stockholders, attorneys, and politicians profoundly skeptical toward labor —and have therefore been hostile or at least embarrassed by the workingman in the same pew, or at the same communion rail, thinking of him not as brother but as a stranger or an enemy. It is this failure of the church that should concern us all. When the sleeping giant awakens and labor comes into its own, it will have no patience with the church unless we in the churches have made some fundamental changes in our attitudes and practices.

A year ago, when I spoke on "Why Labor Shuns the Church," I received several splendid letters. One of them I have saved and I should like to read from it this morning. These are a few sentences from many: "The most important reason for labor's negative attitude toward the church has been the church's traditional role of defender of the status quo. This has been based in part on the church's extensive land holdings, untaxed, and its theological emphasis on the life hereafter. This has minimized the importance of improvements in material goals in this earthly sphere. Labor's tradition has been based on a faith in man's infinite potentialities through the use of his social intellect. Labor therefore rejects supernatural forces." This fine letter then describes the failure of the Catholic church to help workers build a democratic, classless society because of its own commitment to an authoritarian, stratified society. The letter continues with a description of the failure of the Protestant church through its espousal of an intense individualism, which dismissed not only the intermediary of the priest, but also the intermediary of the united workers resisting their own exploitation by the then-developing industrial society. The Protestant church soon became a middle-class church, whatever its theology, and dismissed the bread and butter problems of workers as beyond its purview.

This letter from a member of this church then concludes: "These points of conflict in the Catholic and Protestant churches need not exist in a humanistic Unitarian church. But labor does not know of such a church. We must overcome the ignorance of most workers concerning the Unitarian church which does not point to salvation beyond this earth, which does not ignore the striving of labor for its just demands."

Certainly this must increasingly become the sort of church where a man who works in a shop, on a construction crew, in a service station, on a postal route, feels a warm welcome. The woman in a china factory, at a billing machine, in domestic service should find this to be her church, along with the college teacher, the physician, the business man, the social scientist, and the housewife. Only as all persons in our common civic life discover the realities of which we speak today can we be proud of the Unitarian church.

As I hope to make clear this morning, the Unitarian church has not just discovered the worker in the twentieth century. To be sure, Unitarian leaders have taken their part in labor's struggle over the years. The Unitarian Orestes Brownson, of whom I spoke a month ago from this pulpit, was a valiant leader in the New York Workingmen's Party. He wrote to President Martin Van Buren, successor to Andrew Jackson, "Sir, I wish to thank you in the name of liberty and humanity for the firm stand you have taken during the struggle now going on between the Democracy and the monied power of this country. You are now indeed with the people and the people will sustain you." Soon after, President Van Buren aroused the fury of the conservatives by establishing a ten-hour day for federal employees—this over one hundred years ago, in March 1840.

I would that I had the time for further evidence of the efforts of Unitarians to share in labor's struggle, and of the good fruits of such action when it was forthcoming. The tragedy is that we, as a church in America, have done so little when we should have done so much. We have, in fact, lagged behind some other denominations in this respect.

As I tried to indicate with the Biblical message earlier in this service, there is abundant evidence of religious concern for the worker in our earliest documents of the Jewish and Christian tradition, though there are ministers by the thousand who never use a sentence from them as texts for sermons. While one might attend some churches for a lifetime and not discover it, the truth is that for thirty centuries the exploitation of the worker and his recourse to justice through collective action have been themes close to the conscience of religion. The passages from Deuteronomy, from the prophets, from Ecclesiastes and the Gospels, from the Epistles and other writings of the Old and New Testaments this morning were a brief reminder of this fact. And a study of our Unitarian spokesmen here in America since our organization as a movement in 1825 would further fortify this thesis. We have time today for but one further illustration of this truth a century ago. The greatest of our New England prophets, Theodore Parker, in his Unitarian pulpit spoke often and with crystal clarity of what he called "the laboring classes." From one of his manuscripts I share with you this morning are passages to make clear the long perspective we should have in any consideration of the problem of labor in our own time. Also, because time gives sanction to words which might otherwise burn with too great a heat.

These are the words of Theodore Parker in 1841:

The law of Nature is this: If a man will not work, neither shall he eat. Christianity says man's greatness consists in the amount of service that he renders to the world. Certainly, he is most honorable who by his hand or his head does the greatest and best work for the race. The noblest soul the world ever saw appeared, *not in the ranks of the indolent*, but took on him the form of a servant, and when he washed the disciples' feet, meant something not generally understood in the 19th century.

And Parker continues:

Manual labor, though an unavoidable duty, is both a pleasure and a dignity unless abused by its terrible excess—when it becomes a terrible punishment and a curse. It is only a proper amount of work that is a blessing. Too much of it wears out the body before its time, cripples the mind, debases the soul, and chills the affections. It makes a man a spinning jenny or a ploughing-machine. He ceases to be a man and becomes a thing.

There must be a great sin somewhere in that state of society which allows one man to waste day and night in sluggishness or riot, consuming the bread of whole families, while from others equally gifted and faithful, it demands 12, 15 or 18 hours of hard work out of the 24, and then leaves the man so weary and worn, that he is capable of nothing but sleep—sleep that is broken by no dream.

No doubt there are exceptions, men born under the worst of circumstances, who have redeemed themselves and obtained an excellence of intellectual growth which is worthy of wonder, but *these are exceptions* to the general rule, men gifted at birth with a power almost superhuman: *It is not from the exceptions* that we frame the law.

And I would conclude these references to an address written one hundred and ten years ago, at the beginning of the industrial age in America, with a passage of startling prophetic power. Remember, this was written before the large scale organization of labor, before our government had labor legislation or collective bargaining or a department of labor. Says Theodore Parker:

> There are remedies at hand. It is true a certain amount of labor must be performed, in order that society be fed and clothed, warmed and comforted, relieved when sick, buried when dead. If this is wisely distributed, if he performs his just portion, the burden is slight and crushes no one. It is doubtless right that one man should use the services of another, but *only* when *both* parties benefit from the relation. The smith may use the services of the collier, the grocer and the glazier, for he does them a service in return. He who heals the body deserves a compensation. If the painter, the preacher, the statesman is doing a great work for mankind, he has a right to their service in return. But on what ground an idle man, who does nothing for society, or an active man whose work is wholly selfish, can use the services of others, and call them to feed him, who repays no equivalent in kind, *it yet remains for reason to discover.* Each is to use the ability he has for himself and for others. Who that is able will not return to society, with his head or hand, an equivalent for what he has received? Only the sluggard or the robber. If one cannot work through weakness, infancy or age, or sickness—then love works for him and he too is fed. If one will not work, *though he can,* the law of nature should have its effect. *He ought to starve.*

So spoke the most forthright of Unitarians in 1841. You may read further if you wish. The climax is not for tender ears. He further develops the danger to a people that venerates its oppressors. Boston in 1841 crowded to hear him, but today the end of this sermon of Parker's would lead to unpredictable disasters in Unitarian churches and to a call before some committee for examination. As Henry Steele Commager says so well in his biography of Parker, *Yankee Crusader:*

> To Parker nothing took one back to fundamentals as did the labor question, nothing revealed more glaringly the immortality of the entire social order. There was no sentimentality here. No polite abstractions.

Parker saw with dangerous clarity the barbarism and brutality of the industrial feudalism of the 19th century in America.

I leave this rugged prophet, grandson of the man who fired the first American musket at Lexington Common, with these words he spoke from his pulpit in the Music Hall on Tremont Street:

> When I remember that all value is the result of work, and see that no man gets rich by his own work, I cannot help thinking that labor is often wickedly underpaid and capital sometimes as grossly overfed. I shall believe that capital is at the mercy of labor when the two extremes of society change places.

If this seems out of date, I urge a drive this afternoon—from Soto Street to Bel Air.

Much has changed, it may be said, one hundred and ten years later. It must be for each of us to decide *how much* has changed. It is my thesis today that the most fundamental fact *has not yet changed*: that the remedy for society's iniquitous extremes lies in the hands of labor, that even now the men and women of labor are a mighty but sleeping giant, and that cruel and needless poverty will continue for millions, and fear and frightening insecurity continue for further millions until those at the levers of our social machine are placed there clearly at the mandate of those who toil.

But let us come down to recent times. The words of Parker fell into good soil. Lincoln read them and recast them in his own way. Sixty-nine years after Lincoln, Franklin Roosevelt read them and stated them in his own cadences at the beginning of his first campaign for the presidency. In Wilkes-Barre he said:

> The gains of labor are the gains of all. The new problem is to see that the machine age serves equally well the men and women who run its machines. If modern government is to justify itself, it must see to it that human values are not mangled and destroyed. You and I know that this is sound morality and good religion.

Roosevelt was saying in new words what Wendell Philips said in Tremont Temple, Boston, the day after Lincoln's election to the presidency: "I am sure you cannot make a nation one half steamboats, sewing machines and Bibles—and the *other half slaves.*"

The struggle for justice and bread—which must be identical—has continued from earliest recorded history, as I have tried to say already this morning; but the majority of American workers know this struggle very slightly. It is not taught in the schools, discussed in the homes, explained in the halls of Congress, or made the theme of our films. It is kept a secret from millions; even—I am sorry to report—from millions of men and women in trade unions.

How many union members (a part of the sleeping giant of which we speak today) know Senator George Norris's great words spoken in Congress a few years ago? Here is what the senator from Nebraska who defeated the yellow-dog contract once said:

> The right of collective bargaining has been determined in this country. The opportunity of labor to fight for its rights should not be limited by court restrictions that in practical effect impose conditions of servitude upon men. Never will men's consciences permit them to restore the tyranny and injustice which bound men to the earth in willing and unremitting toil.

If this address today seems inappropriate to anyone, it is evidence that the church has been so far from facing this basic question of who should shape the pattern of society that any elementary discussion seems like an anachronism, seems strangely unspiritual and unreligious. My only suggestion to those who feel this way is a few hours reading of the book of Deuteronomy or the prophecy of Jeremiah in the Bible, or a further perusal of Channing and Parker on labor. We modern churchmen have wandered far off the proper reservation of responsible religion, I fear.

Whenever a George Norris or a Franklin Roosevelt, a Henry Ward or a Claude Williams pleads for the need in our own time for a far more active leadership by labor, for a far greater sharing of the nation's wealth with those who produce it, the cry is heard that this is socialism, that this is preaching class hatred, that this weakens us in the face of external and menacing forces. Let us say in reply: If America's unconscious giant, the men and women of labor, awaken and assume far greater responsibility for the quality of our Congress, for the nature of our laws, for the control of business in the public interest, nothing but good can come of it.

Strife and suffering, civil disorder and war can be the only outcome of further dismemberment of our society, of the separation of the workers from the middle class and the owners of industry. It is for the liberal church, including our own, with special vigor to end the disastrous lie that manual work is undignified, that doctors and lawyers and merchants are not workers side by side with industrial toilers. The perils of class war come from those who maintain great barriers of income between owners and nonowners, between men at machines and men in front offices. These barriers can ruin and destroy the American concept of democracy and equality. It is for us in the house of religious freedom to elevate in the public mind the pride and glory of the worker. "Blessed shall be thy basket and thy kneading trough" cries the author of Deuteronomy. Let us say, "Blessed be the dynamo and the die press," and see to it that these new tools bring leisure and security to those who operate them. Until the truck driver and the orchard worker are given as great respect as the radio executive, the film star, or the surgeon, we have failed in America to fulfill our teaching of the Declaration of Independence—and even more failed as world citizens to fulfill the teachings of the ancient prophets. "It is good and comely for one to eat and to drink, and to enjoy the good of his labor that he taketh under the sun—for it is his portion."

This is no easy exhortation this morning. The presses that will speak of this teaching of brotherhood among all workers are few among us. The pulpits that will preach of such equality are rare. The film producers who will picture labor without condescension are almost invisible. Yet the unconscious giant remains in our midst. The task lies fundamentally at the door of labor. Labor's rank and file must everywhere assert their resolution that the toilers of the earth are one, that war need not slay the sons of farm and factory by the millions, that the schoolhouse and legislative hall belong to all the people, that the church is a temple for every living person without exception anywhere. When this is said by the earth's majorities, here and elsewhere, the ancient deceptions of heaven and hell will be swept away, the ancient pacts between rulers and priests will be broken, and the children of the earth will enter into their proper heritage. This is your task and mine, and cannot be longer postponed. "He hath sent me to heal the broken hearted, to preach deliverance to the captive, and recovery of sight to the blind, and to set at liberty them that are bruised." "The profit of the earth is for all. Ye shall not build and another inhabit. The workman is worthy of his hire." So let it be, not tomorrow, but today.

Do We Have Freedom of the Press?
September 16, 1951

For visitors or members unfamiliar with the working habits of the clergy, I should like to say that sermon subjects in my own ministry are prepared several weeks in advance. Some weeks ago I sketched out my preaching plans in considerable detail through February 1952. This subject today was planned for during August. If there is a felicitous relevance of today's subject to events of the past week, it only indicates that the temper of the social climate can be divined without supernatural powers by those who study such matters. The question of whether we have "freedom of the press" was brought forcibly home to many of us by the death of William Randolph Hearst, but it had haunted me as a sermon theme for a very long time.

Inasmuch as I was a working newspaperman for the Methodist church headquarters in New York in the late twenties, and for the *New York Herald-Tribune* in the same period, and later served as editor of our own Unitarian monthly journal, the *Christian Register* for five years, the relationship of freedom of the press and liberal religion has never been for me either academic or remote. My intention today is to speak, with your consent, in quite specific terms of the indissoluble bonds between the liberated religious spirit and the instrument of the press. It is my purpose to indicate that today all of us who cherish liberty in our democratic world must see the unconditional need for a free press: responsible, subject to the people's control, but free for popular opinion and authentic news to appear. It is my thesis that if the integrity and free operation of the human spirit are our highest religious values, then it is an inescapable correlary that we must have means of communication whereby we may hold traffic with other human minds. Any controls or supervision or restriction set by the people of a country will be only for the purpose of guaranteeing that the traffic of mind with mind shall not be frustrated. The purpose is never half-truth, defamation or falsehood, or mere profit. There can be no veneration for spiritual dignity, for private insight of mind and conscience that is indifferent to the accompanying problem of sharing the discovered truth or moral judgment. Today a book publisher can be a greater servant of truth than a cardinal. I profoundly question the sincerity or devotion to truth of any religious leader, for example, who speaks of the sanctity of religion and who is indifferent to the tragically acute issue of freedom of the press, the film, the airwaves, or the other media of modern communication. A cloistered freedom is a contradiction in terms; an imprisoned truth might as well have never been discovered. All truth, from the prophet's tongue in the sanctuary of religion, or from the laboratory of the scientist, or from the inventor's drawing board, waits on communication.

This is why I emphasize the religious character of the subject of freedom of the press. It is a sacred matter because a venal press injures human souls, wrecks the lives of men and women, paralyzes the mind, and withers the conscience. This has always, under all religions, been called a monstrous evil—and so it is.

To be sure, I begin this matter far back in human history: in the days of the Old and New Testament in ancient Palestine. This was a pre-newspaper world, a pre-broadcasting and pre-television world. (I might say there was something to be said for it—but we must not let corruption or abuse of any tool of science trap us into cursing the value of the discovery.) If the words of Hillel about truth-telling or of Jesus about loving one's neighbor be good news, then they remain good news when broadcast faster than the speed of light around the planet. A poem like Milton's "Samson Agonistes" is no less great and eloquent because a fine actor reads it before a television camera and it is shared with millions. Let us be very clear about this: freedom of the press is as sacred as the high altar or the holy of holies of any religion because it is an instrument for lighting the minds of men and women, bringing them out of darkness and ignorance, and when the magazine, or newspaper, or book becomes a vehicle of filth or slander or corruption of men's plans for a better world, or when the press remains silent on plans that exist to harness a mighty river and prevent untold devastation in floodtime, then a sin is committed, a greater sin than many tabulated in the commandments or pronounced by church councils or proclaimed in encyclicals from a papal throne.

The days of the Jewish prophets and later of Jesus and St. Paul were pre-newspaper days, to be sure, but the principles now undergirding the role of a press in a decent society of free men came into focus in those early days. Listen to David, the psalmist: "I will walk in liberty for I seek thy precepts." Listen to the prophet, Hosea, eight hundred years before Christ: "I was to them as they that take off the yoke on their

jaws, and I laid meat unto them." This is the mission of high religion
and of a democratic state: to remove the hooks from off the jaws of
men and give them meat—materially and spiritually. Jesus on the moun-
tainside near Jerusalem fed the multitude with bread and then delivered
a Sermon on the Mount. There was no newspaper, no radio, no news-
reel camera; but he fed the hungry, then nourished their minds. This
is the task of religion, and it is the duty of all means of communication
to aid and support it that none may languish needlessly in ignorance
or destitution.

Listen to Saint Paul in the Epistle to the Galatians: "Stand fast
therefore in the liberty wherewith Christ has made us free, not using
your liberty for a cloak of maliciousness but as servants of God." Some
of you may feel this has an archaic flavor of speech, but I assure you
that it speaks across the centuries with penetrating moral vigor. Liberty,
in pulpit or in editorial office, is not an unbounded right. It cannot
be used properly as "a cloak of maliciousness." St. Paul knew nothing
of galley proofs or rotary presses, but he knew the temptation to use
liberty for character assassination or for maintaining the trade in idols
in Ephesus rather than for the pursuit of truth and dignity. There are,
happily, members of the working press in all echelons who work with
high conscientiousness, who spell out truth with fairness and honesty,
even if they know the blue pencil will come into play an hour later
on the copy desk. I have met such men in Boston and Los Angeles,
and the delinquencies in the press I speak of today are not of their
making.

In his children's history of the world, *The Story of Mankind*, my
friend and fellow Unitarian, the late Hendrik Willem Van Loon, wrote:

> When I say that the Renaissance was an era of expression I mean this:
> People were no longer contented to be the audience and sit still while
> the Emperor and Pope told them what to do or think. They wanted
> to be actors upon the stage of life. They insisted upon giving expres-
> sion to their own individual ideas. All Italy was filled with men and
> women who lived that they might add their mite to the sum total of
> our accumulated treasures of knowledge and beauty. In Germany Jo-
> han Gutenberg had just invented a new method of copying books. He
> had studied the old woodcuts and had perfected a system by which
> individual letters of soft lead could be placed in such a way that they
> formed words and whole pages. He soon lost all his money in a law
> suit over his invention and died in poverty, but the expression of his
> peculiar genius lived after him.

Dr. Van Loon then draws one of his inimitable pictures of a monk in
A.D. 1400 copying one book in a hundred days, and beside it a sketch

of a printer in 1500 sharing in a process with a press that does one hundred books in one day.

This was one of the great watersheds of history. Ideas—those of the Psalmist, of Hosea the Prophet, of St. Paul, of Jesus, and thousands of other men of creative mind—now began to be shared across continents and oceans. Printing became not just a trade, but a means of grace. Truth found a million tongues and broke out of prison.

Let us come down to the eighteenth century in the United States. Let us limit ourselves for a moment to two Unitarian leaders at the end of the century: Thomas Jefferson, our greatest layman, and William Ellery Channing, our greatest minister. I want to make it clear beyond peradventure of any doubt this morning that when I speak of freedom of the press and its role in a free church and a free state, I speak with some giant figures standing behind me. There is nothing singular or eccentric about a syllable that I am uttering this morning. Freedom of the press is something we Unitarians have long cherished and struggled for in pulpit and pew, and in resolutions of our national body. We do not dismiss lightly the prostitution of the press to lurid advertising or to the special pleading for pornography or political irresponsibility.

Listen to one of the classic statements of Thomas Jefferson: "Difference of opinion leads to enquiry and to truth. We value too much the freedom of opinion not to cherish its exercise."

In a letter to Corey in 1823, Jefferson wrote:

> There are certain principles to which all agree and which all cherish as vitally essential to the protection of life, liberty, property and the safety of the citizen: one of them is freedom of religion, restricted only from acts of trespass on that of others. Another is freedom of the press, subject only to liability for personal injuries. This formidable censor of the public functionaries, by arraigning them at the tribunal of public opinion, produces reform peaceably, which must otherwise be done by revolution.

This statement I hope you all remember and inwardly digest. If we ministers who believe a better life is possible on earth avoid agitation for revolution by the people, it is because men like Jefferson convinced us that there are prior weapons for a free people to employ—and notable among them is the press.

Jefferson was no cloistered scholar discussing this matter. He was a working politician and knew how the press could be abused and perverted. One reminder of his words would help us this morning as we ask, "Do we have freedom of the press?":

The way to prevent irregular interpositions of the people is to give them full information through the channels of the public papers, and contrive that those papers should penetrate the whole mass of the people. But indeed the abuses of the freedom of the press here have been carried to a length never before known or borne by any civilized nation. The Federalists fill their newspapers with falsehoods, calumnies and audacities. We are fairly going through the experiment whether freedom of discussion, unaided by coercion, is sufficient for the propagation and protection of truth, and for the maintenance of an administration pure and upright in its actions and views.

I wonder if you feel as I do a prophetic prediction about some of the yellow journalism of this century in Jefferson's words to Mr. Norvell in 1807 about the newspapers of his own day:

It is a melancholy truth that a suppression of the press could not more completely deprive the nation of its benefits than is done by its abandoned prostitution to falsehood. Truth today becomes suspicious by being put into that polluted vehicle. I really look with commiseration over the great body of my fellow citizens, who reading the newspapers, live and die in the belief that they have known something of what has been passing in the world of their time. Perhaps an editor might begin a reformation, if he divided his paper into four chapters, heading the first, truth, the second, probabilities, the third, possibilities, the fourth, lies. The first chapter would be very short.

I hope by now that you share with me the feeling that if we are concerned with individual and collective reform and improvement in this world, we must watch with vigilant eye the media of communication, for when these sources are contaminated, the health of all is threatened. Before I turn to the current scene on this subject of a free press, I ask your indulgence in one more flashback into history. We Unitarians were united into a body of churches by a gentle, quiet, aristocratic citizen and minister named William Ellery Channing. He is known to all people schooled in the records of religious liberation, for he struck the finest blow for human dignity ever witnessed on this continent, and ended the tyranny of John Calvin's dark and cynical estimate of mankind for several centuries to come. I shall be preaching on Channing later this year. Now I ask you to listen to this Boston prophet on the matter of the press. In 1828 Channing wrote a brilliant lecture on Napoleon Bonaparte, the foreshadow of Hitler, whose blacker deeds are today more generously passed by. Listen to Channing on Napoleon:

Another means by which the First Consul protected his power can excite no wonder. That he should fetter the press, should banish or imprison refractory editors, should subject the journals and more important works of literature to jealous superintendence, these are things of course. Free writing and despotism are such implacable foes, that we hardly think of blaming a tyrant for keeping no terms with the press.

He cannot do it. He might as reasonably choose a volcano for the foundation of his throne. Necessity is laid upon him, unless he is in love with ruin, to check the bold and honest expression of thought. But the necessity is his own choice, and let infamy be that man's portion who seizes a power which he cannot sustain, but by dooming the mind through a vast empire to slavery, and by turning the press into an instrument of public delusion and debasement.

This passage may be one hundred and twenty-three years old, but it has a startling relevance to our problem this morning. I conclude our conversation with William Ellery Channing with one final passage on the press, written into his address in 1812 for a "day of humiliation" in Boston following the declaration of war against Great Britain. I urge your close attention to this passage, not frequently reprinted in these present days. It was delivered before one of the most conservative congregations in Boston—to merchants, statesmen, editors, and attorneys—men of substance and success. I mention this, not snobbishly, but to assure you that Dr. Channing was not speaking before some small, hidden, conspiratorial remnant of malcontents along the waterfront at Tea Wharf.

Nothing ought to excite greater indignation and alarm than the attempts which have lately been made to destroy the freedom of the press. We have lived to hear the strange doctrine that to expose the measures of rulers is treason. We have seen a savage populace excited and let loose upon men whose crime consisted in bearing testimony against the present war. There have been symptoms of a purpose to terrify into silence those who disapprove the calamitous war under which we suffer, to deprive us of the only means left of obtaining a better and wiser government.

The cry is raised that since the war is declared, let all opposition be hushed. A sentiment more unworthy of a free country can hardly be propagated. If this be admitted, rulers have only to declare war and they are screened from scrutiny. In war as in peace, assert the freedom of the press and of speech . . . hold fast this freedom. Cling to this as the bulwark of all your rights and privileges.

You may have concluded by this point that it might have been better if Johan Gutenberg had never discovered that soft lead type of his. But as an old newspaperman, may I remind you that I could make a long and stirring chronicle of the glorious goods that followed in the wake of the printing press: the Bible printed in the common tongues of a hundred languages, the handbills and tracts that aroused millions of men and women to struggle for their rights in two hemispheres, the plays of Shakespeare, the poems of Keats and Whitman. The minds of whole populations have been watered and fertilized by the printed word. Few, indeed, advocate a return to literacy or abdication of the use of our brains —though in the past week two clippings have made me wonder. You may have seen them, too.

The L.A. *Herald & Express* ran a Portland, Oregon, story on September 12, headed, "Judge Harold Medina of New York says loyalty better than brains. . . . Brains are cheap. The qualities that make for success are guts and loyalty." The second story was in that capsule magazine, *Quick*, and quotes Cy Howard, creator of *My Friend Irma*, played by actress Marie Wilson. Mr. Howard's sagacious judgment was couched in these words: "All day long a man competes. When he comes home nights he wants a stupid girl who'll keep her mouth shut and let him look at television." These stories, combined with the newspaper announcement yesterday that Burbank plans a purge of its library, should make us reflect on the cult of antirationalism growing amongst us. The next step to saying dangerous thoughts should be banned is to say brains are really bad themselves.

This week I entertained in my home one of England's distinguished Unitarian leaders, Rev. Henry Cheetham of London. He referred to the fact that English Unitarians who visit this country find Americans distrustful of their own press in giving them world information necessary to understanding the situation in other lands. He was asked constantly by Americans about how affairs are going in England, in trade, civil rights, rearmament, and health services—and he finds us hungry for the unvarnished facts of what Great Britain has done since the war which could and should give great encouragement to liberals here. With tons of pulpwood consumed, we still wonder what is really going on.

Shakespeare somewhere suggests that the dyer's arm becomes the color of his vat. Walt Whitman in one essay speaks of a child that goes forth each day, becoming what it sees. Harry Overstreet, in his book *The Mature Mind*, suggests that people are becoming like that which they see and hear daily on television, radio, in the press, and on film. Psychologically, he notes, we are newspaper-made, movie-made, radio-made people today.

Today we are speaking especially of the press. Permit me to summarize a portion, at least, of the present picture. We do have a free press in the sense that no government dictator, no law, no censor (except in war theaters) decrees what must or must not go into newspaper columns. But it must be said that this does not mean we have a fair, honest, objective presentation of the news. Freedom of the press in practical terms today (and throughout this century at least) means freedom for very rich men to own newspapers and give readers a view of the world through their eyes, the eyes of big business. Whether big business is benevolent or self-centered is not the issue today, but rather the fact that this is one view and not that of the readers, but of an extremely small fraction of the people.

Working men have not the money to buy newspaper plants. No law need make the press unfree. Limited availability of capital makes it unfree. The news we receive is inevitably slanted and colored, or suppressed against the poor and for the rich. The evidence is overwhelming. A daily newspaper costs at least a million dollars as the owners of *PM, Compass,* the *Mirror,* or any other new daily in recent years can testify. I have never forgotten my friend Professor Joseph Fletcher's neat summary of this bias of money in the press. "Remember," he said, "news stories are published on the backs of advertisements."

One witness can stand for many on this point this morning. These are the words of the late Republican editor, a man of great talent and judgment, William Allen White of the *Emporia Gazette*:

> Any newspaper in any American town represents a considerable lot of capital for the size of the town. The owners of newspaper investments, whether they be individuals, bankers or stockholders in a corporation feel a rather keen sense of financial responsibility and they pass their anxieties along to the newspaper operatives whether these be managing editors, foremen, city editors or reporters. The sense of property goes thrilling down the line. It produces a slant and a bias that becomes a prejudice against any thing or any cause that seriously affects the right, title or interest of all other capital, however invested. Newspaper men may lean over backward in their upright attitude toward the obviously unfair demands of some advertisers and still may be poor, miserable sinners when they discuss the stability of institutions that are founded entirely upon the economic status quo.

That quotation, I again remind you, was from the hand of William Allen White, of the party of Wendell Willkie, not from the *People's World*. I underscore Mr. White's reference to upright newsmen trying to be fair and objective. One of the finest letters to me about my present appearance in the headlines was from a staff member of a West Coast Hearst newspaper, and another equally inspiring one was from an able staff member of a large broadcasting company. Yes, there is individual integrity, and lots of it, in the communications field, but Harold Ickes was still right when he echoed Mr. White's viewpoint:

> It is even more a pity that so many newspapers persist in representing a class interest, a money interest, instead of a public interest; that the Bill of Rights, excepting only the right of a press free from government interference or control, means little to them; that they oppose

and misrepresent the working man; that they ignore the rights of the underprivileged to justice and equality of opportunity; that they color news, distort news, suppress news and invent "news" in favor of those with whom they are allied financially, and with those whose objectives they are in sympathy.

Let us realize this morning that freedom of the press is far more than an absence of restraint. It must have a positive aspect also. It must deal with news and opinion of the real issues of life for millions if it is to serve as it should in a democracy, and not be merely a profitable investment for a group of stockholders. Freedom of the press must tackle bread and butter problems, matters of adequate clothing and modern housing, as well as opportunity to cultivate the mind, develop one's personality, and assert one's individuality.

In December 1942, Henry R. Luce of Time, Inc. suggested to Dr. Robert Hutchins, then Chancellor of the University of Chicago, an inquiry into freedom of the press. A year later a commission headed by Dr. Hutchins was at work. It included Zachariah Chafee, Jr., Professor William Hocking, Archibald MacLeish, and several other distinguished American figures. The findings of this prolonged study have been published by the University of Chicago Press under the title *A Free and Responsible Press*. If any here have not read this 140-page book, I strongly press upon you the wisdom of your doing so. It is "must" reading for all who cherish the basic freedoms of our land. Mr. Luce little dreamed he was financing a study that would deal hardly with his own press empire.

The commission set out to answer the question: Is freedom of the press in danger? Its answer was yes. It concluded that the freedom of the press is in danger for three reasons. First, the importance of the press to the people has greatly increased with the development of the press as an instrument of mass communication. At the same time this development of the press has decreased the proportion of the people who can express their opinion through the press. A very few men write the editorials most Americans read. Second, the few who are able to use the machinery of the press as an instrument of mass communication have not provided a service adequate to the needs of society. Third, those who direct the machinery of the press have engaged from time to time in practices that society condemns and which, if continued, it will inevitably have to regulate and control.

I cannot today share with you the enormous stimulation of this report, or the grim facts it represents for strong minds to face, but I do wish to read one paragraph of Dr. Hutchins's comment:

The moral right of free expression achieves a legal status because the conscience of citizens is the source of the continued vitality of the state. Wholly apart from the traditional ground for a free press, we see that public information is a necessary condition of adequate public discussion. Public discussion elicits mental power and breadth, it is essential to building a mentally robust public, and without something of this kind, a self-governing society could not operate.

I would that every publisher in America, of every political faith and every economic view, might remember the commission's words:

> We insist that, morally considered, the freedom of the press is a conditional right—conditional on the honesty and responsibility of writer, broadcaster, and publisher. A man who lies, intentionally or carelessly, is not morally entitled to claim the protection of the first amendment.

I urge you to read the many specific recommendations of the commission: on revision of libel laws; giving the injured person a chance to reply in the paper itself; the recommendations of greater self-discipline by the commercial press; or greater responsibility as a common carrier of information, uncolored and unprejudiced; these and many other proposals of reform to stave off a government-controlled press, every American should read and consider.

Since the Hutchins report, freedom of the press has been under serious attack. Three editors of newspapers languish in prison under the Smith Act, in a fashion that shames the land of Peter Zenger. It is significant that when our government acts against the press, it attacks the unsubsidized minority press, not the giants of monopoly. It is also significant that the cause of a free press is being championed in the courts by a great newspaper, the *St. Louis Post Dispatch*, which feels that no newspaper, however despised and unpopular, should be thus penalized, since a threat to one is a threat to all.

I wish to close by speaking briefly on the legacy to the American people of William Randolph Hearst. There are many of us in the pulpit, as well as in other fields of endeavor, who agree with the classic colloquialism of the great historian Charles E. Beard, some years ago, that "no person with intellectual honesty will touch Hearst with a ten foot pole." Yet flags were lowered and council meetings stopped to honor his passing. No one at his funeral, which was a gathering of many of his long-time enemies as well as his friends in the newspaper business, spoke of his consorting with Nazi officials in Berlin in 1934, or of his relations with the Capone gangsters in fighting a circulation war with Col. McCormick's *Chicago Tribune*. The darker chapters were forgotten, but we should not forget as long as many hundreds of thousands of people use his papers as the channel for news and opinion.

The editorial in the *Nation* for August 25 was the most just and yet unsparing evaluation of Hearst to appear at the time of the publisher's death. I agree with the *Nation* that Hearst was subsidized, that he was imitative and not original, and that he was hopelessly self-centered. Hearst borrowed Joseph Pulitzer's yellow journalism formulas and spent money extending them. His inherited fortune gave him opportunities others could only envy. He was in many ways the poor little rich boy of *Citizen Kane*, so brilliantly played by Orson Welles, a film that might now join the flood of reissues from the film libraries of Hollywood.

The *Manchester Guardian*, one of the great journals of the English-speaking world, wrote the most sagacious obituary for the Lord of San Simeon: "William Randolph Hearst is dead, and it is hard to think of him with charity. Perhaps no man ever did so much to debase the standards of journalism." But, whatever his shortcomings, whatever his deliberate inflation of the lie to a stock in trade of shameless journalism, it should be noted that he should not be made the scapegoat entirely of our own sins and errors and defaults. One cannot call him simply a moral monster and go home. Hearst only helped to fashion the social morality that came as an evil inheritance from his father and his fellow robber barons. We all in America helped to maintain Hearst and encourage him. Few, indeed, boycotted his papers. Few had the courage to denounce his ethics or his highly questionable attitude at the beginning of both world wars. In his resistance to our course in entering the wars, there was none of the high motivation of the religious objector to war, for which one could honor him; he simply manifested a preference for a society composed of an elite and a mass to support it, which in both wars seemed a cause best represented by Imperial Germany and the Third Reich. The works of Hearst are best left unnamed in any hall of fame. But we should all know that this exhibit of degraded journalism highlights the possibility of a fine and free press in the future, if we choose to have it so. I am not disposed to indulge in a shower of invective because it only darkens the air. We Americans are responsible for not working day and night for the kind of a nation that will make yellow journalism and newspaper fortunes founded on gossip, slander, and war-mongering utterly impossible. We, the people, must reject the lifting to a secular sainthood of any man who so abuses a great profession and a needed institution of communication, the public press.

The press in America can be free, and there are millions of us to help make it so by our indestructible resolution and personal efforts. No one of us is too inconspicuous to add his weight. It will be the work of millions of people. You and I have our part to play.

Is Death Row Necessary?
A Reconsideration of
Capital Punishment
November 1954

This sermon today is a polemic against continued toleration of the death penalty in our American society. If I can help to destroy, with even a few persons here, the grip of an incredibly barbarous practice in so-called civilized society, I shall rest content. I am sure I do not stand alone in saying that we Unitarians must join with our Methodist co-religionists, with the Friends, and many others who in recent months have organized practical campaigns to see this form of medieval punishment removed from our moral code, from our philosophy of government, and, more important, from our statute books.

I am beginning with what often comes last in a sermon, a statement of my purpose in preaching this address. I want to bring the death row concept out of the limbo of the accepted, the conventional, and the automatic. I want to judge it against the profession of all high religion. We have seriously and conscientiously committed ourselves in the liberal church to the ideal of reverence for life. It is now time—long past time—that we ended the contradiction between principle and practice. We can achieve only an intolerable schizophrenia if we call ourselves our brothers' keepers, yet continue to play the role of God, destroying, with vengeance, and in the name of retribution, the lives of men and women who have broken our social code of spilling human blood. I hope it can prod many of you to personal action to help us use our legislative apparatus to abolish the death penalty now, in this generation, in America.

As you well know, the cases in this state which ignited the issue into flame this year were two in number: the near-death of Robert Wesley Wells and the still probable death of Caryl Chessman. Several million people were alerted, by a wise and unflagging campaign, to rescue Robert Wells from the state gas chamber this year, and by so doing were compelled to reflect on the whole process of legal killing in our penological system. Mr. Wells had not taken any life. The phenomenal success of *Cell 2455*, a bestseller by Caryl Chessman, a condemned criminal psychopath in Death Row at San Quentin these past six years, aroused still more millions of Americans. It made sharp and clear the unhappy conscience we have as a people on the matter of capital punishment in our present day society. (Mr. Chessman, also, has taken no life. I have read *Cell 2455* carefully and I hope you will do the same.) We are a people deeply divided over the existing laws and the existing emotional attitudes toward this subject. Many of us live with social wounds of long standing: the deaths of the Martinsville Seven, the executions of Sacco and Vanzetti, the death penalty exacted from Willy McGee in Mississippi, and last year the double execution of Ethel and Julius Rosenberg. There are scores of other cases I could mention, with names unknown to most of us. I am speaking of capital punishment, which is accepted as axiomatic, and solemnly defended with biblical citations by ministers and lay people Sunday after Sunday across the land.

We cannot dismiss from today's discussion the espionage and treason aspects of this subject. Our 83rd Congress, just ended in August, wrote the death penalty for peacetime treason into law, and I predict that swift efforts by Senator Jenner and others will be undertaken to open cases for its employment. We have never as a nation in peacetime executed a man or woman for treason. Has something happened to our minds and conscience that we turn back to the dark ages for penological practices? How far has the cult of violence infected us, how many steps have we retreated that we seek to solve our problems of social control with the lethal gas bomb or the electric chair? The recent proposal to take the lives of political heretics, made by Governor Shivers of Texas, is a stark commentary on our own emotional atavism, our own surrender of reason and decency. Let it be manifestly plain that I am not discussing the relative heinousness of any act: treason, murder, rape, political intransigence. I am discussing the efficacy or wisdom of the death penalty; that and that alone is my subject. Is the maintenance of a death row a deterrent to socially unacceptable behavior? Are we advancing the cause of a mature civilization on this earth by the continued employment of executioners?

Remember that classic passage of Mark Twain's in "The Man That Corrupted Hadleyburg"?: "The universal conspiracy of the silent accepted lie is hard at work always and everywhere, and always in the interest of stupidity or sham, never in the interest of a thing fine and respectable." There are all too many silent accepted lies that give moral status and religious sanction to warfare, economic exploitation of the weak by the strong, racial oppression; but today we are speaking of just one of them, the justification of capital punishment for sins against society.

Let me remind you—and myself—that the criminal, no matter how limited by native endowment and inheritance, is enormously conditioned by social factors that you and I produce. His humiliations, his frustrations, his feelings of inadequacy, his hatreds and rebellions are not entirely made within himself. We share in their diabolical fabrication. It is manifest hypocrisy for our society, our own in America or that of another nation using the death row mentality, to wreak vengeance on the offender when his behavior is to a very real degree of our making. Death by the hand of the law may quiet his voice and end his offenses, but the soil of criminal behavior is fertilized with his dust and ashes. No solution is made, and we are a sicker people for the exaction of the fatal penalty. We are not more secure, as we had hoped. Our property is no more safe than it was. Violence breeds violence. Hate breeds hate. Self-righteousness is a hair shirt that neither clothes our moral nakedness nor warms us against the chilling climate of a childish culture that seeks to destroy its problems rather than solve them.

We are not called upon today to present a brief for the guilt or innocence of Robert Wells, or Caryl Chessman, or Willy McGee, or Sacco and Vanzetti. On these matters there is room for much difference of opinion by thoughtful men and women; but we are called upon to explain our own actions in the manner of punishing them.

The late Professor Robert Millikan of Caltech wisely observed that the essential task of religion is to develop the conscience, the ideals, and the aspirations of mankind. If this be true, then we in the churches must bend our efforts with ever fresh energy to this task as it affects the offending member of society. It demands that we ask what we are after—his demolition or his restoration. If we reverence life, we must give life a chance, often under highly controlled circumstances, at times taking maximum security measures for the protection of other people, but still in a principled fashion that assumes that no stone will be left unturned in the possible rehabilitation of a man's spirit and dignity. In the process of doing this our entire society can recover its self-respect and its dignity also.

I wish this morning to speak of some of the trends in capital punishment practices in our world today, giving special emphasis to those here in the United States. We can do something about them here. And by doing our best here, firmly and effectively, we can influence world opinion where it lags behind us. Let us begin by noting that six out of our forty-eight states do not permit the existence of death row; there is no capital penalty for any reason. Let us call the roll; it is an honorable one and worth remembering: Maine, Michigan, Minnesota, North Dakota, Rhode Island, and Wisconsin. Let us note also that murder and homicide rates are downward in their trend in these recent years in the United States. The murder rate in 1933 was 7.1 percent per hundred thousand inhabitants. In 1951 it was 4.9. The homicide rate in 1933 was 97 percent per hundred thousand. It is now 4.5 percent.

In the past 275 years we have seen more progress toward the abolition of capital punishment than in any previous period known in history. In these 275 years mankind has progressed from bloody and severe punishments being the rule, to making them the occasional method. The trend has been away from the gallows, from the stake, the butcher knife, the whip, and branding iron; crushing, quartering, smothering, and boiling in oil, with the single and terrible exception of twentieth-century fascism. We have come to use fines and imprisonment, correction, and rehabilitation. To be sure, the sixteenth-century mentality still exists, as any reading of letters to the newspapers' editors will reveal. My own letter to the Los Angeles Daily News this summer, on behalf of imprisonment rather than execution for the admitted criminal Caryl Chessman, brought me the most vicious and abusive mail I have ever received. There are citizens, nourished on personal frustration and crime movies, hardened by two world wars and the emotional appeals by a Hitler to slaughter a whole race of people, who have not caught up with the social science or the classic precepts of religion, who plead for a return to the subhuman expedients of the rack and the wheel, living burial, and the technological refinements of torture brought in by a decadent science in this century.

There is a trend toward basing abolition of the death penalty on secular principles, on logic, on psychological knowledge, and the social welfare of the community, rather than on the classical arguments of religion. While prophets and sages have long argued for sanctifying life, let us remember that the arguments for capital punishment have, alas, been offered for centuries by Judaism and Christianity (and other faiths) with thunderous invective. The greatest argument for executions today is still the law of "an eye for an eye, a tooth for a tooth," the law of retribution found in the Old Testament. Today we argue, not for expiation of the sin of killing by invocation of a divine law, but for control of a natural crime against society, requiring on our part knowledge and understanding of human behavior, an understanding of social pressures that lead to criminality. It is worth consideration for a moment, by all of us here, that we are all capable of taking human life under certain provocations that can be named and pinpointed in the studies of psychiatrists and criminologists. Let no man be proud, lest he discover some day his own frailty. As a condemned murderer paces his cell at San Quentin, let us all say, "There but for the grace of a loving home, a useful job, and understanding friends, go I."

Yes, science has made inroads into theological territory. The church's advocacy of doctrines of expiation and retribution are under terrific fire today, fortunately. I might add that not only the church (in some quarters) is fighting for these barbaric doctrines, but also the average Hollywood film producer. The theme of retribution is a dramatic asset not lightly surrendered. But advocates of capital punishment are on the defensive, and we should keep them there. They no longer can assume axiomatic justification by the public for throwing the switch at Sing Sing or San Quentin. American juries are increasingly reluctant to find criminals guilty of first degree murder, not because they think them innocent, but because they do not believe in the supreme penalty even if the offenders are guilty.

There has been a trend in the past one hundred years to abolish the death penalty completely. It is now forbidden in thirty countries by law or tradition. There is a trend toward making fewer offenses punishable by death. There is a total of seven offenses in our forty-eight states that call for death by some means: first degree murder, kidnapping, armed robbery, burglary, arson, train wrecking, and rape, with Congress two months ago on the Federal level adding peacetime treason. It is to be noted that most states have eliminated as meriting death most of these seven offenses in law or in practice, eliminating those which are offenses against property, keeping offenses against fellow citizens. In practice, there is really only one capital offense, murder, except, let us admit with contrition, the crime of rape in the Southern states when committed, or allegedly committed, by a Negro.

England deserves note for the best example of a long-time trend away from capital punishment. In 1780 there were 350 crimes in that land punishable by death, ruthlessly enforced against men, women, and children, and for as slight a felony as the theft of forty shillings. As Professor Hartung of Wayne University observed:

> Only the passing of the Roman Inquisition, the greatest single source of executions for heresies, witchcraft and other religious offenses in western civilization, can compare with the English development in dramatically demonstrating the trend toward the progressive reduction in the number of crimes carrying the death penalty.

There has been a trend also towards making the death penalty permissive rather than mandatory. Courts and juries are now given far more initiative in the matter. In 1918 capital punishment was mandatory in twelve states for capital crimes. In 1951 Vermont was the only remaining state which gave no such permission to judge or jury.

There is a trend toward the reduction of executions per year, but I could deliver an entire address on the cruel and class-minded character of selective execution. Today there are fewer executions than in the past for capital offenses, for which we should be thankful. But let it be noted with shame that the death penalty is preponderantly used now against the Negro people, the poor, the uneducated, and the immigrant. I shall give but one example, though I have read considerably more, for documenting this tragic discrimination in the execution chamber. Listen to Warden Lawes of Sing Sing:

> For twelve years I have escorted 150 men and one woman to the death chamber . . . and the electric chair. In ages they ranged from 16 to 63. They came from all kinds of homes and environments. In one respect they were all alike. All were poor and all were friendless. It is an unequal punishment. No punishment could be invented with so many inherent defects. It is unequal in the way it is applied to the rich and the poor. The defendant of wealth and position never goes to the electric chair or gallows. Juries do not intentionally favor the rich, the law is theoretically impartial, but the defendant with ample means is able to have his case defended with every favorable aspect. The poor defendant often has only an attorney supplied by the court.

Thorsten Sellin in 1930 studied the executions of that year in the United States, and found that most of the 155 executions were of Negroes and immigrants. Federal figures indicate that in the period 1937–50 (thirteen years) 1,861 people were executed in this country. One thousand and sixty-five were Negroes executed for murder, rape, and armed robbery. Two hundred and thirty-three were rape cases involving a Negro; only twenty-six rape cases involved whites. The annals of the American Academy of Political and Social Science from November 1952 will provide you with further detailed statistics on this grim and prejudicial discrimination against the nonwhite American who commits the same crimes as white citizens. Women are rarely executed in the United States, but twice as many Negro women are killed as whites.

Let us note in our study this morning that there has been a trend away from public executions. Such exhibitions existed in this country until 1862, and of course long after that when we include illegal executions and lynchings. I shall never forget *Life* magazine's morbid publication of a photograph of a lynching in San Jose, California, by a sadistic mob a few years ago. The news camera and printing press have continued public executions vicariously, as most of us know all too well. As the Elizabethan playwrights proved to the hilt, there is a pathological hunger to feed the mind on horrors, which must be combatted. When one adds the fortune to be made out of peddling such horror, he sees that the sin is twice compounded.

Some of you may have read William Makepeace Thackeray's classic essay on going to see a man hanged. I agree with one student of penology, Warden Lawes, who says that one swift way to end capital punishment would be to make the jury, the judge, and the prosecutor attend the final event in the death chamber. One executioner who had dispatched several scores of people to eternity pleaded eloquently that the sentencing judge should be forced to be present, and help pull the switch. He said he had never known of a judge or a prosecutor responsible for a criminal's death being present in those last tragic minutes.

But let us turn to the alternatives to the death penalty. There is more to our thought this morning than moral revulsion at our protracted moral infancy, our long-cherished primitivism as a race. We need, for our own welfare as a people, to consider more humanitarian methods of dealing with the social offender so long disposed of by the shortcut of the prison grave. Life imprisonment is one alternative. Parole for tested social rehabilitation is still another. The governor's pardon is a widely recognized alternative. These alternatives can and should be studied far more, along with plans for the radical improvement of our correctional institutions, our customs regarding length of sentences, our arrangements for receiving the paroled prisoner back into society at a useful place. I cannot discuss these today, but our church and our Fellowship for Social Justice have a continuing obligation here. We should be interested in the individual treatment of the offending person by the diagnostic knowledges of medicine and psychiatry. Many psychotic and psychopathic persons who commit crimes of physical assault and prey on society with deadly weapons are tomorrow's murderers. Social scientists and psychiatrists believe that detection and treatment of these persons could probably reduce the murder rate by 40 percent. Certainly application of modern psychiatric practices could reduce many of the errors that judges and juries commit with such terrible finality. Hand in hand, of course, must go reeducation of the public. We must learn how to handle the press, the film, and the ill-educated person (whether he holds a Ph.D. or not) who says of Sacco and Vanzetti, "Maybe there is a doubt of their committing the Braintree murders, but they are radicals and foreigners, aren't they? They could have done it. Let's not take any chances."

The psychiatrist and social scientist can help us analyze not only the prisoner, but ourselves to prove the phenomena of violence that cause us to inflict death on a man who commits a crime of which we are all capable under similar provocation. The Victorian illusion that just a little moral advice about self-control will stop our hands has been proven to be a very frail reed. We need to cure sick minds and find them work in a healthy society. The best defense for the community is not more executions or higher walls around the prisons, but a profound understanding of the individual, an understanding which can lead to preventive measures against threats of violence by our fellow citizens.

In the United States, with its humanitarianism and democratic doctrines written into law, with its increasing objectivity in the study of social relationships, with its growing confidence in the powers of science, the death penalty is becoming recognized more and more as an ineffective method of punishment. In its place is a growing recognition of the role of imprisonment under humane conditions. We now expect to achieve large scale personal and social rehabilitation of the prisoner. More and more, people are realizing that love, respect, security among relatives, friends, and business associates, rather than fear of legal penalties, is what keeps most of us from violating the law. We are learning far more about social controls in a modern world. We in the churches have a great part to play in education, in reform of present practices, in exposing the hypocrisy and sadism in our own heart, in using the knowledge about the humane personality previously unavailable. In a real sense, you and I in this church can see how love and not hate can provide for the common defense, and bring that commonwealth of brothers for which we have so long prayed. There is work for all of us. Whether the offenders living in the shadow of manmade death be few or many in our prisons, their right to our understanding, compassion, and assistance is a claim upon us this very day. We can, if we choose, advance the rule of reason and of goodwill. We can live to see this savage legacy of vengeance and fear wiped from the lawbooks of this state and every state within our country. The march toward this goal has been long, and many of our own household of the Unitarian church have played valiant parts. We can complete their labors in this generation if we make it a mandate upon our own conscience. That is why I have spoken to you on the matter this morning. We are on no fool's errand. We can end the curse of blood at our prison gates, so we can close death row and build a nation of men enjoying the fruits of their knowledge and labor in peace and without hatred. This is a reasonable and a commanding obligation as we enter the century of the liberated man.

Are We Accepting
a Cult of Violence?
March 1955

This is a sermon I have long delayed delivering. You may ascribe this postponement to occupational cowardice, for like most ministers I infinitely prefer discussing the good news of life, not the bad. My Quaker parents believed in a most practical fashion that human nature was strangely mixed, and tragically frail, but that it possessed remarkable affirmative powers of love, of reason, of goodwill, of cooperation; and the wise man stressed these things, and tried to order his life by their employment.

Your minister attempts to bring you what he considers the good news about mankind from week to week. I could take my whole time today in such a report. For example, President Eisenhower on Lincoln's birthday named a distinguished Negro attorney, George E. Hayes, to the District of Columbia Public Utilities Commission. Mr. Hayes was one of McCarthy's so-called "red influence targets" because he had defended Mrs. Annie Lee Moss in her successful fight for clearance from the Wisconsin senator's charges of subversion. Or I could report that the Yugoslav government has finally decreed complete separation of church and state. I could remind you that the Associated Press tells us that Denmark, the Netherlands, and Belgium have all reduced the periods of compulsory military training. Or I could report that fifty-six nations have pooled funds for the United Nations technical assistance fund; that a Superior Court ruling in Southern California a few days ago declared that it is unconstitutional for veterans to be required to sign a loyalty oath in order to enjoy tax exemption. I could tell you that West Germany's government signed the U.N. Genocide Convention, the forty-seventh government to do so. (I shall refrain from comment regarding our own government's failure in this regard.) I could remind you that the great physicist and Nobel Prize winner, Harold Urey, stated at a Chicago banquet that Morton Sobell was improperly tried, and that our government's use of professional informers must be stopped. And these are but a few of the items in my file on good news in a naughty world.

But this morning we are facing some news that is far from good. I am asking the question: Are we accepting a cult of violence? And my answer is yes. To an overwhelming degree we are developing such a cult, and unless we can reverse the trend, by understanding the reasons, and by understanding our resources for changing it, our culture and our society are as doomed as the civilization of ancient Rome. And because a few statesmen and their advisors have the power to trigger atomic and hydrogen bombs, this violence can destroy man and all living creatures, and make a planetary dust bowl of this our home. As Jean-Paul Sartre recently said: "History must remove the warhead from the atom bomb, or else the atom bomb will blow up the world. The people must unite against the bomb, and impose peace without ever giving the nuclear weapon the time or pretext for being exploded." He is supported by an extraordinary coalition of voices, high and low. Senator George Smathers, during the recent debate on giving our President unprecedented powers of life or death for millions, declared: "We sit on the brink of a great and fiery chasm. We must end inflammatory and belligerent speeches." So we speak today of violence against a background of threatened violence, which outstrips the imagination of man to describe.

The gravest danger of all this morning is that we come to the subject under discussion numb and insensitive as we face the daily facts of violence: the police brutality, the berserk father with a knife, the lethal self-violence and barbiturates and carbon monoxide, the syndicated violence of the public actions ironically called "comics," the daily dosage of violence on TV screens and in movie houses, the verbal violence of drunken parents and sadistic husbands and neurotic wives. We have become calloused to the arrogant foreman cursing field and factory workers from minority groups, the teenager with his kit of narcotics, the angry high school students in well-to-do suburbs wrecking their building with fire hoses over new cafeteria rules, the Boston prisoners protesting the horror of "the hole" and the hopeless diets by holding their guards at gunpoint for three days; these are but one week's tabulation, and each day seems the same, or mounting in its terror.

It is not sufficient today that we admit the existence of an increasing amount of violence of all kinds in our daily lives. This is all too familiar to every one of us, every hour we live. It is necessary to see behind this prairie fire of violence the effort to capture *consent* for violence, to give it status, to domesticate it. There is a campaign, if you will, to produce in all of us a basic psychological reorientation to accept the increased use of violence, to surrender to an ethic of violence. There is a war going on against the nonviolent mind. To me this psychological warfare to win your consent and mine for a society of violence is worse than the cold war (even as it is a part of it). Here is an assault on our humanity, our self-respect, our higher centers of dignity, love, and creative living. As I speak these words today I am conscious of the victories that the men of violence have scored in the past ten years. They have made all of us more insensitive to the operation of violence in our daily lives. Not only has violence become an instrument of national policy with our naval fleets, our air force wings, our toughened assault regiments, our stockpiles of A and H bombs, but violence has become an instrument of educational policy, of domestic relations, of social intercourse, of entertainment. We are degrading and brutalizing ourselves hour after hour. We are indeed developing a cult of violence and giving it sanctions, approvals, rationalization, and altar blessings.

The rehearsal of evidence could take hours, if we chose. In any such rehearsal it is essential that we remember that here is no visitation of a plague; no policy enforced by an alien emperor upon us, a defeated nation in warfare; no scourge of God sent from the skies by miraculous visitation; this is what we are doing to ourselves! Parents, teachers, politicians, military men, preachers, publishers, film directors, to mention but a few of the perpetrators, are responsible. We are all involved in the guilt of transforming modern man into a beast. This Roman circus, this saturnalia of terror and violence, is of our own making and it will be ended only when we stop our own hands from such blind masochism, or when we have literally blown ourselves into radioactive dust. It could be ended in a few years time if we resolved to have it ended. Doubleday and Company, publishers of Mickey Spillane's work, could be stopped from spreading the subhuman pornography and verbal violence of Mike Hammer. Bloody prizefights could be ended if the city fathers so determined. Sing Sing executions of political prisoners about whom there were grave doubts of guilt could be prevented, if we so insisted.

The cult of violence begins with our children and in our own times is carried through to the systematic extermination of children, the adult, and aged by the million in the ovens of Nazi Germany. The Midcentury White House Conference on Youth and Children in 1950 was right when it said: "Fear and anxiety due to the possibility of war and bombing raids are a national phenomena and affect children and youth." Certainly we in this church heard last Sunday our own cherished youth reveal the blight that the threat of violence in war brings to our high school and college generation. It frustrates education, wrecks plans for a peaceful vocation, paralyzes normal courtship and marriage arrangements. It seeks to dehumanize our own flesh and blood.

The cult of violence is obvious in newsreels on a hundred thousand movie screens each week with its mock battles, its simulated invasions, its briefing on how an army carries through Operation Killer, but I think we forget the indoctrination for accepting this which lies in the school room. Early in 1949 our government published a fifty-four-page document "American Education and International Tensions." It stated that the time had come to revamp our traditional school functions. We should, it insisted, convert the schools into agencies of political indoctrination for the official policies of our government. The report was prepared by a twenty-two member Educational Policies Commission of the National Education Association. It stated that cold war tensions would continue for years to come with the world divided into hostile camps. Our children, it said, will continue for years to live under an oppressive shadow of fear. Nowhere did the report indicate that children should be taught that there was a chance for peacefully resolving international tensions. I quote exactly its words: "The development of an ardent desire for peace with the rest of the world is the least of educational problems. Teaching that peace is desirable is one thing. Disapproval of war, of any kind, and under any and all circumstances is another. A far better educational goal is the ability to distinguish between different kinds of wars." Let me remind you that this was not always the thinking of the NEA. In 1934 a resolution of the NEA had said: "War is the greatest menace to civilization. Children should be taught the truth about wars and its costs in human life and ideals and material wealth. Legislation should be passed prohibiting profits from the manufacture of armaments." Twenty-one years ago we did not have the teachers mobilized for the cult of violence. And they can demobilize themselves now if they will so resolve. But we are at a point where turning back becomes harder every day. Evidence of this difficulty was reflected in the words of Dean Millicent McIntosh of Barnard College, who was quoted in 1951 as saying: "College girls are becoming afraid to advocate the humanitarian point of view because it has become associated with communism."

Our culture, from childhood through old age, appeals to the primitive and the aggressive impulses in our nature with naked candor. I hope many of you have read, or will read, Christopher LaFarge's article in the *Saturday Review* for November 6, 1954, entitled "Mickey Spillane and His Bloody Hammer." It is the best statement on our current literary vigilantism I have yet seen. He reminds us that as of June, 1954, twenty-four million copies of Spillane's books had been sold in this country. Twenty-four million copies of books that pass as literature yet are nothing more than a type of wish fulfillment writing of an immature type, of a potentially destructive variety. While there has been fiction before, some of it well-written, that described sadism, not until Spillane did we get sadism held up as a justifiable means to an admirable end.

Mr. LaFarge then comments: "What troubles me about his manifestation is that Spillane seems to have succeeded in making the character of Mike Hammer acceptable to a huge public. And that portion of the public is repudiating thereby the basic principles on which our country has so far operated. . . . Mike Hammer is the brutal apotheosis of McCarthyism: when things seem wrong, let one man cure the wrong by whatever means he, as a privileged savior, chooses." Mr. LaFarge continues to amplify his thesis that Spillane's books, like McCarthyism in our public life, extend the old and bloody tradition in our country of the vigilantes. He reminds us that the vigilantes began on the frontier with men who were impatient with the remoteness of the law when needed to punish the cattle rustlers and the brigands. Now the vigilante has extended his operations to all persons whose moral, racial, religious, and political outlooks are said to be disliked by the majority of the community. And we have thereby the persecutions, intolerances, riots, and lynchings that mar so much of what is fine in our nation.

The frontier impatience is still with us. In our complex industrial society, in our teeming cities, in our impersonal relationships of factory, shop, and community, we lose confidence in the possibilities of justice and fair play, and thus turn to short cuts, and short cuts mean violence. The end will be, as Mr. LaFarge indicates, the ultimate corruption of a republic of laws. Behind this comment lies of course the tremendous challenge we face to take more time from manufacturing, from war preparations, from commerce and trade, to concentrate on the first business of government: the welfare of our people. It seems absurd that we must remind ourselves that we have schools and courts, social agencies and professional workers by the hundreds of thousands, whose function is welfare, equity, justice. We are not without men and tools, we are simply not using them in our preoccupation with other things sold to us surprisingly as the pearl of great price.

We are tolerating the vigilante mentality, we are building the cult of violence by our own refusal to use peaceful, decent, and proven alternatives. Dr. Frederic Wertham is right when he says we are immunizing with our comic books and TV horror programs a whole generation against pity and recognition of the evil of cruelty and violence. But the comic books that venerate the storm trooper pattern are published by men whom we accept not as gangsters but as harmless businessmen. And we give our children dimes and quarters to buy them. One hundred million comic books were published in 1952. Ninety-eight percent of our American children read them. "They are," said Dr. Wertham of Queens Hospital's Mental Hygiene Clinic, "The greatest mass influence on children." These books fit the designs of the cold war architects. They fit the mind of the growing child to accept violence, savagery, and sudden death. They are a so-called "literature" of destruction and nihilism. And we are mostly silent, the churches are voiceless, the schools passive. How are we to encourage love, affection, equality, tolerance, patience, sanity, and tenderness when the lurid comic book lies in a pool around our homes with crime on every page: stabbings, scaldings, brandings, stranglings, and unmentionable acts of sadism that congeal our blood even to name. I am looking for no easy scapegoats today, but I am saying that it is not only an abstract profit-centered economy that we can blame. We can blame the parents of America, the teachers of America, the writers of America, the merchants of America at the corner drugstore who contribute to this colossal delinquency.

I have a television set in my home. I know Dr. Baxter is there on the screen discussing Shakespeare's *Romeo and Juliet*, that Ed Murrow presents Dr. Robert Oppenheimer, that the University of Pennsylvania offers me an exciting guessing contest by anthropologists and paleontologists identifying ancient artifacts. But I also know that this same screen offers millions of children and adults one thousand acts of violence on seven stations in a single week. (A research organization did the gory task of counting.) We see our fellow citizens as heavy-muscled, trigger happy; as people who solve their problems not with reason, not with law, but with a spray of bullets and a gleaming knife. I know that this is reflected in the news program with gigantic mushroom clouds from a Nevada sand dune after an A-bomb testing. I know it is confirmed by endless hours of maneuvers by our naval and air forces brought to the screen. But I would remind you that this cult of violence, this indoctrination in violence, is of our own making and can be stopped by organized and persistent effort: not by counterviolence, but by our PTA, our city council, our Congress, our courts, our buyers' boycotts of offending programs and products, our resolute and implacable resistance to such seduction of our humanity. There are alternatives, plenty of them if we will shake the sleep from our eyes and arise to duty.

Norman Cousins once said: "Where man can find no answer, he will find fear." This is true. But there are answers, and you and I as advocates of brotherhood, of sanity, of reason, of religion have a paramount obligation to find and employ the answers. I am not being glib today. I know we are dealing with basic tensions and forces in our society that have brought this whirlwind of self-destruction. I know there is the impulse to violence in every person in this auditorium today. Few here are without guilt of verbal violence, of explosive temper that can lead to physical violence against our children, our loved ones, and those who cross our wills in the daily commerce of everyday life. We have read Menninger's *Love Against Hate*, and Horney, and Freud, and Rollo May, and Erich Fromm. As I said on the radio program last Sunday night, "man has spirit, he has a rebel nature. He is a creator and a destroyer." We resent law and order when they are set against us and our desires.

In a machine age, the violence of the law breaker is often idealized by dramatists and film writers and newspaper publishers. Adventure and risk are limited all too often to antisocial action: to warfare, to crime, to brutal spectacles disguised as sport, to revenge against prisoners, to dramas and films about murder and incest, rape and robbery. We conduct a daily campaign to find scapegoats against whom to spend our hostilities. Political demagogues and witch hunters seek to drain off our belligerence in dangerous ways: to offer us victims in congressional hearings, to find spies in atomic plants, to discover Communists in interracial housing projects, to discover subversive eggheads in our colleges, to find underground agents preparing Girl Scout handbooks, to accuse the Ford Foundation of sheltering Reds, the Rockefeller Foundation of being a socialist plot, the churches of being undermined by Moscow— and so the madness grows. The cry for revenge eats away our sanity and our common sense.

What, my friends, is our task in one single church, a pathetically small drop of water in the pond? First, I would remind you that under many creeds and many flags, secular and religious groups of quiet, sober, concerned men and women are doing their part in dealing with this dilemma of aggressive and rebel man in a complex society. I am deeply indebted, as you are, to psychiatrists, writers, teachers, and clergymen of a liberal mind and scientific temper who are also drops of water in the pond. We are not alone as we tackle some of these problems. Let us face certain facts about our human nature. Every one of us is torn two ways: we are members of society who need and desire to belong to the group, unless we are sick or very strangely conditioned by education; we crave the acceptance and love of the group of which we are a part. But we also are driven by a desire to be individuals, to be ourselves, to assert our private convictions and be honored for our own achievements, our own uniqueness. We want to break with society and stand in opposition to its restraints and laws. Frankly, there is no resolution of the dilemma; there is only a working compromise. The acceptance of one or the other alone makes us slaves and robots or, on the other hand, anarchists and hermits.

We all want to be ourselves (especially Unitarians), yet we do not want to be by ourselves or rejected by our peers. But let me say that in my professional and nonprofessional activities, I am persuaded that there are ways of sublimating our impulse to violence or hostility, our aggressiveness. There are harmless dissenting activities, socially useful expressions of our aggressions. We need what Dr. Bronowski of England calls "astringent tensions," which keep our community alive, which keep our civilization advancing to overcome its remaining chaos. As citizens we do not have to attain success and status, even in this competitive economic society with all its primitive traits, by crushing our neighbors in business or social life or in our homes. An economy of uses rather than profit, of cooperation instead of brutal competition, will help tremendously and it is on the way, believe me. But meanwhile, you and I can start some pilot plants of personal and social living thar reject violence, ruthless greed, evil tempers, domestic rages, racial and sex chauvinism.

Every single one of us can play an important role by helping all who work with us, or live with us, to know that we respect each man, woman, and child within the orbit of our influence. We can be a counterforce to the Mike Hammer mentality, the McCarthy mentality, which treats others with arrogance and contempt and even cruelty. We can change some of the practices of our boards of education, our parent teacher groups, our unions, our churches, and our homes, so that people will know that they count, and are honored for their views, their personal qualities, their talents.

I agree with Dr. Bronowski of the BBC in his *Face of Violence* when he says that we have much to encourage us. The size and complexity of modern industrial society has steadily increased the status of the worker. The increase of scientific controls, of mass production techniques and inventions has increased, not decreased the importance of the individual. Politicians today know this well; our legislation for human welfare, for bargaining with labor, for raising the standard of living of the worker is evidence of it. Yes, today "each man is a fulcrum on which the world moves." This is why Africa is in revolt, why China seeks to complete her revolution, and why the CIO and AFL propose to get together to complete a lot of unfinished business for the American worker, who resents having irresponsibles of an old time school of business reach into his pocket and rob him of the fruit of his toil.

With less violence and more law, we can make progress faster. Karl Marx and Karl Menninger are closer together than either of them would probably admit if they could get together. Man the worker must maintain an aggressive attitude against those who enjoy paying him only half his wages, and the psychologist is right in saying there is a science of peace, of man working for himself through paths of goodwill and love. Louis Pasteur noted that the law of blood and death ever invents new means of destruction, but he also noted a law of peace and work and health, ever delivering man from the scourges that beset him. Gautama Buddha, Jesus, Gandhi, and many others have helped us discover the wisdom which John Donne called "This medicine, love, which cures all sorrows." The perennial blossom of cruelty can be overcome; the urge to hurt other people is a cancer of the spirit that can be cured. Freud was right when he wrote: "The voice of intelligence is weak but it is persistent." Knowledge and truth and infinite patience in our efforts can prove stronger, we know, than hate and violence. Dr. Brock Chisholm was right when he pointed out that "maturity represents a wholesome amalgamation of two things: dissatisfaction with the status quo, which calls forth aggressive, constructive effort, and secondly, social concern and devotion. Our morale consists of the merging of the two."

We have a cult of violence, and I think there is no disposition to deny its strength, nor underestimate its force, but you and I also know there are vast and heartening counterforces which it is our task as individuals and as a church to recognize and explore and employ. Remember those words that I read earlier today from our friend Corliss Lamont: "Our permanent rebellion is not a matter of force and violence, it is the daily rebellion of our spirits against the injustices perpetrated by the cruel, the stupid, the selfish and the short-sighted. In our struggle for a better world we find a constant challenge to our intelligence, our ability, our perseverance in the face of heavy odds." Let me close with those ringing words of Karl Menninger's that deserve to echo in our hearts for many months to come: "It is not impossible to conceive of a time when the expression of love will be as natural, as spontaneous and as magnificently organized as is the expression of rage and hate at the present moment." This is my own credo also, and it is yours as we leave this place to resume our daily tasks and pleasures, tomorrow and in the years to come.

The Indian in America Today
May 1, 1955

As one newly come in recent years to a study of the American Indian, it would be my preference this morning to talk to you about his spirit and cultural contribution to our life here on this continent. Nothing would make me happier than to encourage on your part, and mine, an increased effort to understand the Indian heritage: his ancient reverence and passion for human personality, joined with a reverence and passion for the earth and its web of life. The Indians in tribes and societies have had a power for living that much of our modern world has lost. By virtue of this power, the ancient Incas of South America, for example, by universal agreement of their people made conservation and increase of the earth's resources its foundational national policy. If our modern world should be able to recapture this power, the earth's natural resources would not be irrevocably wasted within the twentieth century, which is the prospect now. Let me bring you these words of John Collier, former U.S. Commissioner of Indian Affairs: "True democracy, founded on neighborhoods and reaching over the world, would bring to realization our cherished dream of heaven on earth. And living peace, not just an interlude between wars, would be born and last through the ages."

These words are not airy sentimentality, but the conclusion of a man who has initiated more creative and practical programs on behalf of the Indian groups in this country than any other single person. This morning we have copies of his *Indians of the Americas*, which I hope everyone not now owning it will purchase. . . . If several hundred of you would within the next fortnight digest this magnificent volume, I would feel the hours spent in planning today's address were indeed well spent.

Never have I read more carefully and written more cautiously on a sermonic theme than on today's address. I must confess that as a citizen educated in the first quarter of this century, I was miserably short-changed in the public schools and colleges I attended, as far as knowledge of the Indian role in our history was concerned. I grew to middle age with no substantial instruction about the first citizens of this nation. I was told nothing of any depth about their history, their origin, their ideas, their contributions to civilization; nor was I told the story of our extermination of these peoples, our betrayal of our pledged word, our naked and gargantuan greed for their land. I trust you fared better in your schools, among your friends, in your cultural education. I have a lot of catching up to do.

One of our members longest associated with this church commented that I must be losing my sense of humor, since in my sermon on Africa I favored the African people in their desire to see many white men leave that continent if they could not forsake their ancient imperialistic habits.

"Where," asked my friend, "are the white men to go? Who will take them in?" And now, as I raise seriously today the federal termination policies of our government, and propose returning many areas and resources to thousands of dispossessed Indians, this same friendly critic may chide me afresh and ask me, "Where is the space ship waiting for white men and women exiled from earth?" Let me anticipate myself a bit this morning, and say right now that I believe that in this country of ours, which I have traversed many times, there is room enough for all to live with decency, equality, dignity, and plenty. In this nation of 160 million people, there is room for four hundred thousand Indians without the discrimination, poverty, disease, and misery that is now the lot of the overwhelming majority of them and which is likely to grow far worse if federal termination policies are not reversed.

No one with any sensitivity to human values, no one with a pretense of religious and humanitarian ideals, can study the record of our treatment of the Indian within our borders without humiliation and shame. One reason, of course, our school books are so void of information is that the information, if printed, would destroy much of the pretense about our democratic ideal being a living reality. We are speaking today of our most discriminated-against minority. My remarks can do little more than urge upon you, if it be necessary, a stripping away of layers of ignorance and misinformation, and a facing of the historical realities, and today, at this very hour, the significance of the revival of anti-Indian policies by our government. There have been hours, yea, years of fine insight, splendid policy-making, and magnificent endeavor to practice with our Indian fellow Americans the brotherhood enshrined in our great founding documents. These hours of achievement can be recovered and surpassed. It is because I consider the hour late, but not hopelessly late, that I am speaking to you this morning. The betrayal of the Indians can be stopped by plain Americans like you and me. No further crimes need be committed.

Some of you saw the television program last Wednesday on "Disneyland," "Davy Crockett Goes to Congress" with its thrilling and dramatic story of the Tennessee frontiersman a century ago fighting President Andrew Jackson and the land profiteers on behalf of the Indian tribes. While we cannot leap on a horse like Davy and gallop to Washington to defeat legislation selling out the Indian's rights, we can singly and collectively do the equivalent with our pens, our purses, and our organizations. (Of this more later.) I am happy that we have begun to have films, television, and books in recent years that reveal some insight into the Indian crisis in America today. It is a mere beginning, often crude, partial, and sentimental, still clinging to chauvinistic stereotypes, still rooted in three centuries of defensive hostility based on the conquering invader's psychology. But my remarks today are not set in the framework of a lost cause, far from it. I think the very iniquity of our government policy in the past four years has awakened many slumbering citizens to action. The case is far from hopeless—if we choose to remedy matters.

This is the season of the greatly publicized outdoor drama, "Ramona," being played in Hemet. I would that every one of the thousands who see this romantic play would not stop with this work by Helen Hunt Jackson, but go on to read her book, A Century of Dishonor. It is a book written in the 1880s that deserves high position in the literature on the Indian, and may be the start of an understanding of the continued dishonor which went on until the Hoover and Roosevelt administrations . . . and now, after a few short years of reform and insight, has returned to plague us.

Basically, the "dishonor" Helen Hunt Jackson referred to was the official denial of the right of many hundreds of Indian communities to exist at all, denial of the right of Indians to exist as Indians. This denial was made in the face of several hundred Senate-ratified treaties and Supreme Court decisions. If the pledged word has to die in order to destroy the Indian communities, then let it die: this was government policy from 1870 to 1924, and, under new laws signed by President Eisenhower, it has again become government policy. I speak today in no ecclesiastical vacuum. Great wrongs are being revived and extended. For the sake of oil, fishing rights, uranium-rich desert land, and water rights—things desired by white citizens—thousands of Indians in the next several months face destruction of their tribal communities, the sale of their treaty-pledged lands, the end of federal health and welfare services solemnly promised them. My voice is being raised along with many others far stronger and more widely heard: Mr. Fey in the Christian Century, Mr. Leibling in the New Yorker, Mr. John Collier in the Nation, Mr. Aubrey Haines in Frontier, and many others. Never did so many people offer me assistance in preparing an address as spoke or wrote to me when this subject was announced. And I am grateful to all of them. There is a public conscience developing on the treatment of the Indian today in America, and I am profoundly glad of it. May it multiply a thousand-fold. My one great desire today is to encourage, as wholeheartedly as possible, the acceptance by Americans of the grandeur, the dignity, and the value of the Indian and his culture, to emphasize as strongly as possible the need to help Indian cultures to survive, as well as Indian citizens. During 1933–45, John Collier, as Indian Commissioner, made a great effort to implement ideas and policies initiated by the Meriam Commission in the Hoover administration, policies aimed at preserving Indian societies and culture. The assault from enemies of these policies was colossal. Mr. Collier was accused of wanting to keep the Indian in the Stone Age, of making a museum piece of Indian culture, of advocating a sentimentality regarding the Indian. Defending the Indians' right to believe as they chose, to speak their own language, to exercise self-government was all called sentimentality!

Let us face the truth that for all but the most sophisticated of Americans, the Indian civilization of the Americas does not exist as a knowledgeable fact. Until the Spanish and English and Portuguese conquest of this hemisphere, all is darkness. John Howard Lawson is right in his great book, *Hidden Heritage,* when he writes: "European and American thought places an absolute value on the conquest. In assuming possession Europeans and Americans assume that all that went before was without form and void; God's voice separated the light from the darkness . . . and history begins with the conquest. Our assumption has been that people condemned to servitude or destruction can have no valid past, no culture worth saving, no enduring social achievements."

Only in the most recent years have anthropologists and social scientists and trained historians lifted the curtain on the civilization of the Indian peoples, from Alaska to the tip of South America. I am really furious with myself that fifty good years have passed in my life and I am a mere child in my knowledge of the disinherited red Indians of this hemisphere, that just now I am learning about the Mayan, the Aztec, the Inca, the Toltec, and the Navajo societies. It is partly the fault of my sloth and indolence and inertia to scholarship, a feeble memory, a sluggish imagination; but that is not the whole story. The books were not written, the teachers were not informed, our culture was saturated with a white man's preconceptions and prides. I was fed nonsense about the savage and ignorant Indian tribes that is a part of the rubbish called primary education in thousands of schools even to this day.

Our children have a right to know the heritage of this hemisphere —its peoples, its cultures and civilizations as far back as can be known —centuries before the white intruder arrived. Why was I not told that the Indian had for his foes at first the long-extinct horse and camel, the giant beaver and giant bear, the four-horned antelope, the dire-wolf, and the mammoth? His imperishable artifacts are found—stone arrowheads, spear points, and knives—in caves in Texas, New Mexico, California, Oregon, Colorado, and Saskatchewan. In 13,000 B.C. or even earlier, these migrant hunters moved across the plain of Alaska, which was not ice-covered in the late Pleistocene age. They are found down the Rocky Mountains, their petrified footprints are found in Nicaragua. Their imprint is found in Brazil and Ecuador and southern Patagonia. It is one of the great stories of all history: the growth of these dawn societies of Indians, hundreds of them, of startling diversity and distinctions over ten thousand years ago. The details of the origins and the early millennia are gone, but the inventions, the social forms, the tempers of mind, the devotions, the worldviews, the humanities marched on, and do still march on in our own time. This we should be told and tell our children now.

Let us study this Indian saga with some humility. More than half of our agricultural wealth is the result of cultivation of wild growths by the Indian, none of which have been parallelled by the 450 years of white man's civilization in this hemisphere. Maize or Indian corn, developed in prehistoric times in South America, revolutionized Indian society. The development of corn by prehistoric Indians with the resultant settled societies has been called the greatest achievement in agricultural history, for corn is the most domesticated of grains, the only one that cannot sow itself or take care of itself.

And what of the other contributions of the early Indian civilization: the potato, the sweet potato, tapioca, the pineapple, the avocado, the artichoke, the peanut, the strawberry, the kidney bean, the pumpkin, rubber, chocolate, and tobacco? If one stops to consider the development involved in these scientific agricultural enterprises, the experimentation, the application over many seasons, through generations and ages, he will be less inclined to talk about the childlike savage Indian.

More important even than these major contributions to our health, welfare, and pleasure on the planet from our Indian societies are the inward experiences of these people of the dawn of history. Let it be said clearly, and with full evidence now coming to the surface for our enlightenment, that the Indians have a record of social striving of immense importance. They have demonstrated for centuries upon centuries, and continue to demonstrate today, as John Collier tells us so eloquently: "that intensity of life, form in life, beauty in the human relationship, happiness and amplitude of personality are *not* dependent on a complexity of material culture."

It is very hard for us to grasp this fact. It is heresy and treason almost to allow ourselves to consider that human, psychic, and social values were not created by ourselves as a result of our elaborate material, industrial civilization. The greatness of life, its possibilities and richness, moved in ancient times through structured societies long, long before white men came to this hemisphere. This the Indians from Alaska to Chile and Bolivia are telling us if we choose to listen. The Stone Age, the Age of the Incas, the Mayan world are periods of human achievement we need to remeasure if we are to set our values straight. The Indians of many cultures and ages can teach us much we never knew, or have in some cases forgotten, about the intensity of life, physical and mental, individual and social, and especially its potentials when we become aware of our interdependence upon the natural resources: the soil, the air, the sea, the seasons. We are just beginning to discover and respect the multiple languages of ancient and modern Indian culture, the languages of art, of dance, of ceremonial, of craftsmanship, of ascetic discipline, of song, of chase. As we today begin to conceive of structures like the United Nations and federations of nations, as we begin to think of disarmament and world peace in tough and realistic terms born of terror and fear, we should remember the thousands of years of experiment, eminently successful again and again, of Indian neighborhoods and nations that lived in peace across the continents. The greatest experiment in successful peace organizations in North America still remains the Five Nations of the Iroquois organized in 1570. This commonwealth of Indian nations achieved a social, political, and economic equality that has never been equalled. This Indian league for peace survived over three centuries, an achievement of government never matched in the Western world. The five powerful Indian nations—Mohawk, Oneida, Cayuga, Onondaga, and Seneca—had been at war for endless years, a blood feud of terrible intensity, and it was ended by a peace treaty—ended for 350 years.

Time today forbids more of this magnificent heritage, material and spiritual, personality-centered and society-centered, that comes from the Indian nations in North and South America over fifteen thousand years, but I begin to hope that our schoolrooms and churches, living rooms and restaurants will echo in years to come with far less foolishness about the primitive Indians, the inferior red men to whom we brought civilization and light. Many, many of us have a whole education still ahead of us in understanding the contribution to our world of the Indian peoples: specifically their psychological maturity, their many-sidedness, their intensity combined with tranquility. The Indian sense of values is something you and I have, to a large degree, not yet discovered. My plea today is that we do not permit the decimation of the Indian people, the breakdown of their recently strengthened and reconstituted social structures, before we really know what they represent to Indians, and to much of the non-Indian world as well. While subhuman greed for land, oil, minerals, and water motivates a large portion of the present American government policy, we must also recognize [that] it is supported and made possible by immense ignorance on the part of the American people. This ignorance can be dissipated if we care enough to see it dissipated.

This morning I am insisting that we face a hard fact: the fact is that the four hundred thousand Indians of this country do not trust us. They have suffered so many betrayals, reversals, and exploitations at the hands of white men, from George Sandys of Virginia Plantation in 1625 to Senator McCarran of Nevada in 1954, that our good faith is at a zero reading. If we used modern terms for our three-century assault on the Indian, we would speak of bacteriological warfare, of concentration camps, and of genocide. These are strong terms, and in the light of evidence hard to avoid. During the centuries of colonial expansion of European civilization on this continent, white men's diseases mowed down vast members of the aboriginal peoples. More conscious was the eighteenth-century case in Pennsylvania where smallpox-infested bedding was sent from a pesthouse into an Indian community by colonists who wanted to see the Indians wiped out, as they were by this virulent disease. It was, one might note, a devout Christian community that committed this bacteriological crime.

Historians like Clark Wissler and Carlton Coon tell of the fury of white settlers who found Indian tribes showing strong resistance to white advance. In one case, the Indians were rounded up and cast into a military prison. I am referring to the defeat and surrender of Geronimo in 1886. The United States Army seized all of the Apache men it could find, in addition to 329 women and children, and sent them off to a military prison in Florida, later sending them all to Fort Sill, Oklahoma, where they were held until 1914. Deaths during these tragic years among women and children were double the normal rate, due to poor food and unsanitary conditions and the vicissitudes of such confinement.

In 1864 troops under Kit Carson rounded up eight thousand Navajos in Arizona and took them to Fort Sumner, New Mexico, where they lived for ten years. This was a majority of the tribe. Authorities estimate that three to six thousand more Navajos were slaves, scattered amongst the white settlers of the southwest.

In the 1870s a majority of the Cheyenne and Nez Perce tribes were incarcerated in stockades in Oklahoma. By any definitions worth using, these are examples of concentration camp existence and explain some of the long-cherished hostilities of the Indian peoples to the white invader of his land.

"Genocide" is a new term for an old crime. It must never be forgotten that a systematic extermination of the Indian people was undertaken by the Spanish and later conquerors in the New World. In the mid-sixteenth century Las Casas published the *Apologetica Historia de las Indias*, suppressed in its full nine hundred pages for three hundred years, only portions appearing in his own time. It told the blood-chilling story of the destruction of the Indians in the Spanish colonies: half a million exterminated in Cuba, four million killed in Guatemala in sixteen years; in all the American possessions more than twelve million Indian men, women, and children perished at the hands of the invader.

In Las Casas's famed debate with Sepulveda, he spoke with biblical fury of the quiet of the Spaniards, saying: "The tyranny wrought in their devastations, massacres, and slaughters is so monstrous that the blind may see it, the deaf hear it, and the dumb recount it. God will punish Spain and all her people with inevitable severity."

Las Casas's words were read from one end of Europe to the other, and thousands learned some of the cruel story of sixteenth-century genocide in its grimmest aspects. While the English colonists did not face such large numbers in their campaigns, the extermination of the Indians was just as relentlessly carried out. Listen to Edward Waterhouse of the Jamestown plantation in the early seventeenth century: "Victory may be gained in many ways—by force, by surprise, by famine in burning their corn, by breaking their fishing weirs, by pursuing and chasing them with our horses and bloodhounds to draw after them and mastiffs to tear them."

This is but a small sampling of the evidence we might consider if time and a strong stomach permitted.

I wish this part of my report today were all in the past tense, but it is not. We are speaking in a year of extreme crisis for the Indians of the United States. This is a year of a gigantic takeaway, to use John Collier's term in the *Nation* last October. The United States, he points out, is trustee for Indian properties worth tens of billions of dollars. We as a government are also trustee over the political, social, cultural institutions, and group enterprises of several hundred Indian groups. The administration and Congress are now driving toward the destruction of these trusteeship obligations and arranging for turning over these Indian properties to whites. To use Dr. Collier's strong but informed words: "The demolition goes on behind a smoke screen of fabrications." This is being done through Public Law 280, rushed through Congress in July 1953, without hearings on its essential provisions. As President Eisenhower signed it, he lamented its most "unchristian" provisions, but signed it anyway. Public Law 280 crowns years of infamy against the Indian with new theft and betrayal. It authorizes any state government at its own discretion to substitute its own law for federal Indian law, and its own codes for Indian tribal codes.

Public Law 280 and several supporting laws are a massive sellout of our Indian citizens so iniquitous and enormous that I cannot find words, to say nothing of time, to express my shock and shame as an American citizen. Many of us as Americans were proud and hopeful in 1934 when the Indian Reorganization Act was passed, which reaffirmed and made explicit the bilateral Indian-federal government relation. It empowered several hundred Indian groups to organize for domestic self-rule and for economic self-help. The succeeding years saw 182 tribal constitutions written and 154 tribal corporate charters signed. The act created a revolving credit fund that helped immensely in fulfilling communal aspirations, while meeting individual needs as well. The Indian reorganization that took place was of remarkable promise for the future of the Indian in our nation. Now, twenty years later, through Law 280, history is reversed and a new crime is added to ancient ones. The aim now is to atomize and suffocate the group life of the tribes, a life that is their vitality, motivation, and hope—the greatness of which I earlier hinted at in only the broadest strokes. We are again looting the Indian estate and destroying his communal life, his culture, and his very spirit. And as other areas of the Americas begin to meet the Indian situation with imagination and honor, we return to old and evil ways. Forty million Indians of the Americas are watching us with alert eyes. And they are noting what can be done where conscience, intelligence, and public sentiment work. They note, believe me, that in Bolivia the United Nations Technical Assistance Administration, in cooperation with the Bolivian government, is remapping eight major areas on a twelve thousand-foot plateau for Indian settlement. Dr. Edmundo Flores of the Department of Agricultural Economics of the University of Mexico is the United Nations-appointed director of the project. Families with centuries of peonage behind them will now begin ownership of the land with twenty-five years to pay for it. The Indians there were bitterly skeptical, but are now persuaded that this is truly a new approach of honorable intentions. Dr. Flores said recently: "They are now looking forward to learning how to read, to fulfill a dream of education."

I mention this far off example because only with such visions of democratic integrity and responsibility can we today rise and insist upon an immediate return to the policy of the thirties—of the days of the Indian Reorganization Law. We can, I am convinced, delay and eventually stop this colossal sellout of the Indian people, the theft of their land, their water rights, the fishing and lumber rights, and, even worst, the theft of their social institutions. We can, and must, write to Indian Commissioner Glenn Emmons and to President Eisenhower. All competent authorities agree: only an aroused public opinion can stop this juggernaut of reaction from crushing the remains of Indian society in the United States.

We are gathered here today in a church for a religious service. At the heart of this religion of ours is a profound and controlling respect for the dignity and worth of human beings. This respect, even more this affection for other persons known and unknown in our human family, is our most sacred possession. If we grow calloused to the welfare, the security, and [the] possibilities of our Indian citizens, our damage is not only to them, but to ourselves. Nothing is more devastating to moral health than professions of brotherhood [that] we have no intention of honoring in practice. No matter how wealthy it may be, our society is doomed if our treaties are forgotten, our pledged word ignored, our neighbor's fields and streams and minerals taken for ourselves. We dare not forget the obligations that a higher religion places upon us to fulfill our commitments, to remember our neighbor's hunger for both bread and knowledge. The greatness of the Indian culture is a precious heritage and holds within it wisdom we desperately need in these cold days of automation and nuclear testings on the Nevada flats. There is no time for postponements, for idle trusting, with Micawber, that something will show up. The takeaway is in process at this very moment. The destruction of treaties is going on during these very months. If we are people of principle, we will rise to our feet and act. We can, if we will, live with ourselves, without shame. Let us return to a better day. We are not a docile people when we see injustice being done. We are not fatalists. We are a people who believe our vision of a commonwealth of man is no mirage. We can be brothers, with none under us, and none above us—equal, friendly, free.

Thou Shalt Not Bear False Witness
The Informer in
Contemporary America
May 1955

Earlier today we heard the classic Hebrew statement of the Pentateuch, "Thou shalt not bear false witness"—as well as the magnificent words of Second Esdras concluding King Darius's parable: "Truth beareth away the victory." When ideas so clothed with beauty and conviction cease to move us deeply, we have indeed lost to all that deserves the name of religion, or the name of humanity. Without the keystone of integrity for the truth, our social structures are doomed for swift collapse.

If there is a toleration in high places and consent among the people for tampering with known truth, for substituting lies for facts, for voluntary employment of half-truths—knowing they are half-truths—our culture has already made a choice of death. This contempt for the truth we know has increased in the past decade, and threatens the health of our nation. It has not yet conquered our people, nor captured our government, but it is a malady of frightening proportions in high places. Not since the valiant Edward Livingston in the days of the Alien and Sedition Legislation of 1798 has our country had to face, as it does today, the unholy evil of the political informer as a real danger to our continuing democracy. The evil has returned and blindness to its presence can but spread the plague and multiply the peril.

Today's address is not, for your minister, an exploration of uncharted virgin territory. In this amazing mid-twentieth century the clergyman all too often finds himself the target of the enterprising informer. The victims not only are discovered among men and women in union halls and factory shops, they are also found within the cloister and the churchyard. Bishop Oxnam was slandered and lied about by Harvey

Matusow. Rev. Jack McMichael faced his accusers, Manning Johnson and the Edmistons, government-salaried informers. Mr. McMichael repudiated them as irresponsible people with no truth in them as far as he was concerned. Along with several other New England ministers, I have myself been fingered as a probable subversive by Herbert Philbrick, an FBI informer, whose ingenious fabrications have been named for what they are by bishops, rectors, and ministers of several denominations. Rabbi Wise, Rabbi Magnes, John Haynes Holmes, Bishop Parsons, Harry F. Ward, editor Guy Shipler, and dozens of others have been caught in the net of the hireling witness of whom we speak today. And let me make it transparently clear that I am not concentrating today only on the shabby, quick-witted, headline-hungry, money-loving Harvey Matusow, but far more on the sinister and symptomatic profession he represents. I am speaking of the David Browns, the Paul Crouches, the Louis Budenzes, the J. B. Matthewses, the Whittaker Chamberses, and all their fellow workers in this subterranean industry of lying about men's words and deeds, and doing so for reasons only a depth psychologist could adequately understand; men and women who barter men's reputations for thirty pieces of silver, multiplied a thousandfold by contracts, book royalties, TV appearances, and all the proliferating network of profits associated with communication of hot copy in a cold war.

I assure you I come to this subject of the Ninth Commandment today with no bright and shining face. Having read *False Witness* by Harvey Matusow word for word, and a score of articles and news stories about him, and conversed with one person who has known him, I would wish we might speak of other matters. But we are in a sick society, and if you have any doubt of it, read *False Witness* as I did from cover to cover, and you will have new material for a clinical study in the American fear psychosis, material to go along with Whittaker Chambers's *Witness* and Herbert Philbrick's *I Led Three Lives*. The most conservative patriot of any integrity will be as sickened by these books as the most ardent Communist party member, for we have, in the acceptance of such testimony by our government, our courts, and masses of our citizens, an acceptance of something morally revolting and politically destructive of all democratic values. I recommend the reading of this book by Harvey Matusow with a heavy heart. I never less wanted to say "Read this book," but I say it because there can be no health in us if we ignore its information, if we stand idly by and permit the Roy Cohns, the Herbert Brownells, and the FBI to continue the employment of such persons in their frenetic efforts to stamp out the traditions of free speech, association, and political agitation in American society.

In earlier months from this pulpit I have spoken of the grave dangers of hydrogen and cobalt bombs. This morning we are speaking of a danger no less devastating: the moral degeneration of a culture that complacently tolerates the use of the paid informer in congressional hearings, in political trials, and in the publishing, entertainment, and educational professions. Cvetic, Philbrick, Budenz, and others of their satanic craft have moved from the witness stand to the publisher's office, to the college podium, to the TV studio with ease and acceleration, with bank accounts measuring their success in dramatic and vivid terms. And too few of us seem disturbed. Have we forgotten Titus Oakes of the seventeenth century in England, the archetype of informers, whose lies of a Jesuit plot sent men to prison and the grave? Have we forgotten Ann Putnam of Newburyport, Massachusetts, whose lies sent Salem women accused of witchcraft to the gallows tree? Have we forgotten the ancient Jewish tradition of refused burial in a sacred ground to the informer, the most outcast of men? Have we forgotten the Christian tradition of ostracism for those who play Judas and betray their leaders for thirty pieces of silver? The degree of our moral decadence in this matter struck me a few months ago when a prominent Unitarian minister wrote in the *Christian Register*: "Why all this perturbation about the paid informer? Why shouldn't he be paid?" I must confess a certain shame that a prominent clergyman of my own denomination can so blithely condone this ancient iniquity when the editors of the *New York Times* (who profess less concern for moral sensitivity) can editorialize on what they properly call the "shabby business of the paid professional informer," and warn that "in this semi-political area special caution is needed by government officers."

Before turning to Mr. Matusow's case study in the political informing trade, let me remind you that the reason for our discussing this matter at all today is that the church or temple must assume some responsibility for cleansing our culture of its most deforming sins, or become an accomplice in their perpetuation. My presupposition today is that with civil liberties operating for all our citizens we have a chance of being human beings, otherwise we are merely a part of nature's automation. If you and I cannot advocate freedom for all men, including Communists and socialists, to think, to organize, to propose legal programs of reform and change, we have bartered away our very humanity, our religion, our souls. Lord Acton was right when he said: "Liberty means the assurance that every man shall be protected in doing what he believes to be his duty against the influence of authority and majorities, custom and opinion." This dictum of Lord Acton's undergirds our American traditions of tolerance and latitude for dissenters and nonconformists. If, under a wave of hysteria, or under the whiplash of men who despise freedom and fear people with ballots and books in their hands, we surrender the guarantees of liberty Lord Acton advocates, then we cease to be men and are transformed into gibbering slaves of one tyrant or another. I care not how polished our chrome buildings, how swift our airplanes, how ingenious our food packaging, we are no longer men, but monsters. Judge Learned Hand, one of the truly great American jurists of the mid-twentieth century, has frankly asserted that he believes that "the community is already in process of dissolution where each man begins to eye his neighbor as a possible enemy, where nonconformity with the accepted creed is a mark of disaffection, where denunciation takes the place of evidence, and orthodoxy chokes freedom of dissent."

These are words to ponder as we speak today of the informer in our society and the morality of those who hire him. While I am speaking primarily of the professional spy hired by our government today, let us remember that for every paid agent of the Department of Justice or the Un-American Committee or the Burns Committee, there are hundreds of volunteers, sick souls of whom Judge Learned Hand is thinking in his words just quoted.

Human freedom has never been completely achieved, and it has suffered grievous violations, but the urge toward a greater measure of liberty is the fire that burns in the soul of every healthy and growing human being anywhere. We are heirs of men who felt the irresistible hunger for free thought and militant advocacy of a better government, a better school, a better church. Apathy at this moment of history can send us back to the medieval hovels from which our ancestors so painfully emerged. There are churchmen and editors and congressmen and businessmen who are dedicated to such a backward journey. They despise democracy, they loathe free speech for masses of people, they cherish the ego-consoling myth of an aristocratic elite, and they gladly pay recanting Communists the necessary fees for selling the names and freedom of honest men and women practicing their rights as American citizens. If we do not face the existence of such a block of men and women wishing frankly to see history rolled back to the thirteenth century or earlier, we shall let the world of Jefferson, Lincoln, and Franklin Roosevelt be destroyed. It is the firm intention of such despisers of the dream to destroy our freedom, if they can terrorize enough people into sleep or silence.

The Talmud says at one place, "The search for truth is itself a religious quest." And the corollary is clear to me: the dismissal of the bearer of false witness is a religious duty for every man of conscience. Some of you will remember that on April 10, 1954, the *Nation* published a special issue on "the informer," edited by Frank J. Donner. His brilliant writing in that number makes an excellent preface for Harvey Matusow's *Confessions*, one year later. Mr. Donner emphasized, as I am trying to do this morning, that the political inquisition of this postwar decade is seeking to equate liberal democracy with treason itself. "The informer," he noted, "invests in conspiratorial trappings the normal operations of democracy. New Dealers and Socialists (to say nothing of all Marxists) become plotters. The terms *fellow travellers*, *pinks*, and *parlor socialists* are replaced with the words *spies*, *conspirators*, and *agents*. The informer seeks to freeze the long established, normal flow of democratic thought and activity." His testimony sends men and women to jail, ruins reputations, ends livelihoods, dissipates discussion in union halls, forums, and even churches. Because of him teachers avoid the controversial subject. Because of him friends end the custom of political argument and commentary around the dinner table or in the living room. The climate of a police state is engendered. Truth and freedom become major casualties of the political process. The informer finds himself a prized citizen. The traditional contempt for his activities, the odium of his craft is forgotten. Boston gives the keys of the city to Louis Budenz. Malden declares a Philbrick Day. Bunting and banquets are proffered as tributes from a grateful citizenry.

Alan Barth of the *Washington Post* does not exaggerate in saying: "Today the informer is raised to the stature of national hero . . . his role is transformed into a profession." But the tarnish will not come off. The indecency and the vulgarity of a man betraying his friends, shattering the trust of his fellow citizens, selling his memories and his inventions woven around guesswork and possibilities—this remains! If we cannot have a society where we respect men's conscience and opinions, whatever they may be, and consider the mind an inviolate castle to be protected from invasion, we cannot have a society; we have only a civil war and desolation. It makes no difference whether the opinions be Republican orthodoxy or Communist heresy, we must protect the holy shekinah of a man's mind, or we are doomed jackals. We shall utterly destroy the creations of the centuries. That is why I equate Matusow, Budenz, Crouch, Gitlow, Cvetic, and Bentley (and all their tribe) with the men who cry out for massive retaliation with H-bombs and jellied gasoline; they are men who would destroy themselves and us in a holocaust of hate and destruction unparallelled in all history. The informer is as much a part of the Pentagon *dramatis personnae* as the man who invents the trigger mechanism of the H-bomb; both wish to end the process of free thought, of negotiation, of reform, of social evolution. If you and I and millions like us cannot end the iniquity of the informer in our midst, we will surely guarantee the ministrations of the atomic warrior at some date, near or far. They are of the same evil fraternity. The one shatters the conscience, the other the flesh.

From these remarks you may gather that I am grateful to Angus Cameron and Albert Kahn for publishing, at considerable economic risk, *False Witness* by Harvey Matusow. You have all read, possibly to the point of fatigue, the press reviews of this astonishing paperback book.

Let us not underestimate Mr. Matusow's abilities. One does not merely stumble into such notoriety and success as this twenty-nine-year-old man achieved without considerable intelligence. He was not the darling of Senator McCarthy and Roy Cohn without reason. He did not woo and win the hand of Mrs. Billie Bentley without acumen and a sense of timing almost approaching genius. Senator Jackson, Congressman Walters, Senator McCarthy, U.S. Attorney Charles F. Herring, and many others may now insist that they were duped by this young man, that he is neurotic and irresponsible, and that the Communist party planned the entire operation over the years with superhuman cunning. But the fact remains that Mr. Matusow sold himself to his employers with enormous adroitness—and Elizabeth Gurley Flynn and Alexander Trachtenberg and Clinton Jencks suffer prison or the insecurity of life lived on bail as a result. And even worse, almost every American out of jail looks over his shoulder and holds his tongue because this Bronx-born veteran of World War II found his only job in a lifetime to be the sordid business of selling his friends to the police for twenty-five dollars a day, plus expenses.

Stewart Alsop, the distinguished Washington correspondent, is right when he says: "It is a remarkable political confession which may cause major explosions." It has already done so! I shall not recount the biography of Harvey Matusow this morning. He can tell you himself of his tragic frustrations, his emotional hunger for recognition, his rejection by his friends, his army experiences, his joining of the Communist party, his activities in the American Youth for Democracy, his disillusionment with party discipline, and his phone call to the FBI offering himself as an informer. I leave it to a skilled psychiatrist to chart the drives that motivated this young American who hungered for headlines and money with such insatiable greed. I most certainly do not place all the responsibility for these crimes against free men upon Harvey Matusow's own shoulders. Our culture surely builds its success stereotypes on those who can make and retain the front page, whether by honorable means or foul. This week saw Dr. Jonas Salk and his anti-polio vaccine capture headlines from Senator Knowland and Chiang Kai-Shek, but this is tragically rare, as every editor knows. Harvey Matusow discovered the dubious satisfactions of notoriety, and one of his bitterest days was when his first appearance publicly before a Washington investigating committee was ruined by King George VI dying in London and stealing the front page from the ambitious witness, coached and ready for his day of glory.

No, the fault is far from concentrated on the figure of Harvey Matusow. Murray Kempton in the April issue of the *Progressive* is right in saying: "Matusow has been a runner for a racket mob which has infected the whole of our society, and those of us who thought of ourselves as liberal anti-Communists deserve to feel the shame at the sight of him

that the McCarthyites should." Whether Mr. Kempton has learned that
the Communist must be heard and tolerated as well as the Socialist like
himself or the Republican like Mr. Luce, I do not know, but I hope
there will be much soul-searching by all groups in our land who profess
a respect for the democratic process. This process cannot have exceptions without becoming a house of cards. The blame for a Matusow
must, to a large part, be placed on the shoulders of those who use him,
and those of us, you and me, who tolerate in office elected and appointed officials who use a Matusow unblushingly, and justify it with
facile logic and moral sentiments. It is this surrender of honor and fair
play and elemental justice in public and business life that should shock
and disturb every one of us today. There are all too many clergymen
in pulpits today and editors in news offices tomorrow morning who will
speak in anger of Harvey Matusow, not because he sought to fatten himself on the thoughts and dedications of honorable dissenters and nonconformists who trusted him, but because he finally reached the end
of his own long, elastic conscience, and recanted. Matusow is now out
on bail from a Texas court, not for his iniquitous lying about Mr. Jencks
and a great trade union, but because he was so unwise as to admit he
lied. If he is imprisoned, it will be for his truth telling, not his lies.

Some of you may ask, as others have before you, "Can we believe
Harvey Matusow now?" This problem of credibility, as Mr. Kahn, the
publisher, observes, you must decide for yourselves after reading the
book. Mr. Angus Cameron is a man I trust implicitly, and I am certain
that he and his colleague Mr. Kahn are both convinced that this book
is a true statement from the hand of a man who has written many
falsehoods and who had little to gain in this transaction. I doubt very
much if the profits from this book will keep the fast-spending Mr.
Matusow in beer and skittles very long. Frankly, I am not primarily
interested in the future of Mr. Matusow any more than I am in that
of David Brown, who gathered names by the hundreds in liberal
organizations throughout the city during the past several years. Such
persons usually find a livelihood. I am far, far more interested in their
victims: the men and women who signed their petitions, who telephoned
and stamped letters and did a thousand and one jobs for world peace,
for civil liberties, for racial equality, for all the causes that today must
be done with heroic energy and patience. These people have, because
of Matusow, because of Brown and Cvetic, and Bentley, and Budenz,
and all their ignoble colleagues, lost their jobs, been cut off from their
friends, suffered the disillusionments of betrayal for the humane and
decent trust of a fellow citizen beside them.

I am not particularly interested in the interior fantasies of Harvey
Matusow. He is a brittle plastic product of our faceless culture. I am
interested in the easy acceptance of informers by Americans who ought

to know better. I am concerned that professors of ethics and bishops of the church are, in too great numbers, silent on the immorality of paying our tax moneys to these betrayers of men's reputations. We are all infected by this industry of the stool pigeon and the paid witness.

Only in a time of panic will the informer become a public hero. It is a judgment on our society that Matt Cvetic can earn $15,000 a year for his anti-Communist activities; that Louis Budenz has gathered some $60,000 from royalties, lecture fees, and witnesses fees since leaving the Communist party in 1945, conservatively estimated. But it is not the money made that disturbs me nearly as much as the moral degeneracy encouraged. Matusow explains at length (as did Chambers and other false witnesses) that the informer soon learns to become an *agent provocateur*. He creates lies out of whole cloth to enhance the half-lies he told yesterday. Pages of evidence have been published by the *Nation*, the *Progressive*, and Cameron and Kahn to indicate how the new Titus Oakes of our day, like their infamous progenitor, improve their memories with the passage of time. When Mr. Matusow began his professional duties, he sweated at the naming of each former friend; later, the names tumbled out in generous profusion. One informer for the FBI confessed he recruited his own sisters and brothers into the Communist party in order later to turn in their names. In his almost incredible confession to the Civil Rights Congress, David Brown told how he made up names to fill out otherwise weak and thin reports to the FBI.

The freedom of our country must be measured by our ability to purge ourselves of this leprosy of the informer. Where there is fear there can be no freedom. We are not building the country of Paine and Franklin when we have to stop and weigh every word in public or private, or crawl on our hands and knees hunting for hidden microphones, or check our guest lists for dinner, or eliminate all names in letters overseas, or otherwise walk on eggs lest someone suffer.

This cancer of subsidized lying can and must be cut from our body politic. Every one of us can speak his own mind and write his own letter to the president, to his senator, to his congressman, and insist that the employment of political informers be stopped. The informer is a hangover from a day when there were weak and incompetent police systems. The political informer is a confession of fear of ideas. We have laws to protect us against real subversion and espionage and treason. It is cant and nonsense to say that our country is in mortal danger if we do not listen prayerfully to the jumbled and calculated inventions of former Communists now made fat on falsehood. In the days of Debs and Lincoln Steffens and other outspoken radicals, our people did not tremble at every new heresy proposed. They listened and went home saying, "He's right" or "Nonsense, foolishness—but let him talk." What has happened to our sense of humor, our innate love of justice, our curiosity, our open-minded hospitality to new thoughts? The best protection against internal enemies lies in open discussion, as Sir Erskine May concluded years ago. I am grateful to Harvey Matusow, in a heavy-hearted way, for his grim contribution to our fight against social destruction. His book can be a text to disillusion those who still think that there is room for the political witch-hunt, or that it is a noble inquisition we witness today, and that the motives of the investigators are pure and unblemished. This book will bring a new viewpoint to all who so believe. Our congressmen have emerged from its reading red of face and silent of lip. I do not share John Steinbeck's optimism that Matusow has automatically ended the use of the informer. The informer John Lautner is now testifying in Denver in a Smith Act trial. But I hope Matusow may have started a great revulsion against the fraternity of Judas in our own day. I pray our children may never need to learn the names of Titus Oakes or Harvey Matusow. May they enjoy an early oblivion.

The Contribution of the Negro
Woman to American History
February 1957

Of all the human qualities needed for happiness in this life, beyond empathy for other people—sincere, unmeasured empathy—the most essential quality is stamina or perseverance. How many of us have good insights, splendid starts, wonderful spurts of dedicated energy to this cause or that; and how absolutely imperative and yet how tragically limited is the stamina to stay with our ideas and our causes until we have accomplished the task!

And this leads me into the theme of today's address: "The Contribution of the Negro Woman to American History." As I have been reading for many weeks in the field of the American Negro woman, I have concluded that the most impressive contribution of all has been her perseverance over the centuries, from the arrival of the first indentured colored servants to these shores until this very hour of unabated struggle for acceptance and equality in our American society. I agree with Dr. Ashley Montagu, as he says, "Women have more physical and moral strength than men." I am not trying to denigrate men, white or Negro, this morning. I have before and will again speak here of Frederick Douglass, Denmark Vesey, Booker T. Washington, W. E. B. DuBois, and of their Caucasian colleagues in the struggle for equality: Abraham Lincoln, Thaddeus Stevens, William Lloyd Garrison, and so many others. But at this moment let us give full allowance to the quiet, unrecorded, unmeasured stamina of Negro women over the years, and its continuing power today in America, in the mothers and wives and sisters of millions of Negro men who in their staunch labors would often have lost courage and endurance were it not for such unflinching support.

Let it be noted at the beginning: We speak today of millions of

Americans who have and still do suffer a double discrimination, because of their race and because of their sex. This is no feminist polemic today; we are simply noting the social reality that the Negro woman is in double jeopardy every hour of her life, because she is made aware of her color and of her sex, at the employment office, in the public restaurant, at the college registrar's office, in the political caucus—everywhere she turns.

Today opens Negro History Week. We have observed it in this church since 1949. Mayor Norris Poulson proclaimed it for 1957 last Tuesday at his office. Churches, schools, clubs, unions, and other groups are holding many programs to celebrate the hard-won gains of the Negro people over the years. I wish only that more of the millions of Los Angeles citizens knew of the week's events and shared in them.

Dr. J. Bronowski, in that remarkable article in the December 29 *Nation*, "Science and Human Values," observes that "knowledge is communally made. The path to knowledge goes by the way of correcting concepts." Just so; our knowledge of the contribution of the Negro woman to American life will come through thousands of programs, including this modest one today, by your adding your knowledge to mine and mine to yours, and by correcting our concepts. In 1963 we shall observe the one-hundred-year anniversary of the Emancipation Proclamation. As Jackie Robinson said in this city a week ago: "By 1963 we should have the full equality as Negroes that Lincoln's declaration promised." The National Association for the Advancement of Colored People has a six-year plan to make sure that in 1963 full freedom is possessed. Part of the plan should be a far wider dissemination of facts. Action on your part will grow out of knowledge, and knowledge is communally made. If you do any research and study on today's subject, you will discover the appalling silence of the school books, the anthologies, the histories, the encyclopedias on the contribution of the Negro woman. When you recall, as I do daily, that she is less than a century out of chattel slavery, less than a century out of almost total illiteracy, you will be staggered at the progress she has made against superhuman odds—odds which still operate against her in 1957.

In speaking of the Who's Who of the Negro woman in America, I do not wish to concentrate only on the talented or exceptional woman who by virtue of hard work, self-discipline, and luck became a celebrity. We are celebrity-mad in this land of ours. The pursuit of fame has perverted our sense of human values already far beyond all good sense. I have never forgotten a New York speech in which Paul Robeson spoke simple and moving words on the contributions of the American Negro to the wealth of this nation of ours: the railroad track he has laid, the buildings his toil has raised to the skies, the billions of tons of merchandise his muscles have lifted onto ship and freight car and truck.

So it can be said today that our nation owes much to the Negro woman. We know that slavery forced her into the roles of cotton picker, rice harvester, sugar refiner, domestic worker, and later, unskilled industrial worker, laundress, and cook. This has all been labor that enriched America, with little reward going to the toiler, but it has great honor and calls for more respect than a glamour-seeking culture gives it. Such toil is not over. Let us have no illusions: the wage legislation won, the union contracts signed, the hourly wages increased still must be seen against frightful economic discrimination. The Negro worker, man or woman, is still the last hired, the first fired. As we honor great figures in Negro achievement this morning, let these cruel facts be very present in our minds.

I wish to speak of two periods: first, the Negro woman of the past, especially in the nineteenth century, and, secondly, the Negro woman of the twentieth century up to the present time. I have no immodest thought that I, a Caucasian minister, am instructing our Negro members, friends, and visitors in any new facts today. I am simply mentioning a minimum number of women whom we all, irrespective of our color, should know and honor. Hundreds more could be mentioned, and should be, but time and my lack of erudition forbid. These named today, however, are symbolic of the others and they should be written on the tablets of memory with a pride that they added so much to our nation.

In the Who's Who of yesterday let me begin with Deborah Sampson Gannett, who, disguised as a man, served in the Revolutionary Army, in the Fourth Massachusetts Regiment, the first American woman to enroll in the armed services. Massachusetts later granted her a cash award and gave her a citation for her extraordinary heroism. We have heard of Crispus Attucks, the first Negro to fall in Boston for American freedom. Let us add beside him the valiant figure of Deborah Gannett.

In the eighteenth century there was a peaceful woman of great talent named Phyllis Wheatley whose poetry has survived the years on its merits. Her lyrical and elaborate tribute to President George Washington is in several anthologies. Phyllis Wheatley came from Senegal as a child and was sold into slavery on the dock of Boston in 1761 to a tailor, John Wheatley. She was taught to read and write by the tailor's wife, and at twenty years of age attained some distinction for her poetry. She was later given her freedom and a trip to London where she read before royalty, and returned to become one of the best known poets in New England.

With the nineteenth century came the development of the struggle for freedom from slavery. It is natural, therefore, that most of the great and memorable names of Negro women are associated with this crucial issue. Thousands of the most courageous and indefatigable will never be known, for no adequate records were kept. A few we should know and remember as now we do Nat Turner, Denmark Vesey, Charles Redmond, and Frederick Douglass.

Two women's figures stand above all others: Sojourner Truth and Harriet Tubman. Their biographies should be read by all of us if they are unfamiliar. Sojourner Truth is one of the most impressive and forceful women in American history. Books have been written about both of these great women, though neither could read or write. (Never forget that to teach a slave to read was to court the severest penalties, and few white persons even had the desire to try.)

Sojourner Truth was born Isabella Baumfree in 1797, the property of a Dutch master in New York. Her parents died in her childhood and she was sold to John Dumont in whose services she remained until all slaves were freed in New York in 1827. Even then her master did not want to let her go, so she ran away, reluctantly leaving her children behind. When her five-year-old son was sold to an Alabama owner, she went to court in a rare and bold case and finally won her son back. In 1843 she decided to leave domestic service and took the name Sojourner Truth. She was a deeply religious woman, mystical in her faith. From then on until her death she was one of the most imperious voices against slavery in this land. She also spoke for women's rights, for temperance, for improved working conditions for women, and for suffrage. A tall, dark, deep-voiced woman, she electrified her audiences. Her deep fervor and religious faith, her tact, her singing, her ironic wit and swift repartee to hecklers won her thousands of supporters, Negro and white, for abolition and the other causes so dear to her heart.

The second leader of her sex and her people was Harriet Tubman. She was even more of an irritant to the slave power because she not only spoke with uncompromising audacity and force, she went into the South and organized an underground railway for the escape of slaves to freedom. At one time there was a price on her head of forty thousand dollars, a tremendous sum of money in those days. She was born a slave on the eastern shore of Maryland in 1823. At the age of twenty-five she ran away, leaving a husband, parents, brothers, and sisters behind, a cost in emotional agony we should never forget. She carried a pistol on her whenever she conducted freedom forays, and if a slave on the way north faltered, she quietly said: "You will be free or die!" Strength returned to the falterer. It is estimated that this incredible heroine (whose name we should know as well or better than Harriet Beecher Stowe) guided three hundred slaves to freedom, including her aged parents. Up creek beds, through swamps, she made nineteen separate trips into slave territory on her reckless missions.

Secret stations of the Underground Railway were organized from Wilmington, Delaware, to the Great Lakes—barns, cellars, churches, woodsheds, caves—with white friends to help with food and clothing, and with wagons with false bottoms for trips in harsher weather. Harriet Tubman once said, toward the end of her life: "I never ran my train off the track, and I never lost a passenger." Three thousand workers on this great underground aided Harriet Tubman and her allies to assist seventy-five thousand slaves to escape in the decade before the Civil War.

In so swift a survey as this today, we should make it abundantly clear that Negro women played a very large and brilliant role in the abolition movement, in the Civil War activities of the slaves, and during Reconstruction. I wish we had time to tell the story of Ellen Craft and her husband, William, who were aided by Boston abolitionists in frustrating federal agents of the Fugitive Slave Act, or the dramatic story of Margaret Garner, who resisted slave catchers in Kentucky by killing her two children and drowning herself in the Ohio River rather than return to chattel bondage. Her story is the best answer to those who would tell us the slaves were content with slavery.

What has already been said in these past few moments indicates, I hope, the profound truth of Frederick Douglass's observation in his *Life and Times*: "The thing more than anything else that destroyed the Fugitive Slave Act was the resistance made to it by the slaves themselves." As a child in the early part of this century, I remember stories told by my Quaker family, who came from around Salem, Ohio, about the Quaker leadership in the underground station in Salem fifty years earlier. But magnificent as was the white man's aid to this nonviolent resistance movement, the real credit should go to the Negro slaves, men and women alike. The only other nineteenth-century name I have time to mention today is that of Ida B. Wells, the beautiful and dedicated wife of Ferdinand Barnett of the National Equal Rights League. At the end of the century she wrote a book called *A Red Record*, a three-year statistical report of lynching. She demonstrated that protection of white womanhood was not the basis of lynching, since in no given year had even half of the Negroes who were lynched been charged with rape or attempted rape. Lynching, she contended, was a form of intimidation to preserve the plantation system and the white ballot box. Miss Wells lectured across America as chairman of the anti-lynching bureau of the National Equal Rights League.

And this brings me to our second group of Negro women, those of this century who have extended the range of women's participation, against such stiff odds, into new areas of American life. The way was paved by women like Mrs. Frederick Douglass and Mrs. Booker T. Washington, but new leadership appeared that is still today far from adequately recognized, especially by the white citizens of this country.

It would take a separate address to tell the great story of the founding of the National Association for the Advancement of Colored People early in the century. Suffice for today that we honor the strong and progressive leadership given in the past and present by such Negro women as Jessie Fauset, Goldie Watson, Rosa Parks (whose sit-down resistance in a bus in Montgomery, Alabama, in December 1955 started the great boycott movement the world now knows so well). I think of the martyrdom of Mr. and Mrs. Harry Moore, co-leaders of the NAACP in Florida, slain in 1951. While two hemispheres know the leadership of Rev. Martin Luther King, most Caucasians, at least, do not know the continuous and exceptional leadership of Mrs. King as organizer and speaker. If you ask why there are not Negro women in political office like Congressmen Powell, Dawson, and Diggs, I would remind you that male chauvinism in America observes no color line; it infects all racial groups.

One name must symbolize hundreds when we speak of Negro women in education. The elimination of illiteracy has not been completed in America for any racial group, but we should honor one name above all others (though comparisons are invidious). I refer to Dr. Mary McLeod Bethune. It has been my privilege twice to speak from platforms with this giant of the soul, though she was a woman of small stature physically. On October 3, 1904, this amazing woman single-handedly opened a training school for Negro girls. She began with one dollar and a half, a few orange crates, and a superlative confidence in herself and her race. Today the school, now known as Bethune-Cookman College, is worth many hundreds of thousand dollars and has been the pilot plant for scores of other educational ventures by Negroes for Negroes. In the story of Negro education since the end of the Civil War, the aid given by the Rockefellers and Rosenwalds and Peabodys deserves full recognition, but let it be frankly said that Mrs. Bethune's imagination outstripped those just mentioned, and Booker T. Washington's also, by seeing the new role of equality in the twentieth-century world for Negro women. This is Mrs. Bethune's genius. It was fitting that President Franklin D. Roosevelt chose her as the only woman in his "shadow cabinet" of Negro leaders during the days of the early New Deal. This daughter of slave parents was made director of Negro youth programs in the National Youth Administration. Credit to her should be given for far-seeing programs in the WPA Federal projects in adult education and in the arts, which assisted many thousands of Negroes for the first time to acquire education in many fields. One recalls, for instance, such a sculptress as Selma Burke, and Edna Thomas as an actress in the WPA Federal Theater production of *Macbeth* under Orson Welles.

Mary McLeod Bethune, who should of course be in the Hall of Fame at New York University, spearheaded by her force of mind and social insight the concept of integrated education and would, if alive, be supporting with many practical proposals the entire campaign today to have public schools totally integrated from nursery to graduate school from coast to coast.

The contribution of the Negro woman to the professions in this century is far greater than most of us yet realize, for reasons of noncommunication already alluded to (ironical as it is in a century of such unmatched technical means of communication). Let us think for a moment of Negro women of letters: of Shirley Graham whose life of Frederick Douglass, entitled *There Was Once A Slave*, is beautifully and simply written for popular reading. She is in my judgment one of the finest craftsmen in literature of her race since Phyllis Wheatley. Let us think of Eslanda Goode Robeson with her books on Africa, her astute magazine articles on public affairs, and her present position in the press offices of the United Nations in New York. In the field of the novel, one of several writers of great distinction is Zora Neale Hurston, whose *Moses, Man of the Mountain* is the best known. We need not leave this city to see the stirring spectacle of three Negro women editors of newspapers; Ruth Washington of the *Sentinel*, Patricia Alexander of the *Herald Dispatch*, and Almena Lomax of the *Tribune*, and until a few years ago, Charlotta Bass of the *California Eagle*. How this would have delighted the heart of the late Mary Church Terrell, of whom I wanted to speak at length today if time had permitted: the first greatly educated Negro woman in America, educated in Ohio and Europe, teacher at Wilberforce, first President of the National Association of Colored Women's Clubs, first Negro woman appointee to the board of education for the public schools of the District of Columbia, author, multilingual lecturer, leader extraordinary, who at the age of ninety-two organized and marched on picket lines for abolition of discrimination in Washington restaurants.

In spite of discrimination against women generally in trade union organization in American labor, there have been many women vigorous in advocating the necessity for women in industrial labor leadership. I first learned this from young Thelma Dale, Negro youth leader whom I met at the White House at a dinner Mrs. Roosevelt gave in May 1940 for youth leaders and advisors of the American Youth Congress. Probably one of the trade union leaders whose name will live longest in pioneering in this field is Miranda Smith of South Carolina, organizer in the tobacco industry. Another Negro woman labor leader and one still very active is Louise Tuttle, business agent of the Needle Trades Union in Los Angeles. Since the Negro man has just begun to find acceptance in positions of leadership in the labor movement, it is not surprising that the Negro woman has met such resistance. But doors are beginning to open.

In the theater progress has been difficult, though at times so brilliant that recognition has been forced by public opinion when the chance has been given. One thinks of such outstanding actresses as Ethel Waters, Florence Mills, Rose McClendon, Frances Williams, and Evelyn Ellis.

After decades of discrimination (against all reason artistically) we are beginning to see a tardy breakthrough in opera for Negro singers. Mattiwilda Dobbs, Marion Anderson, Leontyne Price have begun the demolition of this ancient barrier of prejudice. I hope among you there is no failure to recognize that this victory is due in a real way to the earlier successes in folk and popular music fields of such gifted and well-trained artists as Lena Horne, Muriel Smith, Maxine Sullivan, Ella Fitzgerald, and Josephine Baker.

And let nothing I say minimize the continued necessity for struggle in the entertainment industry by all of us to see that the Negro woman artist is given her deserved opportunity in this highly competitive field. True, Dorothy Dandridge in the movies was nominated for an Academy "Oscar." True, Eartha Kitt gets onto TV screens (as well as being asked to dine in New Delhi this week with Premier Nehru), but film and TV are still terra incognita for most Negro women, even the most talented.

In the dance, progress has been made, again against overwhelming odds, by a ballet artist like Janet Collins, a folk dance artist like Katherine Dunham, a modern exponent like Pearl Primus, but real integration is still ahead of us in the cutural arts—all of them. I am sorry time forbids an adequate mention of the graphic arts but again let one distinguished name stand for many who ought to be honored. In oils, probably America's greatest Negro woman painter is Thelma Johnson Street of New York, Chicago, and Los Angeles, whose work I hope we some time will exhibit on our Artist of the Month program.

In the field of medicine and health one name must symbolize several. Dr. Ruth Temple has for many years given herself brilliantly to preventive medicine in the city health department of Los Angeles. Mrs. Mabel Gray has spearheaded the campaign for enlarging the great Taborian Hospital at Mount Bayou, Mississippi, which not only represents the advance of Negro women in medicine and nursing, but is an example of health service to the Negro people of the South in times of cruel and merciless economic retaliation by intransigent white forces.

Two final areas of contribution can be but briefly alluded to, business and sports. There has been advance in this century for the Negro business woman and the white-collar office worker, though it has been painfully slow. Mrs. Emily Johnson here in Los Angeles has been made president of the Consolidated Realty Company, a "first" for a woman of her race. And it is heartening to see her leadership in planning for integrated realty groups. Until people of all races can live together successfully without restrictive covenants and color lines in housing, all these other advances have a fatal handicap. While Jackie Robinson pioneered in male sports talent in big league baseball, and hundreds of Negro men in this generation gained a livelihood in other sports, Miss Althea Gibson in tennis has won international honors. I wish that the state department would not only send her on a tour in Asia and Europe (which it did) but that at home Americans would open the doors to more of her sisters in all sports. It is heartening to see in the 1956 Olympics Negro-American women competing.

Let me close with this exhortation. It is not enough to make knowledge communally (to remind you of Dr. Bronowski's phrase again), as I have sought to do in preparing this address today and circulating it.

If our thesis is right that the next six years should bring us, at the centenary of the Emancipation Proclamation, to the end of Negro discrimination in all the areas of American life, then every one of us has personal responsibility, whatever our work, our color, our creed, our economic status, our political faith. We must know and circulate the facts, and increase our knowledge of them as they grow. We should subscribe to and read at least one Negro newspaper (as we should be reading the papers of other minorities in our community). We should join and renew memberships regularly in the Negro organizations that welcome non-Negro members like the NAACP and the Urban League. We should do all in our power to aid the end of restrictive residential practices. We should help wherever we can to increase integrated employment in private as well as public organizations, businesses, and professions. We should patronize shops, stores, theaters, restaurants, and hospitals that have won the battle for integration. We should work politically to see that Negro women, as well as men, gain public appointment and elective office. We should do all possible to support strong civil rights legislation and establish Fair Employment Practice Commissions in this state and nationally.

And in all this, at every point, we must insist that the victory be double-barrelled, for the minority citizen and for both sexes thereof. The churches, so long guilty of the grossest discrimination both against the Negro and the woman, are beginning to make progress in words and deeds. Our local church and our denomination has much yet to do. We are making gains here in membership, in leadership, but we have just begun, and we need our own six-year plan to be ready for the year 1963. It is not enough to quote Scripture or honor past heroines, or present ones; we must each play our roles with the stamina that is so primary to all human progress. Knowledge is not enough. Stamina is even more basic if the new day is to bring the fulfillment of our dreams and hopes.

In other addresses I have reminded you of the necessity to implement our knowledge. We have in recent months redoubled our efforts to repeal the church loyalty oath, to protect the rights of the foreign-born threatened with deportation, to find qualified leadership for our public school programs, to end the health menace of air pollution, to support the American Indian in his struggle for his social and economic right, and to prevent the exploitation of farm labor from across our southern border or from Japan. As I speak of the implications of today's address, let us realize we cannot slacken in our responsibility in other areas of religious conscience. Building a democratic world is a many-sided task.

On the Taking of Life
Can We Curb Our Passion
for Violence?
June 3, 1962

A man named Dagobert Runes has recently edited a book called *A Pictorial History of Philosophy*. It is no substitute for more thorough study of philosophy, but it is a magnificent reminder from past reading of many giant figures of thought who discussed man's fate. I hope to see a copy placed in our lending library and another in our church school library. In his introduction Dr. Runes makes this judgment:

> Three men have trod the road to inner freedom, and have personified the true character of philosophy: Solomon, the King; Socrates, the vagrant; and Spinoza, the renegade. They deviated at no time for any church or churlish purpose, serving no one but the voice of their own conscience, the demon within their soul. It is still this still small voice of man's conscience that accounts for the only goodness that is left in this world and it is the only substance that makes life more than a mere hacking out of existence among savage nations and selfish people.

I mention this quotation this morning because we are discussing for a few minutes a very fundamental phenomenon in our present world: the enormity of violence and the hardening of men's hearts to the taking of life. If I felt there were no possibility for the sensitive conscience of thinking man to make some changes in his own thought and action on this problem, I would surely not have the impertinence to stand before you now. This is not simply one more address deploring a condition of astronomical dimensions. There is no place better than a free church in which to look at our personal and collective behavior with honest eyes and take stock of the possibilities for changing it—and then taking the next step.

Those of you who were listening to Joe Dolan last Wednesday night on radio KHJ will recall that a local teacher of fundamentalist Christianity severely criticized your minister by name as a hypocrite for continuing to occupy this pulpit without subscribing to a belief in God. Yet, during the entire program, this same gentleman gave no hint that Christianity has a profound moral imperative to help man correct his ethical behavior and put his house in order on this earth—to come to terms with the violence around us and within us. But this imperative has been, and will remain, my own chief reason for being a minister of religion. Anything less leads to what Mr. Dolan several times referred to as barren theological sterility. Let me say Rev. Brooks Walker did a splendid job of defending my rights and activities as a Unitarian minister to the listening audience, calculated by the wise men of the studio at ninety thousand.

I am deeply concerned, more than ever before in my life, at the acceptance of violence and the taking of life in our present society. I cannot make it an acceptable fact of life. We have spoken of this before and will speak of it again. Every enterprise you and I undertake is involved: our making of a living, our building of a family, our participation in a democratic government.

You need not agree with my judgments in these controversial issues, as regular attendants at these services well know, but you do have a responsibility to ask yourself, "What can I do to diminish the acceptance of a culture and a government scarlet with blood stains every hour of our existence?" I am involved as are you. We are all conditioned to a bland acceptance of this prevailing cheap evaluation of human life, whether we realize it or not. The temptation to blame the cold war, the nuclear arms race, and the emergence of colonial peoples to freedom is constantly with us, and must be resisted.

Let me dismiss, if I may, with a few words the argument that the possibility of nuclear annihilation has so cheapened life that no effort by an individual to come to terms with violence and life-taking counts for very much. I realize that Dr. Ralph Lapp's recent statement that "a nuclear war between the USSR and the United States would be over in a single night or at most two nights" tends to cheapen one's sense of human values. But Dr. Lapp is no fatalist, and is doing all that he can, as are Dr. Pauling and Bertrand Russell, to awaken people to the need for total rejection of the atomic answer to world strife. Dr. Lapp is speaking to lead men not into despair and surrender, but to overwhelming resistance to a manmade destruction of the human race.

The same motive impels Claude Eatherly, the navigator of the U.S. plane that bombed Hiroshima, to write his letters published in the book *Burning Conscience*, which I mentioned last Sunday. He has been trying for fifteen years to destroy the hero image of himself bestowed upon him by the press and the government. Listen to his words:

> The truth is that society simply cannot accept the fact of my guilt without at the same time recognizing its own far greater guilt. But it is, of course, highly desirable that society should recognize this. I accept the fact that I am unlikely to bring about that recognition by getting into scrapes with the law, as I have been doing to shatter the "hero image" of me by which society has sought to perpetuate its own complacency.

As I read and reread the hundreds of news stories in my files on the efforts of men and women all over the world, from every walk of life, to reject the dependence of governments on massive destruction, I am persuaded that man can and must return to his full sanity. We have said this together many times before, and many of you act on it with disciplined effort. If the concerted efforts of scores of millions prove successful, the more immediate and visible issues of violence will seem more susceptible of solution. A few days ago in Denver, the American Association for the Advancement of Science held a one-day symposium on the need for a new collaborative "science of survival" to save the human species. It is probably the first time in history that sober and learned men ever had to make such a proposition—that of saving mankind from its own hands rather than from the forces of nature—and it is not a minute too soon! But I am more concerned with the violence at our doorstep, which we can take steps to diminish or expunge from our lives if we wish to.

Have we downgraded our evaluation of human life in this century? Do we think less of life in this technological age than did our preindustrial forefathers? As we learn to extend life through medical and pharmaceutical knowledge, through diet and exercise, through far more exact knowledge of the life process, do we find a man's life of less importance than did our grandparents one hundred years ago, or in the times of the first Christians, or in the century of the European Enlightenment? Were Dr. Dagobert Rune's three philosophers—Solomon, Socrates, and Spinoza—more or less sensitive to the worth of an individual human life than you and I sitting here today?

You and I are brainwashed by Dr. Libby, Mr. Teller, the Pentagon pantheon; we are poisoned in our supermarkets by preservatives and adulterants in our half-filled boxes of food, and imperiled on the highways by motorcars far from adequate in design to withstand the stresses of modern traffic—as Dr. Albert Burke said so well this past week on his TV show. Our violence is streamlined and magnificently packaged, but nonetheless lethal in its power and effect.

All I know is that I am deeply disturbed at the acceptance of violence and the taking of life now, today, in my own city and nation, and often by people who seem to me to have a sensitive conscience on many other matters. Is there some deep and insatiable hunger for cruelty, some thrill appetite embedded in Homo sapiens that cannot be eradicated? Must we accept such a lust for violence and death as a part of our nature to be rationalized and justified when it seeks expression? Are we beasts with a thin skin of decency covering us most of the time, a skin which can be torn apart under sufficient stress? Is the Unitarian advocacy of reverence for life a piece of sentimental idealism? Is it incapable of controlling our own behavior and taming this appetite for contrived suffering in other mortal men and women? Let me speak quite specifically of the kind of violence that troubles me just as much as mass death in nuclear war, or Nazi death camps where the wholesale devastation numbs the imagination and staggers our power to absorb reality.

Recently a young man by the name of Benny Paret was killed in the boxing ring. The slaughter was seen by millions on television. In the twelfth round he was hit hard on the head several times, went down, was counted out, and never came out of the coma. As Norman Cousins of the *Saturday Review* wrote in a very moving editorial, "One question that was solemnly studied in three official probes concerned the referee. Did he act in time to stop the fight? What about the examining physician? What about the manager for Benny Paret; did he rush his fighter into the ring without time enough for him to recuperate from the previous one?"

"In short," wrote Mr. Cousins, "the investigators looked into every possible cause except the real one. Benny Paret was killed because the human fist delivers enough impact, when directed against the head, to produce a massive hemorrhage in the brain. The primary responsibility for this death lies with the people who pay to see a man hurt and TV producers who contract for such so-called entertainment. The crowd wants a knockout." As Mr. Cousins says earlier in his editorial: "Mike Jacobs, the fight promoter, once told me 'The crowd come to see a killer. They don't come out to see a tea party. If they think anything else they are kidding themselves. If you hire boxing artists who don't pack dynamite in their fists, you end up counting your empty seats.' " Mr. Cousins ends his editorial in words I find myself supporting: "Don't blame the referee or the fight managers or the physician examiner. Put the blame where it belongs: on the prevailing mores that regard prize fighting as a perfectly proper enterprise and vehicle of entertainment."

Some of you may also have seen Jim Murray's column in the L.A. *Times* at the time of the fight. In a very eloquent declaration he said: "National television cannot long hope to offer public executions as 'entertainment.' Boxing is in the docks today and the charge is murder. The degree is not important. The indictment is overwhelming, a true bill written in the blood and tears of the victims of the most savage sport known to man since Nero and the lions. It is a sport barnacled with its own human debris. The pot of gold turns into buckets of blood. Prize fights are great theater. But so is hanging. If this can happen to Benny Paret at the summit of the profession, boxing should have to go back to the barges, I am afraid." Concludes Jim Murray: "Its calloused indifference to its own, its disdain for the simple dignity of a human being, has earned it no other consideration. No civilized society can put its stamp of approval on its present form—and its violent kingdom is no more prepared to offer sound medical basis, pension plans, care for the indigent and atonement for its own negligence than the Mafia. A dope addict gets a better break from society than a punch-drunk fighter." This quotation is not by a preacher, but by a sportswriter in a commercial paper.

It is a sad commentary on the state of contemporary religion that editors of literary reviews and sports columnists have spoken out with more fervor in recent weeks on this subject of prize fighting than clergymen from their pulpits, for reasons I can only guess at (none of them creditable)! Just as it was Joe Dolan, a Catholic news commentator, a layman, who last Wednesday burst into a righteous rage at a Christian theological professor who was calmly rejecting the concept of co-existence with the Russians because they were atheists.

I may speak only for myself, but I cannot advocate a religion of reverence for life and accept the barbarism of prize fighting as an optional entertainment in my culture. The two are utterly irreconcilable. A church that finds such a subject beneath its dignity for discussion is indeed lost in sterility for this generation of men and women.

On April 27 a Negro Muslim was shot to death by a policeman, and six others were wounded. Mr. Wendell Green, chairman of the Negro Committee for Representative Government, at a rally of two thousand people at the Second Baptist Church of Los Angeles said: "The Los Angeles policemen acted like a conquering army in an occupied country. We must find a positive program to correct these wrongs." Reverend Mr. Henderson, the minister, added, "It cannot be denied there is police brutality in this city. Anyone who says it doesn't exist doesn't know what he is talking about."

The shooting down of unarmed citizens by the police cannot be ignored by all of us, white or Negro, in Los Angeles if we expect people to listen when we protest violence against freedom riders or citizens of color seeking to register to vote in Mississippi and Georgia. Reverence for life begins in our own backyard, on our own streets, in our own real estate offices. All-white coroner's juries exonerating policemen are no answer to a community's need for security against sadism in uniform. After the zoot suit riots a few years ago, at the time of the Sleepy

Lagoon case, some reforms were instigated in training programs for police officers. Other cities have advanced far beyond Los Angeles in teaching a police force how to be effective and responsible without the taking of life too quickly or indulging in needless violence. To ignore these possibilities is to be guilty ourselves of shocking negligence and irresponsibility.

My files have all too many stories in them over the past years of gratuitous violence exhibited toward Mexican-Americans and Negroes in this city. No editor of a Negro newspaper here in Los Angeles will deny the facts of police brutality and the absence of protest by the great majority of white citizens living within our city limits. To me the silence of the masses of our people is as immoral as the violence of the offending police. The mayor, the city council, and the police commission will act to reform what can be reformed only when you and I play our proper role as citizens. It is acquiescence to the taking of life needlessly that concerns me most this morning.

I am not, for the moment, concerned with the teachings of the Negro Muslims, which are indeed a red herring in this most recent tragedy. After four hundred years of racial segregation and exploitation in this country, it is inevitable that militant and bitter minority organizations will be formed. Our task is to remove, throughout our nation, the roots of injustice that have been nourished by our callousness and hesitation to act. We have a great deal of unfinished business on our hands to be tackled, including the education of our officials and our police as to how to deal with our fellow citizens, especially in tension situations, whatever their cause.

As you now know, the President of Israel refused to commute the death sentence of Adolph Eichmann last Thursday and he has been hanged, his body cremated, and the ashes cast upon the waters of the Mediterranean Sea. The news reports from Tel Aviv told us that the people of Israel were divided, that the intellectuals and professional classes favored life imprisonment and that industrial workers and farmers wished to see the hanging take place. If there is a case for capital punishment, it can certainly be made in the case of a man who sent six or eight millions to the gas chambers of Hitler's Third Reich. What has not been said often enough is the part played by the Jewish Agency during the last war in policies which played into the hands of the mass death of Jews. Until Ben Hecht's book *Perfidy* appeared recently, few knew this unsavory chapter of the history of Hitler's genocide. No people, including the Jews, are without the weaknesses of human flesh and blood. The betrayal of the Hungarian Jews by Rudolf Kastner, who later held a high position in the Mapai government in Israel, is something Ben-Gurion and Sharett have tragically failed to explain to the world.

Let me add, Americans and the British cannot exonerate themselves in this fearful series of events. The refusal of the Allied governments during the war to open their doors to the Jewish refugees makes us all undeniably guilty. I am not trying to oversimplify a complex problem, but I am saying that demanding the death of a criminal is a poor way to control our lust for violence, or to exonerate ourselves from fearful indifference to Allied anti-Semitism in 1942–3.

I am more concerned with the unhappy record of the state of California as first among fifty states in killing criminals in a gas chamber. I would that all of us would read Arthur Koestler's *Hanged by the Neck* and C. H. Rolph's *Hanged in Error* to learn precisely what our record is in the so-called Western world in using the rope or rifle or gas pellet to punish those allegedly guilty of crimes against society. The margin of error is far too great to be ignored. The innocent who die by the hangman's noose are too many to justify this method of handling society's offenders. I have preached before on the immorality of capital punishment itself, and the task is still with us to find more civilized ways of dealing with the anti-social individual. Television, when used by a Bill Stout or the producers of "The Defenders," can help tremendously in reeducating the millions who sit forty minutes or more a day before their TV screens.

There is a great deal that you and I can do to provide substitutes for capital punishment if we make room for such study and agitation in our lives. Capital punishment has been abolished in many different places in the world. For a long time the Soviet Union gave leadership, as well as several smaller countries. This week I signed a letter with Dr. Linus Pauling, Professor William Ernest Hocking, Dr. Martin Luther King, and Professor Henry Steele Commager protesting to the Soviet government the killing of Soviet citizens for economic crimes. Twenty-five such executions have taken place since May of last year. I have read the stories in *Pravda* and *Izvestia* on these crimes and I, like many others, feel the case for rational and socially redemptive solutions is tragically weakened by the new Soviet policy. In my lexicon, no socialist society is justified in the murder of its citizens for any reason whatsoever. Life is sacred, and the worst of offenders can be incarcerated, educated, and oftentimes restored to usefulness. The short cuts of vengeance, public example, and state violence leave me unpersuaded.

I might add, on this particular issue, that only an American who has shown his profound concern for capital punishment in his own country has really earned the right to suggest to the people of another government to clean house. The punishment and attempted rehabilitation of the men and women guilty of currency speculation and bribery has its necessary place in a society anywhere, and it has long been to the credit of the Soviet Union that it sought to return the antisocial citizen to useful service. Abandonment of this policy is a return to an earlier order I had hoped was dead.

But again, I say our primary concern this morning is the taking of life in our own community where, unlike foreign countries, we have some influence. I cannot speak for you, but for myself I think it exceedingly disturbing that Los Angeles has one thousand suicides a year and eight thousand attempted suicides. Dr. Robert Litman, a psychiatrist at the University of Southern California Medical School, who is director of the suicide prevention center at General Hospital, has said that there are twenty-five thousand suicidal crises a year in this city, conservatively estimated—crises where persons seriously discuss or threaten to take their lives. These are not primarily lonely people living by themselves, but people in a social context, 70 percent married and living in a family situation.

Again, let me confess there are many reasons for such a vast load of suicidally-minded men and women. Ministers have more frequent conversations with such folk than many other citizens, and we know well the forces that press upon the emotionally and mentally insecure man or woman. What I am saying this morning is that you and I can play a far greater part than most of us now do play in helping the person who seriously considers taking his own life and who often inflicts violence upon himself short of death. It is morally insufficient to say this is a sick world and only its drastic social and political reconstruction can reduce these appalling statistics. Psychiatrists, doctors, and ministers know that even today, in a corrupt and tension-ridden world, there is much we can do. The indifference and cynicism all too many of us exhibit toward the frightened and insecure citizen with a knife or bottle of barbiturates can be reduced if we so choose. The answer is not entirely medical and psychiatric. I have spent enough time counseling with such people to know that new directions and fresh solutions can be found, often by the person himself, if given the time and understanding called for. If we declare ourselves for reverence for life, we will make room to cherish it in our friends and neighbors. The fault for one thousand suicides a year in Los Angeles is yours and mine in part, and I am enough of a Christian to believe that casting out demons did not end with the death of Jesus and many of his first disciples two thousand years ago. The violence of suicide can be reduced tremendously if we help our own neighbors find fulfilling work, new friends, sympathetic professional guidance, and our own openness to their needs. There is far too much reliance on wholesale reforms—the ending of nuclear tests and tinder-fire wars in Asia—which must be ended by our political pressure upon our government, without realizing that the real job begins at home.

You and I can, as Dr. Karl Menninger has said so well, end the taboo on discussing this subject of self-destruction in our own community. The nature and degree of the internal stress a man is enduring can indeed be found if searched for. I am sure every therapist listening will agree that in almost every case of suicide (where psychiatric counseling was involved) there was a missed clue, an ignored hint, which was possibly determinative in the final decision to employ self-violence. Today I am simply asking that we care about people far more than we have before, and make room for the healing process to occur. Let us begin where we can begin in this survival of mankind, at our own doorstep!

There are various avenues open to us here and now if we wish to diminish the violence in our midst. As I am writing this sermon my radio carries repeated invitations to see a new film where the chief character kills a woman every hour. I do not have to see it. Nor do you. We can stay home in droves. Today I visited a neighborhood market where comic books are spread across the counter, comic books statistically proven to have a very high content of physical assaults, tortures, and murders. The television in my home could, if I wished, deliver me one thousand crimes every seven days, a statistic recorded by Gerson Leyman not long ago. Schramm, Lyle, and Parker in their book on TV in the lives of children have this to say:

> Many parents of younger children are clearly concerned about the amount of violence and crime on television. The more highly educated the parents, the more worried they are about it. . . . But above all, the objection is to the number of crimes and the extent of the violence which can be seen at hours when children view. "If you could prevent certain TV programs from being seen by your children, what kinds would you try to prevent?" parents were asked, and 65 percent of their answers were they would try to cut out programs of crime, violence, and horror. "Why do you object to those?" these parents were asked. Because they frighten young children. Because children tend to keep them in their heads, remember them and dream about them. Because (a few of them said) they see children playing out some of these games. Because it gives children a wrong idea of what life is like. Because it might make for delinquency.

Later in the book, they state that

> television does not necessarily reduce aggression. It is just as likely to build aggression. The vicarious satisfactions of television will not for very long take care of real-life sexual frustrations or other social troubles. More likely, the sex on television will further frustrate an already frustrated child. The violence on television may stimulate the aggression in an already frustrated and aggressive child. Therefore, in some, though not all, of these cases, television may both suggest the tool of violence and help to build up the aggression drive that needs such a

tool. Then, when aggression in a real-life situation is at a sufficient height, the child remembers how aggressive acts were done on television.

You and I can do something about this conditioning of men, women, and children to violence in their so-called entertainment. We are not helpless as local viewers or in the higher levels of action. I wrote to Mr. Newton H. Minow, chairman of the Federal Communications Commission in Washington, last week and received, in time for this sermon, his now famous speech to the National Association of Broadcasters one year ago. Allow me to share one paragraph with you. Said Mr. Minow:

> When television is good, nothing—not the theater, not the magazines or newspapers—nothing is better. But when television is bad, nothing is worse. I invite you to sit down in front of your television set when your station goes on the air and stay there without a book, magazine, newspaper, profit and loss sheet or rating book to distract you— and keep your eyes glued to that set until the station signs off. I can assure you that you will observe a vast wasteland. You will see a procession of game shows, violence, audience participation shows, formula comedies about totally unbelievable families, blood and thunder, mayhem, violence, sadism, murder, western badmen, western good men, private eyes, gangsters, more violence, and cartoons. And, endlessly, commercials—many screaming, cajoling, and offending. And most of all, boredom. True, you will see a few things you will enjoy. But they will be very, very few. And if you think I exaggerate, try it. Is there one person in this room who claims that broadcasting can't do better?
>
> Well, a glance at next season's proposed programming can give us a little heart. Of 73½ hours of prime evening time, the networks have tentatively scheduled 59 hours to categories of "action-adventure," situation comedy, variety, quiz, and movies. Is there one network president in this room who claims he can't do better? Well, is there at least one network president who believes that the other networks can't do better?

He ended his lecture to the broadcasters with these words: "Gentlemen, your trust accounting with your beneficiaries is overdue. . . . I am not convinced that you have tried hard enough to solve your problems."

And there has indeed been some improvement in the twelve months since, as you who intelligently follow the TV guides well know, but the "vast wasteland" is still a wasteland most of the time. Your written support of good shows, and condemnation of bad ones, can accelerate the reform. And the same goes for radio, the movies, and the comic books. We do not have to succumb to the drivel, the salacious, the violent that pours from these media every hour of the day. If we care about human life as a value in our scheme of things, a value beyond profits and indulgence in sensationalism, we can act, and act effectively. Do not underestimate your part in all this.

A few days ago in the city of Hawthorne, a suburb of this city of ours, two carloads of youth and young adults leapt from their vehicles, assaulted a youth they had never seen before, kicked him, horsewhipped him, and ran their cars over his bloody body. As I write, he still hovers between life and death. Such violent rumbles are not only something put to music by Leonard Bernstein for the film *West Side Story*. They occur in this city and for many of the same reasons as prompted the youth of New York to kill one another in that now famous dramatization of twentieth-century reality on the streets of Manhattan.

I am not for an instant today proposing a slackening of your efforts for world peace, for international disarmament, or for pressing for withdrawal of our Marines from Thailand, as my own support of the delegation of our members to Moscow this coming July for the World Congress for Peace and Disarmament should indicate, but I am saying that the goal of survival and humanity must be pursued within our own county limits, wherever we may live. A Hawthorne rumble with its senseless and brutal assault upon a stranger on the street should move the conscience also. We cannot have a peaceful world and a strife-torn city. If we expect and sanction violence, we will surely get it. If we minimize what a concerned citizen can do, or a concerned church can do, we will endure the evil fruits of such apathy many more years than might otherwise be necessary. Our sermons and our hymns, our resolutions and our discussions are indeed sterile unless they move us one by one to appraise the violence within our own breasts, and the taking of life that will inevitably come through our inaction. The passion for violence can be curbed. The first step is to cease defending it as inevitable either as God's will, or society's folly, or the price of being unfinished human beings. Such sophistries are not good enough to stand. The equation can be changed, if we will set about to change it.

All Persons Held as Slaves
The Centenary of the
Emancipation Proclamation
January 6, 1963

Rev. Fritchman asked Bill Walker, distinguished Hollywood actor and member of the First Unitarian Church of Los Angeles, to read the "Emancipation Proclamation" by Abraham Lincoln, and the report of a meeting in Tremont Temple, Boston, on December 31, 1862, by Frederick Douglass. Space limitation dictates omitting these.

*　　*　　*

Last Tuesday, on January first, the President of the United States, John F. Kennedy, called on all Americans to hold special ceremonies marking the one-hundredth anniversary of the Emancipation Proclamation. I hope our president, like your minister, had mixed feelings about calling attention to this event of January 1, 1863. It is rather like calling one's friends together to celebrate the anniversary of the date on which he stopped beating his wife.

It is a shameful fact that as recently as a hundred years ago Americans held other Americans as human property. We cannot observe this centennial without advertising to mankind that this new nation, proud of its freedom, withheld freedom from millions of its inhabitants, and had done so for three centuries—first as colonies, later as an independent nation. This is not ancient history; this was yesterday, as it were. The father of Rev. Lewis McGee, our associate minister until recently, was born a slave. My own grandfather was wounded in the battle of Gettysburg. Lincoln's proclamation, which resulted in the freeing of some—not all—of the four million slaves, was only a first step toward ending the worst

166

single crime of our country, and was a war measure, an act of desperation by a government that was not at all certain it was going to win the civil rebellion of the slave states.

From our own perspective we know that no man or woman should ever have been allowed to land on these shores as a slave, and that this monstrous traffic, once it had started, should have been ended with the Declaration of Independence, or at least when the Constitution was adopted a few years later, after victory over Great Britain had been achieved.

I do not know about your schoolbooks, but in Ohio where I was educated no mention was ever made in my history classes of the fact that, in the first draft of the Declaration of Independence, Thomas Jefferson arraigned the King for waging "cruel war against human nature itself, violating the most sacred rights of life and liberty in the persons of a distant people who never offended him, captivating and carrying them into slavery in another hemisphere, or to incur miserable death in their transportation thither."

No teacher told me that those words were stricken from the Declaration on the insistence of the southern delegation to the Continental Congress. There were Barnetts and Eastlands in those days also! Jefferson's great document said all men were free, but he said it in the context of a slave society—as Pericles had said it in Athens twenty-five hundred years earlier. We need to remember now, as we face the desperate unfinished business of emancipation, that Thomas Cooper of South Carolina stood up at the Continental Congress and shouted, "We talk a great deal of nonsense about the rights of man. We say that man was born free and equal to every other man. Nothing could be more untrue. No human being ever was, or now is, born free."

Not until 1835, to my knowledge, did a southern slaveholder stand up and speak out against the iniquity of this barter in human beings. In that year James G. Birney of Alabama declared, "It has now become absolutely necessary that slavery should cease in order that freedom may be preserved in any portion of the land." It took twenty-eight more years for a president to sign a state paper making this the official position of the government. This Abraham Lincoln did. And even then it was but a partial liberation—freedom for slaves in rebel states and counties only, as the reading by Bill Walker this morning made so tragically clear.

The Emancipation Proclamation has none of the ringing poetry of Lincoln's Gettysburg address or his Cooper Union speech. It reads like a bill of sale. It excludes slaves of the border states, which had remained in the Union, and the slaves of the conquered and occupied South— embracing most of Louisiana, Arkansas, Tennessee, and a large portion of other Southern states. As one realist observed, Mr. Lincoln declared the slaves free in only the places where, at the time, he had no real power to free them. On January 1, 1863, only two hundred thousand slaves were released of a total of four million.

As the historian Richard Current has well said, "It might seem ironic to celebrate, a hundred years later, either the Proclamation or its author. But there is a double irony. Strangely enough, Abraham Lincoln deserves his fame as the Great Emancipator, and his proclamation is rightly remembered as a conspicuous milestone on the long road from slavery to freedom."

While it should have been done years earlier, the fact remains that Lincoln did start the action of freedom—Lincoln who ran for the presidency as a restrictionist, not an abolitionist, and who never believed that Negroes and whites could live together in the same nation. He had many plans for deportation of the freed slaves to Africa or Panama or to some other part of the globe. Yet he signed the first document giving some of them freedom. If we are unhappy that it was tardy and even reluctant, let us save our shame for what has happened in the first hundred years since that January day in 1863, for it is quite clear that we need a second Emancipation.

It is not easy for America in 1963 to talk seriously about the Emancipation Proclamation because it immediately confronts us all with the necessity of looking at the American Negro today, and with the even greater necessity of looking at the American white man today. When such a confrontation takes place, we are too likely to retreat into our own special Nirvanas. Paul Goodman, the city planner and writer, in his new book *Utopian Essays and Practical Proposals*, has observed this phenomenon and says, "A psychologist would say that our people suffer from a compulsion neurosis; they are warding off panic by repeating themselves; inevitably they are very busy and very conformist. There is no effort to remedy the causes, and there is little effort to think up new directions."

I mention this retreat from reality and into mindless repetitive habit because most of our fellow citizens refuse to look directly at the one-hundred-year lag on the Negro question: even liberals, even some of the people who attend this church. We Unitarians have far from achieved the integration goal we set for ourselves fifteen years ago. I learned to my astonishment last week that a Negro woman, attending this church, overheard a white woman say in the women's washroom that it was dreadful that we did not have separate facilities for white and colored! You may dismiss this as the hectic outburst of a visitor unfamiliar with our Unitarian principles, but I must say that hardly a week passes that I do not see some evidence of racial prejudice or ignorance that makes me wonder afresh why so many men and women and children of darker complexion return to our church and put up with such behavior in an institution committed to the brotherhood of all people. We have made progress here, and we should be proud of it, but we should also be radically discontented with the unredeemed areas of our lives where prejudice and ancient habit still operate.

This is not a historical address today. It is too easy to retreat into history and miss the real issue of our time: the bland acceptance of neo-slavery in the United States right now. A visiting Asian journalist recently commented on the splendid contribution of the American Peace Corps to some fifty underprivileged nations, and then he concluded, "But I have been to Harlem and to Chicago's Black Belt and to your southern states, and I am shocked at your black ghettos, which rival some of the worst slums in the world. Can't you spare something for your own underprivileged? You Americans preach individual dignity and equality of opportunity all over the world. Why not extend it to the American Negroes?"

And if I am told, as I will be, that I do not do justice to the great progress made by the American Negro in the past hundred years, I have but one reply: "It is far too little and it is fearfully late—to our abiding shame!" Most of the real gains (which have come only in the past twenty years) have been won by the Negroes themselves.

The editor of the *Progressive* magazine says it well in the December 1963 issue:

> The gains of the past two decades have been achieved by the Negroes themselves. Often with little or no help from their government. In the courts, in the bus terminals, in the lunchrooms, on countless picket lines across the country, Negro Americans, armed with song, prayer and the law, have pressed ever more urgently against the barriers of racial discrimination.

If we had unlimited financial resources, I would have invited two great Americans to speak here today: Dr. Martin Luther King, Jr. and Mr. James Baldwin—both men of enormous strength of mind and character, both Negro citizens who have a great deal to say to all of us, black and white. In their absence allow me to quote their own eloquent words. First I quote from an article, "The Luminous Promise," in the *Progressive* for December 1962, by Martin Luther King, Jr.:

> The unresolved race question is a pathological infection in our social and political anatomy which has sickened us throughout our history. How has our social health been injured by this condition? The legacy is the impairment of the lives of nearly 20 million of our citizens. Based solely on their color, Negroes have been condemned to a sub-existence, never sharing the fruits of progress equally. The average income of Negroes is approximately $3,500 per family annually, compared to

$5,800 for white citizens. This differential, tragic though it is, tells only part of the story. The more horrible aspect is found in the inner structure and equality of the Negro community. It is a community artificially but effectively separated from the dominant culture of our society. It has a pathetically small and grotesquely distorted middle class. The overwhelming majority of Negroes are domestics, laborers, and always the largest segment of the unemployed. If employment entails heavy work, if the wages are miserable, if the filth is revolting, the job belongs to the Negro.

Every Negro knows these truths, and his personality is corroded by a sense of inferiority, generated by this degraded status. Negroes, North and South, still live in segregation, housed in unendurable slums, eat in segregation, pray in segregation, and die in segregation. The life experience of the Negro in integration remains a rare exception even in the North.

We do not have as much time as the cautious try to give us. We are not only living in a time of cataclysmic change—we live in an era in which human rights is the central world theme. A totally new political phenomenon has arisen from the rubble and destruction of World War II. A neutralist sector has established itself between the two contending camps of the world. More than a billion people are in the neutralist arena. One basic reason for the neutrality of these nations is that they do not trust the integrity of either East or West on the issue of equality and human rights. Our declarations that we are making progress in race relations ring in their ears with pathetic emptiness. In India, Indonesia, Ghana and Brazil, to mention a few of the nations which together contain almost a billion humans, the right to vote has been exercised even by illiterate peasants in primitive villages still ringed by the jungle. In some of our cities in the South, college professors cannot vote, cannot eat, and cannot use a library or a park in equality. In Africa, Negroes have formed states, govern themselves, and function in world tribunals with dignity and effectiveness.

Then Dr. King answers the question: "What should be done?"

The key to everything is Federal commitment, full, unequivocal, and unremitting. When the President declares that the security of the nation, its sacred honor, and its future are inseparable from its civil rights, and that every facility of government, every department will operate strictly on that principle, on that day the knell of resistance will ring.

This is not a visionary dream, an ideal conception, an extremist demand. It is practical, as the Emancipation Proclamation was practical, because it is necessary. The time has come. Neither North nor South can endure the Mississippi experience long into the troubled future. When a federal army, virtually all of the regular marshals in the country, the Federal Bureau of Investigation, the National Guard, the Justice Department, the White House staff, and the Chief Executive must all be mobilized as a military force to register one single Negro in college, the ironic tragedy threatens to cancel out the undeniable triumph. The Oxford, Mississipi affair was a triumph because the administration did not flinch, and let no one doubt its determination! But it was a tragedy too, that it was necessary to exert so much effort for but one Negro, symbolic though he be.

Dr. King concludes:

There are twenty million Negroes in the United States. Each lives impaired by a disability not of his making. Our era cries for the moral spirit abroad in 1862 when the Emancipation Proclamation revolutionized an entire nation. There are those who may feel that I am excessively optimistic about the white South. I am optimistic, and I always have been. I place less responsibility on the moderate Southerner than upon the Administration in Washington. Millions of Southerners would have complied with the Supreme Court school decision eight years ago if the sense of inevitability then had been girded by government action. Without federal commitment, they were left to act alone, often to sacrifice everything. Many Negroes could and did do this, but it is neither realistic nor fair to expect it of the Southern white, however, much as his guilt may torment him. Self-preservation survives and surmounts guilt feelings. Yet the federal government had no such agonizing choices. It could have acted but did not. Instead it dissipated vast potential support, and then rationalized inaction as necessary until support could be organized.

The second American Negro who should be in this pulpit today is Mr. James Baldwin, one of the greatest writers of the present century. In the November 17, 1962 *New Yorker* article (which is really a small book), Mr. Baldwin speaks with the voice of profound concern for the future of our nation. No summary can possibly substitute for reading the entire message, and I urge you to find a copy soon and read it slowly and, if possible, more than once, as I have done. It is called "A Letter from a Region in My Mind." I would be surprised to learn of any non-Negro publication in the past sixty years of American publishing that has printed so critical an analysis of the white American image as this one. I salute the editors of the *New Yorker*.

What is Mr. Baldwin telling the American people? Let me indicate just a few of his judgments as we speak today of the centenary of the Emancipation Proclamation.

The Negro is not an abnormally sensitive person; rather, he is a daily victim of incessant and gratuitous humiliation and danger. We must search always for a gimmick for sheer survival—and it does not matter too much what the gimmick; if it is not found, he is destroyed.

By white America's mores, culture, government, and religion, the Negro is taught to despise himself. The world is white and he is black: a stranger to its promises and rewards.

There is a long and impressive section in Mr. Baldwin's article on the Black Muslim movement, which every one of us should read with great care, not because Mr. Baldwin accepts the Black Muslim program, but because he understands the reasons why millions of American Negroes acknowledge the facts that the Black Muslims state with enormous effectiveness. The white man's heaven is all too often the black man's hell —something which few white Americans have ever even thought about.

I have never read more telling criticism of the Christian church than Mr. Baldwin presents in these pages, especially the passage on the Christian nation of Germany in World War II:

The terms "civilized" and "Christian" begin to have a very strange ring, particularly in the ears of those who have been judged to be neither civilized nor Christian, when a Christian nation surrenders to a full and violent orgy, as Germany did during the Third Reich. For the crime of their ancestry, millions of people in the middle of the 20th century, and in the heart of Europe—God's citadel—were sent to a death so calculated, so hideous, and so prolonged that no age before this enlightened one had been able to imagine it, much less achieve and record it. Furthermore, those beneath the Western heel, unlike those within the West, are aware that Germany's current role in Europe is to act as a bulwark against the "uncivilized" hordes, and since power is what the powerless want, they understand very well what we of the West want to keep, and are not deluded by our talk of freedom that we have never been willing to share with them. From my own point of view, the fact of the Third Reich alone makes obsolete forever any question of Christian superiority, except in technological terms. White people were (and are) astounded by the holocaust in Germany. They did not know that they could act that way. But I very much doubt that black people were astounded—at least in the same way. For my part, the fate of the Jews, and the world's indifference to it, frightened me very much. I could not but feel, in those sorrowful years, that this human indifference, concerning which I knew so much already, would be my portion on the day that the United States decided to murder its Negroes systematically instead of little by little and catch-as-catch-can. I was, of course, authoritatively assured that what had happened to the Jews in Germany could not happen to the Negroes in America, but I thought, bleakly, that the German Jews had probably believed similar counselors, and, again, I could not share the white man's vision of himself for the very good reason that white men in America do not behave toward black men the way they behave toward each other. When a white man faces a black man, especially if the black man is helpless, terrible things are revealed.

Mr. Baldwin later asks and answers: "Are things so bad as the Black Muslim says they are? They are worse, and the Muslims do not help matters, but there is no reason that black men should be expected to be more patient, more forbearing, more farseeing than whites—indeed quite the contrary."

Then appears one of the most significant statements of the article and one which I have rarely heard from a church pulpit or in a white schoolroom or read in a white newspaper: "The real reason is that white men do not want their lives, their self-image, or their property threatened. One wishes they would say so more often."

One reason we all need to read James Baldwin's article is that we have not faced the stark reality that the brutal treatment of the Negro in this country, from the first days three hundred years ago in slave transports from Africa until this very hour, cannot be exaggerated. The efforts of the white man to destroy the Negro is not for anything he has done; it is utterly gratuitous. The power of the white world is threatened whenever a black man refuses to accept the white world's definitions.

Mr. Baldwin has a very telling report on his discussion at dinner with the Black Muslim leader, Elijah Mohammed, in which the author could find no rebuttal to the evidence spread before him of the oppression of the Negro, save to mention exceptions—the kind we are all quick to grasp at—Marian Anderson, Ralph Bunche, Jackie Robinson, and Joe Louis. But the state of the world proved the justice of the indictment.

In other lands the Negro has broken many of the bonds that have held him, formed new government, driven out the colonials, and found his self-respect. But after four hundred years in America, he is still not recognized as a human being. Here he remains trapped, disinherited, and despised. The reason for the rise of the Black Muslim movement is not that the program for a new black nation is so compelling, but that Elijah Mohammed and his followers have restored a sense of worth to people robbed of it. People cannot live without it.

Mr. Baldwin is telling us of white America that controls the power at every turn—in government, business, industry, in school and church: whoever debases others is debasing himself. And we of white America are victims ourselves of four hundred years of such self-debasement, as we continue a slavery in new forms for twenty million Americans.

Since the American Negro constitutes but one-ninth of the population, it is unlikely he will ever rise to decisive power in this country, as his black brothers are doing in African countries. Here he is, one hundred years after technical emancipation, the most despised creature in his country, with the possible exception of the American Indian. Only radical and far-seeing changes can possibly affect this situation. And, says Mr. Baldwin with terrible candor, the white Americans are simply not willing to make these changes. Indeed, they are so slothful that they cannot envision them.

"Most American Negroes," he says, "have lost faith that the white American has any such intentions to change things enough to get him out of the ghetto—the menial task and the unwanted jobs of our complex society. Negroes have learned that very few people or government *give* anything; they *get*, they *guard*, they *keep*. And when they give, it is from utter necessity and from fear of losing power."

Only political pressures of the cold war, of rising nations of color overseas, will bring even token reforms such as the Supreme Court decision on school integration in 1954—a reform left to fend for itself without a firm federal support that could be recognized as meaning what it said.

What is Mr. Baldwin saying to us? He is saying that there are many things we do not like to see in ourselves. We like to talk about freedom and equality, but we do not like to grant it if it threatens our present privilege and power. We do not like to examine our institutions or our own hearts. In Mr. Baldwin's words, "We are to our world neighbors an unmitigated disaster, and we are often just that to ourselves. If one doubts it, ask a Cuban peasant or a Spanish poet."

Let me close this reference to a great essay, desperately needed at this time, by saying that Mr. Baldwin is not hopeless about the future. People can be brought to face themselves and shoulder responsibility. Man can face reality and change things, but in this country we have not tried such bracing tasks for a long time; we resist reality with monumental stubbornness. Our responsibility is to life in a tragic world.

We are in sore need of new standards for ourselves, the white portion of America. Little wonder that Negroes do not want to be integrated into a burning building (to use Mr. Baldwin's graphic image), and at present too many Americans are skilled at little more than lighting torches for bonfires of homes of other people, even if it means burning their own to the ground.

This morning as we observe a great moment in American history, I ask that we acknowledge the tremendous contribution the Negro has made for four hundred years in building this nation of ours. Let us dedicate our energies to giving to twenty million Negro Americans what is theirs already: the right to be respected as first-class citizens; to be given that right not as a boon but as elemental justice.

Sixty years ago Mr. W. E. B. Dubois said, "The problem of twentieth-century America is the color line." It is still true. The intransigence and ignorance of the white American can bring the entire structure of our nation down upon us—and this is not empty rhetoric. It is not too late for black and white together—even a minority of them who know what they are doing—to prevent absolute disaster. The alternative to vengeance and destruction on a scale never before seen in this land—for all of the race riots of Chicago and Detroit—is an unremitting effort to break down barriers that have become intolerable and that can be broken by a federal government which has the power, and by millions of citizens who can insist that the human dignity of every person be inviolate. It can and must be undertaken by black and white alike, without delay. The silence of the good can be s⁺attered. The intimidation of the bad can be rejected. This is the only way we can possibly make the emancipation of the slaves in 1863 contribute to our world in the second century of freedom.

Even in this very church we have work to do to make such a philosophy a way of life. Alas, the mores and presuppositions of white America carry over into our life together here—tragically. It is not easy to practice what we preach when our culture does not even want to preach the ideals we have accepted.

I ask, on this Emancipation Sunday, and also on this fifteenth anniversary of my coming to this church as minister, that we make the total brotherhood of men our resolution for 1963, come what may: a resolution by each and every one of us—minister, trustees, staff, members, friends—all of us, with a dedication and a sensitivity never before achieved in our life together in this family we call the First Unitarian Church of Los Angeles.

The Morality of Civil Disobedience
November 29, 1964

On Sunday, November 29, 1964 a special service was held at the First Unitarian Church of Los Angeles, 2936 West Eighth Street, Los Angeles, honoring young men and women in the area who have been arrested on civil disobedience issues. Mr. A. L. Wirin, attorney for the American Civil Liberties Union, gave a short talk commending them for their stand, and then presented scrolls of honor to those present. Approximately fifty arrestees from the Congress of Racial Equality and from the Non-Violent Action Committee have received such scrolls for their contribution to the principles of civil liberties and civil rights, which have resulted in several cases of fines and imprisonment.

The minister's sermon topic that day was "The Morality of Civil Disobedience" (herein printed). In August of this year Mr. Wirin had delivered an address at the church on "Civil Disobedience and Law."

*   *   *

On November 24 in New York City, at a dinner for the *National Guardian*, I heard a thirty-year-old professor from Yale University, Dr. Staughton Lynd, tell an audience of a thousand people that direct action must continue to go hand in hand with political action in America.

Political action, he reminded us, achieved the test ban treaty and the Civil Rights Act. But there is also direct action, symbolized most dynamically today in the civil rights movement in the South. Robert Moses, the tremendously effective director of the Mississippi project for the Student Non-Violent Coordinating Committee (SNCC), sat beside me as Dr. Lynd spoke, and later explained to all of us the absolute necessity for a direct challenge to the state and federal establishments, as is seen in the work of the Freedom Democratic Party of Mississippi.

This young man—quiet, dedicated, with no flourishes of oratory, who has been beaten and suffered attempts on his life—represents the "politics of morality," namely direct action. As Professor Lynd put it, "One way to keep politicians, including oneself, honest is not to surrender the instrument of direct moral confrontation through action. Direct action can dramatize problems, can test out new social institutions, even when it is not regarded as an all-sufficient technique. We should never accept a politics which advocates abandonment of direct action." Dr. Lynd, who taught in freedom schools in Mississippi last summer, then asked, "Should we not indeed make an absolute rule of retaining freedom to demonstrate under all circumstances?"

Could I have had a better preparation for today's remarks to these men and women before me, who are being honored for their employment of direct actions of civil disobedience, than Tuesday night's meeting with a group of leaders from many parts of America, firmly committed to the morality of civil disobedience?

I should like to step back into history for a few moments today to find my own perspective for discussing the morality of civil disobedience, for this subject has a great and important lineage, while it is as timely as any issue on the agenda of mankind at this hour. Nothing so shocks many good liberal citizens as the choices made by other people in deciding what laws compel them to resist compliance. Let me suggest as a basic principle for our discussion today the great words of Henry David Thoreau, "There will never be a really free and enlightened state until the State comes to recognize the individual as a higher and independent power, from which all its own power and authority derives, and treats him accordingly."

This is the very heart of the matter. There is no sense in discussing morality unless men and women are genuinely free to make value judgments both to themselves and their social relationships, are free to advocate minor or major changes in their institutions and habits of living together. If this is gone, then even the most benevolent state is doing no more than managing a vast anthill, not a human society.

I apparently shocked students at a nearby college recently when they asked me, "Do you believe in revolution?" by replying, "Of course, when necessary; that is why Jefferson and Lincoln emphasized its importance in our American ideological arsenal, and reminded all comers that our republic was born in revolution." I ended my comment by reminding them of Emerson's classic dictum, "The highest virtue is always against the law." Emerson, of course, was simply stating in his aphoristic way that law is a working agreement on the minimum in a social situation, never the maximum possible for human felicity.

But back to Thoreau once more, the teacher of Tolstoy and Gandhi and Martin Luther King, Jr. Said Thoreau, "The law will never make men free; it is men who have got to make the law free. They are the lovers of law and order who observe the law when the government breaks it."

I remembered this Tuesday night in New York as Robert Moses of the SNCC Mississippi Project explained why the Negro voters of that state will demand of Congress this coming session that the Freedom Democratic Party nominees elected by them be seated in Washington, instead of the white Congressmen elected under state laws that contradict the Constitution of the United States. The state government violates the Constitution, not the Negro people of Mississippi. And I thought also of J. Edgar Hoover, open advocate of states' rights, representing the Department of Justice charged with enforcing the Civil Rights Act of 1964.

Like Thoreau and Gandhi before them, Robert Moses, Martin Luther King, Jr., Roy Wilkins, and Fred Shuttlesworth are men who insist that advocacy of civil disobedience calls for the highest moral resources of which mankind is capable. Institutional reality (the state and its law) must often, in an unjust, unfinished society, be made subordinate to the morality of man. Man must be the judge, whatever the cost to the establishment, or the feelings of the status quo defenders; man must be the judge of what is morally acceptable, of what seems like progress and growth. And he must say so with action as well as words. It is this fact that we are underscoring today, as we make these awards to men and women involved in acts of civil disobedience.

Let me remind the young people before me today who have taken part in such acts that there is a long history of such resistance to law when conscience rebels. There have been many forms to such resistance, and many diverse areas on the earth's surface where disobedience has taken place. Allow me a minute or two to speak of them. They have heartened me, as I am sure they have many of you.

We must not be too quick to draw lines as to proper and improper forms, proper and improper subjects for rebellion. If there is anything that resists neat categories of what is right and wrong, it is civil disobedience. Some forms of protest are legal, recognized by the rules of an established order; others are illegal. A man of moral sensitivity, with an educated conscience, cannot always restrict himself to the legal protests, the sanctioned ones. I think especially of the conscientious objector to war. The legislators who make draft laws for military service open a very narrow door for the man of conscience to pass through, and it is no surprise to me that the jails have been filled with so many resisters. Since when did a congressman voting billions for military establishments and war ever show a magnanimous spirit toward the conscience of the dissenter to the whole murderous system? What cares he for Gandhi's satyagraha or George Fox's "Inner Light"? Let me mention five historic examples of civil disobedience.

First, I would remind you of the Underground Railroad from 1830–1860 of the Quakers, abetted by a sprinkling of Catholics and freethinkers, which aided some fifty thousand slaves to escape to freedom. It led to the Fugitive Slave Act, which in turn had to be resisted by men like the Unitarian minister of Boston, Theodore Parker, and his friends. I am very proud that on my mother's side I am related to that incredible Quaker, Thomas Garrett of Delaware, who helped twenty-seven hundred Negro slaves get to Canada, even though it cost him his rather sizeable fortune to do so. The abolitionists advocated legal actions, but the underground railroad leadership felt that there was a higher morality to be obeyed and they defied the law. They followed their private star.

Second, I would remind you of that mother of civil disobedience in our time, Rosa Parks of Montgomery, Alabama, who told the bus driver in 1955, "I am tired and I'm sitting up front here where I am." After that, for an entire year forty-two thousand Negro people boycotted the buses rather than face further humiliation. The Congress of Racial Equality became, from then on, a leading American organization for teaching Gandhian techniques of nonviolence to thousands of Americans, black and white together. In 1961 CORE initiated the famous "freedom rides" ending with arrest and imprisonment for many hundreds of people.

Third, in 1957 a group of young pacifists organized the Committee for Non-Violent Action to seek imaginative and dramatic nonviolent actions to supplement the traditional methods of civil disobedience. Many of us remember their project on Hiroshima Day, 1957, when a twenty-four-hour vigil was organized outside the A-bomb testing grounds in Nevada. In 1958 CNVA organized the sailing of a thirty-foot ketch into the forbidden test area of the Pacific. Captain Albert Bigelow's *Golden Rule* was sailed from Los Angeles but was intercepted by the U.S. Coast Guard outside of Honolulu, and its crew of five men arrested and sentenced to sixty days in prison. The moral demand for atomic disarmament was heard around the world!

Fourth, let me turn the pages of history back a little further to Canterbury, Connecticut, in 1831. Prudence Crandall, a young Quaker school teacher, opened a school, a private academy for girls, and admitted in the second year of her school's life a Negro child. Indignant white parents withdrew their children as pupils, and the state legislature passed a notorious "black law" prohibiting the establishment of schools for nonresident Negroes in any city or town of Connecticut without permission of the local authorities. Prudence opened a school for Negro pupils. She ignored the law and kept the school open with the aid of William Lloyd Garrison and Rev. Sam Joe May. She was arrested, tried, and convicted under the new law. In July 1834 she gained a reversal in the higher courts on technical grounds, but local opposition was so great that she had to close this first attempt at interracial education in America. One hundred twenty-five years later the U.S. Supreme Court caught up with the morality of Prudence Crandall.

One more illustration: the woman suffrage advocate, Alice Paul of Moorestown, New Jersey, a social worker and educator who formed the National Woman's Party, which eventually secured fifty thousand members. She believed in direct action as well as education by more conventional methods. Many of the actions she took were illegal, though nonviolent. She landed herself in jail, with her co-workers, several times. One of these actions was a public burning of the unkept campaign promises of President Woodrow Wilson regarding suffrage. The brutality of the prison officials to the protesting women led her into the field of prison reform and the employment of the hunger strike technique. Suffrage for women in America owes much to Alice Paul and her civil disobedience programs.

Now let us return to the problems involved in the employment of civil disobedience. It is not enough, of course, simply to say that the primitive Christians refused to pay taxes for maintenance of heathen temples, or that the Pennsylvania Quakers refused to pay levies for wars against the Indians, or that the colonists in Boston, Baltimore, and New York threw tea into harbors to dramatize an unpopular tax demanded by the king.

To discuss the morality involved in civil disobedience one has to make judgments on the intent and purpose of rebellion against society's laws. When people speak of a "higher law" or a law of God, which takes precedence over society's laws, I find it necessary to say that semantics must not lead us astray. Some of my dearest friends have declared that it is God's will that war be resisted, that the draft be rejected, that the races be treated with absolute equality, and I honor their declaration. But for the purposes of morality, I can equally honor the integrity and conscience of the citizen who declares that after his own hard thought and study (though he is a free-thinker) he must say no to serving in the U.S. armed forces in Vietnam or anywhere else, or that he will not observe the white and colored signs in any school room or hotel or restaurant or swimming pool anywhere, public or private, just because it outrages his moral convictions—nothing else, his sense of human decency.

Let me give two examples to illustrate that the higher moral law, even within religious movements, varies in formulation, but is of the same basic character. The Methodist Church of the United States, on May 4 of this year at its Pittsburgh General Conference, passed a statement on civil disobedience, after three hours of debate, which said, "The individual has a right to follow God's will rather than man's in the rare instances when placed in a position where his conscience will permit him to do no other." As you know, hundreds of militant, thoughtful Methodists have been very active in a wide variety of actions on civil disobedience, and have thereby brought honor to their churches.

On May 16 in San Francisco the Unitarian Universalist Association, at its third General Assembly, passed a resolution that "reaffirmed, defended, and promoted the supreme worth of every human personality, the dignity of man, and the use of the democratic method in human relationships"; urged its member churches and individual members to demonstrate their support of these principles by "defending the right of individuals to engage in nonviolent civil disobedience for greater racial justice."

This second resolution has no reference to a "higher law" or to "the will of God," and I mention these two formulations to emphasize that the integrity of man's ultimate moral authority (in or out of any historic religious tradition) is found in his own inner faculties of thought, whether considered secular or divine. The United States Supreme Court is at this moment deliberating a case of a conscientious objector to military service who denies that the voice of God is required to validate his rejection of the draft board's demands.

So today we should not confuse the moral imperative of the individual and a theological doctrine of a supreme being. The higher moral law is not found in outer space, but in the deep recesses of inner space where Thoreau and Gandhi urged us all to go when faced with life's most disturbing ethical dilemmas. Tennessee prisoners held hostages this week in an act of civil disobedience to secure better mail privileges. Also this week Vietnam Buddhist high school students defied government officials and protested the war policies of the present administration. The religious terms used in phrasing the protests—if religious terms were used —would differ greatly, but the common reality is the same.

A time comes when the Establishment must bend before the voice of the outraged individual, and that voice is often stronger than prison walls or police revolvers. It is that voice which we honor this morning. It represents man at his very best, though it can at times falter, be in error, or bear the stamp of passion and prejudice. This is a risk freedom must always take.

Let me take another area of disobedience that is fraught with immense challenges to the conventional ethic of our class-ridden American civilization. All of the discussion these days about the triple revolution of cybernation, weaponry, and racial rights raises difficult new issues of morality and civil disobedience.

It is admitted, even by the most respectable students of the "war on poverty," that America has a hard core population of many millions of unemployed and youth who will never find jobs. They are the ex-miners in Appalachia and ex-autoworkers of Detroit, and many others. They are often Negroes, many are Puerto Ricans, Mexican Americans, and Indians. They do not work; they do not expect to work again. Many do not want to work. They live on welfare checks. They are the most depressed class in America.

They are proletarians in the old Roman sense, people of no practical value to the social order. As George and Louise Crowley say so well in the current issue of the *Monthly Review*, "These people are no longer even needed as strikebreakers; machines do it better. A government economist has dubbed them the 'no people.' They constitute a real and tragic class in America. They resist the oppression of social relations and institutions, having enjoyed such a minimal amount of its fruits and privileges. They reject the class morality of a society which has no use for them." They perform common actions, without conspiracy or planning, but because it comes to them naturally in their despair, and their ranks are growing.

Their civil disobedience takes various forms. They tear up their draft cards, they dodge draft officials, and, if placed in the armed forces, goldbrick and desert. They resist wage slavery by living on the dole. They resist welfare rules and regulations. Their disobedience comes out of frustration and personal expediency dictated by the rejection facing them at every turn. They utilize social welfare agencies, consumer credit opportunities, and a hundred devices to secure sufficient income to live on in their ghettos. Yes, they are nihilistic and anarchistic, not by philosophical reflection, but out of rebellion at America's unwillingness to put first things first in Congress, in the White House, and in the homes of the affluent millions who feel life is so good.

It is absurd and futile to discuss the morality of civil disobedience with people who are "no people," whom we choose to ignore and forget in the midst of euphoric Te Deums sung to the "greatest civilization in history." But there is a moral protest in this kind of civil disobedience, and we must see it.

There is civil disobedience amongst the rich who engage in pricefixing in major industries in Schenectady and Pittsburgh and New York, and there is civil disobedience amongst the very poor. There is civil disobedience by the disenfranchised Negroes of the old Confederacy, and by the college youth who find nothing being done to end the war system or the cannibalism of national rivalries or the destructive march of automation.

What can we conclude about the morality of civil disobedience? I return to my friend Professor Lynd of Yale. He is right when he says that actions of this kind can dramatize problems we otherwise are tempted to postpone answering. We doubtless will not agree, even in this church, as to which actions deserve the term moral and which immoral or amoral.

I think Thoreau and Tolstoy and Gandhi are telling us that all of us must expect civil disobedience to be with us as long as our social institutions are so blind to men and women's real needs for food and dignity and peace.

Tolstoy looked around him and saw the rulers of his day contemptuous of people and their hunger for life's necessities, including that greatest necessity, self-respect. Do you remember his words? "By means of the army, the clergy, the police, the threat of bayonets, bullets, prisons, workhouses, gallows, the rulers compel the enslaved people to continue to live in their stupefaction and slavery."

The rebellion in Tolstoy's Russia against this tyranny, as you well know, did not come in nonviolent civil disobedience, but in violence and revolution in the second decade of this century. The same may happen again in many countries, including our own, in the years ahead, possibly ignited by the anger of fifteen million people of color, as James Baldwin has warned us in *The Fire Next Time*. Or it may lead to another kind of horror, the dehumanization of millions of Americans into the anthill I mentioned earlier, where food and shelter and transistorized circuses are provided, but no dignity nor worth for people is made possible. This is not the day to discuss the real changes called for by the triple revolution, but I am certain of one thing: Every civil disobedience demonstration that I have mentioned today should make us build with utmost speed a moral social structure for all of our people, otherwise we shall see such a vast escalation of civil disobedience as will stagger the imagination. The morality of the civil disobedience actions being honored today lies in the fact that, in the best of conscience, these people before us here were demonstrating the necessity for change, for freedom now, not tomorrow, and for everybody. Yes, good, comfortable people will always be shocked and distressed at such acts and say it is the wrong time and the wrong method. But the actions remain moral if the protest awakens the slumbering, if it compels them to see the faces they do not see now—in a Jefferson Avenue market, in a Van de Kamp Bakery, in a Torrance realty development, in a Compton Bank of America, in a Palace Hotel sit-in—wherever it may be. Thoreau walks beside each one. Men make laws, not laws men; so we must see the men!

There are many means to be undertaken, some political, some direct action. If the catastrophes of civil strife and war building up are to be avoided, we will listen to the voices and deeds of the children of civil disobedience. The law will never make men free. Only men can do that. There are many tools to build the house of freedom, but if lives are to be saved and society made safe for people, let us see the moral grandeur of wise and well-designed civil disobedience. It flourishes on love and hope, not hate and fear.

Do Women Like It as It Is?
June 29, 1969

One of the privileges and duties of a church like this is to help people draw up a social balance sheet from time to time to see just where we are. Unless we do this, we fall into one of two pits: the pit of simply wrestling with immediate social problems or the pit of repeating broad generalizations, many of them tired and shabby but pleasantly familiar and tranquilizing. Today we are discussing a very timeworn issue: the position of women in the world, but particularly in our own American society. I have spoken of the role of women for twenty-one years from this pulpit, and never with any recognizable unanimity resulting therefrom. Let me share a few conclusions I have come to, some of which I have announced before and others which are new, knowing that there are barriers and distances invisibly raised even in a generous and friendly congregation such as this. Above all, there is a real generation gap which works for difference. Many older men and women have no ear for new concepts on the woman question, and find their children and grandchildren saying and doing things utterly incomprehensible to them and terribly wrong!

Do not think your minister is seeing a woman's revolution where there is none. The reading list in your orders of service is evidence that immense change is now in process regarding the ethics, the values, the habits of women. Barbara Ward is right: "We must de-mythologize our thinking." And the mythologies about women are substantial, tradition-bound, and emotionally charged with a great many people of both sexes.

One of the difficulties that confronts young women is securing a hearing for their ideas from older women whose decisions have been made long ago, who feel that the die is cast, and who see no way of turning back without great upheaval, which they cannot bear to contemplate; and thus the traditional values and practices are defended with vehemence, even if without logic. Let me make it clear we are discussing the position of women in the world today, not just middle-class women in the United States, important as their problems certainly are.

Too often we ascribe male chauvinism to middle-class men, to those of the Lay League and Establishment circles—and one does find it there; but also it is found amongst our youth, or radicals, our minorities. I have stories in my files on its malignant activity among doctors, lawyers, financiers, and also Black Panthers and Students for a Democratic Society (SDS). Many women within the Students for a Democratic Society feel fettered by their sex, and their frustration grew at the SDS convention that ended last June 24 in Chicago. "Within SDS, we are really the only oppressed group," a coed from New York's City College told a "women's caucus" at the Coliseum. "We shouldn't appeal to men to give up their chauvinism—we must form a movement powerful enough to force them to." On the third day of a fiercely factionalized convention, the women smarted over "male chauvinism." They were angry at the Black Panther speaker who said the women's only revolutionary role was sexual; they were bitter over the mimeographing and baby-sitting jobs they had been assigned. "The men make decisions and we make love or coffee," mocked an elfin blonde from the University of Wisconsin, adding that she was "very sick of dirty work." The Progressive Labor Party faction of SDS wanted to detour for the rights of females along the Maoist march to a classless society. "We shouldn't worry about ourselves when the problem is not men against women, but the workers against the ruling class," declared a PLP girl from Berkeley, demure in a blue-flowered frock. But feminists were skeptical that anything can change the status of women within their ranks. She spoke outside the Coliseum, where a nearby nightclub advertises "Live-Live Bikini Girls" and several signs say "Help Wanted Female."

To get into the larger frame of reference, we might look at a remarkable document, a resolution accepted by the General Assembly of the United Nations November 9, 1967, entitled A *Declaration on the Elimination of Discrimination Against Women*. It was passed unanimously by the 126 member nations, some semi-feudal, some socialist, some capitalist. It has been called a Magna Carta for women, and so it may well prove to be in a world still harboring a fantastic amount of discrimination against women. I strongly urge your reading of it word for word, pencil in hand, when the mind is fresh, to check the statements you truly accept and are willing to practice. I find so much smugness expressed by men and women, especially of middle and older years, reflecting a feeling that we have achieved here a society with little surviving male chauvinism, economic or legal or cultural prejudice, that such checking may prove to be quite revealing in exposing pockets of prejudice of which many of us are not really conscious.

I would like to share some sentences from the declaration to establish a base for further comments to be made this morning. Do not think only of Saudi Arabia, or Ethiopia, or Japan, or the USSR, or Sweden as I read; think also of the United States of America and that portion of it called southern California.

> The peoples of the United Nations have, in the Charter, reaffirmed their faith in fundamental human rights, in the dignity and worth of the human person and in the equal rights of men and women. The Universal Declaration of Human Rights asserts the principle of non-discrimination and proclaims that all human beings are born free and equal in dignity and rights and that everyone is entitled to all the rights and freedoms set forth therein, without distinction of any kind, including any distinction as to sex. Discrimination against women is incompatible with human dignity and with the welfare of the family and of society, prevents their participation, on equal terms with men, in the political, social, economic and cultural life of their countries and is an obstacle to the full development of the potentialities of women in the service of their countries and of humanity. The full and complete development of a country, the welfare of the world and the cause of peace require the maximum participation of women as well as men in all fields.

Article 1—

> Discrimination against women, denying or limiting as it does their equality of rights with men, is fundamentally unjust and constitutes an offence against human dignity.

Article 2—

> All appropriate measures shall be taken to abolish existing laws, customs, regulations and practices which are discriminatory against women, and to establish an adequate legal protection for equal rights of men and women; in particular:

> (a) The principle of equality of rights shall be embodied in the constitution or otherwise guaranteed by law;

> (b) The international instruments of the United Nations and the specialized agencies relating to the elimination of discrimination against women shall be ratified or acceded to and fully implemented *as soon as practicable*. [I hope not *all* deliberate speed.]

Article 3—

> All appropriate measures shall be taken to educate public opinion and to direct national aspirations towards the eradication of prejudice and the abolition of customary and all other practices which are based on the idea of the inferiority of women.

Article 4—

All appropriate measures shall be taken to ensure to women on equal terms with men, without any discrimination:

(a) The right to vote in all elections and be eligible for election to all publicly elected bodies;

(b) The right to hold public office and to exercise all public functions. Such rights shall be guaranteed by legislation.

Article 5—

Women shall have the same rights as men to acquire, change or retain their nationality. Marriage to an alien shall not automatically affect the nationality of the wife either by rendering her stateless or by forcing upon her the nationality of her husband.

Article 6—

1. Without prejudice to the safeguarding of the unity and the harmony of the family, which remains the basic unit of any society, all appropriate measures, particularly legislative measures, shall be taken to ensure to women, married or unmarried, equal rights with men in the field of civil law, and in particular:

   (a) The right to acquire, administer, enjoy, dispose of and inherit property, including property acquired during marriage;

   (b) The right to equality in legal capacity and the exercise thereof;

   (c) The same rights as men with regard to the law on the movements of persons.

2. All appropriate measures shall be taken to ensure the principle of equality of status of the husband and wife, and in particular:

   (a) Women shall have the same right as men to free choice of a spouse and to enter into marriage only with their free and full consent;

3. Child marriage and the betrothal of young girls before puberty shall be prohibited, and effective action, including legislation, shall be taken to specify a minimum age for marriage and to make the registration of marriages in an official registry compulsory.

Article 9—

All appropriate measures shall be taken to ensure to girls and women, married or unmarried, equal rights with men in education at all levels.

Article 10—

1. All appropriate measures shall be taken to ensure to women, married or unmarried, equal rights with men in the field of economic and social life, and in particular:

(a) The right, *without discrimination on grounds* of marital status or any other grounds, to receive vocational training, to work, to free choice of profession and employment, and to professional and vocational advancement;

(b) The right to *equal remuneration with men* and to equality of treatment in respect of work of equal value;

2. In order to prevent discrimination against women on account of marriage or maternity and to ensure their effective right to work, measures shall be taken to prevent their dismissal in the event of marriage or maternity and to provide paid maternity leave, with the guarantee of returning to former employment, and to provide the necessary social services, including child-care facilities. [In textile factories in Uzbekistan, medical centers, nurses, nurseries, in the factory—women have deliveries of babies!]

I have been asking women for several weeks whether they feel in this country an inequality of opportunity in education, especially graduate study in their professions, in job opportunities in their choice of vocation, and in rates of payment for work performed. The overwhelming testimony was that they strongly felt these discriminations. I hope it is clear that I am not discussing the American middle-class woman alone or the American college woman alone. I am not urging you to read books by Clare Booth Luce, or Pearl Buck, or Margaret Mead, or Betty Friedan, or Eve Merriam, who so often seem devoid of concern for the millions of working-class women, married or unmarried, employed or unemployed. While there well may be some here who dissent, my own conviction is that the Magna Carta of the U.N. declaration cannot be translated fully into living fact under a capitalist society; and the changeover to socialism will not automatically make it real, either, though it does provide a far better ground for such achievement. I say this both from personal observation of both kinds of societies in recent years, and by reading the history of women's struggles under many kinds of economic and social orders.

I have been told by women leaders in revolutionary groups that even when socialism exists in power around the world, it will take at least several decades to really solve the woman question justly. I think I must concur.

One reason I read today from an interview with Dr. Barbara Ward, the distinguished British economist, was her own expanded understanding in recent years that the world is in for great convulsions as imperialism is recognized around the globe for what it is: the dominance of developed countries that control most of the economy of the world in complete disproportion to the global population. The fact is that 80 percent of the world's wealth is controlled by Europe and America, so that market forces reward those already rewarded. This plus the stagnant state of world agriculture and the growth of technology makes the development of international bodies like the United Nations and a true World Bank essential. Around the world peoples long in colonial dependence on Europe and America are determined to do things their own way. It was interesting to hear Barbara Ward telling students at Pomona College that there is worse to come before it can be better, and that she feels so radical that she cannot be distinguished from SDS. She added this pregnant observation: "I get very tired of people crying that they cannot afford any more taxes. We haven't begun to tax ourselves. As long as there is human need, there must be expenditure. A system is worth keeping only if it is used for advancing humanity. Nothing will be done, radical or otherwise, if we do not have the courage to want a profound transformation of an unbalanced, unjust society and stay with courage for as long as it takes."

I might add that this emphasis on staying with the problem of changing society reminded me of many hours of reading Len De Caux's remarkable manuscript on the growth of the CIO during the New Deal, and the later failure of nerve and patience and courage by millions of Americans who for a few short years had had a vision of a far different America and world. Unless we can stay at the job of transforming our economic and political institutions to rectify gigantic inequalities of income and opportunity, the woman's role will remain as miserable and shameful as it now is for the majority of the female sex in this and many other nations.

This is not a statistical sermon today, but a sentence or two of documentation may help the skeptic on this matter of wage differentials (so roundly excoriated by the U.N. declaration from which I read). In a report in May 1967 from a commission on the status of women, it was stated: "Twenty-nine million women over 16 years of age in this country work . . . which constitutes 37 percent of all workers. Forty-one percent of women over 16 in the United States are workers." (This means the civilian labor force and does not include millions of very busy housewives, a separate subject that calls for extended examination which we cannot give today.) One of our members, Mary Inman of Long Beach, makes a very strong case for wages for housewives in any society calling itself equalitarian and just. But these figures I quote are of women outside of the home.

The median wage for full-time working women in this 1967 report was $3,973 as against $6,848 for men. In the same year (1966) 61 percent of the full-time working women received less than $3,000 income compared with 27 percent of the men. And at the upper levels, 4 percent of the women received more than $7,000 compared with 7 percent of the men. The great differences here are not salaries entirely, but in bonuses and commissions paid to men.

It boils down to the fact that women do one-third of the labor and make one-fifth of the income. So on the economic level, the answer I get from women is that they do not like it as it is. Little wonder that there is a renewal of the women's revolution started by Susan B. Anthony and Elizabeth Cady Stanton.

But the changing models for being a woman are not only in the field of economics and jobs. The rebellion against outmoded models by millions of young people, both working class and middle class, are dramatized for us each new day. Let me take an example from an unexpected source, the department of psychology of a very conservative religious school, Fuller Theological Seminary. Dr. Lee Edward Travis of that school recently spoke to the University of Redlands Woman's Club and the Scripps College Alumnae on Women in a panel on "Our Changing Society."

> Is femininity just a bill of goods sold to women? If the answer is yes, what else is there for women to be? You bought this bill of goods because it paid. Have you considered that the price you paid was too high? We have considered you to be glamorous, sweet, 34-24-34, dainty, sweet-smelling, dependent, passive, affirmative, supportive, submissive, coy, becomingly inhibited, socially poised and skillful, a loving homemaker. You are to gratify and nurture those around you; and you may occasionally give in to hysteria and emotional outburst.
>
> Did you decide all this? Who told you to do this? The answer is that a male-dominated culture carved out the role for women, providing rewards for those who bought the system and rejection for those who didn't. You bought this because it paid. You got more out of it if you did this. You were more popular if you did this. The philosophy that brought you here is the Judeo-Christian theory of the dominance of the male, the implication that a woman is a bit subordinate, a bit inferior. Western culture has always held to the supposition that the male is the dominant quality. But does this work? Will your dynamics of being passive, submissive, becomingly inhibited, tolerate your assumption of responsibility?

Dr. Travis attributed much of the standardization of womanhood to the "model concept," that of a mother nurturing a family and passing on to her daughter the same role, with the same rewards. He suggested that some of the results of the system in question brought about not only inequities but injuries in modern society. The undesirable results, at least from the woman's position, are that the attractive role of the male devalues the role of the female, the inhibition of sexual impulses restricts a woman to romantic love, that a woman's sexuality becomes a bargaining principle, that competition grows between husband and wife:

Might I propose a symmetrical relationship? Might I suggest we consider the futility of sexual roles? There is wholeness only in union. This is a fundamental law of life. We should bring an end to competition, in which somebody wins and somebody loses, and replace it with a congruent relationship where it is impossible to determine the head of the house.

I would not quote Dr. Travis at this length were it not an accurate index to the changing role that is rejecting former models for feminine behavior across America. One could take the questionnaires issued by the burgeoning mating organizations here in California to see how swift is the change in women's value in the past few years. The male world is under fire because it has produced an untenable culture, one offering lip service to equality and justice for men and women but actually prohibiting participation on equal terms by women. Anyone who counsels with people, married or unmarried, over any length of time, discovers how extensive is the male control pattern in our society, and this two generations after suffrage was granted to women and a century after education became open to women.

Let us speak of the changing model for women made effective by increased contraceptive control through the Pill, and the demand for legalized abortion, which will make it possible for women to give consent to their being used for human reproduction. The sexual revolution of which we hear so much has far more implications than we can explore in a single sermon, or a series of sermons, but a few factors seem to mark a great departure from centuries of social practice, in fact a great departure from practices I found prevalent when I had Dr. Kinsey speak in this church twenty years ago.

We are having to rewrite some of the definitions Dr. Will Durant said, in his *Story of Civilization,* "that marriage is an association of mates for the care of the offspring." This is no longer true for many people who enter into marriage. It is certainly a diminishing factor since smaller families come with increased education, with increased knowledge of the control of child-production, with deepened awareness of the perils of overpopulation in today's world. I agree with my friend Rabbi Leonard Beerman when he says that childless marriages place a great strain on the partners, for they have one less crutch for an often meaningless relationship. Marriages without children should force two people to face the reality of their relationship.

The pill and other contraceptive knowledge and the growing acceptance of the ethical right to legal abortion open up a new type of freedom to make individual choices never before possible on a large scale. Whether we make wise and creative use of these new challenges for human felicity remains to be seen, but certainly millions of girls and women who did not like it as it was may have a chance to make a new society where freedom and equality are more than words. The Judeo-Christian, Puritan Protestant ethic on sex has shown its bankruptcy to this generation, and Hawthorne's *The Scarlet Letter* is relegated to high school English courses as a part of our literary past, beautifully expressed but morally and socially unconvincing. There are many people of middle and later years who have no intention of having children; who ask, why marry? They say, "We can have sex without marriage if we do not intend to produce a family." This view, of course, has prevailed in many nations in the past and in our own century, as many political revolutionaries of the 1905 vintage can confirm; but today the new pharmaceuticals, as well as the declining power of church and temple taboos, make such views far easier to accept. I have read some of the literature of the sexual freedom groups and am far from certain that more happiness is in store for many now in transition from an older ethic to a newer one. I see the exploitation of thousands of lonely and frustrated people by racketeers and dollar-minded cultists and I pray that here, as in other areas of the market economy, people can show some judgment and self-direction. The growth of prostitution and venereal disease and an out of control drug culture that threatens the health of many young people are signals I feel we need to take very seriously.

On the more optimistic side, I find the temporary postponement of marriage by our young people, in and out of college, a definite decision to find their own identity. As a minister, I have seen many young people in the past repeat their parents' mistake of premature marriage, often under social coercion in a stricter church-controlled culture. Today, many young women tell me they intend to wait for marriage until they find their own values, their own potentials as persons as well as marriage partners. This is something the Pill has made possible, as well as the new insights of psychology and liberated religion.

I agree with the many professors, psychiatrists, clergy, and writers who say the newer freedom is not leading to more promiscuity than in past generations, but to a far better conscience, shorn of grandfather's hypocrisy and practice of the double standard. The women's revolution is far more than sexual, but it is also that—and the ancient timbers of a male-dominated society are creaking and shaking as never before. The women who say they "do not like it as it is" are achieving a maturity not even encouraged a generation ago, so they may have it better than it has ever been before, especially if the liberated women can play the role of Lysistrata and end the madness of war and demand the end of poverty as well. Men have failed on both scores. Possibly the new generation of men and women together, both with new perspectives, can do what most of us have been unable to do: build a good society without a so-called inferior people to make it go—slaves, peasants, illiterates, or overly-docile women. Bellamy and Lenin thought such dreams were possible—so why not a Unitarian too? Most of my colleagues in the Unitarian ministry support a great deal of what I have said today, even if they wait until they retire to write their autobiographies and say it out loud.

I have of late been reading *Born Female* by Caroline Bird. As some of you may remember her statement: "Traditional marriage can be as corrupt as prostitution, so often based on economics instead of love." And she continues, "The social costs of keeping women down are far greater than we like to admit. The demonic practice of keeping vast numbers of brilliant and intelligent women cataloged as housewives goes on and on. A change in sex roles hurts men and women, but women suffer more and have to do most of the adjusting as things are now organized."

It is in the same book, I believe, that Marshall McLuhan is quoted as saying, "In the new age there may well be little need for standardized males or females, the whole business of sex may become again as in the tribal state, play. It will be freer, but less important."

I have discovered that many men admit that women have a real gripe, especially if they are far enough away, like Iran or Brazil. It's a little harder to see in the United States where habitual patterns make prisoners of us all with all too few exceptions.

There are many things that a minister can say on this subject, even though he will be put down as simply another man talking by some of his listeners. For example, he can say it is wrong morally to make gifted women prove they are twice as good as men. To give every woman a chance, I would say that marriage and men and work must change many patterns. This is part of the women's revolution today and there is far more than can be said in the usual thirty sermonic minutes. But do not think it is an invention of my fancy, it is a very real revolution as the panel we shall eventually have on this subject, made up only of women, will spell out most clearly. If anyone doubts that there is a women's revolution, ask your friendly neighborhood teenager or, in most cases, her enlightened mother. There are many differences on tactics and dynamics of advancing women power, but it is not something found only in Alice's Restaurant or even the Women's Federation of the American Unitarians and Universalists as they get ready for next year's meetings in Portland, Oregon, where the women's liberation movement will be the theme of the week.

It is important that we all, whatever our sex or age or condition of servitude, accept challenge of a predominantly male civilization in most of the countries of the world today, and most certainly in the United States. The thing that is new is the insistence that there be changes and that they be made now, in the home, in the school, in the office, in the factory, everywhere where women participate. It calls for intelligence and compassion for it is a painful process for both men and women and certainly for the children who are far more affected than we often like to admit. Not every proposal of those advocating woman power will be equally creative and realistic. As in all other revolutions, there will be nonsense and wisdom intermingled. There will be angry resistance from men and also from many women, I have discovered, when this subject comes up. Those that have it made now are less impressed with the need for the radical changes at many points in the lives of women, especially working class women, though I find the exploitation of the female sex is in all classes and in all economic categories. Let us not despair the democratic dream; the equalitarian dream is not dead. We can all come to terms with our chauvinisms with varying success, but it is not an impossible dream.

Part Three

Government

How Free Should Free Speech Be?
August 6, 1950

On a hot August day in 1852, in humid Concord, Massachusetts, Ralph Waldo Emerson sat down and wrote in his diary: "If you take in a lie, you must take in all that goes with it. England takes in this neat National Church, and it glazes their eyes, and bloats the flesh, and deforms and debilitates, and translates the nervous young England so far into false, magisterial old Polonius." Now, to be sure, this address today on "How Free Should Free Speech Be?" is not intended to discuss the National Church of England, but is rather to remind ourselves that the acceptance of any institution, sacred or secular, that freezes thought into a creed, that issues thirty-nine incontrovertible articles, that dismisses the dissenter with excommunication or its equivalent, is no friend of modern man in search of truth. I quote our own Emerson, our Unitarian prophet of whom we are so justly proud, because this Concord philosopher speaks blunt Anglo-Saxon truth desperately needed at this hour. In the frenetic and panic temper of too many Americans today is a peril that the surrender of free speech will be considered without counting the terrible price involved.

This morning I am not discussing the Korean war, or the imminent Mundt-Nixon police-state legislation, or the ten-million-dollar loan voted this week by the Senate to dictator Franco's Spain, or the mob violence against Willy McGee's defender in a Mississippi hotel room, though these recent events are in my mind and yours, I dare say, as we discuss together this fundamental issue of free speech. This pulpit, like Unitarian pulpits for four centuries in many lands, is dedicated to the responsible and honest pursuit of wisdom, in fragments or in large pieces, in part or in related patterns. The known lie has no place in our midst for we know, as did Emerson, that the lie, issued by a single individual or hallowed by national institutions, "glazes the eye, bloats the flesh, deforms

197

and debilitates." Spiritual values, if they exist at all, exist intimately and inseparately in the troubled life of man, in his struggles and aspirations, in his work, in his conversation, in his affections and his searchings.

Speech, freely spoken without fear of reprisal and repression, is the tool of this process of human progress. No spiritual gain, no material advancement, can possibly be achieved without its fluid operation, its creative work upon the mind and conscience of men. Can I make it transparently clear this morning that this is no heavenly abstraction, this freedom of speech and thought of which we speak? It is the means of human progress, the artillery of the spirit, the air and water and sunshine of growth for ideas, working ideas of men building families and societies.

John Haynes Holmes recently stated an embracing principle of our free religious fellowship when he declared: "Religion must be used in furthering great works of justice and reform. It must be used to abolish poverty, the breeding ground of all misery and crime, by distributing equably among men the abundance of the soil. It must be used to get rid of war and to establish enduring peace. Here is the supreme test of the effectiveness of religion." And such a ridge-pole concept for religion cannot be erected without authentic freedom by the builders. Fear of punishment for honest thought, or capitulation to half-truths, cannot possibly insure a religion such as Dr. Holmes defines.

These are hard and demanding days and none of you who gather here, whatever your individual convictions on any single matter, do not wish this church to preoccupy itself with the mere trivia of religion. We are all hungry for substance, or that which will refresh the heart and mind, and give nourishment where so many have only straw to offer. The Unitarian tradition is built upon the necessity for freedom of speech as a tool of liberated men. This is a season when we all need to be fully conscious of our great resources. We need to know the limits of free speech. We need first, however, to know its extent and possibilities.

This is a very elementary address today. I wish to speak of our Unitarian tradition of free speech, our historic American tradition of freedom of thought and word, and finally, to ask a few questions on the limits of freedom—for I would not for a moment disguise my conviction that in a very relative world, a growing, expanding, exploring universe, there are no absolutes, and that every tool is subordinate to man its user; it is not his master. A freedom that would destroy one is not freedom but the utmost tyranny.

Do you remember that eloquent passage in Pierre van Paassen's *Why Jesus Died*, in the chapter on the Eternal Gospel, which reads:

> Five hundred thousand long years ago man was alternately up on his
> hind feet and dropping back on all fours. At last one of his young
> was born that no longer supported itself on its hands. Man was up

for good. *Anthropus erectus!* The greatest moment in the history of civilization: man walking erect and his eyes looking upward. He shapes a stone into an axe, he hews down the wilderness, and his plow cuts through the loam. His brain begins to grow. He has imagination. The élan is in his mind, the eternal restlessness, the living spark of the cosmos, the Creator Spiritus. It drives him through the wilderness, through darkness and tempests. *He is out to conquer chaos.*

That is the business of high religion. That is the task of millions of living men, and it includes the work of the Unitarian today. We have been at it a long, long time, with many reverses and heartbreaking defeats, but for this man exists beyond the beasts of the field: to conquer chaos. He yields to the impulse of spirit in his body and brain. When we are in greatest need of our tools of progress, we should refresh our memories, teach our children our first principles, and rebuke those who would bury in the ground our chief means of salvation. There is not a man or woman amongst us who can afford to ignore this heritage of freedom, for by it, above all else, are we going to make order out of chaos, and confidence out of fear.

To those unfamiliar with our Unitarian story let me say this morning that we count as our landmark of religious liberty the hill outside of Geneva, Switzerland, called Champel, where a religious dictator named John Calvin ordered the burning at the stake of Michael Servetus for his advocacy of religious liberty, and specifically for the doctrine of the unity of God. We consider Servetus the father of our Unitarian faith, its first heroic defender. On August 13, 1553, this first murder of the Protestant Reformation took place and aroused the conscience of the Christian world. One of the boldest and clearest defenders of Servetus at that time was a professor at the College of Geneva named Sebastian Castillio. No name save that of Servetus shines more brilliantly down the corridors of history when it comes to liberty of mind than that of Castillio, as you might know well if you have read Stephan Zweig's life masterpiece, *The Right to Heresy.* Two years before the burning of Servetus, Castillio wrote these words: "To seek truth and to utter what one believes to be true can never be a crime. No one must be *forced* to accept a conclusion. Conviction is free."

This is the cornerstone of our Unitarian edifice over the centuries. We have never claimed infallibility, nor denied committing errors in logic, nor pronounced our facts as irrefutable and complete, but we have said that in the mid-sixteenth century in central Europe, under the whiplash of Calvin and Farel, a few giant spirits discovered the imperishable necessity of free speech; and defended it, some to the death, some a little short of destruction. From such clarity by a few, millions have found their way to integrity and honor, to the satisfactions of a reasonable belief, and today the discovery of unhampered searching for truth as a primary human enterprise still goes on. In 1950 men are able to say, as did Socrates centuries ago, "No harm can come to a good man, either in life or in death."

Fifteen years after the death of Servetus, another great figure arose. This time in Kolsovar, Hungary, a bishop named Francis David led the forces of the Unitarians, proclaiming in a period of hysteria and fear not unlike our own today, "There is no greater piece of folly than to try to exercise power over conscience and soul, both of which are subject only to their Creator." The heart of the Reformation soon came to be this matter of individual liberty in mind in contrast to the dogmatic power of either Rome or Geneva. The progress in intellectual freedom, which took the form of religious controversy during these centuries, rests upon men like Servetus, Castillio, and David who valiantly clarified the issue for hundreds of thousands whose minds were cramped and deformed by generations of authoritarian church leadership.

I would at times that we had the New England tradition of the seventeenth century on Sunday mornings, with the two-hour sermon, for it would take such a timetable today to tell the barest outlines of the story of free speech in religion here in America alone. But you and I today stand in what liberty we now possess (the most any generation has ever known) because inflexible and gallant men of iron consciences declared the primacy of free speech for theologians, for plain citizens, for social heretics. There was Jonathan Nayhew in Boston two hundred years ago, our precursor of American Unitarianism, stating that tyranny must be resisted and oppression stopped as a religious duty. There was Tom Paine with his *Age of Reason*, Ethan Allen with his *Reason the Only Oracle of Man*. There was Elihu Palmer with his *Principles of Nature* and his network of free-thinking societies.

We Unitarians have known many struggles for liberty under many flags. It should be a source of great pride that free speech in religion has been so central a principle in our history that in various lands we are still called not Unitarians, but "Remonstrants"or "Nonsubscribing Presbyterians," because in earlier days we remonstrated against Calvinism and Lutheranism, and in Ireland and England refused to subscribe to the articles of faith of the dominant Presbyterian church. Our roots sink deep in nonconformity. We used our tongues for religious and humanistic independence in Poland and Holland, Hungary and Denmark, England and America. Free speech is our language of Zion, and never was it more needed than at this hour.

These are days when it is not a privilege only to read our Unitarian statesman, Thomas Jefferson, but our basic duty. We need to memorize, as men once memorized the catechism, his words to Alexander Hamilton: "Our people took their freedom in their own hands so that never again would the corrupt will of one man oppress them. You cannot fix fear in their hearts, or make fear their principle of government." A few years after Jefferson died, the founder of organized Unitarianism in this nation, Dr. William Ellery Channing, proclaimed in Boston the foundation theme of our churches to this day: "Freedom of opinion, of speech, of press, is our most valuable privilege, the very soul of republican institutions, the safeguard of all other rights. Nothing awakens and improves men so much as free communications of thoughts and feelings." Then he concluded: "If rulers succeed in silencing every voice but that which approves them, if nothing reaches the people but what would lend support to men in power—farewell to liberty. The form of a free government may remain, but the life, the soul, the substance is fled."

These are indeed prophetic words from the most vigorous advocate of liberal religion in all America a century ago. We would do well to write them on the tablets of our hearts. I was invited, in the midst of writing these words, to speak on a television forum on the subject "Should We Imprison American Communists Now?" I could not but remember how familiar the mentality has always been, in Channing's day or ours, to incarcerate the Jacobin, slam the prison door on the Populist, imprison the Debs, and execute the Vanzetti. If we are competing for the earth's billions, we cannot succeed by denying liberty of speech to those here or elsewhere who challenge our policies and economic institutions. This is not to sanction the Communist thesis; it is to say that the non-Communist cannot build his case in any land on imprisonment of the heretic. We have through the Voice of America, through national network radio programs, and through millions of magazine articles proclaimed the power of our constitutional rights—with its cornerstone of free speech. If it be true (as I think it is) that absence of free speech in Russia is a weakness of that system of government, something they could well learn from our Bill of Rights, then we are the losers, not the victors, if we surrender freedom of speech to those who ask for such surrender in the struggle of ideas today, a struggle bidding for two billion living persons on this planet.

We began with political liberty in our revolution of 1776. Russia in 1917, in a feudal nation unmarked by any tradition of democracy such as we inherited from the Cromwellian civil war, began with economic reform. She had added suffrage to those disenfranchised by the Bolsheviks, including priests of the Orthodox church. My own opinion has been that Russia has grown strong enough to tolerate even more civil liberty than she, with a long feudal heritage, has yet permitted. Certainly we will not speed more toleration of dissent in Russia by liquidating this central asset of constitutional democracy. If the free trade of ideas advocated by Justice Holmes is sound, we could win far more than we could lose by giving freedom to the Socialist and Communist to speak. Our *Los Angeles Daily News* of August 2 makes this cardinal point as it warns against the moral weakness of passing the Mundt-Nixon bill. A man convinced of the superior merits of capitalism should be able to defend them against attack with something more persuasive than a concentration camp. This is something we ought to say to our government at this hour. Superior arguments alone, on which we now spend billions, cannot win the world to our system in contrast to a socialist system. A free and open encounter of the two systems in serving starving, landless, but proud peoples on every continent is needed, not an encounter of guns and the bodies of our youth.

A year or two ago a distinguished Methodist official, Dr. Ralph E. Diffendorfer of the Methodist Board of Foreign Missions, long known as a strong opponent of communism, wrote: "So long as communism offers Asia, Africa, and Latin America a new and classless society, based not on exploitation but on brotherhood and economic justice, and so long as our western civilization does not fulfill these needs of mankind, there will be no respite from 'communism's challenge.'" Without free speech by Americans, capitalist or socialist in conviction, there can be no planning to meet this crucial challenge Dr. Diffendorfer presents so clearly.

I want to make it clear beyond all debate today that I speak in the best American tradition, the best free world tradition, in this basic plea for keeping open the doors of liberty, of speech, and though I care not if this address seems too filled with quotations from other voices, let us hear these voices and engrave them on our memories. I am reminding you that we are many, they are few, we who care for the operation of man's mind freely, as against the foe who fears the word of challenge and criticism, who seeks to block the proposal for man's next step in civilization. We, the plain citizens, are sovereign, and our use of free speech is a right more precious than rubies. It is our guarantee of survival. Those of us familiar with Jewish and Christian history know that this dependence on the free voice of the people is the core of our religion. Jehovah tells the young Samuel centuries ago, "Harken unto the voice of the people in all they say unto thee." David, the Psalmist, cries, "I will walk at liberty." The men and women who formed our institutions took those ancient injunctions and many like them with high seriousness. They wrote their covenants and articles of government with a sense of the sacredness of the people's voice. We may have altered our metaphysics and our theologies since Samuel's day, and even since Roger Williams's day, but I hope we do not alter our respect for the freedom of opinion they engendered.

Today the distinction between religious free speech, such as Castillio and Servetus defended, and secular free speech concerning politics, economics, and social welfare, is a very low wall of separation. Today we Unitarians, with many others, believe all life affecting man's destiny is religious. As I now remind you of our freedom tradition here in the Western world, I would remind you that it no longer is limited to the matter of creed or theology; it affects every area of life without exception. Today one is less likely to be imprisoned for contradicting the idea of the Trinity than he is for proposing to take seriously Premier Nehru's proposal of mediation of the Korean war. Both, however, require freedom of speech, if we are not to capitulate to the very totalitarianism we profess to abhor.

If all else be forgotten today, I urge you to remember that we Americans traditionally, if we be true to our unmatched heritage, stake our case to the world on the words of the late Justice Louis Brandeis:

> The right of a citizen of the United States is to take part in making Federal laws and in the conduct of government includes the right to speak or write about them, to make his own opinion, to teach the truth as he sees it. Were this not so, the right of the people to assemble for the purpose of petitioning Congress would be a right totally without substance. Like the course of the heavenly bodies, harmony in national life is a resultant of the struggle between contending forces. In frank expression of conflicting opinion lies the greatest promise of wisdom in governmental action, in suppression lies the greatest peril.

I agree with the editors of the *Saturday Evening Post* on July 29 when they wrote of the Truman administration and the Pentagon: "It is difficult to see what area for free discussion remains. Freedom of criticism is now more important than ever, but it will take stout men to defend it." The *Post* editors are thinking, as the editorial makes clear, of Senator Taft, but their plea is as applicable to the extreme left. We Americans cannot afford to silence the American Communist or the American Republican unless we are prepared to surrender the very heart of our American gospel of freedom. There are Americans who would imprison nonconformists, including Communists, justifying their action on the grounds Communists in other lands brook no opposition. The areas of free speech in socialist countries are greater than most Americans believe, but it remains true that teaching capitalism is forbidden. I am not defending the Soviet limitations of free speech today. I am saying we Americans believe in free trade of ideas in all fields, including the economic and political. To exclude the left wing is to deny the validity of our thesis, and to confirm the Communist teaching that it will not work. We are more obliged to prove our case that we have in free speech a tool of superior merit, and one that works pragmatically. Let Senator Taft speak and let the left wing editor speak, or labor leader, as well as all other Americans, and out of such conflict of opinion win the admiration of the world. As Archibald MacLeish so wisely said recently, "Freedom is not something to save, it is something to use." This is worth more than atom bombs in our arsenal or B29s in the sky. With it we are able to discuss the kind of assistance that will win us friends in the Asian, African, and Latin American struggle Dr. Diffendorfer describes.

This is no time to forget the healthy American pragmatism of our free speech tradition enunciated by Benjamin Franklin two centuries ago: "When men differ in opinion, both sides ought to have the advantage equally of being heard by the public, and when truth and error have fair play, the former is always the overmatch for the latter." It was Dean Wilbur Bender a year ago at Harvard College in Massachusetts who stated Franklin's thesis in modern words when he said, "I know of no faster way of producing Communists than by making martyrs out of a handful of Communists we now have. Forbidding them to speak would be treason to the ancient tradition of Harvard and America; it would be proof we have something to hide, that we have lost faith in our principles."

In one of his famed dissents, a great Unitarian, Justice Oliver Wendell Holmes, wrote in 1918:

> The best test of truth is the power of thought to get itself accepted in the competition of the marketplace. Truth is the only ground upon which men's wishes can be safely carried out. That is the theory of our Constitution. It is an experiment; all life is an experiment.

Unitarians are committed to the unrestricted use of reason in the working out of human welfare. They have a profound skepticism and distrust of what John Stuart Mill once called "the deep slumber of decided opinion." Our as yet partial and elementary approximations of world justice and equality should prevent us from the diabolical conceit that we can afford any smugness about our own perfections. We have much to offer the world as Americans: incredible genius in production techniques, organized scientific skills in industry and agriculture, astonishing advances in health and medicine. But it will take all the free speech we can summon to make such resources available to the world's millions in peace and goodwill.

I for one am convinced, after a month of reading every possible source open to me, that if we Americans had shown in South Korea a determined will to support the people there in their postwar plans for land reform, trade union organizations, industrialization, and cooperatives, and helped them dismiss their Japanese-trained police, there would never have been an incident at the 38th parallel. When a right-wing CIO member of the ECA mission in South Korea returns to America, as Stanley Earl did last week, to write in the *Portland Oregonian* on our miserable bungling in occupation policy the past five years, free discussion of such errors is the height of patriotism. Mr. Earl, known for his anti-Communist sympathies for years, stated that he returned because as an American ECA official he refused to participate in Korea in the liquidation of the working-class movement in that country. No American who cherishes the good will we once enjoyed in Asia is obligated to defend a program by our occupying forces in Korea that engenders hatred of America for its setting back the clock of democracy and welfare for twenty million people in that troubled nation.

It may be argued that dictatorships are more efficient in the short run, benevolent emperors have had their advocates as superior to democracies and congresses of the people, but America has had a century and a half of experimenting with free speech by the people. Our people have criticized and applauded, supported some wars and rejected others like those of 1812 and the Mexican war. Our people won freedom for the slaves. To be sure, Elijah Lovejoy was murdered for supporting abolition through free speech and a free press. But the victory of liberty was clear. A few months ago the Universal Declaration of Human Rights had written into its corpus this Article 19: "Everyone has the right of freedom of opinion and expression; this includes freedom to hold opinions without interference." This is no time to retreat from a world declaration we by precept and example helped to frame. We Unitarians have in our national assembly, in our local churches, and in our pulpits declared that there is no health in us by retreating to repression, hysteria, and fear. The sentiment we fear today may be tomorrow's honored commonplace of free men. It is our own thesis that we are capable of measuring ideas on their merits, irrespective of the advocate, his origin or party. There is no surer way of losing immeasurably our prestige, won over two centuries of hospitality to liberal and radical thought, than to fling into discard or prison every nonconformist and dissenter. This is to build our own police state, to commit our own treason, to wreck the work of giant builders of the race whose very names make our hearts sing: Samuel Adams, Thomas Jefferson, Peter Altgeld, Wendell Phillips, Theodore Parker.

Are there limits to free speech? This a citizen has a right to ask and receive an honest answer. I am a Unitarian who believes in no absolutes. My universe is like that of Heraclitus: one in flux, one growing, changing, developing. The effort to freeze generalizations, even the best, into absolutes seems counter to the nature of the universe itself and the record of man's half-million-year struggle to be human. I have tried to say that the employment of free speech is more needed today than the restriction of it. Most people are in danger of using too little rather than too much. Silence is more likely to destroy us than responsible expression. We have not reached the degree of civilization we now possess by the sealing of lips of scientists and teachers, statesmen and prophets. The road marked "thought-control" points to the jungle of the anthropoid and the bear garden of Neanderthal man.

Our founding fathers and later leaders recognized the right of extreme economic and political proposals. Jefferson and Lincoln, as is well known, declared the right of a people to change their government, if need be, by revolutionary action. Our distinguished American poet Archibald MacLeish, not too long ago an assistant Secretary of State, recently asserted: "Revolution was once a word spoken with pride by every American who had the right to claim it." Under the present Smith Act (if it had been enacted by the British government in 1775), Washington, Patrick Henry, Benjamin Franklin, and Thomas Jefferson would have been imprisoned and fined, and the revolution aborted.

I might add, since in these days people make inferences on the slenderest of words, that I am not today advocating revolution. It is my own contention there is much of reform this side of revolution that calls for stout and courageous men. Controlling the hand of greed, providing rents a working man can afford, keeping our youth at peaceful occupations, permitting other nations to solve internal conflicts without intervention, supporting the suffrage of minority groups, these and a thousand other projects a long sea mile this side of revolution should consume our energies. But the right of revolution is written into our institutions by word and example by those whose tombs we erect and whose names we crown with glory. As in 1776 and 1861, so today it is still an unfinished country and unfinished world.

So we Unitarians have with many other Americans sought to keep the channels of freedom of speech open to all men and to oppose only those men and groups who have openly or by indirection sought to use freedom of speech to assault fellow citizens whose race or creed or nationality offended them. And this is not a limitation of freedom of speech, but an insistence that *all* men enjoy it, and that any fascist mentality that teaches a gospel of exclusion of man for reasons of race or nationality or creed has thereby itself sought to limit free speech, saying there are people unworthy of it beause of their heritage. This is arrant nonsense.

The men of the Third Reich who cast millions of Jews into the ovens of Buchenwald, the Japanese who cast the Philippine guerrillas into concentration camps and beheaded their leaders with swords in the last war, the Ku Klux Klan that lynches and burns the Negro workers who form unions or seek to vote are the only persons whom a democracy should limit, not so much for their words, but because their words impel men to violence for no other reason than that the victims are Jews, or Negroes, or foreign-born. In January 1946 I wrote an editorial, as editor of the *Christian Register*, on this matter of civil liberties for fascists, which aroused considerable controversy. I quoted in the opening sentence Lincoln Steffin's morbid epigram about the character who would defend civil liberties for everybody until the last tongue was cut out. Free speech is not an abstract right and absolute right. A democracy with a Bill of Rights like ours has a moral obligation to see that it works for every citizen, not with exceptions. It tolerates no "except for Jews, except for Negroes, except for people born in Yugoslavia." I lived in Boston and saw the emotional and explosive speech of Father Coughlin and Gerald Smith incite and inflame audiences so that for weeks afterward we suffered waves of terrorism and physical violence in Roxbury and Dorchester against Jews and Negroes. This, I contended then and do now, was not a matter of the right of free speech by Gerald Smith. It was incitement to violence, which followed in terrible ferocity. It was inversely limitation of speech to decent, law-abiding Jewish and Negro citizens. This intimidation was the result of a false concept of freedom. No man under our doctrine of the Bill of Rights has the right to advocate violence against our people, or ideas that directly lead to violence to our people because of their race, or creed, or nationality.

To permit such advocacy is to turn free speech upside down. It is advocacy of murder, suppression, and intimidation, and several million people in this generation are dead in Europe because we let fascism pass as a political theory of government and did not recognize it as a theory of race extermination of so-called inferior peoples. As a Unitarian I believe we have more to gain by freedom of advocacy of ideas than we have by repression, censorship, and incarceration of the nonconformist. Unless we claim our present society in its political and economic and cultural patterns is the best of all possible worlds, we must believe that all voices should be heard, making only the exception of the man who preaches race and religious hatred. There is no ethnic group on earth we can afford to exempt from the privileges of speech. The dark-skinned majorities on the planet know it. We dare not be ignorant of it. The man who would imprison or destroy any man because of color or origin is our enemy, for he would return us to the barbarism from which we painfully emerged.

If this limitation seems like a small exception, I would simply say, "I would that it *were* a small exception, but I fear there are many who have yet failed to extricate from their policies and economics and philosophy, and even their religion, the poison of race hatred. Any political philosophy by any name, left or right or center, that includes in its platform this exclusion of some from the blessings of free humanity can be the undoing of our liberty as a people. I have long considered myself an anti-fascist Unitarian because the dismal record of fascism in slaughtering its foes seemed the greatest contradiction to my religion and my American democratic faith. The only limitation I believe we can afford on free speech is the insistence that no man, under its banner, exclude others from its privileges because he does not like their pigment, their homeland, or their religious heritage. Such exclusion is a betrayal of man himself.

When we Unitarians speak of freedom, let the trumpet sound a clarion note. We mean freedom not only to believe a doctrine, but to practice a deed. There will be many desperate men with no concern for American traditions of freedom and no interest in the common good of all, seeking to turn America over to a privileged company of plunderers. It can happen, and many devoted and sincere American leaders in both parties are desperately afraid it has begun to happen. The tumult about silencing Communists is so loud these reckless adventurers in high places hope they can use it to seal the lips and end the activity of the millions of solid citizens who want to solve the gigantic problems of our nation so long neglected since the end of World War II. Free speech should be free enough to let every serious citizen, right and left and center, add his skill and energy and wisdom to the progress of America.

I am still wedded to the words of one of the most valiant Americans of a century ago, Theodore Parker, when he wrote: "Though all the governors of the world bid us commit treason against man, and set the example, let us never submit."

Statement Before the House
Un-American Activities Committee
in the Hollywood Roosevelt Hotel
September 12, 1951

I am profoundly shocked at this first example to my knowledge of the committee's calling before it of a parish minister. Every clergyman in the land should be equally alarmed. As a churchman and as a citizen I am appalled and indignant at this invasion of my duties and privileges as a minister of religion. Through long struggle, America finally won a separation of church and state to the continuation of which every priest, rabbi, and minister is dedicated.

Representative Jackson said on Monday at this hearing that the purpose of these hearings was to "determine the extent of infiltration of communism into the film industry." This being the case, I can see no reason whatsoever for my being subpoenaed by the committee. I have no knowledge whatsoever of the matter. My opinions are an open record, being expressed in the pulpit and on the air with predictable regularity. There is no need for a subpoena to find out my views on loyalty or my ignorance of Communist infiltration into the motion pictures. I am frankly indignant at being called before the committee when its avowed purpose is a matter about which we in the churches know nothing.

Such questionings as this can create great jeopardy for parish ministers of every faith. We of the churches and synagogues have a relationship of intimate confidence in the confessional and study, which is recognized by custom and tradition in this land. If this House committee can invade that confidence, men and women will have little reason to believe the sacredness of the minister-parishioner relationship is inviolate. Some one hundred forty thousand clergymen of all religions in this country value this hallowed custom of privacy and have no intention of surrendering it in a period of hysteria and intimidation. The clergy are not to be regimented into any party's program of witch hunting nor can they be expected to betray the confidences of those coming to them for moral and spiritual guidance.

We ministers do not all preach the same religious doctrines, nor do we all share the same political views, being Americans conscious of our free heritage. I happen to be a birthright Quaker now serving the Unitarian denomination, which has officially taken a position of disapproval of the work of this committee. Many of my fellow ministers in the Unitarian churches and in other fellowships have frequently protested the work of this committee. Now, with this subpoena, you actually seek to invade the realm of religion. The churches will not, I predict, accept such an effort to achieve among the clergy a deadly uniformity through defining what are dangerous thoughts. The history of religion in America—Catholic, Jewish, and Protestant—has been one of healthy independency and.it must remain that way.

It has been the prerogative of the clergy since the days of Moses to sift and weigh all ideas and programs for their moral merit. We in the church have no tradition of docile conformity to other men's statements of loyalty and sound patriotism. If this committee should succeed in subpoening the ministers of this country and intimidating them, both American democracy and unfettered religion as we have known them for one hundred sixty-five years will vanish. I wish to have no part in such a disaster and I shall do all I possibly can to prevent it from taking place.

*   *   *

Mr. Fritchman, in a statement given over KECA of the American Broadcasting Company at 6:05 P.M., September 12, added to this statement:

> It has been suggested that the committee was not investigating my work as a minister, but rather as a citizen. I am a minister twenty-four hours a day, like any other responsible clergyman, and further, the committee did inquire into speakers, meetings, and the activities of my church. I naturally refused to discuss church matters with the committee.
>
> The field of religion has thus been invaded by the committee and this does provide a real attack on freedom of religion. The first amendment protects freedom of religious speech and association.

Statement Following a Service at the First Unitarian Church of Los Angeles Concerning the House Un-American Activities Committee
September 16, 1951

In addition to the statement I filed with the Committee on Un-American Activities and gave to the press, September 12, 1951, it may be desirable for me to make one or two clarifications based upon the hearing itself. My first statement was, of course, prepared in advance, before I knew the nature of the interrogation.

It has not been stated in the press or on the air that this was my second appearance before the committee, the first being on October 23, 1946, in Washington, D.C. At that time I answered all questions. At that time I was editor of the *Unitarian Journal*, the *Christian Register*, in Boston, and not a parish minister, an important distinction.

In October, 1947, while preaching in the Los Angeles Unitarian Church as guest minister, I reported at a clergy meeting on the many activities I participated in as a Unitarian clergyman: speaking and writing on behalf of world peace, civil liberties for all citizens including members of the minority parties, Spanish democracy, labor's rights, etc. These activities had been widely mentioned in national magazines and were in no way unfamiliar to the members of the church who, a few weeks later, called me as their resident minister here in Los Angeles.

At that meeting in October, 1947, I told the Unitarian group that I was shocked by the then developing persecution of the "Hollywood Ten" writers and directors—and that I would not again participate in a barbaric inquisition regarding political affiliations. I discovered here in the Hollywood investigation by the Committee on Un-American Activities that the purpose was the blacklisting of talented writers and directors and the making of them into political pariahs. One's party affiliations are a private matter, and the destruction of that privacy for a Socialist or Communist can lead only to a later destruction for all parties not in power. My earlier disavowal of membership in the Communist party was not the main issue in the questioning. It has since become a primary matter for the inquisitors in their many hearings and could lead to the destruction of all semblance of democratic dissent by those advocating change.

In view of the present situation and of my interpretation of the rights of a citizen under the Constitution, and in view of the fact that "guilt by association" is now the technique used to blacklist and ruin innocent people who possess some taint of nonconformity, I am now obliged to refuse to answer under the Fifth Amendment many questions of affiliation and membership, however innocent they may seem at first glance. Mr. Howard McGrath's list of so-called subversive groups is very long and covers almost every area of human responsibility for justice.

I am one who believes Congress has proper authority to make many investigations, but I do not believe it has the power to ask citizens to surrender their privileges under the Constitution and the Bill of Rights: rights of freedom of worship, association, speech, and communication.

Representative Jackson seeks to separate my ministerial from my civic life. He protests he is not questioning me as a clergyman. But he has already questioned me on officers, speakers, meetings, and activities at the Unitarian Church, not only groups renting rooms for meetings, but actual events under the auspices of the church itself. He holds the strange opinion that a minister is only a minister when robed for services or when listening to the troubles of his mind in the sanctity of his study. A reading of the Old and New Testaments would remind him that for centuries religion has taken the minister into the marketplace, the forum, the parliament, and the streetcorner, wherever he could strike blows for freedom and aid his fellows to diminish "man's inhumanity to man." Religious work is far more than presiding at the altar or uniting men and maidens in the marriage bond. Any minister who must disclose the words and activities of his church people or himself before a governmental committee has surrendered his leadership as a moral guide. Our founding fathers made the wall of separation between church and state very high, and so it must remain if the clergy are to avoid being abject sycophants before the administration in power. I would remind Mr. Jackson of Cromwell's efforts to proscribe the religious leadership of John Lillburne. The indemnity paid by Parliament to Lillburne has long symbolized the importance of free association in a democratic state by religious leaders.

We ministers, priests, and rabbis may be conservatives or radicals, but with exceedingly few exceptions we are not craven puppets of any administration's political orthodoxy. With Isaiah in ancient Israel, we in the twentieth century still proclaim: "Woe unto them that decree the unrighteous decrees, and to the writers that write perverseness, that turn aside the needy from justice, and rob the poor of my people of their right, that widows may be their spoil, that they may make the fatherless their spoil." We are ministers at work when we repeat these words before film writers, or Kiwanis Clubs, or congregations on a Sunday morning. Religion is not a Sunday matter only in America.

These are days when the summer soldier and the sunshine patriot find the going hard, but I am immensely heartened by the many evidences of understanding received this week, from workers in fields of press, radio, and religion, from housewives and trade unionists, doctors and teachers. I especially appreciate the unanimity of our trustees in this church. It is heartening to know how many of you wrote of your sentiments not only to me and to our trustees, but to the congressmen on the committee, John S. Wood and Donald Jackson. They need to know how American citizens feel about this attack upon all organized religion and its prophetic function in a free society. If we all employ the liberties won for us by our forefathers, men who had felt the whiplash of tyranny themselves, we will restrict congressional investigations to their proper sphere.

Statements by Rev. Fritchman and the Board of Trustees of the First Unitarian Church of Los Angeles Concerning HUAC and the National Conference of the Committee for the Protection of the Foreign Born

November 1956

According to then-Congressman Clyde Doyle, in the *Los Angeles Times*, November 21, 1956, thirty-one subpoenas have been issued by the House Committee on Un-American Activities for a hearing on December 5 in Los Angeles. This brings the hearing into the week of a National Conference of the Committee for the Protection of the Foreign Born. Many of those summoned to the hearing are active in the work of this organization. Mr. Fritchman is an honorary president of the local Committee for the Protection of the Foreign Born.

* * *

It is almost unbelievable that in free America in 1956 a congressional committee has the impertinence to subpoena a minister, an attorney, a trade unionist, or anyone else, to appear and answer for their civic dedication, their zeal for effective democratic activity. Yet the subpoenas issued this week in Los Angeles, and the statement to the press made by Congressman Clyde Doyle would seem clearly to indicate that this is the Un-American Committee's purpose here. As a member of a liberal church, of a denomination known throughout the world for its commitment to freedom of the mind, to social justice and peace, and as a citizen of the United States I am shocked at being subpoenaed for the apparent reason that I have joined thousands of Americans in efforts to amend or repeal restrictive legislation against the foreign-born. This is a cause which has enlisted the conscience of many clergymen and laymen of all faiths. But apparently what was appropriate for President Eisenhower in his State of the Union message last January becomes unlawful for a plain citizen to propose. Senator Kuchel or Congressman James Roosevelt have quite properly urged radical changes in the Walter-McCarran Act, but it seems to be cause for a subpoena if a parish minister does the same. To what absurdity will the logic of the Un-American Committee next lead? Are the thousands of rabbis, priests, and parsons and their parishioners who seek revision of laws supporting racial discrimination to expect a police officer at their doors with a call to a government hearing? What remains of freedom of religion, what remains of citizenship under the whole Bill of Rights if the very act of proposing legislative change is called "subversive"? It is time indeed for the American people to demand the abolition of a committee so fantastically out of line with the American way of life as it has been practiced for the past two centuries. My own Unitarian denomination asked for the abolition of this committee at its annual meeting in 1946. I see no reason for any revision of their judgment in 1956.

STATEMENT BY THE BOARD OF TRUSTEES OF THE FIRST UNITARIAN CHURCH OF LOS ANGELES

The Board of Trustees of the First Unitarian Church of Los Angeles on November 21, 1956, having heard and considered the statement of its minister, the Reverend Stephen H. Fritchman, on the matter of his subpoena to appear before the House Committee on Un-American Activities on December 5, 1956, unanimously reaffirms its full confidence in Mr. Fritchman. The Board recognizes the right of every member of the church, both lay and ministerial, to engage in activities as citizens in accordance with the dictates of his own conscience.

Why I Am Not Cooperating with the Hearings of the House Committee on Un-American Activities
Statement Before the Committee
December 6, 1956

The House Committee on Un-American Activities has stated through press channels that its purpose is to investigate persons and organizations who have been agitating for reform or repeal of the Walter-McCarran Immigration and Naturalization Act. Thus the committee has made the main issue today the right of persons to influence public opinion on congressional legislation. Interference with persons who seek to influence legislation (be they right or wrong in their opinions of the proposed changes or repeal) is clearly forbidden under the First Amendment. This was decided by the United States Supreme Court in the now famous Rumely Case.

On the basis of the above, I refuse to cooperate in any way with the House Committee in the present hearings or to answer any of their questions on the grounds of pertinence. They have no right to inquire into the matter. My refusal is based both on the First and Fifth Amendments.

We in the churches have been protesting for several years about the discriminatory and racist character of this omnibus act. The denomination I serve, the American Unitarian Association, passed a strong resolution on May 22 of this year, saying "The Walter-McCarran Act employs origins quota systems which perpetuate the concept of superior peoples, contrary to scientific knowledge, and to the interests of the people of this country." That resolution expresses my own conscience and judgment also.

216

Not only are quota systems un-American in spirit, so also are the shocking deportation clauses of the act. I stand in firm support of Rabbi Simon Kramer, president of the Synagogue Council of America, when he says, as he did, "Deportation used as a penalty is inhuman and medieval." I also stand with Father Joseph C. Whalen of the Catholic Diocese of Grand Rapids, Michigan, when he says: "The provisions of the Walter-McCarran Act that jeopardize an opportunity for a fair hearing for those faced with deportation are not consistent with the record and reputation of America for fair play for all."

I know well that we have stumbled over the years in our immigration legislation, as Japanese, Chinese, and many other minorities can tragically testify. But on the whole, from the beginning of our nation, we followed Benjamin Franklin's conviction that "strangers are welcome, because there is room enough for them all, and the old inhabitants are not jealous of them."

Has Mr. Walter or this committee forgotten that we are a nation of immigrants? I am not a full-blooded American Indian, nor is Congressman Walter (so far as I know). His law, which he co-authored with Senator McCarran, had it been in force in the early days of this nation, would have excluded his forebears and mine, also. I am profoundly opposed to a law such as the Walter-McCarran Act that violates the early American ideals of hospitality of the foreign-born of all races and creeds, and that violates even more the deepest insights of the Old and New Testaments, which it is my privilege to teach as a minister of religion.

For these reasons I see no reason whatsoever for cooperating with your expressed intention of investigating my rights to agitate for a substitute law more consonant with our American heritage.

Discovering Our Arab Neighbors
An Address on the Aspirations of the Peoples of the Middle East
May 19, 1957

Rev. Fritchman read three poems by Arabic writers at the morning service: *The Will to Live* by Abu-el-Qasim el-Shabi, *The Cottage* by Abd-el-Wahhab el-Bayati, and *My Soul Distracted* by Fadwa Touqan.

*   *   *

"The area of the Middle East is today one of the danger spots of the earth. The great powers of the West and the East may very likely be dragged into a Third World War by their half-hearted satellites and the Jews and the Arabs as well." These are the words of Dr. Ernest Simon, one of Israel's leading intellectuals, a professor at the Hebrew University now on a teaching visit in Los Angeles. It was my privilege to speak with him at some length in late December. These words, just quoted, by a very sensitive and world-minded citizen of Israel were from his article in the magazine *Liberation* in September 1956 (before the renewal of war in Egypt by the Israeli, French, and British forces). I shall refer to this article later, but the quotation seemed to me the appropriate beginning for our discussion for *two* reasons: first, it is true that the Middle East is today a danger spot of the earth without equal as far as a possible World War III is concerned and should keep us from any casual or academic approach to our subject, and second, Dr. Simon is one of the outstanding Jewish leaders of the world who has for several decades worked on the Arab problem in Palestine and the Middle East, often in opposition to powerful majorities of his own Israeli compatriots. His understanding of the magnitude of the issues is tragically rare in

218

the world today, and we need to share his insight with gratitude and support.

This is the first sermon I have ever preached on the Arab problem in the Middle East though I have, of course, spoken several times on the Moslem religion and the contribution of the Mohammedan peoples to world civilization. I am ashamed of this tardiness for I know that it reflects a pattern of provincialism by a Westerner that should give us all pause. Until recent years the Arab world was not a present reality in the life of the average American, not even the average American student and professional person. Our ignorance of the Arab people and their problems is still colossal. We all need a far more informed mind regarding the Arab world if we are to make even modest progress toward the one world of peaceful people to which we so glibly pay homage with our lips, personally and collectively. I am happy to say that some fairly popular nontechnical, nonprofessional magazines have in recent months sought to meet the vacuum existing on this subject, notably *Holiday* magazine, the *Atlantic Monthly*, the *American Mercury*, and in its own perverse way, *Life* magazine, and in its rather pious way, the *Christian Century*.

It is no exaggeration today to say that most of us, I fear, come to a study of the Arab people with both illiteracy and some prejudice. Very little material filters from our press, our films, our television, our government releases, or our churches, which reflects either objectivity or profound sympathy with the forty millions of Arabs in what was formerly called the Near East, more recently the Middle East, and now by Premier Nehru, West Asia. It is judicious, I think, to repair this mental lag of ours if we are to avoid new disasters—if not total annihilation—in the decades ahead. That Third World War Dr. Simon referred to is not just a journalistic tour-de-force; he was in complete earnestness, as I am today. It is too late to be parochial in our minds or our habits as Westerners. There is an enormous ferment in Arab society which we *must* understand. Quasi-feudal, preindustrial, premodern patterns are changing rapidly from India's western borders of Arabia to Morocco on the Atlantic Ocean. The transitional period will be long, but every single day of our remaining lives will mark changes that affect us all. Sheer self-interest, as well as faith in the brotherhood of all peoples, should impel us to catch up with history and find solutions of equity, goodwill, and understanding. The beginnings of the present crisis in Arab affairs that we read of in our papers every day in cartoon and article go back at least to the breakup of the Ottoman Empire at the end of World War I. The Ottoman Empire had long straddled the Middle East. The greater part of the peoples in this large area are Moslems (though Jews and Christians are also considerable factors in the human situation involved). Since very few of us here are Moslems, we have never really felt the urgency of the twentieth-century crises in this part of the world. The religion of Islam is a great unifying force in the Middle East, something like Confucianism in China as a philosophy that prescribes a certain uniformity of conduct. Islam emphasizes that men, *merely by being men,* are brothers and equal in the sight of God, and have dignity even in extreme poverty. Islam has given the Western world an atmosphere of romance, evoking memories of the Crusades in the Middle Ages. It provided for many years a mixture of monotheism, picturesque nomadic life, deserts, Bedouins, camels, caravans, fanaticism, and a tradition of male gregariousness. Our local film industry has for years exaggerated and maintained this mixture of fancy and romance. The Arab stereotype has been constructed and deeply implanted in the Western mind—a stereotype that flatters our pride and consolidates our prejudice. Most of us have been unwilling (until catastrophe and oil shocked us awake) to recognize that the old order is changing in the Middle East.

Religion, specifically the Moslem religion, has played a large part in the present crisis in the Arab world. We Americans too glibly think the entire matter can be dismissed as a war between rival oil corporations and empire-minded governments and Arab leaders distressed at the pilot plant democracy of Israel in their midst. Such oversimplifications do violence to sober realities we have preferred to leave unexplored. The patterns of the revolution of the Arab peoples is not the familiar one we have seen in Europe, Asia, and Africa in this century. It violates many of the axioms Russian, Indian, and Latin-American radicals have been taught. It seems perverse and irrational when compared with developments in Israel, Ghana, or Guatemala. But it is revolution nonetheless and cannot be dreamed away. In all of the articles and reports I have been reading in recent weeks, a common generalization has emerged. We Westerners underestimate the power of the Moslem religion with the Arab masses, even if it be a religion in decadence. Need I remind you we, too, are in a culture where religion, Christianity in our case, is in decadence, yet is playing a considerable role. The Moslem religion ties together peoples of many nations and is a major force in their resistance to Western civilization. Of course, it is true that many leaders in the Islamic countries are secular and reformist, but they work in a matrix of hostility from the masses which is nourished by the traditions of their religion. We need not only to understand economic, military, and nationalist factors, but also the importance of the Moslem brotherhood and its oftentimes violent resistance to new world forces.

I referred a moment ago to the fall of the Ottoman Empire as the start of the present great crisis in the Arab world. Let me add that no single dominant political force replaced the breakup of the Ottoman Empire. A series of independent and relatively weak states became rivals attempting to fill the vacuum and united only in a vehement resistance to great Western powers: Britain, France, and, more lately, the United States.

These Western powers assumed at the end of World War I that the new states were too weak to stand alone and needed a guiding hand. So the League of Nations, unable by world opinion to let them become direct colonies of the Western powers, established them as mandated territories under the supervision of Britain and France. They became client states or puppets of these powers. Britain had controlled Egypt since 1881, but after World War I the League of Nations mandated Iraq, Transjordan, and Palestine to Britain, and to France mandated Syria and Lebanon. Of Arab lands only Saudi Arabia and Yemen were left free. This happened, need I say, before the vast oil wealth of these arid desert lands was even suspected to exist.

In customary imperial fashion, the British thought of themselves as the liberators of the Arabs from the Turks, but we should now not be surprised that the Arabs simply thought of them as *new Turks*—Turks, if you will, with an Oxford accent. From this point on after World War I, the nationalism of the Arabs was directed against Britain and France, whom they felt had cheated them out of their rightful independence that they had been promised. This new nationalism had as its purpose to liberate the Arab peoples, to establish eventual equality with the West, and to secure their sovereign independence. To be sure there were some governing groups in the Arab lands (and they still exist with power) who saw an advantage in accommodation with the Western powers, but the underlying pressure remained with the millions of Arabs to achieve these purposes. As Professor Robert Neuman at UCLA has said very plainly: "Arab nationalism is not just a wild emotion, it is a form of the struggle for men's liberation." And he adds: "We who have had our own liberation struggle long behind us often feel that the Arabs are attacking the wrong enemy, that their true enemies are want, fear, and disease. It may well be hoped that they, too, will see this, but this calls for a calm, detached, and rational attitude, and the time for such a rational attitude can come only after the Arabs have conquered their complexes." Let me immediately say that Dr. Neuman betrays a certain condescension here. It is the Western powers [that] have greatly contributed to these so-called "complexes." I'm sure George III in 1776 used the equivalent term of complexes in discussing Sam Adams's, Ben Franklin's, and George Washington's intransigence about independence and national integrity.

The Arab struggle against the West expressed itself during the twenties and thirties in periodic collisions in Egypt and a growing unrest in other countries, except Jordan, the slowest to awaken politically. Britain and France were both thought of as overlords—for such they were —even if at times they wore a velvet glove. The Arabs, for all of their differences among themselves, and they were many, felt this foreign imperial hand distorting the course of their political growth. They blamed the West for keeping alive out-of-date monarchies and feudal classes. We Americans, who in recent decades have seen our government place confidence in reactionary dictators and kings in both hemispheres, should understand the bitter resentment of such habits by the Eastern world and understand why they turned to Bandung and similar combinations in the East for their salvation from second-class status in the world.

The Arab intelligentsia, the college-educated generation, have been even more hostile to the West than the masses, if that were possible. Unlike the Chinese or Indian intelligentsia, trained in many Western universities and by Western Christian missionaries, the Arabs received little Western influence in constructive and liberating aspects. The West has made very little effort to transform Arab society in a peaceful fashion with legal, industrial, agricultural, educational, and health contributions for their benefit, as was true to some degree in China and India. The Arab students have long since concluded that Western officials and businessmen have had but *one* purpose: to exploit every advantage for their own ends at the greatest possible speed. Arab nationalism has grown amid ramshackle governments, corrupt cliques, socially irresponsible officials, and military dictatorships, and the West has cooperated with them shamefully. We are now reaping the harvest of this greed and irresponsibility.

All of this might have been gradually corrected had not something sensational happened immediately after World War II. Oil, in vast abundance, was discovered in the Middle East. In 1938 the oil traffic carried through the Suez Canal was five million tons—and this is but the beginning. The discovery was made that a high proportion of the world oil reserves were in the Middle East, probably two-thirds of them.

In this introductory address today, I want to stress above all else that Western powers, all of them, failed to understand the force and meaning of Arab nationalism as a passionate longing for the assertion of full sovereignty and equality. There were many objectives of the new Arab nations after 1917—independence, unity, social reform—but the first became the dominant one to be pursued: independence. In Arab countries, one after another, there was a tragic story of bloodshed and sacrifice and increased bitterness that was eventuated in an anti-foreign and, especially, anti-Western feeling. A whole generation has grown up nurtured in an atmosphere of suffering, insecurity, and defiance of imposed authority. However high the cost, the wars of independence have not been in vain. By 1950 some eight Arab states have attained independence, six of them have become members of the United Nations. During this period of strife (which has had its parallels in Asia, Africa, and South America), a new generation of dynamic, educated young Arabs has come to maturity, men who are hard at work bringing far-reaching changes in a reformed Arab society. It is a long, slow process in a long feudal and backward area of the earth, set amidst many natural handicaps in resources for diversified agriculture and industry. Old established patterns of social, economic, and political life are being altered in government and economic organizations as well as in social and cultural customs. There is a renaissance of literature, art, and other aspects of the humanities, as my readings evinced this morning.

Twelve years ago I met one of these young Arab intellectuals, an official of the Egyptian government assigned to the United Nations and doing graduate studies simultaneously at Harvard University. He has become a warm personal friend and I have had my own eyes opened to some of these realities of which we are speaking this morning. As I have attempted to understand the new society in Israel from its young leaders I have met, so from Zaki Hashim of Cairo I have had made available to me developments in the Middle East, which it is hard for most of us to get from our own press and institutions or from the releases of our State Department in Washington. You heard a young graduate student from Saudi Arabia from this pulpit at a recent Forum, and I hope we shall meet many more in the years ahead who can bring us more than the stories that come over our teletypes and TV channels about King Ibn Saud, slave economies, and oil manipulators of either Eastern or Western variety. The continuation of an age of ignorance can bring an age of annihilation as none of us need be told, I am sure.

It is high time that you and I know that Arab feudalism has received mortal blows in recent years that billion-dollar oil cartels cannot repair. Arab society is at the dawn of a new period we must try to understand, as we are attempting, I hope, to understand the new societies in India, China, and Southeast Asia. Land reform measures have already begun in Egypt and Syria, and less radically in Iraq. These measures have already begun to reduce the power and stature of many feudal families—and a start toward more social justice for the millions of landless poor. Five countries—Syria, Lebanon, Iraq, Jordan, and Egypt—have followed these antifeudal measures with more positive programs of economic development to raise the living standards of the undeprivileged families and the general community. Boards of central planning and supervision are actually speeding up (within desperate circumstances economically) an overall economic development. While Americans look askance at President Nasser of Egypt for many of his actions, they rarely read objective reports of marked reforms and developments that resemble our own ambitions toward social responsibility within the context of a welfare state. We are in a poor position to criticize Nasser when we remember our long support of such a corrupt regime with no social conscience as that of ex-King Farouk. There is very little of the democratic ideal yet operating in Egypt (and the British cannot complain it was because their seventy-year occupation tried, and failed, to teach democracy). A government like ours that loans millions of dollars to a Chiang Kai-Shek or a Franco can hardly call Nasser kettle-black. If we spent one-tenth of the money now invested in military bases in the Middle East on industrial and socially useful developments in Eygpt, our righteous indictment of Nasser might have a less hollow sound to the ears of our Arab friends.

Educational and health facilities are being amazingly advanced in recent years. The liberation of women in a Moslem society has begun, and government assistance to men and women alike to secure higher education has made phenomenal strides within the historical context of this area. New electoral laws in Syria, Iraq, Lebanon, and Jordan have started a process far more democratic and representative than would have been thought possible even two decades ago. Mr. Dulles and Mr. MacMillan may not like the political opinions of this younger generation at all times, but the Arab people, like their neighbors in China and India and Ceylon and Indonesia, no longer feel obliged to satisfy the tastes of these empire-minded gentlemen. Our own Negro citizens often better grasp the significance of the Arab awakening than do our sons and daughters of Harvard and Princeton, Vasser and Bryn Mawr (except their Negro alumni).

If we truly grasp these new developments in the Arab countries, we will not fall into the trap of thinking [that] the solutions for this part of the world are to be found in what Guy Wint in his book *Middle East Crisis* calls "pactomania" or in more and more Nike-studded military bases. What is needed is remedy after remedy for the Middle East's economic and social diseases. These remedies call for capital investment, in loans from the World Bank, for trade with Arab countries on favorable terms to them as well as ourselves. It calls for cultural exchanges and exchange of citizens and experts, in particular, who can help with acute problems of development other than pipelines for oil. It calls for far more study of Arab culture and history on your part and mine, and for objective courses on these subjects in our schools and colleges. It calls for a final interment of chauvinistic films, TV serials, and cartoons about the Arab, all as denigrating to their pride as have been, for so long, our portrayals of the American citizen of African descent.

I am not today discussing the particular problems of Israel and the Arab peoples, but if you are interested in today's introduction, I should like in the fall to have a morning address on this subject. Suffice today to say that there have been, and still are, Israeli leaders who care desperately about a far more intelligent and objective solution of this basic problem than a majority of Zionists have given it. My friend, Dr. Simon, whose article I list in the order of service today, has summarized the efforts of Theodore Herzl in his later years, Dr. Joseph Horowitz, Dr. Arthur Ruppin, Dr. Judes Magnes, and Javrel Stern, and we need to know them better. In the context of today's address, I simply want to say that there have been militant Middle East-minded Jews from the beginning of the Palestine settlements in this century who have believed in a bi-national Palestine without second-class citizenship for the Arab and who believed it possible and necessary to live [in] equality with Christians, Moslems, and other faiths in the Middle East. Dr. Magnes was well-esteemed by the younger Arab intellectuals (of whom I spoke a few moments ago), and had he lived, some of the recent developments within Israel that have widened the breach might well never have occurred. Dr. Magnes was deeply dedicated to the bi-national state; Mr. Ben-Gurion was *not.* There are many changes necessary if Israel is to remain a state in the Middle East. Of these possibilities we shall speak, if you wish, another time, but let us recognize today that there are Arabs and Jews alike who see many new and peaceful alternatives possible in the years ahead if a war of annihilation and humiliation for either side is prevented. If humanitarians, if religionists of many faiths who believe in the flexibility of human behavior work together with unrelenting devotion, disaster can be avoided and a new measure of justice achieved.

There are no quick solutions, and we who are an impatient people resent this. We also are faced with our own problem of holding back greedy hands and short imaginations in America, [which] see the Middle East as a new garden of lush profits for prosperity-intoxicated investors. You and I, with other values in mind, can play a role of reconciliation in this part of the world. We need no passports to the Middle East to aid our friends in those nations. We can here in our own city, state, and nation help to restore freedom in the marketplace of ideas and liberty to those blacklisted and pursued by the demons of fear and prejudice. Our Arab neighbors have more recently than we broken with many of the evil legacies of European feudalism. Some of the social enemies the Arabs still must face we never had here in our own land. But of recent days we Americans have lost immeasurable respect and admiration in the Middle East by our return to the habits of Torquemada and Cotton Mather.

There are hundreds of thousands of young Arabs who would welcome a rebirth of freedom in America that they might fight more bravely and hopefully in their own lands. It ill-behooves us, who despise the absolutism of desert kings, to preach democracy in our world broadcasts from the State Department and in our mass media while we silence millions with security checks, teacher's oaths, blacklists, and test declarations of orthodoxy.

Our Arab neighbors are awakening in this mid-century and many of them would like to find allies in America: allies not of petroleum magnates, but of heirs of Jefferson and Lincoln. Are we ready for companionship with this emerging leadership around the fertile crescent of Arabia, our cradle of prophetic religion twenty-six centuries old? Or are we imprisoned in our own cells of conformity and fear? There is work to be done here if we are to play our proper role in the Middle East. Let there be no condescension in our voices until much of the past ten years in America has been revoked. Iraq and Lebanon can detect hypocrisy even in a foreign language.

This church and its members can have a real part through well-directed programs and activities that will inform and inspire us to play the world neighbor more effectively. We can lower the temperature of feelings engendered by partisan advocates, we can educate ourselves and our neighbors on facts carefully hidden from public view. We can pull the fuses on explosives that can end all hope of sanity, brotherhood, and peace. To such a task I hope you will with me commit yourselves from this hour onward.

Celebrating Our Test Oath Victory with a Forward Look
September 1958

We are gathered this morning for the second Sunday of our new church year. This month opens, I confidently believe, a new era for our family here in the First Unitarian Church. Four years of exhausting litigation and valiant struggle have come to an end. As Dr. John Haynes Holmes wrote me in August, this church's name will go into the American history books whenever the story of religious freedom is told. Thousands of members and friends can feel a legitimate surge of pride in a task courageously undertaken, pursued, and victoriously completed. We have every right to say to ourselves and to our friends: "It pays to wage a battle of the spirit on behalf of principle. It can be done collectively as well as singly." We gave courage to other fighters for liberty, and our Unitarian friends around the world have told us of the leadership this church has provided in a season when many were silent or paralyzed.

I have said before, and I say again now, our debt to the men and women of this church during these years is beyond exaggeration. Mr. Murrish, Mr. Wirin, Mr. Okrand, Mr. Brock, Mr. Altman, our attorneys; Mr. Hall and his Committee on Religious Freedom; the late Paul Kelley and his successors as presidents of the Board, Mr. Schmorleitz, Mr. Borough, and Mrs. Koller, all gave us unflinching leadership in a long and costly campaign. The solidarity and staying power of this congregation were the wonder of our churches from coast to coast. You need no words of mine today to spell out the significance of this victory. Justices Black and Douglas have done it in concurring statements from the United States Supreme Court that will live for centuries, I truly believe. The host of friends who gave with utter sacrifice of money and moral support shall be in my memory until my final breath is drawn.

227

But we are here to speak of today and tomorrow. What does a new era for this church mean for all of us in this society of ours called the First Unitarian Church? What is the new perspective we need? We have perforce been, to a great degree, men and women concentrating on a single purpose for four years. Failure in that struggle could have weakened or destroyed our church and robbed us of our common home, this building and all it provides as a center for our many tasks. But we have now determined the security of that home, and a new program is called for. On Wednesday, October 8, at an all-church dinner opening our annual canvass, I shall speak further of this prospect that confronts us with such pregnant possibilities. We never had reason to be more hopeful as a company of Unitarians and friends of the liberal spirit.

We need some fresh exercise of muscles not used in the past few years. We were by necessity often preoccupied with a single task, even though your minister and lay leaders tried to continue serving at our many stations. But we did sacrifice breadth for concentration on religious liberty. We have no cause for apology in all of this; it was a strategy forced upon us by those who sought the destruction of all independency of conscience by the church and temple in present-day America. We now can recover a perspective befitting a church that has won new prestige in this city and throughout the world. We can, with pride, invite friends to join with us. Each month hereafter we plan to welcome new members simply and warmly before this pulpit at the end of the service. We need, above all else, to see that we employ the freedom so dearly purchased, and employ it in many, many tasks appropriate to a church that serves under a banner of humanity, undivided by race or class or party or nationality.

As a parish minister for over a quarter century, I have sometimes seen the tragedy of a good man who feels robbed of his cherished grievance. He stands naked without his familiar enemy, and it often proves to be his undoing. May no such disaster strike us in our time of victory. We have labored together for a splendid cause of freedom and won our battle with a splendid vindication. Can we now turn to new tasks calling for our spirit and dedication? I hope we have no nightmares like those of the evangelist who dreams the devil has died and left him with no adversary to curse. There are, believe me, new fields to harvest for the welfare of the human spirit. We should all rejoice that a barrier is down, a roadway opened, a new territory added for our labors; it is now entirely up to us to speak in words all men can understand of peace, of full humanity, of unfettered thought spoken openly.

Let me speak of three objectives for us as we enter a new era at this church. The first is a greatly broadened welcome to our fellow citizens who want association with a liberal church. They need friendship and understanding. We need in this new era to communicate a sense of warmth and hospitality to young and old who come to us for the first time, not asking anything of them but sincerity in the search for truth and service to mankind. I cannot too strongly express my hope that we will shed all surviving vestiges of narrowness and sectarianism, of intolerance and partisanship. People will come, and should come, at many stages of progress toward a faith in one world, one universal philosophy, one brotherhood. If our practice is as good as our profession, we will have vast patience with those who find but a beachhead of understanding when they first come.

This is a church with no intellectual elite, no political or social elect who determine what shall be the correct view within our church life. All men and women of every and any view, of any background are welcome here to attend services, to enter our activities. We believe in education and growth by the exercise of the listening ear and the controlled tongue. I am no official spokesman for First Church doctrine, nor are you in the pews. We are men and women, young and old, sharing our convictions, expecting new light, and infinitely patient with those of diverse opinion. We not only believe with Scripture that the lion and the lamb can lie down together, we believe that theists and humanists can attend the same church, that capitalists and socialists can love one another, that reverence for life is no idle phrase from the lips of Albert Schweitzer, but a fundamental statement of our attitude toward all persons, and can lead to the greatest progress in human relations, not excluding our own here in this society, this auditorium, in the patio, in each and every room of this building.

I left New England a decade ago, grateful for a congregation that had called me to California because I felt that here the self-love of an elect in-group would have no welcome. Our growth and our success, so far as we have had growth and success, have been due to our power to assure all sorts of people that we require no shibboleths for fellowship within these doors. When we have lost friends, it has often been because we seemed to deny this principle of toleration for the growing mind at its several stages.

Many forces today weaken our self-disciplines and we need to be aware of them. As we enter a new era in the life of this church, we need to be sufficiently introspective to avoid needless failure in our personal relationships. We are not invulnerable to the forces that disintegrate character. There is a certain "eat, drink, and be merry, for tomorrow we die" philosophy in the air today. It is probably all over the world. Not having used my passport yet, I cannot be sure, but I know it exists in the United States. It breeds callousness and self-indulgence and irresponsibility in human relations. One in every ten Americans suffers from some form of mental illness or personality disturbance, according to the National Health Education Committee; ten million Americans have emotional difficulties ranging from mild but clinically recognizable disturbances to grave illness. We of this church can help them and the less disturbed in many ways. And one of the best ways is to know that for centuries religions of many kinds, Stoic and prophetic, ancient and modern, humanistic and God-centered, have helped countless generations of men to find disciplines and methods for daily living that protected them from degenerative forces. Believe me, as you shall discover in a moment, I am a frightened man when I listen to our president commit our nation to policies that can blast us into atomic ash. I am a frightened man when I see an economy, the richest in history, pour its treasure into weapons manufacture while schools are being closed and millions are jobless. I do not minimize the impact of a sick and corrupt environment on the human spirit, yours and mine and our neighbors, but I do say that we must never underestimate the resourcefulness of a group of serious people employing the skills of character we call religion, ethics, philosophy, culture, manners. We are not humanoids, we are humans; our brains and our bodies are lubricated with blood, not machine oil. We have memory and imagination, will and resolution in our equipment. We do not lie down quietly to be punctured with a hypodermic of patriotism or piety on orders from above or below. We do not say "love" is enough. We do not dismiss the matter with some magic word like "acceptance" or "fellowship" or "togetherness." We know by the testimony of centuries and our own best insights today that our only salvation is to be found in the use of our minds, the achievement of mental and emotional growth, the hammering out of new social institutions that will not devour us as a leviathan. We do not settle for existentialist apathy that so conveniently seduces the fatigued mind.

We Unitarians do not think the most pressing project of the race is conquering outer space if it robs us of treasure needed to serve the necessities of those on earth desperate for food and the schoolroom textbook. We are a people with a strange heresy: we believe there are mysteries of inner space many have not yet explored. I, for one, still prefer Emerson to Von Braun and Tagore to Teller. If I listen to a scientist, and I do, it is to an Einstein or a Shapley who insists that I face the delinquencies of my own human nature, who offers me no panacea of a spaceship, who urges me not to buckle on an oxygen tank for a lunar trip, but to find out why I have such hostility toward the man next door who commits television fourteen hours a day.

I said there were three objectives in our new era. The second is the need to achieve far greater intellectual maturity. We need to be fortified with the knowledge and the methods of clear thinking that can aid us immeasurably in the overwhelming tasks that confront us. Unitarianism does not have a creed, an official doctrine, an announced ortho-doxy, but it is a religion that insists that we learn how to recognize real-ity and live with it and, if possible, enjoy it. I meet men and women who cannot live with grief, who cannot pick up threads of duty and obligation after a loved mate or child dies tragically. I meet people who are destroyed by a broken marriage, or a good position lost. But if we can consistently and ably help ourselves to think straight, to know the experiences of others in similar circumstances, if we can recognize a trap when we see it, if we can detect a drug or a poison, be it intellectual or chemical, we are better prepared for these devastations that strike all of us.

I think Mr. McGee shares my thinking on this. He has been in the humanist movement as well as the Methodist and Unitarian churches, and he also knows that too many people shy away from the word "intellectual" as though it were an egghead term for a few privileged folks out of this world. The truth is that we Americans have kidded the word "intellectual" long enough. We have discovered that good scientists and great statesmen are not created by public relations or the assumption that all we need is a large enough inventory of freezers and motor cars to attain the kingdom of God. We have neglected our schools and colleges, transformed them into gymnasia, playgrounds, and country clubs, and wondered why the Russians can send up one dog for every mouse we can send into the ionosphere. It is still an advanced position, alas, to come out forthrightly for reason in religion. The names of churchmen that have encouraged a forthright use of the mind to secure truth in theol-ogy and philosophy are mighty few: Duns Scotus Erigena in the ninth century, Berengar in the tenth century, Peter Abelard in the twelfth cen-tury stand out like blazing suns in the Christian firmament.

Far more often, the great figures, Catholic and Protestant alike, were intolerant toward the free mind at work. It was the reformer Martin Luther who cried out on one occasion: "Beware that silly little fool, that Devil's bride, Dame Reason, God's worst enemy." The Unitarian, the Universalist, the humanist still finds the world surprised that he claims to be religious yet intends to exercise intellectual independence. The anti-egghead campaign started long before our time. It has deep roots in the Dark Ages.

Let me state very clearly that my reading of the history of Unitarian-ism teaches me that it is possible to have a respect for intellect and not lose touch with reality, in fact, that there is no way to reality that ne-glects the use of the human mind. From Servetus to John Haynes Holmes our Unitarian experience has been that the use of reason is imperative and that it takes time, effort, and self-discipline to wrest the answers we want from the place where they may be found. Our own John Milton, three hundred years ago, put it in great prose when he said:

> To be still searching what we know not by what we know, still closing up to truth as we find it, this is the golden rule in theology as in arithmetic . . . not the forced union of cold and inwardly divided souls. Give me the liberty to know, to utter and to argue freely according to conscience, above all other liberties.

Milton swept aside the scholastic barbarism of centuries of theology with his modern temper. He fought arduously against kings and bishops so that he might help men use reason to discover reality. We have the same task today in new contexts.

Intellectual maturity is not attained by mere injunctions to read more books and articles, nor take more courses in university extension, desirable as such practice often is. I am asking that we respect and use the mental equipment that we possess to find, not exclude, the real world in which we live; and this is an enormously hard task. Whole battalions of devils seek to keep us from such a common-sense program.

I shall make no apology this year in asking you to think with me here on Sunday mornings about the contradictions of our society and our philosophies of personal conduct. I know, as Herbert Muller put it recently, that the paradoxes of our age tempt men violently to oversimplify the issues. It is his contention, and mine today, that there is more to contend with than monstrous folly and evil. It is our Unitarian faith, our faith as human beings believing in enlightenment of the human species, that hard and careful thought can save us if we maintain the enterprise of problem-solving.

We have a positive faith in reason and science and emotional maturity. These are not fictions, but things men can find and employ. Creative criticism, imaginative social vision, dedicated effort come out of seasons of serious thought on the issues that determine whether mankind shall live or die on this minor planet that is our home. We enter a new year and a new era for this church, and I propose no small tasks. When I speak of intellectual maturity I am not referring to rare and special minds of genius, of Einstein or Schweitzer, but of plain people we know, and have known, who used with all their strength the mind they possessed for the good of themselves and others, and rejected all blandishments of despair and hedonism. We lost three such persons from our ranks this summer: Henry Putnam, Charles Tanner, Ollie Brunswick —an insurance advertising executive, a plumber, a housewife—all intellectuals by my definition. They were searching, honest, and humane. We who survive can well grieve for their passing from our circle, and we can maintain the fire of their spirit in our own lives, for they left us much unfinished business.

The final thing I would mention today as a task for this new era is the discovery of a local ethos adequate for the needs of twentieth-century mankind. Let me state the problem with a reference to a talk made in Pasadena at Cal Tech, at a Conference on Science and Religion, by Ludwig von Bertalanffy, a distinguished biologist. Listen carefully, for he speaks of your problem and mine today:

> Operating the colossal social structures of our time—from businesses to national states to humanity as a whole—with the ethical concepts of a nomadic society of 2500 years ago is like operating an atomic reactor with the technology of a bushman. Never before was the individual so entangled, controlled, and governed in his most private affairs by impersonal and often inhuman social forces.
>
> The main problem is to complement the traditional code of values as expressed in the Mosaic decalogue and the golden rule with a broadened code applicable to our time.

We church members, like this biologist and thousands of other thoughtful people, do not accept with resignation the plight of modern man enmeshed in this matrix of social forces. The Nuremberg trials ten years ago were an evidence that mankind, when sufficiently revolted, can and does reject the ethics of the Nazi party. The United States Supreme Court on Friday again rejected the ethos of a small minority of racists who counted on the silence of millions of so-called "good people" to defy the laws of our nation regarding equal education for all children irrespective of their ethnic origin. On the whole, most of the time most of us have not looked too closely at the ethos of big business, or colonial enterprise, or the apparatus of state power until they break out in murder or genocide; but if we are to survive, we must look at them continuously and reform them before they destroy us. We cannot longer run the risk of war by accident, which is a present danger every hour of our lives, as Carl Dreher tells us so eloquently in the *Nation.* A nervous, psychotic, or fanatical launch officer can trigger off an accidental war today if he misreads a fugitive shadow on a radar screen. I may speak only for myself; I never attempt to speak for this congregation, as you well know, but I am frightened by the words of a president on television using concepts of outmoded nationalism and injured pride in explaining the need for American warships and aircraft in the Formosan Straits. Any social ethos worthy of construction in these dangerous years through which we are passing cannot be justified if it thinks of anything less than all mankind, American and Formosan, Chinese and Russian, and all the rest of the family of man. Our prestige as a national power is a fantastic anachronism if it leads the entire earth into a war of annihilation, a very real possibility in the days ahead. Yet for this we are now risking the peace of the world.

I feel so strongly that the Unitarian conscience is important in the present critical juncture that I sent to President Dana Greeley of the American Unitarian Association in Boston a telegram on Friday morning. As president of the Pacific Coast Unitarian Ministers Association, I sent copies to my seventy-one colleagues in pulpits from Vancouver to San Diego and from Hawaii to Salt Lake City and Albuquerque. This is the text of the wire:

September 12, 1958

Dr. Dana McLean Greeley, President
American Unitarian Association
25 Beacon Street
Boston 8, Massachusetts

After reading President Eisenhower's Thursday address, I'm deeply concerned lest America find itself in a war that is morally unjustified and without a single supporting ally. Cannot the churches of America show some prophetic leadership at this time? I feel that they must do so with so much at stake. Can you, as our Unitarian leader, invite other heads of denominations to join in a letter to the president insisting upon no war action of any kind and continuous peaceful negotiations? I believe your leadership at this moment might well receive great national support. Millions of Americans are seeking evidence of leadership sufficient to pull us back from an abyss of self-destruction. If this were not a matter of such extreme urgency, I would not trouble you at this season when we all are so preoccupied with church reopenings and programs.

Sincerely

Stephen H. Fritchman

On September 19 Dr. Greeley sent a telegram to President Eisenhower and to Secretary of State Dulles as follows:

I believe religious leaders of America would strongly insist there must be negotiations and further ethical consideration more significant than threat of force in establishing United States leadership and preserving world peace in Far East. We urge avoidance of war and brink of war, and ask full use of United Nations for just and fair settlement of problems.

Copies of this telegram were sent to a number of leading American churchmen by Dr. Greeley.

Do not misunderstand me. I have no overriding, compulsive rescue-complex as my monitor today. I am open to all possible persuasion that our president is doing all that can be done with the state apparatus of which he is the nominal head. But because I can entertain correction, I must not thereby surrender to the perils of "other-directed" living. We must assume responsibility for constructing and using a social ethos that will produce rational, not irrational, behavior as a nation. Otherwise we are but tinder for the final conflagration. If we do not believe that we Unitarians, and our Quaker friends, and our Jewish friends, and all the other people of goodwill in this world who love life and want a civilization of peace and decency can slow down the behemoth of government sufficiently to speak our piece, we have no business here. If the church is not simply a vast ecclesiastical hypnosis, then it must aid us in our condition and empower us for our next step toward the sunlight of our new Eden. True, indeed, stopping the dogs of war on both sides of the Formosan Straits is but one task, and there are many more; we think of Little Rock and Montgomery (where a poor handyman will soon die for a paltry theft of $1.95—enough to make Charles Dickens return to earth in celestial anger). Yes, there are many issues that call for a new social ethos fit for a space age, but the multiplicity of issues does not exempt us from decision regarding those most threatening our survival and our progress. Quite the contrary, the very number of problems that confront us require a fresh assault by mind and conscience. We must take speech more seriously. It is a part of our social engineering. Speech is a weapon, words can transform men's hearts and wills. Silence can be as destructive as a bomb, as final as a hangman's noose. Thomas Mann knew this; remember his words in *The Magic Mountain:* "Speech is civilization itself. The word, even the most contradictory word, preserves contact—it is silence which isolates."

This is indeed a year that ushers in a new era for our church. We did not carry on this litigation for anything less than a chance to renew our work as a society dedicated to the total man. Edouard Herriot was right when he said upon his election as president of the French Assembly in 1951: "You must dispatch the past, ensure the present, and prepare for the future. You are condemned to be heroic." And so we are standing in this place today, in year one of the unfettered church. We are condemned to be heroic.

Address at the Plenary Session of the Tenth Congress of the World Council of Peace in Stockholm, Sweden

May 12, 1959

Mr. Chairman, sisters and brothers of the World Council of Peace: The distinguished delegate from England, Mr. Pritt, confessed on Friday that there were problems of adjustment for Great Britain in learning how to be a colony of a former colony, and in learning how to forget the ancient habits of playing empire-builder to the world. Caesar divests himself of his prerogatives but not without some awkwardness in the performance. May I assure our friend from Great Britain that the new imperium in America has its embarrassments as well. Certainly the group of Americans whom I represent despise the empire mentality that some of our elected and appointed officials seek to thrust upon us with such enthusiasm, always disclaiming their intentions as they test the crown and finger the ermine. As in the days of Balshazar, so today those above the salt are having to decipher the handwriting on the wall. "Mene, mene, tekel, uparsin" has more translations in this atomic century than ever crossed the imaginations of men in Babylon, Rome, or imperial England.

We have come from New York and San Francisco, Brooklyn and Los Angeles to report to you in Stockholm, all of you from China and Japan, the Soviet Union, Europe, Africa, the Middle East, Latin America, and so many other lands, that the new American empire of nuclear armaments and cold war stratagems does not enjoy the unanimous consent of the people of our great nation. It is exceedingly hard to know how great or small is the consent to the present policies in Washington because the greatest communications system of film, radio, TV, and press ever devised in history falls silent when men and women speak out for peace. A New York release by Dr. Albert Schweitzer on nuclear fallout receives a scant two inches in the early editions, while a mere holding of hands by Liz Taylor and Eddie Fisher rates headlines in countless cities, including the Scandinavian. We notoriously voluble Americans have learned the virtue of holding our tongues if we want to get elected to office, hold a job in a university, or get clearance for a job in industry. Even so, there is a great deal more conscience expressing itself at present in the fifty American states than you would ever learn from *Life* and *Time* or the releases from Mr. Herter's State Department in Washington.

If you forget all else I say today, I hope you will remember that the American group speaks with a great deal of humility to this assembly. Millions of Americans, many millions I assure you, will carry to their graves a sense of overwhelming guilt for the bombings of Nagasaki and Hiroshima. I could not stand before you if I did not say this with all the force at my command. To be sure, we were not asked by President Truman in 1945 whether we wanted to have those bombs dropped on the people of Japan. Distinguished scientists who knew of their existence urged President Roosevelt not to use them, and after his death continued to plead for some other form of testing their deadly power. But they *were* dropped and we all in America bear responsibility and blame. The chief executive who gave the order was reelected to our highest office.

With Mme. Blum may I agree from the heart that there is no merit in merely beating the breast and crying "Mea culpa, mea maxima culpa," but it is exceedingly important that there be no ambiguity about the matter. Millions of Americans know that their country must bear a weight of guilt for centuries for this monstrous act at Hiroshima, and no actions or explanations can ever wipe out the stain upon our honor by this horror. It would be easier to say this, dear friends, if we in America had not added to that crime the added actions in Korea with flaming napalm, and the continued deeds of the cold war which have been so fully catalogued here in Stockholm. We Americans are convinced that these things will end—with aid from our fellow Americans, which is growing apace, and from the lessons taught us by every nation represented here at this assembly, and many others not here.

The cold war will end because the peoples of the world, including the people of the United States of America, cannot longer endure its postponement of their hopes for a united, free, and equal community of nations.

Let me assure you that capitalist America has peace forces that receive no great publicity in foreign news dispatches and rarely in the magazines you read from our country. Let me mention two or three of these evidences, with great modesty I assure you, after listening to reports of peace activities in the other nations represented here. I speak in no mood of boasting nor of apology, but simply sharing information.

You have a right to know that we have no united peace organization, but a great many separate forces that need to find a common voice. We Americans are all going back to propose such union of forces of the friend of peace in our own land.

Dr. Holland Roberts, chairman of our delegation, in his address spoke of SANE, the nationwide network of committees advocating a sane nuclear policy to which Mr. Norman Cousins and Dr. Linus Pauling have contributed so much. Thousands of scientists have united under Dr. Pauling's leadership to urge the American people to call for an end of nuclear tests. In colleges and universities from the Atlantic to the Pacific, hundreds of thousands have learned of the mushrooming cloud of nuclear debris that filters leukemia, bone cancer, and genetic infirmities into the present and future generations. Many American citizens, innocent of political thought for decades, are now beginning to organize because their own families seem threatened. They are truly worried for the first time in their lives. Mayors, governors, and senators are speaking out against this monstrosity—the devil of strontium-90—entering their homes without a warrant, and, like the angel of death in ancient Eygpt in biblical days, slaying the firstborn of Pharaoh's people.

Let me report in this brief statement that the churches of America are a far greater force for peace than you might suspect from reports on our revival of religion. In spite of Mr. Dulles's protest and warning given in person, the Fifth World Order Conference of the National Churches of Christ, meeting in Cleveland last December, called for swifter progress in total disarmament, for the suspension of nuclear tests, and for a real working coexistence with socialist countries. The Methodists, Baptists, Episcopalians, Unitarians, Congregationalists, and many other bodies have spoken with passionate insistence on the need for immediate and effective programs of peace, and the clergy in thousands of pulpits speak to their people in the same vein. Above all, the Quakers—the Society of Friends—in no wise a socialist movement but one of profound humanity and tenderness of conscience, leads all other religious organizations in America in the call for the end of both cold and hot wars. Quakers, and others with them, organized fifty ministers last August 6 in San Francisco for a prayer vigil on behalf of victims at Hiroshima and for the end of all such intercontinental catastrophes in years to come.

We of the American delegation would tell you of the growing interest in peace by sections of the business community. Cyrus Eaton, the Cleveland industrialist, father of the Pugwash Conferences, is best known; but Vice Premier Mikoyan of the USSR could tell you of a very large number of manufacturers, industrialists, and businessmen whom he met in America who want peace, world trade, and coexistence—*not war!* The trade unions of America are more and more echoing this cry. Workers in America, like small businessmen and farmers, want to live, want to enjoy health, welfare, and culture, as do millions in other countries. And they are beginning to discover that they must say so in state capitals and in Washington. The voters of the United States are teaching this lesson to candidates for public office. The victories of the people at the polls last November were a beginning of more to come, we believe. A sleeping electorate is waking up to the fact that one cannot have an economy resting on warplanes and missiles, upon the repression of colonial peoples, upon NATO threats out of Washington, Paris, London, and Berlin every twenty-four hours.

For the first time in a decade, the students of America are beginning to think about peace, to insist upon talking out loud, marching in public with placards for peace, and writing editorials and radio scripts for university broadcasting. This is new to the present, so-called "beat generation."

There is a new sound in America today, and it is not coming from Cape Canaveral or the nuclear submarines at Groton, but from men and women and youth protesting after far too long a silence on the issues of war and peace, on racial equality, and social welfare of all peoples everywhere. Freedom of speech was for fifteen years under a terrible assault, known to you as McCarthyism. That was a time when many teachers and editors, ministers, and film writers forgot everything decent and fine they had ever said during the years when together with the Soviet Union, the Chinese, the British, and the French and others they fought and defeated worldwide fascism.

We Americans have yet to build a great monument as have the German people at Buchenwald in honest contrition for a colossal crime against humanity, but I believe we will some day do so with the words "Hiroshima and Nagasaki" engraved upon it. Meanwhile, we are finding our tongues! A former president of the United States has castigated with purple prose the inequities of the Committee on Un-American Activities, which closed the lips of scores of thousands in every walk of life for a generation. The United States Supreme Court has given strong opinions over and over again that dissent is *not* treason, but the very essence of freedom. They have ruled that passports are a right of all Americans. That is why Dr. DuBois, Paul Robeson, Linus Pauling, Rockwell Kent, and thousands of other Americans are visiting your countries and speaking for peace at every opportunity. Americans have sailed peace ships, the *Phoenix* and the *Golden Rule*, into nuclear testing areas and will, if necessary, send protest planes into the stratosphere and diving bells into the sea to say *No more war. Stop the tests. Let us recover our common humanity. Let us with others join the human race and not slaughter it.*

Go back to your peoples, dear friends, next week and tell them that not just seventeen Americans, but millions of Americans are learning how to distinguish between loyalty and aid to Franco, between freedom and guns to Chiang Kai-Shek, between patriotism and economic loans to General Trujillo. They are learning to speak up on those matters. I profoundly believe that the America that is learning painfully how to make integration of the races the enforced law of the land will soon learn how to live in an integrated world, where India and Africa, Argentina and China will be fellow members of a totally united nations organization with all *fed*, all *healthy*, all *educated*, all *cultured*, all *equal*, and with no man holding a knife at his brother's throat. *This is no idle dream.* This is possible in the swift future, not in some distant utopia. The dearest vision of Dr. Joliot-Curie shall come to pass in our children's lifetime. To believe less is a sickness of the soul, a cancer of the human spirit. Long life to the World Council of Peace.

Our Bad Conscience about Panama
The Discovery of a Lost Word— "Imperialism"
March 8, 1964

As members of this church well know, your minister is opposed to token racial integration: a few handsome Negro clerks in department stores or hotels, or as agents at the airline counters, or as handmaidens to princesses in Rose Bowl parade floats. To be sure, tokenism is a step toward the goal of freedom. But to settle for tokenism is to lose the battle. We have had a century of miniscule, hesitant tokenism. And it is not enough!

But there is another tokenism today that troubles me equally. It is "token liberalism." Editor I. F. Stone in Washington used the term to describe the recent statements of President Johnson: his call for a war on poverty, followed by a modest $800 million for new obligations— four-fifths of 1 percent of the national budget of $100 billion. The president calls for diminution of arms expenditure in the light of our present twenty-five times overkill capacity in nuclear weapons. But the 1 percent cut he recommended in the $50 billion arms budget is token liberalism, and bears no resemblance to the fantastic overkill capacity that Ralph Lapp and Seymour Melman have been pointing to as so excessive and provocative. There is no proposal to cut back our apocalyptic inventories of uranium and plutonium.

But now I am speaking of another example of token liberalism: the president's apology for U.S. armed violence against the Panamanians last January 9 over the flag controversy in the Canal Zone, followed a little later by his statement that the so-called "perpetual" treaty with Panama cannot be rewritten in the light of present conditions.

One of our most devoted and long-time members was distressed last Sunday that I criticized our president for his refusal, on the grounds of national interest, to let lard or dried milk into Cuba. My friend reminded me of how severe is the John Birch Society campaign against Mr. Johnson. I mention this now because it is my feeling that there is nothing more needed in the White House at this moment than valid, intelligent criticism of policies that violate its own professions and platform declarations, thus magnifying cynicism and resulting in defection from the ranks of the friends of the administration.

The Birch Society could ask for nothing better to serve their ends than for the president to advocate token liberalism, but perform so modestly in actual fact that things would remain about as they were—or go backward. Mr. Johnson, as I. F. Stone has well said, needs nothing so much as a left opposition. I hope today's address will help make clear to my critic of last week and to any others who share his view that the answer to the John Bircher is a record of *real* reform, which will strengthen America in the eyes of the entire world and meet the critical needs of its citizens at home.

It is extremely important for us to understand the Panama crisis so that we may understand all of Latin and South America. The Latin phrase, *multum in parvo* (much in little), seems especially appropriate. The explosions in Panama on January 9 and 10 may prove to be more important than the problem of Castro's Cuba. The kind of trouble we are facing in a critical stage in Panama is being duplicated throughout the hemisphere from Canada to Chile. Long-dormant antagonisms are taking visible shape. The flag-raising incident was only a symbolic incident, apparently superficial but dramatically characteristic of the situation in many countries north and south of Panama.

On another Sunday soon I plan to talk very candidly about Canada. Meanwhile I urge you to read the March issue of *Holiday* magazine, which is devoted to Canada. *Holiday* is a Curtis Publishing Company magazine from Philadelphia. It has no radical connections and is a succesful free enterprise publication, yet I am glad to use *Holiday* in attempting to spell out the meaning of neo-colonialism and streamlined imperialism.

Allow me to quote from the opening statement of the editor, Ted Patrick:

> The Canadian nation came into being largely out of fear of violence from the United States. That fear goes back to Revolutionary times and it was kept alive all through America's warlike past, which is the story of too much bloodshed and too much jingo, including the pseudo-heroics of Manifest Destiny and Teddy Roosevelt's bully Big Stick. If some of that ancestral apprehension survives in Canada today, it may well be because our nation has not yet cleansed itself completely of

colonialist attitudes—witness what can happen in Panama, and, even worse, what could happen if Washington embraced Senator Goldwater's belief that Cuba must one day be attacked with arms.

I am suggesting that we discover the potency of deep resentments —layer upon layer—that have been accumulating for a century, at least. We are discussing the feelings of a small and dependent nation toward a prodigiously wealthy and powerful neighbor. Beyond these feelings are the reflex actions of nations from Canada to Chile, which see something fundamentally wrong and immoral and eventually self-destructive to America's own interests in our relationships with our western hemisphere neighbors.

One thing that is wrong is that the United States has not persuaded these nations north and south of the Canal Zone that we are interested in them, or that we respect their opinions; that we have any curiosity about their culture, their art, their traditions, or even about their people.

South Americans, Mexicans, Panamanians find us arrogant and motivated by our own comfort and profit. We mark up the price of our cars that we ship for sale to our neighbors, to be paid for by people whose wages are far, far less than our own. We set up military and intelligence stations in Guantanamo, in the Canal Zone, and elsewhere to train guerrilla fighters, to stockpile weapons, to supervise and survey all that goes on in our neighbors' backyard. We see nothing in all of this that is wrong or significant until an explosion occurs as it did on January 9 in the Canal Zone. Even then we wait for it all to blow away.

The Panamanians feel that, despite some recent modest improvements in relations, their country is a protectorate of the United States and that they are colonial subjects of Yankee imperialism. They deeply resent the American presence "in perpetuity" and the American "sovereign" status in the Canal Zone—concessions wrung from the infant nation by President Theodore Roosevelt half a century ago.

Today let us ask: What is colonialism?

If I thought our schoolbooks spelled it out adequately, I would take the answer for granted this morning. But I do not have that assurance. Panamanians are faced daily with the contrast of life in the ten-mile-wide strip that is the U.S. Canal Zone and that of the rest of Panama. The Zone resembles a well-manicured country club with its beautiful homes, spacious lawns, abundance of golf courses, tennis courts, bathing beaches, and fishing facilities all for the exclusive use of Americans. Across the road are the squalid slums and the grinding poverty of Panama.

Bitterness runs high as the Panamanians witness the snobbishness and arrogance of the American settlers who act the role of the colonial master. This colonialist mentality among the thirty-six thousand Americans—60 percent in the military—seems all too familiar to that of the French colonies until recently in Algeria, to the French in the Congo, and to the Afrikaners in South Africa. These second and third generation Zonal residents have angrily protested the mild improvements in recent years, such as the merit system in Canal employment, the desegregation of public facilities in 1960, and then, in 1963, the two-flag agreement to have both Panamanian and American flags on schools and other public buildings in the Zone.

Panama, as an American colony in all but name, has during the past half century had a docile and obedient local government on either side of the Canal Zone. The top Panama administration has been that of a small white oligarchy that controls native-held commerce in Panama. Following the United States' ostracism of Castro's Cuba, Panama broke diplomatic relations with Cuba in December 1961. The Communist party is outlawed and the national front functions as a military police. About sixty local proprietors own one-eighth of the land of Panama and dominate the fifty-one-member parliament. The vast majority of the one million citizens of Panama live in poverty as squatters on unused land or in squalid slums within view of the sheltered suburban homes of the Americans in the Zone. President Chiardi is a millionaire sugar and dairy producer, and the son of a former president.

Meanwhile, colonialism in Panama means the presence of large industrial and commercial corporations owned outside of Panama: Chase National Bank, National City Bank, Sears Roebuck, Pan American, Eastman Kodak, RCA, Goodyear, Conoco and Gulf Oil, and United Fruit with its Panamanian holdings of sixty thousand acres of bananas and cocoa. In addition, Panama offers a tax refuge for five hundred U.S. corporations that maintain a mailbox there.

The U.S. administration of the Zone, including both Canal and military installations, employs about fifteen thousand Panamanians, 83 percent of them in the low-paying jobs. The top fifteen hundred positions are filled with Americans for security reasons, it is claimed. Several AFL-CIO unions in the Zone have barred Panamanians from membership. In addition, U.S. employees receive a 25 percent overseas differential, enjoy the use of special commissaries for tax-free goods, and low-rent housing. Little wonder that in this format of colonialism there has recently been a Panamanian demand for equal pay for equal work.

Panama was literally our creation in 1903 out of the country of Colombia, and it has remained such ever since, including the corrupt local ruling clique, ruthlessly suppressing over the years any efforts of the people to improve their lot in their occupied country.

As in all colonial adventures, the profits are high. Besides the private investments already mentioned, it should be remembered that the total operating net of the Canal comes to some $51 million annually, of which 4 percent goes to the Republic of Panama and the balance goes to the U.S. government to cover the cost of operating the Canal and maintaining a U.S. military government in the Zone, and for payments to the Pentagon and to American banks that handle the paper on the Canal investment, as well as the various recipients of the profits from this so-called "public utility." Mr. Victor Perlo recently stated that the accumulated corporate profits at the end of the fiscal year 1964 are placed at $143 million, or about five times the total rental payments to the Republic of Panama over the entire half-century operation of the Canal.

This is the familiar picture of economic imperialism anywhere, but Mr. C. L. Sulzberger of the *New York Times* said in his Panama editorial: "Colonialism is the thinly disguised inner issue of the crisis in Panama."

Except for the *New York Times*, American newspapers last January chose to say little about another major aspect of American colonialism in Panama: the military side of the picture. Military officials have long said openly that the Panama Canal Zone is of no strategic importance as a naval passage between the Atlantic and Pacific Oceans. The Forrestal-class supercarriers are too big for the locks, and, besides, the Canal is a relatively easy target for a missile strike. The Canal, however, is a major U.S. military center. The uniformed forces of the United States number 9,750 men. They are not there for the protection of the Canal only, but as a mobile force to cope with any emergency in Latin America.

The U.S. military headquarters at Quarry Heights, Canal Zone, is the Southern Command, a unified command under General P. O'Meara, reporting directly to the Joint Chiefs of Staff. In recent years the United States has developed special training programs in the Canal Zone for military men and, by invitation, for Latin American officers and men. These programs include guerrilla-warfare training by the Eighth Special Forces, an army unit, and training in jungle rescue operations by the Air Force Jungle Training Center. Americans have been trained here for guerrilla warfare in South Vietnam.

I mention all of this detail in order to make it quite clear that the occupation of the Canal Zone is by no means simply a local instance of outmoded colonialism. It is much more than that. It is "the pivot and the anchor of the entire United States empire in Latin America." There is no better example in the world today of what imperialism— American imperialism—looks like. American students please note.

We must look at the Canal Zone crisis—the demand by the Panamanians for a new treaty—in post-Cuban crisis terms, not simply as the long-standing problem of increased payments to Panama from Canal tolls, or as a demand for better wages and living conditions in Panama. The military installation and the training programs mentioned above are understood by all Latin Americans, if not by citizens of our country "back in the states." These are seen—and correctly so—as the flexed muscle of imperialism.

Trevor Ambrister has written an illuminating article on "Panama: Why They Hate Us" for the *Saturday Evening Post.* For over a century the *Post* has been a conservative middle-class publication, yet it helps us to understand the causes of Latin American resentment in Panama today. Mr. Armbrister writes:

> Panamanian anger against the United States grows out of a situation which most Americans take for granted, but which most Panamanians consider outdated, unjust, and immoral. Every schoolboy in Panama learns that American marines landed in Mexico, Nicaragua, Haiti, and the Dominican Republic—and that U.S. troops helped to settle a 1925 rent strike in Panama City in favor of the landlords.
>
> The natural dislike of the have nots for the haves is not unique in Panama, but it is aggravated here by the presence in the Canal Zone of more than 35,000 U.S. citizens whose tidy homes, shiny cars, and frequent arrogant attitudes remind Panamanians of their inferior lot.

There is no disguise possible—the naked contrast is there for all to see in its terrible starkness.

Governor Fleming of the Canal Zone is quoted in this *Saturday Evening Post* article as saying:

> The overwhelming majority of Americans in the Zones are moderates and passive, but there are also some 200 or 300 members of the radical right. They have been isolated so long that they have developed a reactionary mentality. Their whole attitude is that nothing should be changed in the best of all possible worlds. It's the perfect situation for the guy who's 150% American—and 50% whisky.

This is the evaluation of the Canal Zone's top administrator! If this is his frank statement, imagine the thinking of the citizens of Panama on the other side of the fence!

Let me say, before we speak of possible actions to be taken, that justice in Panama seems so utterly impossible that the Panamanians themselves dare not demand its full enforcement. This hopelessness derives not from lack of merit, but from the presence of overwhelming U.S. military force. M. S. Arnoni of the magazine, *Minority of One,* has well stated the demoralization of the Panamanians over the decades since the Canal opened in 1914. He says: "Our national record involving Panama is so deplorable that it is hardly surprising that the mere study of it is considered subversive by many flag-waving 'patriots.'"

But you and I cannot leave it at that.

There has been a growing assertiveness by Panamanians in recent months. The failure of the White House to fill the vacant post of U.S. Ambassador to Panama has permitted deterioration. President Kennedy postponed action, even when Governor Fleming urged an enlightened appointment and warned of the deep unrest.

I do not intend to speak in any detail of the flag-raising incident, for it is quite familiar to all of us. We should remember that an agreement had been achieved between the Zone officials and the Panamanian government that *both* flags or *neither* should be flown. The flag-raising incident, set off by Canal Zone American high school students, was symbolic of U.S. contempt for Latin American nations and for treaties between nations. Here is the very essence of unscrupulous colonialism. Here indeed is a David-and-Goliath situation where the smaller power comes to the end of its patience. When on January 9 U.S. forces fired on the Panamanian students in the flag incident, the indignant students fought back with garbage cans and whatever else was available. But behind them, and they knew it, was the powder keg of the entire Latin subcontinent. Meanwhile, the United States is finding that its NATO allies, remembering the Suez Canal crisis, have no interest in defending the Goliath of the North.

As I have pointed out, the government of Panama has been a docile taker of orders for decades, but the violence of the U.S. military in firing on unarmed men and women students ignited a new courage, a new resistance. The forty deaths and two hundred wounded have united all factions in Panama. A new era is here.

Now that the government and the people of Panama have been united—right and center and left—let us see what they are demanding. First of all, there is an insistence that a new treaty be written. There is a demand for the nationalization and neutralization of the Canal. The Panamanians do not wish for the Canal to be used for U.S. aggression against Cuba (in spite of the fact that there are no diplomatic relations between Panama and Cuba) because the Canal would be a prime target for nuclear weapons in any conflict. The Panamanians are asking, modestly enough, for nationalization after five or ten years, and that during the intervening period the U.S. military base be dismantled. Panama's President Chiari is being compelled by public opinion to take a firm stand on the writing of a new treaty at the risk of a revolutionary change of government if he reverts to former habits and thinks too much of his cattle and sugar investments and too little of the welfare of the entire country. If the present Chiari government continues the imperialist game (as the Latin American press bluntly calls it), there will surely be popular resistance and violence.

It is true that Panama is at the mercy of the United States economically, as Cedric Belfrage has indicated in his dispatches from Mexico City. The U.S. can stop purchases in Panama for the Zone. Our government can cut off water for Colon and Panama City. The Panamanian National Economic Council has called for an emergency drive for trade relations with all countries, irrespective of ideology, and the government has instituted austerity measures for a country on a war-footing.

There is danger of an American-engineered coup, using right-wing Panamanian officers trained at the U.S. Fort Gulick School. This danger is real, but a coup could go either right or left, for rank-and-file Panamanian soldiers cannot be counted on to support a right-wing coup. A bloodbath could result from a mood of desperation. Today we should be aware, as never before, of a new spirit in Panama. The inferiority complex of a little and miserably poor nation has begun to vanish at an accelerated tempo.

Washington does indeed face an acute dilemma, no less so because this is an election year. We need more from Thomas C. Mann, called by President Johnson from his post as Ambassador to Mexico to be Assistant Secretary of State for Inter-American Affairs, then a repetition of the role he once played in Guatemala in the overthrow of the government of President Arbenz by U.S.-backed Guatemalan exiles. That episode greatly embellished the imperialist image that South America already had of the United States.

There is no sane or just course for the United States but to negotiate a new treaty, as Panama Ambassador Moreno has asked President Johnson to do.

In 1947 a great Unitarian peace advocate, Emily Green Balch of Massachusetts, who had been awarded the Nobel Peace Prize the year before, proposed that the polar regions and all waterways of strategic importance be administered by the United Nations. The International Executive Committee of the Women's International League for Peace and Freedom sent a petition to the United Nations, asking for a study commission to explore the question of the United Nations' control of international waterways and such narrow straits as the Dardanelles and canals like Suez and Panama. If some action had been taken by the UN, the tragic events of the Israel-Suez Canal area, as well as the present perilous confrontation in Panama, might have been averted.

Also in 1960, Senator Aiken of Vermont proposed a revision of our U.S.-Panama relations, and suggested that we share with others the political liabilities inherent in maintaining and operating the Canal. One means, said Senator Aiken, would be internationalizing the Canal.

This was a constructive proposal, but four years have passed and now it is not enough. Today, Cuba, Venezuela, Brazil, Chile, and Mexico (to mention but a few cardinal examples) are nations which are insisting on entering a post-imperialist era. The conditions vary, but the age of Teddy Roosevelt's gunboat-big stick-U.S. Marines colonialism has come to an end, though the expiring may be long drawn out and painful. We as American citizens cannot longer afford to be ignorant or foolish.

Jim Jenkins, high school senior in the Canal Zone, who led the students in the flag-raising episode of January 9 with the approval of his father and mother, may or may not be one of the two or three hundred John Birch contingent, but his actions may have started a wave of violence and resistance that could make the French colons of Algeria seem pikers indeed. I hope not, but it is ominous that the latest Gallup poll indicates that 45 percent of those polled in the United States felt that we should continue a "firm" policy in Panama. Only 9 percent thought we should pay more rent to Panama for the use of the Canal, or draw up a new treaty to nationalize or internationalize the Canal.

There will be many efforts to bypass the colonialism issue, such as proposing a new canal in another country. There will be proposals, if not action, to pay slightly higher wages to Panamanians working in the Canal Zone. But as long as the gold-versus-silver pay scale and purchasing scale continues, as long as the military base remains on our Zonal strip, the revolution in Panama against the Americans will deepen. You and I can see that the issue of Panama is faced frankly by the two political parties in their conventions next summer. Meanwhile, every letter, every telegram, every phone call to senators, to congressmen, to the State Department, and to the president is valuable. This is a year when many a Washington ear is to the ground. Every straw in the wind is being watched. This is a vote-sensitive year. I can only say: Use your prerogatives!

More than anything else I fear the good citizen—passive and kindly —who is indifferent, who says: "What is the Canal Zone to me?" Who says: "We aren't imperialist. This is the American century of freedom and opportunity." I cannot but remember the words of Stephen Crane in that classic story, *The Red Badge of Courage:*

> Indifference is a militant thing. It batters down the walls of cities and murders the women and children amid flames and the purloining of altar vessels. When it goes away, it leaves smoking ruins, where lie citizens bayoneted through the throat. It is not a children's pastime like mere highway robbery.

Let no Unitarian ever underestimate the peril of indifference. It is the cradle of war, the nursery of death.

The Curse of Vietnam
Brutalization of the American Soul
March 19, 1967

Abraham Lincoln once told the story of the man who was being carried out of town on a rail by some aroused fellow citizens; when asked how he felt, the man replied that if it were not for the honor of it all he would as leave not have had the experience. I feel the same about being last speaker in this international seminar. Surely no one in his right mind expects me to say something novel. I am clearly here because I speak as an American for a segment of our people not always heard from, and not represented in that 67 percent favoring the present policies of President Johnson (which his favorite necromancer Dr. George Gallup tells him is the present count in the Great Consensus.)

It was a profound tragedy that one of America's leading peace crusaders, Rev. A. J. Muste, completed his witness a few weeks ago, just days after returning from North Vietnam. His death took from our ranks a giant conscience we could ill spare. Some recent words of his keep echoing in my ears these days, and I would like to take them as a theme sentence for my remarks tonight: "The people of Vietnam have been shot and bombed from various sides for decades. If only somebody could stop killing them!" And to those words I would add his earlier remarks given in December of 1965 to a federal grand jury in New York, following the arrest of some young men who had burned their draft cards: "It is impossible for me to cooperate with the grand jury in its present

---

Address presented at "Vietnam: An International Seminar" at the University of Victoria, Canada. Other speakers at the seminar included: Sen. Henry Jackson, Washington; Miss Joan Baez, California; Ira Sandperl, California; Prof. Mordecai Breimerg, Vancouver; Prof. Laurence Evans, Vancouver; Rev. Ray N. Hord, Toronto; Tom Hayden, New Jersey; Dr. Gustavo Tolentino, Toronto; and Warren Allmand, M.P., Quebec.

investigation of draft-card burning. The idea of the freedom and dignity of the human being, of his responsibility to God or his fellows or to history, is an empty mockery, if, precisely in such matters, each individual is not free to think and to decide for himself, and free to obey or disobey orders of so-called superiors. In the presence of these ultimate issues, no man is superior to another." Let me anticipate my final conclusion tonight with these words of Dr. Muste's written in *Liberation* magazine two short months ago—a moral declaration that I believe has been echoed in this great seminar here in Victoria. He said: "If we love life more than we do our pride, if our responsibility to all of humanity can overcome the fear of chaos, which leads to greater chaos, then we will be able to commit ourselves to a noble alternative." As one who knew and honored this elder guide in the ways of peace, I am here in Canada because I am certain there is a noble and a viable alternative to the prevailing madness that wears the colors of official policy in my country. I shall be speaking of it during the next few minutes. I know it is hard to discuss morality when we are aware of the monstrous cruelty going on in Vietnam: the beheading of prisoners, the burning of women and children by the Saigon army, American mercenary troops, the Viet Cong. The war is a dirty one, indeed, but we must discuss morality or become in fact neo-fascists of the worst sort—dismissing ends and means as obsolescent and irrelevent.

A young girl in Vancouver Friday night at a public meeting asked me: "Why do we just talk and talk? How can we stop the corporations that make so much money out of the war?"

There was a time when I felt a trifle self-conscious, in our chrome and glass jungle of modern society, to speak of moral values or to urge a frank, naked confrontation with ethics—it was so "square," so out of keeping with the present tempo of thought. But as the militarists and politicians multiply their barbarous agendas for beefing up the slaughter, I find no need for apology. Herman Kahn has taught me to think about the unthinkable by telling me that American national interest is an ultimate goal—and to me that is a moral abomination. We have now come to the point where so-called political "realists" insist that moral considerations are the cause for the shortcomings of American policy. Dr. Hans Morgenthau has gone so far as to say that the detractors of the president's policy are guilty of moral perversion. This is indeed the pot calling the kettle black.

In what context do we listen to such words? North America is an island of material prosperity unmatched anywhere else on this wretched planet. How easy it is in a Las Vegas and Hollywood tinsel paradise to yield to an ethic of moral relativity, of live and let live, which quiets the conscience of the privileged, the educated white Americans who follow its tranquilizing dictates. Our commentators and columnists, and even our clergy speak of "orderly, gradual change" by which they mean no change at all. All they really want is to be safely insulated against the horror of the world in which we live.

I come here tonight to say that by any of the surviving historic ethics I have discovered—Christian, Jewish, Buddhist, humanist—there is one moral principle that seems universal and objectively grounded: the idea of equality. It suggests that every person has a right to be recognized as a moral agent capable of living his own life. When, by the sheer superiority of the nation's military power over other people, we deny them that right, we commit an immoral act.

It is this conviction which motivates my frank and total resistance to my government's war policy in Vietnam. When a man is denied that equality, that right to be a moral agent, he has a right and obligation to resist the arrogance of power exercised over him. The symbolic myth of David and Goliath has not survived without reason.

Possibly the poet says it better than the moral philosopher. I recall the words of our California poet, the late Robinson Jeffers:

> Unhappy country, what wings you have . . .
> Weep, it is frequent in human affairs, weep for the terrible
>   magnificence of the means . . . the ridiculous incompetence
>   of the reasons, the bloody and shabby pathos of the results.

Before we can understand our role as citizens in today's world it is essential that we face the many forms of self-deception and hypocrisy which mask our actions, and I am speaking of my own country specifically. The growing lack of concern for truth mounts ever higher as the months pass. The lying is more presumptuous and daring. I think of Arthur Schlesinger's characterizing American policies in 1954 as "part of our general program of international goodwill." Would any uninstructed reader know that those bland and idealistic words are an effort to rationalize and escape the fact that Americans have no right to be in Vietnam, that the Vietnamese have a centuries-old passion for freedom and independence, that we have been backing a despotic regime in the South, and that we Americans insist that any measures are justified to prevent a so-called Communist take-over there?

The Third Reich's legacy of Mr. Goebbel's big lie appears almost daily in our press as President Johnson denies that Hanoi has ever responded to his overtures to sit before a conference table. With solemn countenance Secretary Dean Rusk denies our violation of the Christmas and Tet truces.

Malcolm Browne, for five years an AP correspondent in Vietnam, in your *Vancouver Sun* gives the truth and not the lie about U.S. actions in that unhappy country, and blames Congress and our average citizens for being ignoramuses with respect to Asia. To spend a million dollars an hour on this, which my country does, and be so ignorant about the issues involved is stupidity raised to the Nth power, as well as immorality equal to that of Ghengis Khan. My fellow citizens grow fat and affluent as they remain ignorant—content to have it so.

This self-deception, this standing morality on its head has been going on for a long time—long before Vietnam was the defoliated and blasted wasteland we have made it today. If I were a historian and had the time, I would remind you of Woodrow Wilson in 1902 telling the Latin Americans that it is America's "peculiar duty to teach colonial peoples order and self-control, the drill and habit of law and obedience." I would tell you of American missionaries in the 1840s describing the Opium War in China to be "a result of a great design of Providence to make the wickedness of men subserve his purposes of mercy toward China and break through her wall of exclusion, thus bringing the empire into more immediate contact with Western and Christian nations."

I am not a historian, and we do not have the time. But the dehumanization of my fellow citizens south of your border has had a long history. I know you are aware of it, and are aware that there have been resisters. Abraham Lincoln, when a freshman congressman, steadfastly refused to sanction the Mexican War at the peril of political suicide. There have sometimes been moral men in power, and they have changed history, and they have won mass support, but it has taken almost superhuman striving—and it still does, at this tragic hour in the nuclear age.

Let me assert as clearly as possible that I am not saying that America is worse than all other countries. Our evil consists of believing that we are better than others, that we have a moral right to be teacher and policeman to other nations. And it also consists in the fact that we could be much better than we are, that we could transform this self-image into reality if we put our minds to it. I still believe this, for I think my country has made great contributions to the world.

This seminar gathering is an occasion to mention, though obviously not to explore in detail, the fact that our demoralization has been a long time growing. The material well-being of a large section of our population in the United States has become our highest priority, and a great majority of our people do not see how fully absorbed they are with its demands, its increasing cry for gain, and the apotheosis of the sixteen-hour-a-day consumer. Industrial capitalism—rarely so named—has become our new religion, and before its altar all else is sacrificed whenever the high priests chant their petitions with solemn regularity.

Only the youth, especially the students and the Negro young men and women of the many ghettos, north and south, have insisted upon rejecting the holy faith of wealth at any price. They have taken the ideals, the moral values of freedom, equality, brotherhood, and peace with a terrible seriousness and have acted upon them. They are angry rather than cynical at this worship of opulence in the midst of a starving world. They, the youth, first said no to the war in Vietnam, and they are still saying it—in a great crescendo of resistance that mounts daily, at times with dignity, and at times with understandable discourtesy for the men in striped pants or encrusted with many medals, because these young people insist that they must be heard. They have a world at stake— and their own lives at stake. If their parents and congressmen cannot distinguish between Mammon, God, and Caesar, they can and they will.

These young people are now doing more than their share—so that I feel, with the late A. J. Muste, that the least we ancients can do is to support them and help to share the burden, because it must be borne if we are to live.

Young people in my country, as you doubtless know well, are standing quietly in peace vigils day after day (along with older citizens of similar conscience) carrying signs that call for an end of the killing. They are sitting in at doorways of the diabolical factories where napalm is manufactured, and at dockside where munitions and planes are shipped to Vietnam. They carry signs reading "Thou Shalt Not Kill" down the aisles of New York cathedrals during Mass. They will be heard. The Sunday New York Times recently carried the largest political protest advertisement (over two pages) and most costly in the history of the paper, with more than sixty-six hundred signatures of teachers and professors demanding an end to the war. They are determined that children and youth shall not be the ignoramuses their parents are.

The youthful clergy in growing numbers are learning from these young people, these students, who have moved from the campuses to the streets. Nearly three thousand clergy and lay leaders, mostly young men, marched around the White House in early February. They came from over forty states, men and women of all faiths. They are moral citizens, and they issued a declaration that shows that the protests of the youth are not unheard in the carpeted and quiet sanctuaries of the church and synagogue.

In their declaration in Washington they insisted that Congress cease offering only military answers to political and ethical questions. They called for an end to a spurious kind of patriotism that ignores the historic tradition of dissent and that ignores criticism of a national policy which offends the nostrils of decent men. They declared that the war in Vietnam is frustrating the timid, modest war against poverty in America's cities and countryside, the war against racism and ill health among the masses of our people. The delegates also called for an end to the draft, to the new mercenary army we now have, half a million strong, in Vietnam and surrounding theaters of action. They called for an end to the clergy's traditional exemption from the draft, and for seminars between plain citizens and congressmen, to help them discover those facts of economics and morality that have been crushed as the behemoth of the Pentagon took over the shaping of American policy.

Professor Douglas Dowd of Cornell, now Fulbright professor on loan to the University of Bologna, Italy, is right when he says of these young people who resist the war so bravely and boldly: "They see, if they cannot always explain, a society that—lacking the guts even to face it—pursues the possession of things as though it were the godhead, or the holy grail." These young people, black and white, have in recent years opened our country's eyes to the widespread poverty and the obscenity of warfare from the air and on the ground that with diabolical technology destroys everything before it—hell bent for Armageddon.

It has been the young people of America who have rejected the insane pageant of politics, which John Emmet Hughes calls so rightly, "the miracle play about the unique United States, virginal and vulnerable, bravely struggling to save its purity from a seductive world and rapacious foe." The shabby charade is not impressing the students of America, and their informed and searching analysis is becoming contagious, I am glad to say, with many of their elders. And this is our hope: that there will be a great enlightenment of the masses of our people before the brutalization of which I speak runs its fatal course to global incineration.

I find in every state I visit, on every campus, new sophistication in spite of the massive propaganda of government and public media. I find new voices asking the necessary questions.

Is it moral to go to the other side of the world to build vast walls of containment, armed bases, military pacts, economic blockades around the two largest nations of the world? Is it moral to squander nearly a trillion dollars worth of our resources on military expenditures while our productive industries stagnate or decline? Is it moral to abandon the American Revolution, which led the world for a century, and now to proscribe all revolutions lest they turn Communist? Is it moral to maneuver Congress again and again to write blank checks for the administration to make war in any degree it chooses? Is it moral to forbid all revolutions—in Cuba, in Santo Domingo, in Brazil, in Vietnam—and to break international covenants and circumvent the United Nations because we possess the military thunderbolts to do so?

The young people are saying no to these questions. So are others, including some of the military now in retirement. For example, you may have seen the words of General David M. Shoup, U.S. Marine Corps, retired, recently spoken at Pierce College, Los Angeles, and reprinted in the *Congressional Record*: "I don't think the whole of Southeast Asia, as related to the present and future safety and freedom of this country, is worth the life and limb of a single American. I believe," continued the General, "that if we had kept our dirty, bloody, dollar-crooked fingers out of the business of these nations so full of depressed, exploited people, they would arrive at a solution of their own. That is what they designed and want. That is what they fight and work for. And if, unfortunately, their revolution must be the violent type because the 'haves' refuse to share with the 'have nots' by any peaceful method, at least what they get will be their own, and not the American style, which they don't want and above all don't want crammed down their throats by Americans." The clergy, I am glad to say, have no monopoly on moral indignation. It is good to hear such words spoken by a general, as well as by students on campus after campus of North America. Not every voice has yielded to the blight of silence.

Some among you may boggle at the bluntness of speech of General Shoup as you may boggle at the four-letter words of some of the student generation today, both of whom are trying to awaken the submerging conscience of the masses of voters in our land. Let me say candidly that I prefer such Anglo-Saxon bluntness to the ambiguities and sophistries of the establishment and all of its sycophants in press and radio and film. George Orwell once commented on the tendency of military men and politicians to use polysyllabic Latin words to cover obscene realities. I think of that as I read of the credibility gap, escalation, pacification, and the calculations of national security. I prefer the honest knavery of the dictator, the blood-thirsty violence of a Cromwell about to purge a king and crying, "If you do God's will you can't be too particular." The students and the rest of us know where we are with such men; they are easier to refute than such slippery rhetoricians as Herman Kahn and Arthur Schlesinger.

For two days now you have been discussing what can be done. The question is even being asked in the highest chambers in Washington. There is a somewhat acrimonious conversation going on between President Johnson and Senator Robert F. Kennedy, who seems to have recently discovered Senators Morse, Fulbright, Gruening, McGovern, and Hatfield. It is of great interest to me that Senator Kennedy, who has never hinted that he wishes to bow out of politics, finds it expedient at this time to take issue with the leader of his party. Does he hear something else than does Dr. Gallup when he puts his ear to the ground? Where do the rumblings in the earth come from that make a Kennedy to bridle at the president's intransigence? From all of us who will not keep quiet as flaming gasoline spills onto the hapless women and children of the Mekong delta and Hanoi; from the footsteps of my own church's men and women in Los Angeles who keep a vigil every Wednesday noon before the Federal Building. Do not tell me Robert Kennedy failed to see the two-page advertisement I referred to in last Sunday's New York Times demanding peace now—the largest of its kind in the history of the newspaper.

I think the senator has discovered the political fact that we cannot win the war militarily in Vietnam, that massive power alone cannot bring victory. It can kill—it cannot win. But of these speculations I do not wish to speak further now. Rather, I should like to do what every one of us must do: come to his own private conclusion about the solution to be found for ending this fearful and immoral carnage. May I speak of my own conviction, well aware that in this audience are many who have other answers, viable ones held in good conscience? It is not enough to express one's sense of outrage and anger at the moral shambles in which America finds itself today in Vietnam. What does one propose?

I propose American withdrawal from all of Vietnam—unilaterally and now. I agree with Professor Howard Zinn of Boston University, in his just published book *Vietnam: The Logic of Withdrawal*, that this is not a war of freedom, that the Ky regime has no claim to our allegiance or support. Our wholesale destructiveness in that country is supported by no persuasive reasons for remaining. The imperative is clear: we must withdraw. Defeating the Viet Cong will not prevent Communist expansion throughout Asia nor the rest of the world. The roots of Communist success are indeed indigenous.

Communism is primarily an ideological force, where German nazism was a military one. Munich analogy is sheer absurdity. "The domino theory," as Professor Zinn so well says, "does not explain Cuba's communism. Burma, unprotected by the United States, and sharing a thousand-mile border with China, is independent and at peace, while Thailand and Vietnam, under our 'protection' are in turmoil."

I shall not develop tonight the oft-presented thesis that withdrawal would cause fearful loss of prestige and face for America. Mr. George Kennan, testifying last year before the Senate Foreign Relations Committee, told Senator Hickenlooper: "Withdrawal would be a six-months sensation, but we would survive it in the end."

New York Times reporter E. W. Kenworthy, in the summer of 1965, found that many of the silent senators in our Congress felt that America should never have gone to Vietnam in the first place and wished our country could get out. Billions of dollars have been spent, thousands of lives have been lost, the moral respect of our long-time allies around the world has been lost, but we "must not lose face"!

I agree with Dr. Zinn and many other Americans that there is a kind of prestige that our nation should not worry about losing, that which is attached to sheer power, to victory by force of arms, devoid of moral content. Which is more terrible? To have people in the world say that the United States withdrew from an untenable situation, or to have it said, as is now being said everywhere, that the United States is acting foolishly and immorally in Vietnam? There is need to lose a certain amount of face and to find a new face resembling man—not the devil.

I know that there are those who propose partial withdrawal to en-
claves in Vietnam. Kennan, Gavin, and Morgenthau all advocate this
position; but the assumption behind it is unconvincing, indeed: that
America would salvage a fraction of prestige, giving us time to negotiate
our way home. It is too late for such maneuvers. We are told that after
Diem's assassination in November 1963, Hanoi was willing to discuss
a coalition, a neutralist government in South Vietnam. But Secretary Dean
Rusk rejected a French proposal, you will remember, for a neutral,
independent South Vietnam, and in July of that year the United States
rejected a suggestion by U Thant, accepted by France, the Soviet Union,
Peking, and Hanoi, to reconvene the Geneva Conference.

President Johnson, I believe, does not wish to negotiate at a bargaining table now because he knows that the time has past, that the political struggle is lost already. So five thousand more U.S. soldiers must
die in 1967. Seven thousand, five hundred have already perished there.
Many more thousands of civilians in that land must perish, and the land
be scorched to utter desolation by fire and chemicals. The Viet Cong
in the South and their friends in the North now feel they have sacrificed too much since those days of rejected offers in 1963 and 1964
to settle for anything less than a South Vietnam in which the National
Liberation Front plays the major role and from which American troops
have completely withdrawn.

The United States, as she departs, could and probably should take
with her those Saigon government officials and military officers who fear
for their lives when the new government comes in. These people could
be resettled elsewhere, though I hope not in California. "It is not our
obligation," as Dr. Zinn so well says, "to go around the world protecting
semi-feudal dictatorships from the wrath of revolutionaries." We have
a sorry record indeed of not developing political freedom in those parts
of the world under our protection, which we call the free world—Latin
America, Spain, the Congo, Greece, South Korea—to mention but a few.

The best way we could demonstrate a genuine concern for political liberty and economic security would be to withdraw from Vietnam
militarily and send, instead, billions of dollars now earmarked for death,
and leave them to be invested by a new people's government of a united
Vietnam. Then "face" could truly be saved for the United States. Such
withdrawal would be neither abdication of responsibility nor isolation-
ism; it would be economic and cultural internationalism—long overdue
from a nation once honored as humanitarian.

The Johnson government has not gained prestige by its war policies. If President Johnson went on national television, after announcing
in advance he was going to make a major policy speech, he could proclaim his intention to withdraw American military forces from Vietnam,
giving the logical reasons for such withdrawal. I believe (as does Dr.

Zinn) that the American people would unite behind his action. Editorials would support, commerce and industry would support him. The angry cries of fanatics would be drowned in a vast wave of relief. If Mr. Johnson does not do this, some other president will, or we shall enter into the final valley of death from which there is no return.

Do you believe this to be fantasy? I would remind you that Lyndon Baines Johnson was overwhelmingly elected because of his rejection of Senator Goldwater's slogans of escalation of the war. The constituency for peace remains, and is even larger today. There is a growing generation of youth who would rather fill the jails in rebellion against this folly in Vietnam than fill graves in veterans' cemeteries. Such an action as is proposed by many today—of immediate and unilateral withdrawal of our forces—takes immense courage, but that is what leadership means. The war can be ended with honor, and the slaughter can be stopped. You and I can play our part to give our leaders in Canada and the United States support to advocate such action by the Washington administration.

We do not have to consent longer to the brutalization of the soul of man anywhere. There are great alternatives of peace and equality for all men. They can and must be undertaken—now.

The Colossus of the North
The United States in Latin America Today
May 21, 1967

*While this sermon is primarily not a book review address it does refer exten-
sively to The Great Fear in Latin America by John Gerassi. The factual
material, quite aside from the author's strong personal judgments, is invalu-
able for a better understanding of the crisis in South America today.*—SHF

Professor Arnold Toynbee wrote in the *London Observer* April 23:

America stands at the parting of the ways and her choice between the
alternatives that confront her will be momentous, not only for America herself, but for the whole human race.

. . . There are pessimists who foresee the so-called free world being transformed step by step into the American counterpart of the Roman Empire. The power basis of the Roman Empire was an alliance
between the Roman "Establishment" armed with invincible Roman
military manpower and the rich minority in the foreign countries that
had been conquered by Roman arms. In World War II terms the Roman accomplices were Quislings. They cooperated with the Roman nobility and Roman business corporations in exploiting the peoples of
the Mediterranean basin. American pessimists see a similar coalition
between American business corporations and a privileged minority in
those tracts of Asia, Africa, and Latin America over which the American corporations have spread their tentacles.

If you desire to follow the thinking of Professor Toynbee further,
you will find the entire story in the Opinion Section of the *Los Angeles
Times* for April 23.

I believe that today the nations of Latin America illustrate this thesis
of Toynbee's better than any other example in the world. We have been

so understandably preoccupied in recent years with the war in Vietnam that most of us have not followed the developing crisis in South America. But the truth is that we cannot afford thus to narrow our vision of the world scene, however compelling may be the reasons to do so. It is my unhappy feeling that new active Vietnams are apt to emerge this very year in Latin American countries. We cannot afford to be unprepared for such explosive developments.

If I were to give this sermon a text it would not be from Fidel Castro or Chairman Mao, but from the late President John F. Kennedy who said: "Those who make peaceful revolution impossible will make violent revolution inevitable." The similarity between that sentiment and many of the words of Che Guevara of Cuba may have helped to speed the death of Mr. Kennedy.

Let us refer to another president, this one living and in power, President Eduardo Frei of Chile, writing in the North American magazine *Foreign Affairs* for April of this year. He says:

> The Latin American Revolution has clearly defined objectives: the participation of the people in the government and the destruction of oligarchies, the redistribution of the land and the ending of feudal or semi-feudal regimes in the countryside, the securing of equal access to cultural and educational facilities and wealth, thus putting an end to inherited privilege and artificial class divisions. A main objective of the revolution also is to secure economic development, coupled with fair distribution of the products and the utilization of international capital for the benefit of the national economy.

I would remind you that President Frei wrote this article to help express his ideas about the Alliance for Progress just before the summit meeting at Punta del Este. He writes as a non-Marxist nationalist. Yet even from this non-Communist position President Frei, in the statements on the purposes of the Latin American Revolution, is tabulating goals that our American government, our press, and much of the academic community call "Communist-line ideas." Unless we Americans can move beyond this muddled logic, there can be no understanding of the titanic forces operating for change in Latin America today. We North Americans are conditioned daily to think of world affairs in cold war concepts: the United States versus the Soviet Union, and capitalism versus communism. But this is not the way the rest of the world looks at world affairs, even if our newsmen and commentators say it is; they are buttering their own American bread and present their thoughts in the tattered clichés familiar to their readers or viewers. But President Frei tells us that the peoples of South America see world affairs as a struggle between the rich and the poor, the powerful who are few and the weak who are many. He notes that the Soviet Union grows ever more power-ful and prosperous; the poor nations identify with her less and less. Professor Marshal Windmiller of San Francisco State College is an ex-pert in this field who also observes that this decreasing prestige of the Soviet Union among the poor nations of the world comes from her preoccupation with peace rather than with revolutionary justice. It is a judgment we all need to ponder.

This point must be understood, whether we agree or not with the primacy of revolutionary justice over peacemaking in an atomic age. It is imperative that we listen to Premier Fidel Castro when he tells the university students of Cuba: "Let us condemn the imperialist aggression against Vietnam, but let us also condemn, starting right now, the future Vietnams in Latin America . . . the Venezuelan President Leoni, who will be the Premier Ky of tomorrow."

Whether one listens to a Latin American democratic President Frei of Chile or a radical Fidel Castro of Cuba, he can hear the insistent demand for economic and social justice in Latin America now. I am not asking that you choose either nationalism or communism as the ultimate answer in Latin America, but rather that you and I know well the urgency of the demand by all responsible popular leadership south of this country; for speedy change to remedy intolerable poverty, op-pression, and injustice. As for the protests of our next-door neighbors and friends about the "red menace," which you will doubtless hear, they can be answered with the cutting words of Dr. Edgar Friedenberg in the current issue of *Look* magazine:

> People in this country certainly fear and hate what they have learned to respond to as "Communism," but they don't know a damn thing about Communism. It seems to threaten their claim to status. It im-plies a loss of virility and of small bits of status in a competitive society. It is this that is feared, not a loss of real freedom. There are very few people among the strong anti-Communists who prize freedom or re-spect other people's privacy.

I mention Freidenberg's comments because I am now well persuaded that the John Birch Society and similar militant anti-Communists know the goals of the Latin American revolution that Frei and Castro spell out so clearly; they know them better than many liberals; they simply reject them. They have no feeling of identification with the exploited peoples of Bolivia or Peru or Guatemala. In fact, I feel that they have no sense of human identification with the poor and rejected citizens of nearby Pacoima, Venice, Watts, or east Los Angeles.

I wish now to turn your attention to a book which I strongly recommend for reading as soon as possible. I refer to John Gerassi's

The Great Fear in Latin America. . . . I am not necessarily supporting all of the solutions listed in his concluding chapter, "A Policy of Re-Conquest," though they are excellent, advanced, and urgent proposals and deserve very careful study. What I plead for this morning, as we are so preoccupied with Vietnam, Israel-Egypt, and Kashmir-Pakistan conflicts, is a study of John Gerassi's facts, thousands of them, and most of them unfamiliar to us.

Let me read a few paragraphs from this book whose author was formerly the Latin American correspondent for *Time* magazine, later editor of *Newsweek*, and is now teaching at Columbia University.

> Latin America's social and economic structure is decadent, corrupt, immoral, and generally unsalvageable.

> That a change is coming is obvious. That it will come about through revolution is certain. That revolution entails the possibility of violence is unavoidable. What remains an enigma is: Who will lead the revolution?

> The choices are not enigmatic—or, at least, should not be.

> No real social change can be effected by what we in the United States are too readily in the habit of calling—erroneously—Latin America's "democratic forces." It is not by accident, that the continent's modern-minded empiricists refer to political crooks, phony reformists, and "enlightened" oligarchs suddenly addicted to the preachings of the Alliance for Progress as just "another bunch of democrats."

> Nor can the change in structure be brought about by those who emulate us, no matter how hard we try to convince ourselves that they can. Latin America's history is not our history, its inheritance not our inheritance, its concepts not our concepts.

The United States ruling class, the "Colossus of the North," has worked out a high-sounding, reform-demanding Alliance for Progress whose small black print prohibits true reforms and whose much-ballyhooed loans and grants rarely filter down to the needy. This American industrial elite has adopted a policy of branding as "Communists" all reformers who carry out exactly what we claim we want to achieve through the alliance. Sooner or later, the revolutionary leaders of Latin America will lead their people to claim that which is denied them: their inalienable rights. To secure these rights they will convert Latin America into an area belonging to Latin Americans, by the gun if necessary. Today, it belongs to foreigners, mostly to citizens or companies of the United States. The great movement that has already begun to form to secure Latin America for its own citi-

zens will be what John Gerassi calls "the Reconquest of Latin America."
Its overpowering assault is inevitable!

Mr. Gerassi writes:

> Our current Latin American policy makes sense if, and only if, we
> are prepared to wage—and win—the Third World War before the full
> strength of that assault comes down. If so, the immediate advantages
> gained—and there are many—are well worth the dirty names we are
> called (and the occasional premature revolts). If not, it is a policy of
> suicidal shortsightedness, a policy of disaster. Our own rights will never
> survive a rebellious Latin America united against us.

I can assure you that Mr. Gerassi does not want a Third World
War, as you will realize when you read his book. He is simply saying
we had better face the realistic alternatives in the southern hemisphere.
Let us in our fresh look at these nations remember that

> Latin America is bigger and potentially richer than we are. Its borders
> begin at the Rio Grande and end at the South Pole, more than ten
> thousand land miles away. It is made up of 20 sovereign states of French,
> Spanish, or Portuguese origin. These 20, according to very optimistic
> examples, have an average yearly per capita income of $253. In Peru,
> for example, more than half the people live outside the money econ-
> omy altogether, bartering whatever goods they manage to grow. Of the
> other half, 80 percent earn $53 a year, while 100 families own 90
> percent of the native (as opposed to foreign) wealth or $1,334,000,000.
>
> In Lima, the capital, whose colonial mansions enveloped by ornate
> wooden balconies help make it one of the most beautiful cities in the
> world, half of 1.3 million inhabitants live in rat-infested slums. One,
> called El Monton, is built around, over, and in the city dump. There,
> when I visited it, naked children, some too young to know how to
> walk, competed with pigs for a few bits of food scraps accidentally
> discarded by the garbage men.
>
> In Chile, unemployment stays doggedly above 17 percent. One-
> third of the 2,000,000 people that live in Santiago, the capital, are
> crowded in squatters' huts made of earth or stray planks, with no wa-
> ter, no electricity, no transportation facilities, no municipal garbage
> disposal system, and no medical attention. One of these slum areas
> is in the dead center of town, a dime's throw from the fashionable
> Crillon Hotel.
>
> Such scenes are repeated over and over in every Latin American
> country. Millions of people barely subsist, while occasional oligarchs
> exhibit a wealth superior to those who in our country can afford yachts,
> private planes, and houses in Florida, Virginia, and Hyannis Port. Latin
> American oligarchs manipulate their respective countries' governments
> to their advantage. To them, the plight of the masses is just "so much

sentimental hogwash," as they themselves put it, and you and I foolish bleeding hearts to care.

[In] Brazil's Northeast, where men die of old age at twenty-eight, parents feel fortunate when they are able to sell their children into slavery. "My daughter may be used as a prostitute and my son will probably spend the rest of his life working very hard and very long on a Sao Paolo plantation," one father told Mr. Gerassi. When he asked the man why he had sold his two children, [the man] replied, "At least they will eat. My other six children were not so fortunate. They stayed here, and they died."

Why is the United States to blame, if it is, for such conditions? Or more important for our sakes, why must the revolutionaries who try to change conditions hold us directly responsible? One reason is easy for the traveler to notice, it is envy—not of what the United States may be like, but of the luxury United States companies in Latin America create. As one Buenos Aires slum resident said: "When I go to el centro, I see many pretty things, things I want so badly to take home to my wife. But I can never afford them. I will never be able to afford them. They are all United States products."

If our press misrepresents the facts in Latin America, if our economic policies disregard Latin America's needs, if our political policies support Latin America's oligarchs bent on profiting from such disregard, then perhaps we can understand why Latin Americans hate us and are determined to overthrow the present order of things.

If our interest is the interest of all of us, if we want to survive with our freedoms and our dignity, if we are concerned more with our unalienable rights—life, liberty, and the pursuit of happiness—than with the extra billions of dollars of a few selfish men, then we must realize that sooner or later the peoples of Latin America will demand the very same rights.

That time has come. They are demanding. Soon they will take. And they will be fully justified in doing so. As Jefferson said, "it is the right of the people to alter or abolish" that which denies them their unalienable rights.

For three quarters of a century the United States has attempted to secure economic and semi-political hegemony over the Latin American nations under many guises. It has been an imperial dream which never really could find acceptance among the liberty-cherishing and proud people of South America. The latest U.S. effort of course has been the Organization of American States (OAS). Witnesses of Punta del Este last month reported they knew that they were watching the beginning of the end of a great dream by the Colossus of the North. The conflict of interests between the United States and the governments of the twenty states of OAS was laid naked to the public eye. For years Washington hoped to lend the appearance of an international consensus to unilateral United States manipulation. Six years ago the U.S. could literally buy the vote of Duvalier of Haiti in order to get a majority for the expulsion of Cuba. By this maneuver the OAS vote transformed a private American vendetta with Castro into what seemed like a continentwide repudiation of the Cuban premier. In 1954 our CIA, as we all know, moved in against President Arbenz of Guatemala and seven years later masterminded the miserable fiasco at the Bay of Pigs in Cuba. Both actions were undertaken with consultation or assistance of the OAS. Many millions of Latin Americans have during these years had their eyes opened to the real purposes of the OAS, and they are repudiating them as the many explanatory rebellions against shaky regimes testify almost daily. The growth of guerrilla movements in Bolivia, Peru, Brazil, Venezuela, and Guatemala (to mention the most familiar) indicate that in these countries there are really two governments existing. New billions of dollars promised in economic aid from the U.S. through the Alliance for Progress, channeled through the OAS funnel, are now seen for what they have always been: an effort to control the markets of South America and the ruling elites benefiting from the commerce in those markets.

But nothing can be done now to save the shaky status quo in Latin America. It is doomed morally, economically, and politically. These countries are determined to change the power faces, as President Frei said so clearly in the article quoted earlier in this sermon. They are determined to be free, to be self-respecting and self-sufficient. If present rulers cannot achieve these ends, new ones will be found, not in the distant future, but as the immediate months pass. They will do it alone, if need be, as did China and Cuba. There will be misery and bloodshed and torture. There will be civil war and probably American intervention. It is my conviction, as I read the dispatches and the books and listen to the newscasts and talk with delegates at conferences who come from these nations, that nothing can stop the new Algerias of the Latin countries, the new Vietnams. The Colossus of the North must go.

You and I have enormous responsibilities. It is our country that tries to keep ancient and feudal powers in control. It is our tax money and our corporate investments there that delay the eventual freedom of these people, and thus will soon add to the casualties of Latin Americans and also our own young men, who will be sent there to prevent the victory of the exploited and oppressed, as is now done in Vietnam.

Two weeks ago today I sat in the living room of Rev. John Morgan of our Toronto Unitarian Church and listened to his report on a month's visit in Cuba from which he had returned a few hours earlier. The evidence makes it clear that the revolutions are but started that will shake the hemisphere for years to come. The great Liberator, Simon Bolivar, was right about American intervention, and his successors understand it well. Imperialism destroys itself. It gives rise to national bourgeois governments, local entrepreneurs so well described by Arnold Toynbee in the lecture we began with today as "affluent Quislings." The national bourgeoisie enjoying the privileges of the new Roman Empire is the first step in the revolution, and only that, be it long or short, mild or violent. Let none of us here today, as we conclude this discussion, ever forget that the Marines of the United States burned one town in Nicaragua twenty-six times to get the rebel leaders. The same is a murderous but authentic parable. The clock cannot be turned back. The only questions is how fast it will move ahead.

Does it make any difference what you and I think or do? I think it does. Having listened to Mr. Saul Alinsky in Denver and to Rev. John Morgan in Toronto, and having read John Gerassi, I am persuaded that citizens here, if well informed and courageous, can lessen the agony of the Latin American revolutions. We can be a part of a public force exposing the true character of our American political and corporate establishments and insisting upon the end of such imperial operations as the OAS and the Alliance for Progress and the CIA. We can resist sending military aid to corrupt establishments in Brazil and Colombia and the other consenting puppet regimes. We can resist sending our own sons to die in new Vietnams south of the border. We can disabuse our children of the fantastic fictions about the Monroe Doctrine, which is today, as it always has been, but gilded rhetoric for American colonialism. We can see to it that our people learn the lesson of President Vargas's suicide in Brazil and remember his words, found beside his body: "The United States controls our economy." The truth is becoming clearer every day.

NBC showed a film a year ago about the sale of American napalm to the Peruvian government to scorch an entire mountain in efforts to destroy the guerrilla movement hiding there. You and I are people who believe that the cruelty of social struggle can be shortened and mitigated by power pressures on an aggressive government by popular protest and action. I would beg you to remember the efforts of Frenchmen a few short years ago to end their government's policies in Algeria, efforts which greatly aided the independence forces there to gain eventual freedom from long colonial rule. I would remind you of the magnificent efforts of the National Liberation Front in Vietnam and of dissident Buddhists and of other rebels in sectors of the Saigon government, efforts to settle the fearful civil strife there. It will probably be, as one Unitarian minister freshly returned from South Vietnam told me in Denver, a coup d'etat by these anti-Premier Ky groups that will sooner or later give President Johnson the excuse to call the whole thing off and come home. *Newsweek*, on April 9 in its Periscope predictions column, prophesied that this unilateral withdrawal will come within twenty-four months. I mention this, not as a diversion, but to say that every mobilization, every Vietnam Summer campaign, every demand by you and me upon our congressmen that we redraft our foreign policy means a shortening of slaughter and further devastation of a foreign people's homeland. So in Latin America. You and I can help indigenous Latin American power to become a reality. If you have stock in companies heavily invested in South American countries, you can vote that stock for withdrawal from such markets. If you have not, you can be a part of a growing resistance, moral and political, to policies that can no longer tolerate the light of public exposure without consequences of great significance.

We have great tasks to perform, and the time is now. The work of Bolivar is far from finished. The courage of Jefferson can be contagious. The years before us will be difficult and costly, but not without immense rewards if we truly cherish the brotherhood of all mankind.

Toward Sanity in the Israeli-Arab Struggle
What Have We Learned in the Past Four Months?
October 8, 1967

Dr. Robert McAfee Brown, Professor of Religion at Stanford University, a few days ago said: "The church will lose tremendously in numbers in the next few years as it takes specific stands on specific issues . . . and this may be its salvation. Those who remain will become the cutting edge in the community, a real creative minority."

I am sure that Dr. Brown is right about the losses, and I hope he is right in his prophecy that the survivors will be a creative minority. We Unitarians have known for years that if a church or temple really takes a position on controversial social issues, it will alienate some people but will usually gain new friends and members. I believe that we have, in hundreds of our Unitarian societies, become a far more creative minority than we used to be. But we have a long way to go before we can do any boasting about it.

Never in my ministry has there been greater need for courage and honesty than in the discussion of the continuing Israeli-Arab conflict. A number of our churches, according to newsletters received from around the country, are undertaking dialogues on the subject. If any of you think me tardy in my presentation of my views, it is only because of a three-month vacation that delayed the study I felt was essential before coming to you. It is inevitable that some of you will take issue with what is said today, whatever it is. This is quite predictable on a matter that involves deep emotions, personal experiences that go back many years, and differing convictions regarding the issue of Israel as a national state in today's world or the merits of Zionism as a solution. Some may feel that there is little to be gained by a presentation of so controversial a subject. I cannot agree. The churches have, for too long, by-passed the hard questions disturbing mankind. I would far rather have some of you reject my own conclusions out-of-hand than feel that it was too difficult a matter to bring into a Unitarian pulpit. During the past twenty years, I have spoken and had guests speak here on Jewish problems, on anti-Semitism, on the place of the Arab (Christian and Moslem) in history and in today's world. Jews and Arabs have been equally welcome here, and will continue to be so as long as I serve as your minister. Otherwise, our reason for existing as a radical church evaporates. The attempt to speak the truth in love and with candor is no idle cliché; it is our most cherished principle, as near a creed as we ever come.

The very talented and humane Ilya Ehrenburg of the Soviet Union, who died a few weeks ago, a man I was privileged to meet several times over the years, wrote in his final memoir:

> When travelling in America I toured the Southern states, in 1946, one year after the collapse of German racism. I saw racism in another form. The whites have too long insulted national and human dignity in America, in Africa and in Asia; there has been an accumulation of hatred and accounts have been settled in the same currency. I understand now that one must see the world as it really is and not mistake one's wishes for reality. Naturally, I continue to think that solidarity among men will overcome intolerance, racial and national arrogance, and brutality, but now I know that the road is long and that strenuous efforts and great sacrifices will be required.

All of this applies directly to the crisis and continuing conflict in Palestine. Hence my own determination to contribute what I can to forthright, but I hope compassionate, discussion and advocated action. The fertile crescent from the Euphrates to the Nile is not a concern only of the Jewish and Arab peoples. We must all see this area as a possible cockpit of World War III, threatening the existence of each one of us. And if we consider all mankind to be our family, we will accept the present conflict as a claim upon our minds, and even more upon our hearts and wills.

Some of the anger and hysteria of the seven-day war is fading, I am glad to say. Some of the irrationality of normally rational men and women, Jewish and Arab alike, is passing. This is fortunate because Israel cannot forever survive by force of arms, surrounded by hostile neighbors. Great powers with their military armaments and fleets can be fickle in a world of cold and hot wars of annihilating ferocity. I believe that a reconciliation of even bitter enemies is possible, that Israel can be recognized as a state by Arab nations, that international waterways can be used by all states including Israel, that the Arab refugees can be humanely settled and not herded into cruel reservations like American Indians, and that the childish dichotomy of good guys and bad guys can be ended.

Today I need not take the time to tell an intelligent congregation that in the past four thousand years Jews and Arabs have both added enormously to human civilization. The era of clichés and stereotypes about Arabs or Jews from anyone, anywhere, must end if the furnaces of war are to be chilled. A progressive and independent Middle East is possible. This is my article of faith.

I agree with Professor Marshall Windmiller of San Francisco State College when he perceptively reminds us: "One of the difficulties we are confronted with is that the hawks in Egypt and in Israel both won over the doves in their own lands." And let me add immediately that nothing is gained by thinking a man is anti-Semitic or unsympathetic to the fearful threat the citizens of Israel felt last June when he faces the hawk-like character of the present government of Israel. The spectacle of General Dayan terrifies any advocate of peace, as does the presence of Gamal Abdel Nasser in the president's chair in Cairo. Friends in London commented more than once to me in July that it was an alarming sight to see doves in America struggling so hard for peaceful solutions in Vietnam, yet playing the hawk in defense of General Dayan in Israel. We will not make much progress in understanding a very difficult area of international affairs in the Middle East unless we can come to terms with our own moral and political schizophrenia, wherever it exists. It is the same kind of schizophrenia which our founding fathers faced in the seventeenth century in driving the Indian people into the wilderness, where they eventually were slaughtered or starved to death, or the schizophrenia of the writers of the American Constitution who left the black slaves out of the guarantees of freedom.

I have read, as have many of you, the article "Israel, A Nation Too Young to Die" by James Michener in *Look* magazine for August 8. One needs to read it to understand the state of mind of Israel citizens in recent months before the war occurred. One would be less than human not to respond to the descriptions of the fear and terror that prevailed. But this brilliant article does not fully come to grips with the great issues involved in Palestine, nor does it close the door to careful study and thought. We will get nowhere unless we start with a confession that catastrophic mistakes were made, and are still being made, in both Tel Aviv and Cairo and other Arab capitals, as well as in Great Britain, the United States, and the Soviet Union. *Let this not be forgotten.*

There is little to be gained by such a vehement rehearsal of Arab threats to destroy Israel as appears in Mr. Arnoni's overreactive article in the *Minority of One* this month, just as there is no excuse for the anti-Semitic cartoons in some Soviet publications. I referred earlier to a few articles I have recently read that present some real diversity of judgment, but are all marked by a profound effort to face the stubborn realities of the Arab-Israel conflict, and to do so without passion, without hatred, and in an effort to bring forth material almost impossible to find in the commercial press of the United States. If you are really interested in today's difficult subject, I strongly commend your reading these articles, which can be found in your library with a little effort or secured from the publishers, who are indicated. There is enough *ad hominem* argument already, enough hostility and defensiveness on all sides, and I do not wish to add further to it today or at any time. I deeply resent intellectual terrorism as I do physical terrorism. Too many ancient and modern mistakes have been made in the blood-soaked fertile crescent from Mesopotamia to Egypt for anyone to offer simplistic formulas which will settle the entire matter. Solutions can be found; there are answers, but it will take a long time to work them out, and it will call for a maximum expenditure of sanity and goodwill within Palestine and beyond its borders.

Stripped of sentiment and special pleading, the Palestine problem is the struggle of two different peoples for the same piece of land. The establishment of the state of Israel was for the Jews a return. For the Arabs it was another invasion. Dr. Fred Engreen, last Sunday at our morning discussion group, filled in many of the often-forgotten details of the four-thousand-year-old struggle, which we must know if we are to understand the depth of feeling on both sides today. He outlined for us the economic, demographic, and political reasons for this warfare-and-migration movement in the cradle of civilization. While many people do not know the history of the Palestine problem, they do know that there have been three wars in the past twenty years between Israel and the Arabs, each ending in victory for Israel. And with each victory the size of Israel has grown, as has, also, the number of Arab homeless.

I find myself agreeing with I. F. Stone when he notes that: "The conflicting ambitions of Arab and Jew in Palestine cannot be fitted into the confines of any ethical system which transcends the tribalistic. This is what confounds the benevolent outsider anxious to satisfy both peoples. The two contenders seem to live in separate universes where the simplest fact is capable of having diametrically opposite meanings." Information should help to replace passion with reason and knowledge, but this, alas, is not always the outcome of sharing information, as I have discovered in the many conversations I have had during the past four months. Yet I see no other choice but to work at the herculean task of employing the rationalist tradition in the service of universal humanistic values. Anything less will simply extend violence and hatred into the limitless future. Vast numbers of Jews, including Israelis, have concluded from the Hitler experience (to go no further back in history) that when threatened, one must kill or be killed. The Arabs concluded, from their Algerian experience with the French colons and their armies, that freedom from inferior status and grinding poverty comes only with the gun and the incendiary bomb. Both Israelis and Arabs have come to the grim judgment that only force can bring justice. And let us Americans not righteously deplore all this from some Olympian height. We, as a people and a government, did far less than we might to save German, Polish, and many other Jewish nationals from the ovens of nazism. We did almost nothing to prevent the death of Algerian Arabs from French terror and torture. It is mostly our doing that Jew and Arab are on a collision course in Palestine. I speak not only of vast imperialist forces at play of which we shall say more in a moment. I speak more of our own individual washing our hands of responsibility for Jews in the thirties in occupied Europe, and for Arabs in Algeria in the fifties.

I have been surprised that some Jews who have not used the Old Testament for polemical purposes for decades, if ever, defend the existence of the Israeli state with biblical authority, little realizing that this logic is a double-edged knife. I mention this fruitless and sterile argument only to dismiss it from the point of view of serious progressive persons of any faith. I hope that the Bible is rarely used in this pulpit for such purposes. The Old Testament, Genesis 15:18, has God saying to Abraham who came from Ur of the Chaldees: "I give this country to your posterity from the river of Egypt up to the great river Euphrates." This to fundamentalist Jews has been evidence that the Promised Land is theirs. But the fundamentalist Arab believes that the "posterity" referred to in Genesis includes the descendants of Ishmael, the son of Abraham by his concubine, Ketirah, the ancestor of all the Arabs, Christian or Moslem. I have no intention of saying that this settles anything; I simply record that both sides are convinced that their real estate deed to Palestine is ancient and valid.

Certainly I. F. Stone is right when he reminds us that the Bible is a book full of ethnocentric fury, that nowhere in it, for instance, can one find a syllable of compassion for the Canaanites whom the Jews slaughtered in taking possession of their land. For fifty years I have had to admit, as a minister, that the Bible is a book that contains many bloody tales of conquest, and that, alas, the religion of Judaism, for all of its grandeur at so many points, has too often justified fratricidal strife. Palestine, for neither Arab nor Jew, deserves to be called a land of peace.

Finally, in this biblical frame of reference, let us note that the Jews have been going in and out of Palestine for over three thousand years. They came down from the Euphrates with Abraham, they returned with Moses from Egypt and later settled the land under Joshua, they returned again after the Babylonian captivity and were dispersed in 70 A.D. when Jerusalem fell to the Romans. This twentieth-century return is the third. The Arabs feel they have a superior claim; they just stayed put. This is, alas, a costly and bitter sibling rivalry that no one can win.

And, as you well know, it continues with unabated fury. Nasser sees a war on Israel as a means to achieving Arab unity, while Dayan and Ben-Gurion see Arab disunity and backwardness as valuable to Israeli security and growth. There are far too many leaders on each side who seem quite willing to seek an apocalyptic solution at the expense of the other's existence. I am saying today that possibilities of peaceful settlement must be continuously pursued or the crossroads of Palestine will mark here mankind's plunge into the bottomless pit.

One thing I think we should have learned since June 4 is that a settlement must be found that does not demand another exile for the Jews, nor the further exile of the Palestinian Arabs, nor their denigration as second-class citizens.

Unpopular as the subject is with many Jews, in and out of Israel, the situation of the Palestinian Arab must be discussed. From the first days of the Zionist settlement the Arabs feared being driven out by Jewish migration. Neighboring Arab states were deeply agitated as possible territorial expansion by setting up of a new state. It was the intent of the British to allay Arab fears on this score that precipitated a struggle between the British and the Jews. The Balfour Declaration in 1917 promised a Jewish national home in Palestine, but it also included a sentence that said: "Nothing shall be done which may prejudice the civil and religious rights of the existing non-Jewish communities in Palestine." British White Papers in 1922, 1930, and 1939 tried to fulfill this companion pledge by steps that would have kept the Jews a permanent minority. Jewish leaders have many times recognized this legitimate Arab concern, but the present Israeli government and more ardent Zionists in many lands have chosen to forget the second half of the Balfour Declaration regarding the rights of the Arabs.

It is important, I feel, for us in America and for the peoples of Europe and the Soviet Union to recognize our possible role. If anti-Semitism can be radically diminished in these countries by you and me and our governments and neighbors, refuge in Israel will be less necessary. The more nationalistic Zionist can then drop the politics of a world in gathering of all exiled Jews, and the peril, as the Arabs must see it, of indefinite expansion of Israel can be eliminated. With Jewish migration to Israel decreasing in recent years, it is a good time to allay this Arab nightmare by ending the necessity for Jews, who mostly wish to live where they are, to think of going to a national homeland in Palestine.

The early Zionist, Herzl, in his book *The Jewish State*, dealt with working hours, housing for workers, and a possible national flag—but had no word about the resident Arabs. For so many Zionists, then and now, the Arab is an invisible man. Achad Ha-Am, the Russian Jewish philosopher, in 1891 tried to point out that Palestine was not an empty land, and that this posed problems. The great Jewish scholar, Martin Buber, and Rabbi Judah Magnes, who learned this lesson well, tried to advocate unity with the Arabs. Alas, too many chose to accept the words of Israel Zangwill about "a land without people for a people without land." (We used a great sentence from Israel Zangwill in our service today, but not *that* one). I. F. Stone tells of Max Nordau, hearing for the first time that there was an Arab population in Palestine, running to Herzl and saying: "I didn't know that, then we are committing an injustice!" On this subject there has been a painful and long moral myopia, and it continues to this hour.

General Dayan, on June 11, in a TV broadcast, "Face the Nation," was *not* in the tradition of Rabbi Magnes nor Martin Buber as the following dialogue from the telecast makes clear:

> Sydney Gruson (*New York Times*) asked: "Is there any possible way that Israel could absorb the huge number of Arabs whose territory it has gained control of now?"

> General Dayan: "Economically we can, but I think that is not in accord with our aims in the future. It would turn Israel into either a bi-national or a poly-Arab-Jewish state and we want to have a Jewish state. We want a Jewish state like the French have a French state."

I have a feeling that many Israelis and many Jews outside of Israel cringed at that flat-footed declaration with all that it implies. King Ferdinand and Queen Isabella in expelling the Jews and Moors from Spain four hundred years ago were saying they wanted Spain to be as Spanish as France was French.

Four months after the war, many writers and religious and political leaders are seeing that world Jewry faces a moral schizophrenia. In the outside world the welfare of Jews depends upon the support of a secular, nonracial, pluralistic society. Our own country has set it as an ideal and made sufficient progress to attract millions of Jews within its borders for over two centuries. The Soviet Union seemed to make strides in this direction for many of its first fifty years, with a tragic backsliding under Stalin and continued failure to press the principle under recent leaders of the Kremlin. But Israel presents us with a society in which mixed marriages cannot be legalized, in which non-Jews have a lesser status than Jews, and in which the ideal is racial and exclusionist.

To Jew and non-Jew of liberal values anywhere this is intolerable. One cannot labor for nonexclusion in America or the USSR or England,

and defend it in Israel. It seems to me that in four months many Jews should have discovered the wisdom of Uri Avnery, a Jew who migrated from Germany in 1933 at the age of ten. He became a right wing nationalist in Palestine, a member of the Irgun terrorists in the struggle against the British, and then swung far to the left and is now a champion of Arab rights, as well as Israeli rights. He even helped a decade ago to organize an Israeli committee to aid Algerian rebels.

I mention Uri Avnery as a contemporary Jew who seems to have grasped the finest insights of the Jewish prophets about the universality of human values and the terrible disasters that follow in the wake of ethnic exclusiveness by any one of any race or creed. Israel must learn this or the warfare will continue forever. So must the Arab. So must you and I, for Israel would not have been developed had there not been a Hitler, the greatest racist of this century, whose spiritual progeny live on in America and other lands in frightening numbers.

Those of you who have listened to me over the years know the importance I ascribe in world affairs to economic factors. This is true also in the case of the Israel-Arab struggle. I am thoroughly convinced, and have been for a long time, that Israel is being cruelly treated as a pawn by imperialist powers, most notably the United States and Great Britain. She is being used as a policeman of the United States in the Middle East with cynical indifference for the welfare of the peoples of Israel. I shall not develop this theme at any length today, but I do hope you follow the reading list I suggested as a start. There is a bitter contradiction here. The United States has supported with arms sales and economic aid sheiks, sultans, and other reactionary figures to prevent nationalization of oil, as in Iran, or of a canal, as in Egypt. The truth is that our government has done everything possible to discourage reform and progressive economic planning in Israel or the Arab nations. Hans J. Morganthau I believe is correct when he writes:

> The officials responsible for our Middle East policy have consistently followed a pro-Arab orientation, qualified by a consideration of the Jewish vote in this country. They have considered Israel a nuisance, which made it impossible for the United States to pursue a straightforward policy among the Arabs.

It is the Arab states that have the oil, not Israel. The *Nation* magazine of May 9, 1966, revealed that the CIA funneled money into the pro-Arab, anti-Israel organization called the American Friends of the Middle East. The hostility of the oil companies to the establishment of Israel has been documented fully in Robert Engler's *The Politics of Oil*.

President Johnson's administration was, I feel, relieved by the swift victory of the Israel forces for it made unnecessary a painful decision regarding open involvement on Israel's side. Our oil monopolies have favorites and foes among the Arab nations, and find at this moment, four months after the war, that the United Arab Republic and Syria still have governments opposed to the goals of the oil consortium. It is well to remember that in 1953 the Mussadegh government of Iran, which had tried to nationalize the oil resources of the country, was overthrown by the aid of the CIA. As a consequence, the previously existing Anglo-Iranian Oil Company was replaced with a consortium in which 40 percent interest is held by American companies. In 1958, when an anti-imperialist regime came to power in Iraq, the United States responded by sending troops into neighboring Lebanon. A storm of protest arose over this intervention thinly disguised as protection of Lebanon from the threat of an alleged attack from the new Iraqi government. The recent establishment of an anti-imperialist government in Syria led the United States to organize plans, with Israeli aid, for overthrowing this government. The story of this effort is now fairly well known. Hyman Lumer's booklet *The Middle East Crisis* develops this material in more detail than I can do this morning, and especially discusses the role of the Soviet Union in the Middle East. Whether one agrees with Mr. Lumer's Marxist presuppositions or not, the relationships of the United States with the oil interests of the Middle East need to be understood. To know reasons why our government and the corporations it represents support the Israeli government, as well as the governments of several reactionary Arab states, is to dispel illusions about any great concern of the power elite for Jewish national independence or the social and economic development of the Arab peoples.

I am not today making a programmatic presentation of what needs to be done. But I am pleading for a point of view that liberal and radical citizens, including Unitarians, Jewish, and non-Jewish, should consider. If we believe in the right of a state such as Israel to exist with freedom and security, then we must be equally dedicated to the right of all peoples to have the same chance for freedom and security: Arabs, Vietnamese, Bolivians, and all others. To pit Jew against Arab is to take a road to destruction for all mankind. The Jewish state, if it is inclusive of Jews and Palestinian Arabs and Christians and any others who wish to live there, can survive and prosper in the Middle East. It has a community of interests with the Arab peoples. This is possible only if Israel cuts its ties with Western imperialist powers that make a colony of its people. I believe this profoundly.

A modern independent Middle Eastern world, in which Israel under progressive leadership shares, is not a hopeless vision. There are radical, dedicated, socially-responsible Jews and Arabs enough to do the job. I have met some of them over the years. They are not rooted in the past, but in the promise of the future. They are not hawks of any kind.

There are no easy paths. But if further fratricidal warfare can be avoided, such leaders can and will come to power. They will not be of the school of Nasser or Dayan. There is no possible hope in a rationalized oppression of the Arab peoples by Israel. The day of the Indian reservations is over. The day of the ghetto is over. Until all are free, none are free. It is true in Vietnam, it is true in Mississippi—and it is true in Palestine.

And Who Are Our Allies?

February 1, 1981

There is nothing more devastating than people who remind us of that mythical creature the salamander, having the power to endure fires unharmed. But other salamanders live in caves and lose their sight. What kind of salamander are you? As I ask this morning, "Who are our allies?" I recognize that every religious institution has its own human salamanders —the heat-hardened, the blind in caves. This is no time to deny that some of them exist within our own Unitarian Universalist movement— else why am I here?

I wish to spend my allotted time today in discussing our allies among the Christians and Jews and other faiths with whom we need to get far better acquainted. We have been too isolated for too long. We need them, and they, I like to believe, need us, a small but historically significant sect called Unitarian Universalists.

I should like to begin with a quite personal word about my own background as a premature ecumenical, since many of you during my ten-year retirement do not know much about my religious odyssey. It is not exemplary, but it is relevant.

Like many of you, I came to Unitarianism from another denomination. I was born into a Quaker Christian family, proud of its two centuries of practicing the quite strict ethical teachings of that intrepid dissenter, George Fox of England. For demographic reasons alone, my father, his sister, and his two children joined a Methodist church in Cleveland Heights, Ohio, about 1905. I was an active, leftward leaning Methodist until 1930, when I jumped the theological fence and became a Unitarian. By that time I had gone to a Methodist college, a liberal Presbyterian theological seminary in New York, and had become an ordained Methodist minister and charged with editing a journal at Methodist headquarters for several thousand Sunday school teachers across the

279

country. Later, in the mid-1930s, as a Unitarian minister in Bangor, Maine, I managed to persuade some fifteen mainline orthodox Christian clergymen to protest to the city school board the continuance of a compulsory military training program in the high school. It taught me something about multi-denominational coalitions. We all preached on the subject on one agreed-upon Sunday. In Boston, while a staff officer at Unitarian headquarters in the late '30s and early '40s, I discovered the necessity for joining with black and white clergy in fighting a violent and continued outbreak of anti-Semitism targeted at Jewish school children. My friendship with Rabbi Joshua Loth Leibman and Rabbi Stephen S. Wise had given me a new understanding of the possibilities of cooperation with Jewish congregations. Again, during the New Deal, and later, the World War II years, I helped to organize the United Christian Council for Democracy, which was a novel experience. Later, I found new friends through association with Rev. Guy Emery Shipler, editor of the *Churchman*, a liberal independent Episcopalian magazine. Now, thirty-five years later, I am still an editorial board member of the *Churchman*. I might add that I am still a member, after fifty years, of the Methodist Federation for Social Action, a very progressive national organization started by Winifred Chappell and Dr. Harry F. Ward. This will suffice for some of my own past efforts to work with allies in religion. It was late in my career that I found a genuine welcome from Roman Catholic clergy. It really began with the priests and nuns who welcomed us Unitarians at Selma, Alabama, at the time of Rev. James Reeb's murder during the civil rights struggle in March of 1965.

Let us recall that the late Pope John XXIII was a great help in opening doors to new ecumenical relationships with non-Catholics. No encyclical will ever attempt, I hope, to weaken this historic achievement. Rev. Daniel Berrigan, who preached Mr. Zwerling's installation sermon in this church, spoke to me that night with a warmth and understanding that equaled any I ever received from some of my own colleagues over the years.

After Philip Zwerling's stirring address on "Surviving Reagan" last Sunday, I desire to concentrate on our religious allies' new struggles coming up. It is important, of course, not to forget the tremendous impact in recent years of the religious rightwingers, led by figures like Fred Schwartz, George Benson, Carl McIntire, Billy James Hargis, Pat Robertson, Billy Graham, and Jerry Falwell, claiming with impertinent arrogance to be the "Moral Majority" of Christians in this country. They have all been around a long time, but only with the 1980 elections did they renounce their contempt for political social action and urge their electronic-media and church-member followers to learn about registering as Republicans and going to the polls. What we must not forget is that their targets were not only liberals in the Senate like Church and

McGovern, but also the thousands of Christian ministers in many main-line-orthodox denominations who have worked conscientiously through their own socially liberal organizations and through the National Council of Churches of Christ and the World Council of Churches with often courageous and quite progressive programs. It is essential in these coming four years to realize that the "Moral Majority" followers have their sternest criticisms for those in the Christian churches who refuse to indulge in red-baiting, who reject the "right to life" campaigns, who support women being ordained as ministers and holding high office as lay leaders, and who welcome the racial integration of their churches. These churchmen are allies in great numbers, who support peace programs and freedom from American interference in national affairs in Latin and South America and Third World countries. These are allies we need and should know far better. Our long history of being rejected by the orthodox churches, because of our independence from the trinitarian dogmas, is changing, and now we are working more and more on issues, on ethical consultation on many major problems. UUA President Pickett could give many examples of this. It is a new scene. We are not alone.

A new situation provides us with possibilities for real cross-fertilization between faiths. There is a very real peril of fascism emerging, not only in other lands, but in our own. It will not be so named. We need now to recall the words of Bertolt Brecht in his play, *Arturo Ui*: "The womb from which Hitler crawled is fecund still." Our present government has made it manifestly clear that it will expand its aid to military dictatorships and put on hold any serious concern with human rights, since our nation's task is to save ourselves and other nations from the mortal disease of communism. And I am sure they mean it. Such a purblind policy has been pursued before with fatal effect, and will now be intensified. It can put our American rulers on a sharper collision course with those peoples of the world who resent and reject the myth of America as the imperial master of the planet. The brainwashing of the American people will be accelerated, I believe, unless we find many allies, including our religious brothers and sisters in many faiths.

There are some church leaders, including Catholics and Protestants, who will go along with Mr. Reagan and his cohorts, including right-wing fundamentalists, as so many did in the days of the Nazis in the '30s and '40s in Germany. But today I would stress that in all of these religious institutions, within and beyond our country's borders, there are men and women totally dedicated to antifascist resistance in ideas and in personal and collective action. Many of them far surpass us Unitarians and Universalists in ardor and alacrity. As I write this, a letter comes from our Unitarian Professor James Luther Adams at Harvard Divinity School, telling me of plans shaping up with his leadership for a large coalition of Catholics, Protestants, and Jews to look at the economic order, present and proposed. We Unitarians will have our opportunity to share in this second annual conclave, made more urgent than ever by the change in administration in Washington.

Why have Unitarians found cooperation with orthodox Christians a difficult task? It is not perversity. There are historical reasons.

In almost every Unitarian church and fellowship I know, there are some members who are filled with what the classic Greek playwrights centuries ago called hubris, overweening pride, a conscious or unconscious arrogance. We should not be proud of being loners, proud of having broken all ties with men and women of character and concern for humanity who are dedicated Methodists, Baptists, Catholics, Jews, or Buddhists. Our track record isn't that impressive. We are liberated, but often isolated. Detachment is no great virtue. Coalitions call for no surrender of our cherished freedom from irrational doctrines. We have no monopoly of ethical values and morality; we all confront powers and principalities that seek to turn the clock back to the days of veritable slavery and naked class oppression—unquestionable feudal elites. We need to recognize our brothers and sisters now facing threats of dehumanization and death. Mature, intelligent Christians of many creeds, and Jews, orthodox and reform, are as troubled as any Unitarians. We cannot afford to stand separately, if we are to be effective together.

The United States can become a Uruguay or an El Salvador if we blind ourselves to the social realities of life for millions of our people. Secretary of State Alexander Haig admits that he shared in the plans to defeat Allende in Chile. He bluntly said we should have considered using the "unthinkable" weapon, which means the nuclear bomb, in demanding the return of the hostages from Iran.

Let me emphasize, the world is larger now than we have ever known before. There are new constellations of cultures. A multiplural world is already here—and growing. It is no longer a bipolarized United States versus the Soviet Union—a scene many of us, who are older, knew so much of our lives. I believe that the Third World, unaligned, involving two-thirds of mankind, will shape the twenty-first century. And there are few Unitarians in the Third World. They do not know our contributions of civil liberties, racial equality, and peace, in the past or present. But we need to know them far better than we do. And our hubris, our pride, has been a high wall between us. I feel, as does Rev. Marjorie Leaming of our Santa Paula Church who recently spoke at the Women in Religion Convocation in Lansing, saying: "I am glad I am a Unitarian Universalist. I couldn't be anything else. Ours is a fabulous religion in terms of freedom and its possibilities for the individual." She then offers an example of our hubris, our cutting ourselves off from millions of dedicated Christians who are not any more enamored of Jerry Falwell's Moral Majority Christians than we are. Marjorie Leaming puts it this way:

Neither the right-wing evangelicals, nor the left-wing evangelicals, nor
the orthodox and mainline Christians have a corner on Jesus. If they
seem to have such a corner, it is because we let them have it. I hope
that we can transcend our Unitarian Universalist bias against Christianity and see that it is worthy of being reinterpreted for many of
us and put to good use in the process of liberation of the whole human race.

Our Unitarian hubris has kept many of us from separating the gold
from the dross in current Christian teachings. We need not recant any
of our ideas about the evils of powerful church institutions, or the misuse of Jesus as a supernatural figure and member of the Trinity. Let me
take another example of the need to know our church history better and
recover the true Jesus. The late Rev. J. Spencer Kennard, Jr., a born
fundamentalist who in his youth rejected its rigidity, later declared himself a religious and political humanist. After his studies at Yale, the Sor-
bonne, and Strasbourg, he tied his politics, which were radical, to his
liberated views of Christianity. I knew Dr. Kennard during my years at
Unitarian headquarters, and admired his bold, scholarly, and politically
realistic years of service. His recognized biblical scholarship convinced many
of us of the need for courageous declarations. He stated that the historical Jesus was in actuality a freedom fighter and political humanist.
The deification of Jesus, he declared, "was an insult to the Galilean teacher.
Jesus was absolutely political. Religion and politics were one."

Today we are discovering in Latin America, in South America, and
in parts of Europe and the United States that there are priests and lay
men and women in the Catholic church who share this concept of Jesus.
Rev. Philip Zwerling has reported on this to you several times after his
visits to Cuba and Nicaragua. He has told you, as has our friend, Professor Blase Bonpane, that the assassination of Salvadoran Archbishop
Romero last year was more than the martyrdom of a brave priest wit-
nessing for social justice. Politically, it marked the loss of a moderate
voice in the revolution rising all over Central and South America. Archbishop Romero was responsible for the fact that unrestrained capitalism and police-state government were condemned by the General Conference of Latin American bishops at Pueblo, Mexico, in January 1979.

For many of us in the United States, for the past forty-five years
an American Catholic editor, Dorothy Day, of the *Catholic Worker*, was
an indefatigable advocate of human worth who knew that bread and dignity were both necessities about which religions must be concerned. When
Dorothy Day died in late November, our Unitarian minister at Arlington
Street Church, Boston, Victor Carpenter, wrote: "She was a Mother Te-
resa with a political consciousness." Victor had met her as she was organizing, in Baltimore in 1968, support for the defense of the Catonsville

Nine. He wrote at the time of her death: "I can still remember Dorothy Day, her eyes blazing as she leveled her scorn and passion upon those persons that were upset at the burning of draft papers but were able to countenance the napalm burning of children halfway around the world in Vietnam." Victor is not guilty of hubris. He knows well that we Unitarian Universalists need to find our place with all those who live with a burning conscience, and take the ideas of Christianity, Unitarianism, and humanism and make them operate in our own churches.

My last example is of a Christian who has aided me enormously in Nanking, China. His name is Rev. K. H. Ting, a graduate of Union Theological Seminary in New York, an Episcopalian bishop in Nanking, formerly Dean of Nanking Theological Seminary. When Mrs. Fritchman and I met him and Mrs. Ting in 1973 in Nanking, we felt already acquainted. An American former YWCA worker for thirty years in Shanghai, later a staff member of Mme Sun Yat-sen's Children's Welfare Council, had been sending Bishop Ting my printed sermons for many years. The bishop is now, after several years of enforced inactivity during the reign of the Gang of Four, extremely active in China under the new dispensation. I want to quote from a sermon he gave in November 1979, based on the New Testament story of Jesus feeding the five thousand: "The disciples thought that Christ's work consisted of *talking* about the kingdom. As to feeding the multitude, it was none of his business and therefore none of theirs either. The disciples said, 'Send the crowd away. Let them go their own ways and get whatever food they can.' " But Bishop Ting reminds us that Jesus said, "Give them to eat." What the disciples were advocating was the principle of looking after oneself, each doing his or her own thing. If this is put into practice, as it was in China in the past, and elsewhere, the result inevitably is for the strong and mighty to dominate and for the common people to be their victims. It ends up in full-fledged capitalism. Bishop Ting then reminds us of John Maynard Keynes's definition of capitalism as "the extraordinary belief that the nastiest of motives will somehow work for the benefit of us all. And we know it hasn't worked out that way."

Bishop Ting is a symbol of the alliance, the coalition, the cooperation which we in the responsible churches of all faiths must form in the immediate years ahead. I think of Rev. James Lawson of Holman Methodist Church, here in Los Angeles, the strongest voice of black churchmen in this county today, and president of the Southern Christian Leadership Conference in Los Angeles, as well as a leader of "The Gathering," an organization of black liberal clergy in this area. Some of you will remember that it was James Lawson who twice went with me to speak to the district attorney during the trial of our own member, Philip Allen, in Philip's behalf. I would like to think that a majority of the pulpits in our own denomination had men and women speaking with as much directness to the issues of this very year as do K. H. Ting in China and James M. Lawson in the United States. We Unitarians and Universalists do have voices of courage among us, and I know it and rejoice, but we need to share the tasks with those of many of our own and other faiths and denominations, and for many this thought will be hard counsel.

Eleven years ago Philip Slater wrote a book, *The Pursuit of Loneliness: American Culture at the Breaking Point.* I reviewed it enthusiastically from this pulpit. In that book he stated:

> When the system as it stands is no longer viable, the mechanism must be exposed for the swindle it is; otherwise the needed radical changes will be rendered ineffectual. . . . Militant activism is task-oriented, and hence partakes of certain old-culture traits such as postponement of self-gratification and ceasing a preoccupation with power.

Militant activism is task-oriented, indeed, as Slater declared so clearly. It means in America rebuking the scandal of millions unemployed, millions of mothers with dependent children being told they must accept reduced welfare support for food and shelter, even as ten million dollars are spent in an obscene Roman holiday during the inauguration of Ronald Reagan. Militant activism means that Christians, Jews, Unitarians, humanists, American Moslems, and others within the religious spectrum of society must join with trade unionists and aroused professionals to demand the end of galloping KKK intimidations, the end of swastika graffiti on temples and Jewish institutes for Holocaust Studies. We give prime-time TV focus on torture, physical and psychological, toward the American hostages in Iran, but offer scant attention to the wholesale torture and death meted out by the late Shah's Savak police against thousands of impoverished students and workers in recent years of struggle. The protest against such violence must come from more than outraged Moslems. The voice of all men and women of conscience must be heard like thunder. If the true believers in all religions cannot speak and be listened to as they name the present crimes in every land, including our own, we are as sounding brass and tinkling cymbals. The time for naked rhetoric is past. This is the hour for militant activism, united resistance, unrelenting protest against the march of fascism. The syndrome of irresponsibility must end. The practice of our moral precepts must take priority over the self-serving proposals of our new and many of our old leaders and their docile and cruelly-deceived supporters.

Unitarians and their allies today cannot be lotus eaters, or blind cave-dwelling salamanders. We liberals and radicals are not alone. We shall be welcomed where the struggle is most intense. Martin Luther King's words still ring in our ears: "We shall overcome!"

Part Four

The Human Condition

Out of This World
The Curse of Cynicism
September 30, 1951

The text for my address is found in a great hymn of the Christian Church:

> O Master, let me walk with thee . . .
> Help me the slow of heart to move,
> By some clear, winning word of love.
> Teach me thy secret, help me bear
> The strain of toil, the fret of care.
> Teach me thy patience, still with thee,
> In closer, deeper company,
> In work that keeps faith sweet and strong,
> In trust that triumphs over wrong.

That was written in 1879—yet it is still sung on Sunday mornings by millions of Christian church people and, for all its sentimentality and easy rhymes, it sets a note of moral vigor and refreshing confidence in man's powers that contrasts with the sour and the decadent atmosphere that envelops much of our current life. I am speaking today about the curse of cynicism. We shall be dealing with some very personal and inescapable facts, for this is no matter of archeological interest. This is not a problem in Shakespearean criticism; it is as personal and intimate a matter as your breakfast this morning, or your income tax.

You may wonder why I quote an unfashionable hymn as a text, why I propose keeping faith sweet and strong, or suggest that trust can triumph over wrong. The air we breathe is so infected with cynicism and defeatism and contempt for altruism or idealism that even a minister of religion has to warn against too complete a surrender. The maintenance of moral stamina is a major religious problem.

289

290 For the Sake of Clarity

The hardest problem brought to my study is not that of the foot-
loose husband with a wandering eye, nor the check-writing wife who
pays no attention to bank balances until the law catches up with her.
The hardest problem is that of the father who spreads a daily rumor
in the home, before his family, that nothing counts but money; that
every man has his price; that no possible state or institution can serve
people without gigantic corruption; that, of course, students cheat at
West Point, or in the high school around the corner; that everybody
is a shoplifter if given a chance; that no woman is ever faithful if her
husband is a thousand miles away.

I am talking today about something far more dangerous than cya-
nide, or marijuana, or 100-proof whiskey—I mean the acceptance of the
poison of cynicism into the human mind. This is not to speak lightly
of loose morality or a preoccupation with strong drink, but I put first
things first. Cynicism is self-defeating, self-crippling, and kills more people than Los Angeles traffic. Cynicism is an excuse for joining the side-
lines, what a radio writer calls "the cult of avoidism." Cynicism is not
so much a surrender regarding others, or a conviction of the hopelessness of struggle, but the exemption of one's self, a cover for fatigue or
laziness, an excuse for letting down effort.

Note well: the cynic is often justifying his own predatory and acquisitive actions. Cynicism is a thin veneer of justification for amoral actions,
a lowering of the terms for living together. A cynical father, shattering
his children's good faith in others, is worse than a man caught in theft
or tampering with the seventh commandment. Cynicism is a moral drug.
It distorts, betrays, enfeebles people with real talent and power.

Cynicism is a curse because it tells a lie about man, individually
and collectively. I am not asking for a varnishing over of harsh reality
today. You and I know that congressmen can be bought to support
legislation; that wives and husbands vulgarize marriage with deception,
and go to the altar often to improve their bank accounts; that there
are great corporations that hire gangsters to keep workers docile; that
bribery has been found in both capitalistic and socialist countries. I read
the papers and see a Costello treated gently by the government, and a
brilliant professor dismissed from his livelihood for the sin of nonconformity in economics. But I also know that decency and faithfulness to
duty, and struggling for peace, and paying one's bills are not front-page
copy to a city editor. And it is very important that we give ourselves
and our children a picture of human life that is not distorted and out
of focus.

This sermon was started in early August at the home of my friend,
the artist Max Band, who said: "Why is every evidence of man working
for a decent and beautiful society called 'out of this world'? A great
film, a wonderful book, a fine painting lead people to say 'It's out of

this world.' It's no such thing, and *it's in this world.*" I enjoy a glorious painting by Mr. Band hanging in my study at home, the head of a rabbi in meditation on the Day of Atonement. It stirs and strengthens my mind every day—and it is in this world!

The curse of cynicism is in direct conflict with fundamental Unitarian theories about man. Without avoiding the worst around us, without denying a great deal that shows man as a hyena or a jackal, we Unitarians say, in our long-held heresy, that the Christian theologians have lied about human nature—it is not contemptible. If you have never read *Against Calvinism* by William Ellery Channing, I urge you to read this classic sermon on resistance to traditional Christian cynicism about man.

I agree with Robert Louis Stevenson in his essay on Walt Whitman: "I hate cynicism a great deal worse than I do the devil, unless perhaps the two are the same thing." We Unitarians say with Balzac: "Man makes his own history." We do not simply issue vituperation against cynicism —we seek to get at the roots of cynicism. I mentioned the Christian theologians who, on the whole, have been more cynical than the original cynics [such as] Diogenes and Aristeppus. The churchmen have slandered man for twenty centuries. Our Episcopalian friends in their prayers still say regularly: "There is no health in us." They are wrong, and Balzac is right: man makes his own history, good or bad, cheap or glorious.

We of the humanist tradition have for centuries rebuked the Calvins and Augustines and St. Pauls with their emphasis on man's weakness, avarice, and lust. When not pushed to the wall by hunger and fear, man's outgiving nature asserts itself magnificently. We Unitarians properly urge men to rely on their inward strength. We say man is potentially good, not a worm, and that there is no reason why he should not be actually so. And note, contrary to what orthodox pulpits assert of us, we do not say men are gods or fallen angels. We say they are men—not more nor less. We can be well-prepared and competent to live splendidly, not out of this world, but in it.

Let this be very clear: To prove man's dignity and even heroic quality is refuting the cynic. I do not turn to the sermonic cisterns for classic illustrations. I do not speak of Captain Scott at the South Pole dying on the frozen waste, nor of Mallory climbing Mt. Everest, nor of Galahad in poetic legends. I say, look around you at the repeated daily facts of generosity and good will not out of this world, but in it: Women sewing in this church every week for children in need, college students building a rest house for tuberculosis patients in the Ejido El Porvenir in Mexico, busy family men going up to Ormsby Village to set a deep freeze locker and build a kitchen, energetic members of this church spending weeks in volunteer service repairing and restoring this building and its furnishings. Are these less truly real than the theft of sixteen thousand dollars by an income tax collector in San Francisco, less real than the murders spread on the front pages of the daily press? I watch the clerks in our stores, the drivers of buses, the postmen on their routes doing the friendly act beyond the call of duty, being patient with the chronic grouch, helpful to the arthritic veteran, and I ask, "Is this less frequent than the fixing of basketball games, less easily found than the lynching of black men in Georgia?" It is not. The cynic points to man's errors, his failures, and generalizes that this proves man's incompetence to fulfill his ideals.

We need a straighter presentation in our schools of the facts of human nature. Man progresses by his errors. They are a sign of strength, not weakness. The weak hesitate to make the effort. The spiritually and mentally strong experiment—and this involves error—but the progress is in the direction of victory.

On December 7, 1903, Wilbur Wright, in a pitifully fragile machine, rose into the air a few feet for fifty-nine seconds. A heavier than air machine had actually flown. The papers stressed the failure. Wright saw the success and its promise. Today, you can attend to business in two or three cities in a few hours because of that so-called "failure" of the Wrights.

The Christian theologians could not accept as a part of normal human existence the facts of error, illness, moral failure, or death. They wanted a perfect man. We have moved a long way from that theory in our liberal churches. We see man as growing, conquering, slipping back, faltering, and resuming his pace. This is man's way of working. We can add obstacles or remove them. We Unitarians believe that we can join with millions of ardent, realistic people in many lands of many various traditions and creeds to extend the means of progress, removing roadblocks that needlessly handicap all of us and remain only because a few find them profitable to themselves.

It is imperative that we note today that cynicism does not enter us by heredity in the genes or in the bloodstream. It is bred into people by events and external habits and institutions. I select an illustration from television. A recent TV magazine reported that in one week in Los Angeles TV programs presented 127 murders, 101 justifiable killings, 93 kidnappings, 11 jailbreaks, 3 human brandings with hot irons. Seventy-two percent of these events were on programs designed for children. This is what I call "force and violence," even if the Smith Act finds it elsewhere. Such programs breed cynicism and the expectation of violence—and they can be prevented. They will be prevented if parents and teachers insist.

The rules of our society today play into the hands of cynics. This is not a political speech for socialism. A Swede or an Englishman, as well as a Russian or a Chinese could equally well say it. The fact is that mankind everywhere, including the United States, is asserting the necessity for revising the rules to prevent abuse by a few against the many. Republicans, Democrats, and Communists in America are beginning to say in unison that Teapot Dome and Tideland Oil scandals, gangster-loving mayors in New York or Florida, mink-coat nepotism, and billion-dollar profits out of warfare must and can be stopped.

The young grow cynical when there are no jobs available unconnected with war industry or war itself. Girls grow cynical who find employment in many professions or trades closed to them because of their sex. Nisei or Mexican Americans grow cynical when they find housing restricted and vocational advancement prevented on grounds of racial origin. Film writers and playwrights grow cynical when they are asked to avoid ideas, problems, or politics, and write only of backstage jealousies, prize fight decadence, or Confederacy romances of the 1860s.

This kind of cynicism is as remediable as yellow fever or smallpox. The bacillus is known. The breeding ground can be cleansed. It is not a sin inherited from Adam and Eve; it is within our power to end it.

We are coming to the place in every land where great aggregations of citizens are saying, "The predatory man must be removed from our midst. He has too long enjoyed legal sanctions and social adulation."

The peoples of Eastern and Western countries alike are spending millions of dollars on jet planes and bombers. The nation that refuses to abolish atomic weapons or to risk multilateral disarmament is doomed by the judgment of plain men and women. Most people in India or America or Argentina are not cynics and are determined to throw out the men in power anywhere who spill blood needlessly and make money doing it. The patience of the masses of people is running out. We shudder alike with shame at Gen. Van Fleet boasting of our wholesale power of destruction in Korea, or at reports of Chinese slaughter of American prisoners.

Ideas are the great weapons of men everywhere—greater far than planes and guns. Men and women have often been forced to earn their bread under terrible adversity. They have been chained and whipped and beaten, and a certain number have become cynics and informers and joined the taskmaster, but the vast majority have turned to ideas—their most inalienable possessions—and forged new tools with which to liberate themselves.

This is the real answer to the cynic. He has been rendered obsolete. He flourishes in a society where corruption is winked at, where the golden calf is worshipped, where sex and sensational scandals replace the arts and letters as man's natural nourishment. Such decadence is being outlawed from pole to pole, and we are watching it occur. Much religion today is rejecting the church cynics: the Calvins and Neubuhrs who see man as a fallen creature whose righteousness is but filthy rags. While men breathe, they think. This is the immemorial answer to the cynic, and we need to remember it today as never before.

We are now changing the face of the earth to make it a place where cynicism will have no swamps in which to breed. The true patriot has moral energy and vast imagination. He is always aware of the promised land, not two hundred years away, but near at hand, awaiting his children's entrance.

The wholesome element in the ancient traditions gives us courage to drive the evil men out of power everywhere and to end the rule of the cynic, who has so long covered with fine words his own self-justification for greed and indifference. High religion has long set the pace for ethical advance. "Cain, where is thy brother? His blood crieth unto me from the ground." "I am the Lord thy God, I brought thee up out of the land of Egypt, out of the house of bondage." "Thus said the Lord, for three transgressions of Israel, and for four, I will not turn away the punishment thereof, because they sold the righteous for silver and the poor for a pair of shoes." "Proclaim liberty to all the land, and to all the inhabitants thereof." "He hath sent me to heal the brokenhearted and to preach deliverance to the captives, and recovering of sight to the blind, and to set at liberty them that are bruised." "Woe unto them that join house to house, that lay field to field until there be no place, that they may be placed alone in the midst of the earth."

There is moral anger, and resolute commitment! The religious spirit sees a complete contradiction between the blighting wind of cynics and the warm pulsating power of human self-confidence. Both cannot dwell in the same man. With Seneca, the Roman poet, the truly religious man says, "I am not born for one corner—the whole world is my native land." No people, no nation, no faith is our natural enemy. A patriotism less than global is becoming treason to humanity.

The opposite of the cynic is the free man declaring his own independence, saying Emerson's words: "Speak your latent convictions, for the inmost in due time becomes the outmost, and our first thought is rendered back to us by the trumpets of the Last Judgment." This is the record from Iknaton to Gandhi.

There is much in our present world around us that spawns a cynical design in men: the cheap display by people of wealth and fashion, the hard contempt shown by men of power for the toil of those on whose shoulders they ride, the suffocation of culture by grade F movies, and the intellectual press vacuum created by much in the press and on the air. Yet, it is our task to say: "People can take the helm, and employ their liberties, and set miscreants back, and depose leaders who fail to lead." This can happen in state and church, in education and the arts. The cynic is deposed by the people rising in their wrath.

One of the Benda brothers in Stefan Heym's great book, *The Eyes of Reason*, declares: "There comes in everyone's time the hour when he must decide for himself, the moment when circumstances and objective conditions and laws counterbalance each other, and when the scale is tipped by the human will."

This the cynic denies; this the free man asserts, and in his assertion marches forward to alter his own and his neighbors' destiny. Our own half century is replete with evidence.

The cynic is a psychic hazard in our struggle today. He is sick and disturbed, however arrogant his words. He can poison a thousand minds and cripple the ardor of all who meet him, but let us not be dismayed. The resolute, unwavering, steady work of the most modest citizen for the cause of human equality and brotherhood can put a dozen cynics to flight. If you act upon the principles of reason and goodwill, you disarm the cynic beyond all rehabilitation. He cannot bear a man of hope, or a woman quietly doing deeds of service. This is his nemesis and his end.

These next few years are going to demand a great deal of the Unitarian, the free thinker, the humanist of every school. But there are millions of plain men and women ready for the task. There is wealth and talent, energy and thought quite adequate for every need. The greatest obstacle is the frightened man who has lost his humanity itself: the cynic steeped in his own apathy and self-love, defeated before he starts and unwilling to add his weight to the common cause. His sickness is contagious and must be cured, not by argument, but by the example of the advancing power of a healthy mind in love with progress and the promise of a world made one. It is your privilege and mine to share in such a mission now, a mission never more commanding since the dawn of time.

Are Mixed Marriages Successful?
March 26, 1961

To our visitors today I should like to say a word about the theory of Unitarian preaching. It sometimes takes strangers by surprise, whether in King's Chapel, Boston, or in First Church, Los Angeles. It sometimes, I'll confess, takes me by surprise. At its best, this is the hour of truth during the week which many of us Unitarians cherish with great anticipation, even if we find ourselves speaking hard and self-critical thoughts that draw blood.

The purpose of a Unitarian sermon is to stir deep waters in a person's mind and conscience, or to change our metaphors, to rehabilitate a lost or forgotten truth. Like some of the Old Testament prophets, we Unitarian ministers feel no divine compulsion to speak comfortably to Jerusalem, but rather to speak the word of the Lord (the phrase is not mine, but Isaiah's) as we find it. We seek also to rehabilitate the man pilloried for one thing and who is never remembered for something better he has said or done. Most of us, for example, remember King Canute in eleventh-century England for stupidly commanding the waves to roll back from his feet as he sat enthroned on the beach, but it is our Unitarian perversity to remember him even better for his great declaration: "I want no money raised in my kingdom by injustice."

Today, for example, I am speaking about mixed marriages. Probably few ministers in this state of California have performed as many as myself. Jew and Gentile, Catholic and Protestant, Mohammedan and Christian, Negro and Caucasian, Chinese and Mexican, Japanese and American: these are but a few of the partnerships it has been my privilege to unite over the past thirteen years. I do not know how many of the six hundred weddings I have solemnized can be called "mixed marriages," for, in truth, practically all marriages are mixed if we explore very far into them. I, a guileless Methodist, was yoked to a New England Unitarian thirty odd years ago, and if you think this is not a mixed marriage, you are indeed innocent of life's more subtle realities.

Before I speak of some of my conclusions on this theme today, allow me to express my sense of gratitude to scores upon scores of couples —young and old, foreign-born and native-born, dark-skinned and light-skinned, symbolic of many traditions and cultures—who have given me courage and wisdom in reconstructing my philosophy of marriage over the years. I am, above all else, saluting the mature mixed marriage, paying my respects to the strong, the independent, the confident men and women who have lived on the frontiers of a new society, setting examples for many young people who will be following in their footsteps in the next few decades, and doing so with greater ease because of these pioneers, even though we all know that there have been mixed marriages since man began to settle into tribes and nations, to worship many gods and celebrate their faith in a thousand rituals.

Candor compels me to confess that some of the mixed marriages I have performed have failed, sometimes miserably, ignominiously, and I bear the wounds of such failures on my soul, whether justifiably or not. It is certainly true that some people are not made of the stuff for a successful mixed marriage, who yet may be able to weather the vicissitudes of matrimony within the confines of their own tradition or culture. I need not say that there are men and women, some quite well along in years, who have no apparent gifts for sharing a common roof with anyone, even of their own sex, or their own culture group.

I believe it was Walt Kelly, the creator of Pogo, who once said: "As we fiddle with the dials to thaw and so digest the prefrozen thought of the taste-makers, we no longer stop to think that the delight of the eye can be the death of the mind." This morning I am talking to people who are genuinely disturbed at the death of the mind that is going on today. Those who are untroubled at such a disaster will not be interested in any of the distinctions we are making here today on marriage or any other subject.

Last October, when I first planned today's address, I sent a letter to a dozen couples of mixed marriages whom I had united over the past decade. In my judgment they were twelve couples who had made a success of their partnership, not without some reverses and minor tragedies in several cases, but still with as high a success factor as people of a common tradition. I could have written many more letters, to be sure, but twelve seemed enough for one minister to digest and absorb in preparation for a single address. What is reported today is dependent at many points on the very thoughtful and intelligent responses I received. Several of the couples are here today.

The questionnaire asked three basic questions: (1) Do you think interracial and interfaith marriages can succeed in America today? (2)

What special problems arise that persons contemplating such marriages should consider seriously? (3) Do children of such marriages have particular difficulties to face?

It may be necessary to remind some of you in the congregation that certain religious bodies refuse to sanction marriage between persons of different faiths, and there are ministers who, in spite of the new marriage legislation in this state, voluntarily refuse to marry persons of different ethnic groups. The rejection of such couples by the clergy is a very real source of anxiety and frustration to many men and women, as I have frequent occasion to know at firsthand.

Let me state with as great care as possible three principles I have held with increasing conviction in my years of experience in this area of interpersonal relations since coming to Los Angeles. (It goes without saying that in a Unitarian pulpit I speak only for myself, and there will be many gradations of agreement or disagreement, even within this church, which seeks to practice a life of equality with persons of every faith, race, and cultural heritage.) First, a man or woman should be free (when of age to make decisions maturely) to marry the person he or she wants to marry. I am convinced that the day of the Shadchen is over. No human relationship should be more independently made. Religious background, racial or national origin should not be allowed to frustrate a union that two persons feel has every chance of bringing happiness and satisfaction to them.

Those who have heard me speak on matrimony before know well that I have no sympathy with St. Jerome's fifth-century judgment that "Marriage is always a vice and that all that can be done is to excuse it and sanctify it, thereby making it a religious sacrament." And I equally reject Percy Bysshe Shelley's dictum; though he was a great English poet, a fine humanist, and social prophet close to my own heart, I have no sympathy with him when he declares that "A system could not have been devised more studiously hostile to human happiness than marriage." I would be a scoundrel indeed if I felt that way and continued to sign over six hundred wedding certificates in the state of California.

My first principle was never better formulated than by my beloved London curmudgeon of the eighteenth century, Dr. Samuel Johnson, who wrote in that priceless journal, *The Idler*: "Every man should regulate his actions by his conscience, without regard to the opinions of the rest of the world. This is one of the first precepts of moral prudence." This advice may seem at times to be costly, but in the long run there is none better, in politics, religion, or in the privacy of the marital relationship.

Second, diverse religious or racial, national, or cultural backgrounds can add a larger dimension to a marriage. They are not to be thought of simply as handicaps or obstacles to be handled with dexterity. They can be positive assets in a relationship. They can bring two people closer together and open to them greater ranges of satisfaction than many other people ever experience.

I am reminded of what Dr. Clyde Kluckbohn says so well in his book, *Mirror for Man:* "The world must be kept safe for differences. Human life should remain as a home of many rooms. There can be allegiance to common purposes as well as enjoyment of great varieties of cultural patterns." Need I remind you married couples who are of identical or similar backgrounds how real is the temptation to be ingrown, self-righteous, superior, and exclusive? Is any snob more offensive, for example, than the Anglo-Saxon snob?

Someone may well be saying at this point: "But can a Roman Catholic have a successful marriage to a Protestant or a Jew? Can an orthodox Jew be happy with a free thinker or a Presbyterian?" I have long since concluded that a person thoroughly committed, emotionally and intellectually, to any orthodox religion has erected beliefs and values, and usually a set of personal habits consistent with those values, which are extremely difficult for a nonconformist marriage partner to live with over a long period of time. It can be done, but only by a deliberate agreement to dismiss religion from the area of shared satisfactions. If there are children, the orthodox religious body makes claims that are not optional for the couple to reject. Such mixed marriages start off with a severe handicap and, in a majority of cases in my experience, one partner, the dissenter from the orthodoxy, finds himself or herself captive to the demands of religious law. It takes an immense amount of human insight and other shared values to compensate for this invasion of the marriage by the demands of the church or temple, to say nothing of the conservative relatives with their pressures of conformity.

Members of liberal Jewish or Christian bodies do not have this problem in such aggravated forms, and, as many of you here today well know, long and rewarding marriages are possible between persons from widely different creedal backgrounds. If a creedal faith is a rigid, fixed possession for one member of a marriage, it is hard for a person uncommitted to such a system to maintain authentic dialogue with his or her partner. Every area of human living is apt to be infected. It is therefore to be questioned whether two persons with so different a concept of life are likely to grow closer together as the years pass; at least I continue to have strong reservations. When the physical attraction becomes less central in the marriage, the intellectual differences often become unendurable. The exceptions are too infrequent to make the general practice a wise one. Unshared areas of thought and experience can become a source of increased tension as the years pass. It is no new observation that a truly orthodox religionist finds being yoked to an unbeliever a severe tax indeed.

All of this which I have said confirms, not denies, my second general principle: that diverse religious, racial, or cultural backgrounds can add a larger dimension to a marriage. But this is true only if there is a respect and acceptance of each partner's quality of mind and conscience, with no yielding to the external compulsions that the church has for centuries brought to bear for the sake of the institutions it serves. I quite agree with Count Keyserling when he says: "Marriage sets up an indisposable state of tension, and its very existence depends upon the preservation of this state. In marriage men and women form an indissoluble unit of life, based upon a fixed distance. A man and woman should never endeavor to be completely merged in one another; on the contrary, the more intimate they are the more they should cherish their own individuality." This is why, as many of you know, I read a great passage from The Prophet by Kahlil Gibran in the marriage service I use, which poetically expresses this need to preserve separate identity in wedlock.

The remainder of today's address will concern itself with the integrated marriage, the interracial marriage if you prefer that term. This second principle I have mentioned applies here; let me repeat it: diverse racial heritages can give an added dimension to marriage. Men and women marry, if they are wise, for the richness that a life together can bring to two individuals. Some of the interracial unions I know are stirring examples of this principle. In the decades ahead I hope thousands instead of hundreds of such marriages will add fresh evidence to this generalization. On the other hand, one should never marry just because the partner is from another race; yet this is sometimes done, as I know all too well. Some guilt-ridden Caucasians, for instance, have married Negroes from motives I would call immature and unhealthy, to prove something to themselves or to the community. This does the cause of racial equality no service, believe me. And, alas, in interracial marriages, as in other marriages, people sometimes marry for highly discreditable motives: for status, for money, or for protection from the demands life makes upon us as adults. Such marriages are built on quicksand and will most probably collapse under the added tensions that interracial marriages all suffer from to some degree.

Let us be very frank today: There is a hostile social climate in many parts of America, and some other parts of the world, for the interracial marriage. For example, the Hollywood Motion Picture Code, adopted March 31, 1930, states bluntly: "Miscegenation is forbidden." This symbol of prejudice can, alas, be found in many other parts of our social fabric. There are heavy economic penalties for many who marry across racial lines. The member of the majority group must learn to live with this fact, day and night, all of his life. And prejudice can come, and at times comes with shocking surprise, from the colored minority group aimed at the Caucasian intruder. Acceptance of the outsider by a long oppressed minority has to be earned by infinite skill and patience. The all too frequent rejection of the partner of color by the dominant Caucasian group is expected, its dismal history is better known, and one prepares himself for it in advance. However, the alienation of a Caucasian from his own group and from the minority group as well is an experience that does occur and that calls for a strong heart and penetrating sympathy.

The third principle I wish to mention this morning can be stated in this fashion: One marries one's partner, and in the last analysis, only one's partner. One does not marry the family, or the neighbors, or the friends at the office, or any other fringe people who are a part of one's day-by-day living. The reactions of family and close friends to an interracial marriage should be discussed and sensibly considered, but no one should go into an interracial marriage if he or she cannot, if need be, stand alone against society, including cherished parents, doting grandmothers, angry siblings who feel threatened, or anyone else! If this cannot be accomplished without panic or contention with one's mate, the marriage project is better abandoned. To be sure, this is true of all marriages, but doubly so of the marriage that defies prevailing convention and in some states even the marriage laws.

Some couples can face the known fact of lower pay for colored or minority citizens, yet are not able to accept the quiet or vehement resistance of long-time relatives or friends. If I have found it hard, over thirty years, to have some relatives I love deeply get angry at my politics, I should be able to understand the character demanded of someone who is rejected by close family members because a mate comes from another ethnic grouping. Happily, time often heals this wound, but sometimes it festers throughout life.

I was deeply moved by the statement a Caucasian husband of a Negro woman made to me this week: "Mr. Fritchman, the two members of an interracial marriage have a great deal to do with finding the acceptance they rightfully desire from others. If one's manner and bearing is one of dignity, of self-confidence, of assurance, others will in most instances respond with dignity and maturity." I have seen this happen, may I add, in many places, with many mixed couples. I have seen it over and over with young people whom I have married from different racial backgrounds. The defensive, insecure, anxious couple will discover hostility, tension, and overt rejection with tragic frequency. It is important to remember Ralph Waldo Emerson's great dictum: "A good man carries his own atmosphere around with him." A chip on the shoulder is no asset to an interracial marriage.

The interracial marriage today has far better chances of succeeding than it did a generation ago, precisely because struggles for equality of opportunity and privilege have been so persistently carried on. Couples marrying across their own racial lines should assume and expect acceptance. They will get it only if they do so walk and speak with assurance, prepared to handle rejection if it comes, but not assuming it as normal. It is normal only in an authoritarian racist society. Democracy provides the assumption of equality. No one should marry a person of another race unless he can proceed upon that premise. Let us remember one is entering a marriage, not enlisting in an army.

In this century, fantastic racial myths have been exploded, colored nations are coming into great strength around the world and in the United Nations. Victories have been won in the courts and Congress for racial equality. The unions are breaking down color bars. Government is lowering, not raising higher, the color bar even in upper echelons of administration. Hawaii, our fiftieth state, is a symbol of the new America. Interracial marriages there are as natural as its glorious sunshine. And the children are the loveliest in the world; I have seen them.

Let me for a moment speak of the children of these interracial marriages, for they must inherit a far better America than we have yet achieved. Negro children in Little Rock, New Orleans, Montgomery, and Clinton (to mention but a familiar few among many others) have been carrying the future of America on their small shoulders, in a way that has made strong men weep with shame and pride. Certainly their reward should include the expectation that all children will soon live together without any prejudice whatsoever because of a dark, a light, or any other color tone of skin. This is no idle dream, no quixotic Utopianism. Like disarmament, it must come fast or we are truly lost, and so is the whole enterprise of civilization. Apartheid spells nothing but death for the children now living. There is no room for it in our philosophy as Americans or as members of the human race.

The children of an interracial marriage must find love and acceptance at home, whether this be hard or easy. This is imperative and worth sacrificing for. So runs the testimony of all those I questioned. A young Japanese mother wrote me in her questionnaire: "Children of these marriages have a unique opportunity. They are born into a heritage of two different cultures and they can gain a better understanding of racial problems and become equipped to cope with them, including being tolerant of the intolerant."

The Caucasian mother of several children in a mixed marriage wrote me: "Our children are taught reverence for life, courtesy, the need for discounting physical differences and the ability to acknowledge cultural contributions from whatever source they come on their merits." She then discusses at greater length than I can report the value of friends and a church that practice interracial brotherhood. Such outposts of tomorrow's world are essential for the children who must have experiences even more than precepts.

At this point I would add my own experience in this church. There are some children and youth of our own membership who have learned the lessons of equality in our church school, in our youth groups, in our larger church services and activities, who find their parents still unprepared for this new world of equality. I admire and cherish those parents of my generation who have grown, with their children, in these recent years, for it has not always been easy. There are parents—some Negro, some Caucasian, some Asian—who find their children's friends of the opposite sex less than promising as prospective life partners. When these friends are of another racial stock, the tensions can multiply with furious pace. There are no easy answers, no glib solutions. Sometimes the resistance of a parent to a marriage is not because of the problems the young person will face if he marries across conventional lines of race; it is because the parent, often unconsciously, is unprepared for his or her own share of obloquy or ostracism. I have, with a sad heart, married young people who were clearly ready for an interracial marriage, while the parents could not face the prospect. Again and again the young people have proved to be correct in their appraisal of themselves. Time and habit too often cripple our powers of experimenting and adapting to difficult undertakings. Some parents have lost these powers.

Of course, young people can fall in love and marry the wrong mates, even of other ethnic groups, and this can break many hearts, but this phenomenon also occurs within one's own group and it is imperative that we remember this fact today, lest it muddy the waters of our thinking on interracial marriage. There have been times when I had a trace of a suspicion that a young girl was marrying a man of another race as an act of rebellion against fifteen or twenty years of parental authority poorly handled. But such cases are the exception, not the rule. Let us realize that the day of the interracial marriage has come; it is gaining prestige in our laws, in our churches, in our communities. The walls of Jericho are tumbling down. There will continue to be ill-formed unions, frivolous marriages, impulsive wedding plans made, and we shall need counsellors of wisdom, and parents with clear heads and loving hearts to talk with their growing young people. But the principle remains: We must marry those we want to marry in our best moments of decision, after careful reflection and a wide exploration of the possibilities within, or beyond, our own heritage.

There is no substitute for a clear head, or for several months of friendship with the best of candidates for marriage. Of course, if you be disciples of [George] Bernard Shaw, you will tell me that women do the courting in their own upside-down, wrong-side out fashion, and I should really advise men how to avoid entrapment. That is another sermon. Today it is sufficient to say that interracial marriage is not for the unprepared, the timid, the insecure, the belligerent. There is a price exacted for nonconformity. As long as America keeps racial minorities in second-class status and penalizes a man for the color of his skin, the country of his origin, or the accident of his religious heritage, we will need dissenters of great courage, superhuman patience with our fellow men, a very deep compassion for the frailties that flesh is heir to, and an uncorrupted dedication to rational thinking in hours of crisis. Such people are all too rare, but you have known them, as have I, and their numbers are growing. They need our friendship and our strong support.

Frozen and Bleeding Hearts
November 15, 1964

In many quarters today nothing is more suspect than compassion and humanitarian proposals for our own citizens or those in other lands. What lies behind the great assault upon the "bleeding heart"?

This address today is not a philosophical sermon, not a sermon aimed at the intellectual or the theologically curious. It is what I like to call a *homily*, a rather direct, practical discussion of a problem that has haunted me for months and which I may solve better if I discuss it openly with you. I come in a mood not of bitterness or cynicism, but of great perplexity. I am troubled at what is happening to so many of us, to all of us to some degree probably, myself included. Our choir will tell us on Christmas Sunday in the words of Cardona-Hine that "Man Is My Song," but at times I feel I must say "Man Is My Nightmare."

Like some of you, I was nurtured in childhood on the parable of the Good Samaritan in the New Testament. The Samaritan, who stopped and bound up the wounds of the stranger attacked by bandits on the road to Jericho, after being ignored by a priest and a Levite, was projected for me as the model of humane character. It was axiomatic that this empathetic man of Samaria should be my guide in all the years yet to come. Whether one is told this story as a Christian or as a non-Christian, it is a part of our cultural heritage, and endless millions of parsons have preached from the story in Luke's gospel (10:31–37). But someone has kidnapped the Good Samaritan, and in our jet age he is very hard to find. So I raise with you the question of the frozen and the bleeding hearts.

By the *frozen* hearts I refer, of course, to the man or woman who has closed off his sympathies from his fellow men, consciously or unconsciously, and has decided to fight his own jungle battles without the handicap of tender sentiments of any kind. With occasional exceptions toward his kin to long-time friends, his private elite, he is out for number one, himself. If questioned, he says it's a rough world and one's first duty is to take care of oneself, for it is certain that no one else will. Every man must play the panther.

By *bleeding* hearts I refer to those dismissed as the soft and sentimental ones who talk as though we were our brother's keepers, bound by some obligation to worry about the other fellow and his troubles.

This is no Western movie I am talking about today. I am not trying to hang white hats or black hats on any of you, or any of my fellow men beyond the doors of this church. I am simply trying to find out what is happening to a great many people, some of them our dear friends and sometimes close relatives, who are changing their ideas and ideals about their responsibility for other people. Why are so many people cold as ice to other people?

By now most of you in this congregation know that I do not share Dr. Arnold Toynbee's grand moral design of history, with his bland assurance that nothing is wasted or lost in the human drama, and that chance and accident are mere illusions, not facts, over the millennia of years of human struggle.

On the contrary, I am convinced that Dr. Toynbee, like many theologians and philosophers, was trying to cushion the shock of reality, the cruel reporting of history that tells us of the steady frustration of the minimal demands of the great majority of human beings, of the mighty torrent of violence, of the rain of misfortune on the just and the unjust alike. It is not easy for sensitive minds to live with these facts in any age. To deny their existence, to turn one's eyes away from the full spectacle of man's misery is a great temptation.

But the important truth is that we do not preserve our ideals by confusing them with the facts. The churches have been telling us for nineteen hundred years, and the Jewish temples for a thousand years before, that we must accept our responsibility for man's welfare collectively—not just our own welfare, or the jig is up; a man cannot make it alone. I happen to believe, as a major premise of my life, that mutual aid is not only good religion, but essential to an enduring political order, to a growing scientific civilization, to finding the heart of any culture deserving of the name. But this is an emerging faith, an ideal, not a proven fact, and millions of people either do not believe it, or feel it will not work in the world we now have, or that its price is too high. So their hearts freeze up.

Let me be very plain about it this morning. We are encountering a great increase in frozen hearts and the rationales to defend them against the protests of the so-called bleeding hearts, the people of compassion who talk about and really take responsibility. The increase of people with frozen hearts is not necessarily deliberate and calculated, but it is taking place, and no church or temple with any sense of obligation to our humanitarian heritage can shrug it off.

Let me turn to an example or two of what I am talking about when I speak of the frozen heart. Here is a quotation from a column by Paul Coates in the *Los Angeles Times* for October 22. You may have seen it.

> The quality of medical mercy is apparently a bit strained in this town. It happened again just this week to a young couple newly arrived here from Detroit. Shortly before midnight last Sunday, Mrs. Jeanne Fox smashed her fingers in a car door. Her husband rushed her to a nearby hospital, a private institution contracted by the city to give emergency aid.
>
> In the receiving room Mr. Fox was asked by a nurse if he carried medical insurance. He explained that he was a member of the Blue Cross plan in Detroit and showed his card. She told him she was sorry, but she couldn't verify his membership at that hour of night. And she suggested that he take his wife to the County General Hospital for treatment.
>
> The doctor on duty looked at the woman's hand, but according to her, and from the medical report which was read to me later, he made no effort to treat it. Mrs. Fox, in tears from the excruciating pain, begged the doctor for "something that will put me out." She received no sedation, and was again advised to go to the County Hospital.

A friend of this church told me on Friday of his efforts as an officer of a union here in California to assist one of the workers in a local plant that had recently concluded a strike of several weeks. Like many other workers in the factory, the man found a large part of his first paycheck after the strike was garnisheed by one of his creditors. My friend phoned the creditor to explain the simple facts that here was a man with several children to feed, that strike relief had been modest, and that a little patience on his part would help enormously. To which he received the reply: "Who are you to shed tears over these union slobs? I want what he owes me."

Or let me turn to the *New York Times* for October 25, and a brief story reporting on the frozen hearts of some United States officials. The Reuters dispatch to the *New York Times* reads:

> Saigon, South Vietnam, Oct. 22 (Reuters)—Communist guerrilla forces in South Vietnam have developed an efficient and well-equipped medical service to care for their rising battle casualties, according to a new intelligence estimate. Evidence shows that the Vietcong are well supplied with modern drugs, including anti-biotics, and their facilities include large base hospitals and medical training centers.
>
> Vietnam Government forces say they know the exact sites of sev-

eral of the hospitals. Some U.S. officials are mystified at Saigon's apparent reluctance to take military action to put these hospitals out of operation. They say this would provide a major psychological setback to Communist troops risking danger in combat.

Now let me turn to an incredible column in the *Los Angeles Times* by Russell Kirk, October 22. It speaks for itself. I read a portion only, but not out of context, I assure you. The next few paragraphs are Russell Kirk and not your minister speaking:

> Never before were the Christian and Jewish religions so distorted by confused sentimentality as they are today. This writer hears all sorts of well-meaning people uttering slogans which they sincerely believe to be religious injunctions—but which, actually, are silly heresies.
>
> I confess to being particularly annoyed when some self-righteous sentimentalist informs me, "You are your brother's keeper!" I'm not, and I'm not sufficiently arrogant to desire any such station.
>
> For what is a "keeper"? Well, a keeper, as one may learn from any dictionary, is a jailer or warden who confines and supervises people. I don't want to be my brother's jailer; and I don't desire to turn the world into one great lunatic asylum or prison, where everybody is "kept" by sanctimonious Pharisees.
>
> Only God is a keeper of souls; and even He ordinarily works through the operations of a general providence, not through miraculous intervention. If we are bent upon our own damnation, He doesn't ordinarily keep us from ruin.
>
> So I protest, sentimental chum, that I am not the keeper of every Chinese coolie or Congolese cannibal or Skid Row inebriant.
>
> I don't mean to drench my pillow in nocturnal tears because daily, somewhere or other, every moment, somebody is wandering from the fold. Not being divine, nor even an archangel, I can't be held responsible for failing to set aright the steps of every Hottentot.
>
> God doesn't expect us to be their priggish "keepers." Persistent interference with others is a usurpation of divine authority.

After finishing that fragment of the gospel by Russell Kirk, I remembered some words of George Bernard Shaw I had read and written down years ago: "This is the only true joy in life: the being used by a purpose recognized by yourself as a mighty one; being a force of nature instead of a feverish, selfish little clod of ailments and grievances complaining that the world will never make you happy."

Who more accurately describes the human condition, Russell Kirk or [George] Bernard Shaw? In which direction are we going? I am sure many of you think about this as often as I do and are making your own evaluations.

It might help to stand back and look at the world as it is now emerging, to get a little perspective. The large-dimension screen of current history has a great deal of encouragement to offer. Did you read, as I did, the fortieth anniversary issue of the *Saturday Review* last August, and specifically the article by Buckminster Fuller in which he said:

> The will of history reads "for everybody or nobody," and since we balk at "for nobody," it has to be "for everybody." And that is the way it is going lickety split and the world around. We will soon penetrate the ocean depths, enlarging our world three fold. We will float large colonies of humans around the world in tensegrity geodesic cloud-island spheres, taxi-serviced by helicopters. The scientists will soon increase the overall efficiency of the world's mechanical devices from the present 4% to 12%.
>
> Computers will eliminate war as an evolutionary function by providing wealth to supply all mankind.

There are scores of studies being published today from the United Nations, from private foundations in various countries, capitalist and socialist, indicating the predictable developments in human productivity and technological efficiency and wiser use of the natural resources of the earth. But all of this is of little value unless we understand our roles toward one another. The interpreters of the elections last week seem to have considerable agreement that the welfare state programs of this country are accepted by the American people as is their commitment to world peace as the first priority. This apparent consensus is a gradual development for a people with an intensely strong individualist tradition, with a frontier philosophy of every man for himself. But let there be no mistake about it: welfare and peace assume that we are, indeed, our brother's keeper, that "we are in the same boat, brother."

The long-term conscience seems to be maturing in this country. We have discovered that we cannot prosper privately unless we manage to help everyone else to prosper and survive with us. But it is the immediate short-term conscience that concerns me this morning. I am still haunted by that kidnapped Good Samaritan, that bleeding heart, who is treated so scornfully by Mr. Kirk and his large confraternity who are so contemptuous of being our brother's keepers. Of course, the whole semantic by-play on the word "keeper" by Mr. Kirk is foolishness. He knows well that the Bible was not talking about our being jailers, but being good neighbors, friends, and allies, one with another.

What about the short-term conscience that leads you to the immediate act of assistance and compassion? Has this outgrown its value in today's world? A member of this church's staff fell and injured her leg on a public sidewalk a few days ago. No one stopped to aid her to her feet, or to call a taxi, or even to take her to a nearby bench. Suddenly everyone was blind, all priests and Levites, as in Luke's parable. You have seen this myopia almost every day of your lives.

Certainly a minister learns quickly in his professional life that this world seems to great numbers of people to be a heartless place in which to live, that time to be compassionate and concerned is the hardest time of all to find. Has something happened to us, or to our world, to make it so much harder to listen to the cry of our brothers on the highway of our world when they lie bleeding there?

Certainly the very character of our immensely complicated industrial society has made it far harder to become involved, even if the reach of our concern with man has broadened enormously within the span of a century. I was aided in my thinking about this problem with a few words by that extremely sensitive professor at Columbia University, Dr. Charles Frankel, in his book *The Case for Modern Man*. His comments are perceptive and relevant to this problem of the frozen and the bleeding hearts. Listen:

> Contemporary industrial society is an elaborately interconnected affair; large-scale organization plays an inevitable role in that society. This means that decisions made in *certain central places* have consequences that flow out farther and wider than the decisions made by most absolute despots in past centuries.
>
> The Madison Avenue account executive does not think of himself as an educator; the industrialist with factories in a dozen states and foreign countries who believes that men who are out of work should be willing to travel two thousand miles to find a job, does not think of himself as advocating an unsettled home life. They do not know they are making the kind of broad social decision they are making; they neither intend, nor can they foresee, most of the consequences of what they are doing; they are likely to feel as much caught in the drift of events as the rest of us.
>
> Technological developments have eaten out the social texture of modern (capitalist) society. To begin with, the simple physical mobility of an industrial population makes social ties impermanent and thin. When a man's place of residence depends mainly upon his job, and when jobs are changed frequently, community pressures are weakened, and community affections diluted. But even more important, the kind of social relation into which men tend to enter in an industrial society has changed fundamentally.
>
> If there is now a widespread sense of guilt and failure, it is in part because humanitarian feelings have indeed increased, and because the moral sympathies of many ordinary men and women now have an immeasurably greater scope than the sympathies of any but the most exceptional leaders of mankind in the past.

The paradox is real. Our scope is worldwide, but our power to see the injured neighbor at our doorstep has lessened. It is easier to give an annual check to the United Fund or the Red Cross than to visit our friends in the hospital or prison ward.

I am glad at the expanded conscience that makes us more sensitive to the needs of people once beyond the ken of our compassion. My desk is covered with recent stories that time forbids my using: headlines reading "Reforms Demanded by Bolivian Labor Leader," "Surgery Gives Sight to Five Blind Brothers in Sicily," "Communists in Mexico Bemoan Life's Cruelty," and many more from sections of the planet about which my grandparents knew little, and hence never worried about. I was invited a few weeks ago to be in New Delhi, India, this November at a conference on peace and anticolonialism, a bid which I was sorely tempted to accept for some of the reasons I hope are apparent this morning. When one meets leaders of movements face to face, the abstraction fades and the realities of a three-billion world population grow personal and humane. We will never thaw out frozen hearts with sermons or government publications, or even the best of legislation. We need the legislation, here and in all countries, and no man more ardently advocates militant agitation for such advances than myself, but let us recognize that we end the fearful reign of the cold-hearted only with personal relationships.

There is, indeed, much, as Professor Frankel indicated, that makes for impersonal ordering of our social and political life today: the so-called Wall Street, or Madison Avenue, or Downing Street, or Kremlin distance from the people themselves. But the real test lies in the acceptance by a government of responsibility for what happens to people. Our test of a political or economic order should not be its label, or its location, or its prophets and saints, but its power to create in the people themselves a sense of urgent concern for the other living peoples around them. We will never get back to the simplicity of the hidden farm in the hills, the village intimacy of our grandfathers.

New billions of people must be fed and clothed, educated and cared for in a fashion that calls for enormous technological coordination of machine power and human intelligence and social institutions. But our homes, our schools, our industries and governments, to say nothing of our churches and temples of all faiths, can play a part far beyond their present effectiveness, and specifically in our own country, in changing the relationships between people, one by one, day by day.

Reluctantly, at the present moment, I am convinced that a majority of my fellow citizens in America do not wish to become involved when they pass a motor accident on their own street where they could save a life by pulling a driver from a burning car, or in a factory workshop where a man has a heart attack and needs instant medical attention, or in the neighborhood organizations for extending playgrounds and clubrooms for the children at loose ends while both parents work. We are too busy, too detached, too preoccupied, too emotionally barricaded to stop and act. We are afraid of having to testify in court, of having to lose time from the job, afraid of being sued for damages. So we turn the key once more on the cell where we have imprisoned the Good Samaritan.

It is a splendid thing that our sympathies are broader than they ever were before, that we can feel profound empathy with the Japanese workers protesting the arrival of a nuclear-powered submarine from the United States, that we can feel shock at a UN report this week that American and British interests are a major blockade to ending apartheid in South Africa; this is, indeed, the compassionate and educated heart we need so greatly. But this same compassion must find expression in our daily lives, even with all the difficulties we face in a compulsive, profit-oriented society that does, indeed, at times penalize us for stopping to be human. If you have a modest window card saying to all comers to your home that you welcome neighbors of every creed, nationality, and race, you may find vandals spraying your walls with paint and obscenities. But without the privilege of asserting and practicing one's common humanity, there really is no life at all. There is only the mockery of words and the routine of sheer survival.

We need almost superhuman patience in trying to live today as though we were already in the good society. This is our major task, as I see it, for a long time to come. The obstacles may be harder here in America than in some other parts of the world; I am inclined to think this is the case. But be that as it may, this is the place we are in, and here is where our work is called for.

I am not belittling for an instant the complexity of pursuing the ideal of brotherhood in a transitional society. That happens to be the problem before us; I am persuaded that it can be done, and it starts with each of us at this very hour. We will not always be successful, and our milk of human kindness will often sour, and our tempers grow frayed. But we at least know what is happening, and we can take care to preserve our decency and love of the brethren, privately and inwardly, and usually without a psychiatrist to help us, or a preacher to pray for us, or a banker to loan us money. The much-aligned bleeding heart is our only hope, and I trust we will soon find a better name for it, less touched with the neurotic guilt of the Russell Kirks of today or tomorrow. I think the conditions for being decent and happy will improve, but that is only one man's guess. We may have to go through Pilgrim's Slough of Despond before we cross over to the other side.

Let me end with the words of a great old winter soldier of the last century who was often called a bleeding heart by his foes, Theodore

Parker, the Unitarian firebrand of Boston, who hid fugitive slaves in his cellar, and burned himself out, to die at fifty. This is what he said:

> Several times in my life has it happened that I have met with what seemed worse than death, and, in my shortsighted folly, I said, "Oh, that I had wings like a dove! for then would I fly away and be at rest." Yet my griefs turned into blessings; the joyous seed I planted came up discipline, and I wished to tear it from the ground; but it flowered fair, and bore a sounder fruit than I expected from what I set in the earth. As I look over my life, I find no disappointment and no sorrow I could afford to lose; the cloudy morning turned out the fairer day; the wounds of my enemies have done me good.

Such words from Parker brace me greatly.

You may play a large part or a modest one in the transformation of the world from a predatory battlefield into a community of friends. You may not see the men and women of avarice and cynicism diminish in great numbers in your lifetime. You may meet few people who seem to justify the eons of evolution of man from the mudflats and the swamps. The percentages may be changing with fantastic speed as self-knowledge and new skills accelerate apace, but be that as it may, you and those immediately around you can begin at this hour to practice the joys and compassions and delights of the sympathetic and understanding heart. Nothing can really stop that but death itself. The great men keep coming on.

The Challenge and Delights
of Getting Older
May 31, 1973

Keynote address at the Facing Life Forum of the Division of Career
and Continuing Education of the Los Angeles Unified School District

Portions also given January 19, 1974, at the Neighborhood Church
of Pasadena for the Second Workshop on Aging of the Pacific Southwest
District of the UUA.

I stand before you a wolf in sheep's clothing. I am not an expert geron-
tologist. I am a rank amateur, a sort of poor man's guru on no Himalayan
mountain peak, no white Rolls Royce, no flowing beard. So, you may
well ask my qualifications. As Dr. Marshall indicated, I am old enough,
I am an activist, and I am having a wonderful time.

Dr. Marshall has told me that the basic theme is "Facing Life," which
is the best possible subject. While I believe millions of Americans have
a paranoid fear of talking about death, to say nothing of making any sensible plans for its inevitable arrival, I frankly am glad you had that discussion last year, because I would prefer to talk about facing life in our own
later years, whether it be in our relationships with our children or young
people or middle-aged folk or older Americans. Dr. Marshall wrote me
that there are seventy-two classes for older adults organized by the Los
Angeles Unified School District's Division of Career and Continuing Education. She told me the members of these classes varied from the low
sixties to the mid-nineties—those are *ages*, not *grades*, you understand.

I am honored and delighted to be here, and I warn you that I shall
be candid; I will be kind, but candid. I am now unemployed, except
on piece work. Happily, I have no mortgage payments. I have a very
patient and intelligent wife, who is better to me than the six wives of

314

Henry VIII, and, like me, she believes in people's liberation—for both men and women—of all ages. What I want people to be liberated from will appear within the next few minutes, I hope. The one thing I assume we can agree on is that once a man or woman has acquired a real taste for education; a little wading in the waters of a second career; or explored his long-buried talents, maybe because nobody ever helped dig them out, or because the boss had no place for them in his shop or office; or once a woman or man starts traveling across this great land of ours and sees its glorious beauty, including Utah and Vermont, that man or woman will never again settle for the old rocking chair.

The other day I ran across a line from that great poet, Pablo Neruda of Chile, who got the Nobel Laureate in 1971, I think it was. He said, "I would become what I am, in some place and in every time, established and assured, and an ardent witness." That is what I hope all of us increasingly become: an ardent witness. I am weary indeed, after nearly half a century in the ministry and teaching professions, of older Americans being treated as nonpersons, as sort of plastic people. We are all of us, unless utterly disfigured and destroyed by contempt or neglect, human beings, flesh and blood and bones, with lighted minds aglow with life and joy and compassion; and that is why I am happy to be here with you today. I believe that, and want it to be a reality with all adult people.

My subject is "The Challenge and Delights of Getting Older." I mean just that! I've been trying out so-called *retirement* for size for six-and-a-half years now. I loathe the word *retirement*, as you will soon discover. It has to me sort of Forest Lawn overtones. But I have had six-and-a-half years of being my own man, writing my own ticket, admitting, as did the great British actor Laurence Olivier on TV recently, that I have a dreadful temper, that I like to have secrets, and ignore forty-five years of living by tight agendas and crowded calendars. I come to this podium a free man—so much so as one can be free and still love his fellow man and fellow woman. I am thoroughly enjoying myself. I need a lot of time to cover the ground still untraveled, which, I am happy to say, for my wife and me this year includes three weeks in the People's Republic of China, that mysterious Middle Kingdom, where we have been invited by that government to visit in September. I have been to other countries and had a great time in each of them. I have worked at jobs in Ohio, Maine, Massachusetts, New York, and California; and I have no major surviving complaints—just a few bruises. I happen to love *people*—white, brown, black, red, and yellow—and now find myself discovering the Mexican Americans and Indians of the Coachella Valley, where I speak once a month. And I understand a little better now the young Indian whose car I saw recently in Santa Paula with a bumper sticker reading, "America, love it *or give it back!*"

I shall be saying this morning that I feel we have run the individualism we prate about too far into the ground. The only way to be a happy person and a good person from now on is to have a strong feeling for the group: for other people, for our families, for our adopted or expanded families, for new communities of people, here and anywhere else we meet them. And we who have been around a while know how basic that truth is. There is no room anymore for hating the Jews or the blacks or the Asians or the Latins—or even the Unitarians! We are all children of the same glorious universe: skylabs, milky ways, the debris-littered moon, and all the rest.

Maybe some of you will understand what I mean when I say that at seventy-one it is easier not to be intimidated by my own mistakes or by my unshakable dreams. At seventy-one one need not feel obligated to apologize for those lost opportunities, or for the many errors of judgment. I am having a great time these days as I say, usually but not always politely, that some of my teachers in elementary school, high school, and even in college often taught me a lot of fantastic half-truths because they felt the whole truth might hurt me, or offend the superintendent's feelings. It took me fifty years to learn a lot of things that kids today are learning in grade school or high school about sex, religion, politics, culture, and many other subjects.

It took me twenty-five years to get over the idea, taught me in Ohio in my childhood by some charming but muddled people, that I was in danger of falling into the hands of an angry god. Then, fortunately, I met some other religious people, just as nice and a little more open-minded who, I found, had lettered in big gold capitals over the organ, "God Is Love," and I felt much better!

Fortunately, I had a quite bright family, even though they had very little schooling on either side. They never made me feel that I had to be a winner and make a lot of money, and believe me, I never did! Two deadly sins I never succumbed to because of that Quaker training at home were envy and jealousy. I have done a lot of wrong things, but I think I have never really been envious of anyone else, or jealous of anyone, and it is a great freedom, believe me. I know some grand millionaires, and have even tapped them at times, but I have never wanted to be one. I have seen many people far more successful than I—bishops, presidents of Rotary International, college deans, writers who get Pulitzer prizes, and actors who get Oscars—lovely, exhilarating people, but I honestly never felt jealous. Thank God for that!

I shall not now describe my sins: the time is too short. And I feel less bad about them at seventy-one than I did at forty! They bothered me for a long time. I have not been a winner or a loser really, but a very happy participant, an incurable extrovert who likes to read books and enjoy conversations, as well as do little jobs in the town or country that seem important and always lack enough hands. If America survives, it will be due to the volunteers, not the people on the payroll. That is what I have learned as a minister in fifty years. These are some of the delights of being older at any age, and at any income level, and from any cultural background.

So let me end this ego-trip section of my talk by saying that I am enjoying my so-called old age in spite of some obvious infirmities: a decaying memory, a tendency to get fatigued a few hours earlier at night (so I miss those midnight hours of reading when the phone doesn't ring). I'm now doing things I postponed far too long: gardening, walking, listening to people more and talking less myself—but still upsetting a few applecarts, rejoicing that the truth about Watergate surfaced so we can clean up the mess and get on with our work.

It's great fun to be old enough to read banned books, see an occasional X-rated movie (not that I ever learned anything from an X-rated movie that I didn't know before seeing it!), and vote a split ticket. In short, to mix responsibility with play and feed my insatiable curiosity. And, oh! if I could just have a third of the energy of Justice William O. Douglas at seventy-five, my long-time friend. I have just read the interview he gave Eric Sevareid on TV last September. I saw it at the time, but just to read it makes me feel I am good for another twenty years. I felt the same about my beloved friend, no longer with us, Dr. W. E. B. DuBois. I last saw him when he was ninety-four, editing the *African Encyclopedia*. He felt that at 92 it's time to pick up a new job, so he took on the Encyclopedia of the African people. He had one of the sharpest minds. I wish many of my students, when I was a professor, had had such a mind at eighteen or twenty as he had at ninety-four!

So now let me speak for a few minutes about old age survivors' benefits. There will be a chance for you to talk back later, I trust, because I may be wrong on a lot of this. I'm having far too much fun for someone whom the Social Security Administration has told to go and sit down on the bench and wait.

A few facts are very important. For example, we must keep in mind that 10 percent of our American population today is over sixty-five years of age. Just seventy years ago it was 4 percent. That's a big switch, and a very good one, if that increased number—that is getting ever larger—is happy and well-cared for and enjoying their bodies and their minds as they should. What I am really talking about this morning are the perils of postponement of enjoying new experiences, anticipating and meeting change, as we get older. My motto, written on the lintels of my doorpost, is "Do It Today!" even if you turn out to live to be ninety or one hundred. Of course, I am biased.

I feel strongly about wasting our precious years. We are in trouble as long as only one-half of our elderly citizens have ever finished elementary school, and only 6 percent of them have finished college. Now don't misunderstand me, I make no fetish about a college degree. I have enough of them to know how unimportant they are, except for providing the disciplines and delights of opening doors that extended reading can give anybody. My parents worked very hard to encourage me to go to school and college. I earned most of my way through. In those days there were few scholarships. The privilege of a relatively lighted mind was sought by many of our ancestors. It was the reason for their coming to this land: our educational system was the envy of the world.

The real issue is whether people have helped you—parents and friends —to learn how to use the forebrain, that wonderful part of the body that makes us human and keeps us from just being fish. They lack a forebrain, and they have been here millions of years longer than we have, and there are times when I think they will be here a lot longer than we will. They may survive us, but who wants to be a fish? The great crime of affluent America is its failure to give people education and jobs to make life worthwhile. This can and must change in our time.

One of the reasons I am so happy in these later years is that the horrors of the competitive society have ended. Keeping up with the Joneses is no longer important. Things become far less important than people as we get older. If we are sensible, we have gotten over our pathetic pack-ratting of this and that in the trunk and in the closet. The consumer mania slows down partly because our income slows down, but also because we know we can consume just so much and the rest is junk. We have begun to learn the proper enjoyment of matters that count when we are older: the open-hearted, open-minded sharing with people, with children, with our peers, with our neighbors; learning how to get along with half as much money, and usually, with not nearly as many of our beloved contemporaries, and learning how to get along with new friends. Those seventy-two classes in continuing education excite me because they are opening doors for many people.

The reason I accepted this invitation was because I realized the elderly are really going through a revolution. Thirty years ago the so-called senior citizens were pushed aside, shelved, rejected. A man's life expectancy for my father's period was forty-two years: today it is seventy-one. I've made it! I've made the average. It's a revolution for older Americans because we now know that the brain cells are not lost in old age. Yes, the mind slows down, the synapses are not quite as quick, but the mental tools have been sharpened and expanded, and in the seventies and eighties we can have the efficiency of the thirties, they tell us in the Gerontology Center, unless we are unhappy victims of actual physical deterioration. I am glad to know this, because I have grabbed hold of a little wisdom, a little weighing and discriminating and choosing, after years of experience. This no teenager can have, nor a twenty-year-old, no matter how gifted. These are survivor benefits!

As a minister emeritus, let me make a confession: the churches—Catholic, Protestant, Unitarian, the Jewish and Buddhist temples—all have too often reinforced the old myth that we become dependent in old age, that schedules and programs are not essential, that we must be thought of as on some kind of shelf and need to be cared for. We know better now, and the centers of gerontology are helping to sweep that myth away. There is a Christian denomination at the University of Georgia where a foundation has been set up to help the churches learn how to join the revolution of the aged, for the aged to learn to be themselves and take care of themselves. Freedom for the elderly! It is just a century or two late in coming.

This is not a talk about death or dying, though I have written many such and feel they are important matters for people to talk about. There is a taboo in America, more than in many other countries, on mentioning death, as though we were all Olympian immortals going to the mountain top, never to die. There is even a taboo in religious circles on the subject. But this address is a talk about life, life for older people, and I do not accept the official government figure of age sixty-five as proof positive that one must retire. That is one of the most absurd and arbitrary numbers ever drawn out of a bag. Rather, let me say people over sixty-five, all the way up to ninety and one-hundred and five, are my concern today and most days. I am *not* discussing the issue of euthanasia, which I am for, under safeguards that keep the White House and the CIA out of the decision-making process! And I am *not* discussing the medieval, barbaric, high-profit-yield industry of funerals and all the fringe benefits of those conglomerates, about which I am an expert who has won his wings. I have seen almost everything that can happen at the time of death.

We are entering an era in which a greatly expanded aging population produces problems for which society has few traditional guidelines because these are new problems. That is why meetings like this are needed. As Dr. James Birren and his colleagues at the Andrus Gerontology Center at the University of Southern California make very clear, "Until 1900, Western man was primarily oriented to what is now only the first half of life. Personal goals then were predominantly to establish a career and family; economic survival was the dominant issue." This is not true any more. Trends toward earlier retirement now indicate that in a few years Americans may spend more than half of their lives outside the labor force.

That thought terrifies many people: they are trapped by the work ethic. I liked my two professions, but they weren't everything in life, and they shouldn't be. Young people have to learn how not to be frightened at not being on the labor force for many decades of their lives. Rapid technological change, which will make much education and many careers obsolete, complicates the picture for the twenty-first century. Note that right now, with a promised cutback by the president of welfare and training and job programs, millions of youth and middle-aged will discover that life without work can be grim, grubbing for food, shelter, and part-time unskilled work, with no leisure opportunities. Let me say once again: poverty is never anything but misery. And the second half of life must not be ruined and made self-destructive by poverty.

Back to my friends at the USC gerontology center—the only really great one in America. I am told Dr. Birren and his staff ask, "What will happen to the middle-aged and older adults whose job skills are no longer needed?" "How many individuals avoid feeling alienated when they are no longer a valuable part of a youth- and production-oriented society?" "Where is the meaning of life to be found by gray-haired Americans who are no longer in the mainstream of productive society?"

In one sense, a longer life is a hard-won victory for Americans, and for people in other lands as well. Only recently have we seriously studied the biochemical, social, and individual problems of the aging, and we will be talking about that later today and in future conferences. We have been grossly ignorant and cruelly indifferent to the biology of aging of the human organism, including the genetics of aging and the effects of the physical and social environments on how we grow up and grow old. This is exciting material to cover, and I wish I had the time to do it now.

For us of the "middle class," who possess some margin of security and resources for mobility, change of scene, and renewed contact with distant families or friends, it is too easy to forget the realities that constitute life for our nation's poor, and unless we keep our eye on this total picture, our ideas and usefulness are irrelevant. In 1968, five short years ago, about a quarter of all older people were living in households below the depressed income figures considered by the U.S. Department of Health, Education and Welfare to be the poverty line. Thirty percent of these families had incomes of less than $3,000 a year. Forty percent of those persons who lived alone or with nonrelatives had incomes of less than $1,500. That was five years ago. The real income of these poor aged citizens has declined since then because of inflation. With food stamp programs not reaching nearly enough of those in greatest need, and new housing being cut back for the elderly, and medical aid made more and more difficult in recent months, both in terms of dollars for the programs and the ability of the aged to get to facilities, the crisis deepens, like something out of Dante's *Inferno*. Dr. Birren visualized an adequate, decent income throughout life as coming from many sources but being *assured*, and this we must have and will have. Every politician knows it, every educator knows it, every minister knows it. Some form of an annual income guaranteed in the second half of life is part of the revolution of the elderly, by whatever name it comes. With the changes taking place, many professions are on the way out. I am not sure there are going to be preachers much longer, to which you may say, "God be praised!"

What is good news—and I see it daily—the refusal of more and more Americans to accept without protest the situation of lowered income in days of inflation, inadequate wages for hard-working people. There is among the elderly, as well as the youth, a militancy we have not seen for a long time. It isn't only the long-haired younger generation who can march and carry picket signs and pack city council chambers; the white-haired grandmothers (who can remember Susan B. Anthony and Emelina Parkhurst's work?) are even better militants because of the experience that age confers. It was Mike Gold, years ago, who wrote that America is the only country in the world where old age is regarded as a disease that makes a person unfit for useful life and the respect of the community.

There are today many places I go where old people are right in there with vigor and passion and intellect, saying things will be a lot better sooner if we do our part, both with suggestions and in protest. And I say this as one just off the picket line in Coachella Valley with Cesar Chavez and his United Farm Workers. It is mighty hot on the picket line, let me tell you. There is a rising voice of demand for change by what some call "Senior Power."

You and I see older people at peace marches, poverty and welfare meetings at city hall, at the state capitols, and in Washington, more than ever before. Heaven be praised! The gray-headed Americans, poor workers, and middle class all refuse to fade away like MacArthur's old soldiers. They have formed three thousand clubs throughout the country; there are millions of members in the National Association of Retired Persons, and many others in many clubs of the National Association of Senior Citizens. They are a very real lobby in Washington, as politicians are finding out.

Let me say that my basic thesis today is that we older Americans, above all else, should do what we can to enjoy life, share in the social process of our culture and active citizenship, and feel good about ourselves, enjoying a legitimate self-love and self-respect, and achieve a sense of real usefulness to as many people as possible. For many years I have advocated the importance of getting the young people into the political scene. I rejoiced when the eighteen-year-olds got the right to vote. Now I am equally concerned that the eighty-year-olds *use the vote*. It is up to us to see that the vote gets out. The appalling figures on nonuse of our voting privileges are an indictment of our political process and our

social unawareness. And if the senior citizens raise the voting percentages, we will get more of the good things we want. That I do believe.

I come from a long line of English and British ancestors who fought
royal arrogance toward the common man, and as religious dissenters came
to America before the Revolution to build a different kind of community. It included getting the vote and getting an education for all of us.
Now we have both for many of our people. To be sure, some of it
is pretty shoddy schooling, and some of the voting doesn't seem to make
much difference; some politicians seem not to listen, the streets still have
potholes, and the landlords still don't understand about rats. Some ten-
ants develop hunger pains, cynicism, and apathy about voting. We older
Americans can help change some of this. I'm still for the eighteen-year-
old vote, but I just want the eighty- and ninety-year-olds out there, too.
Between the two, maybe we can turn some things around.

Older people tend to seek out their mirror images, their friendly
peers who sympathize and listen and share. Younger people underestimate their problems such as coping with new environments, difficult
transportation, far-off health clinics or doctors' offices, bewildering shop-
ping centers, the remoteness of movies or theaters or churches. These
are important issues. Urban planners, architects for public housing, and
designers of new developments should take into consideration such factors as these far oftener. Not everybody drives a car or wants to. Who
wants to be carrying all that smog-making around with him or her all
the time? We should be able to do our thing with relative ease and
convenience if half our nation is going to be old people.

The range of options must be kept as wide open as possible for
older men and women. They have lived a long time, they have strong
views. They want to be heard and to be listened to. Americans for years
have hated to admit they are ever going to be old. They have distorted
and often very stupid ideas of what the older years will be like. They
therefore deny their own aging, refuse to write wills or listen to nutri-
tionists or doctors or psychiatrists—or even clergymen!

And this brings up new agendas for the aged. With far improved
health, stronger minds and bodies, and greater longevity, many millions
of our people will be finding new vocations and service opportunities.
Some will work for pay, but most will be doing volunteer work for
pleasure and a sense of usefulness. Voluntary services are now crying
for aides and helpers in child-care centers, playgrounds, craft groups,
recreational and health organizations, in political parties, and, as I well
know, in churches.

Most senior Americans refuse to be put into cold storage or even
into warm storage in Florida or southern California, or tucked away in
compounds of the rich in hills and valleys away from the noise and
smog of the sprawling cities. And millions can't afford it anyway.

The most important item on any agenda for the elderly is to be free to find an interest of one's own choice and talent, and to pursue it, knowing you are never too old to count as a human being, and have fun doing it.

Many people are making a career now of working with the aging, and they are bringing knowledge, skills, and ideas to bear. As the members of the faculty of the Andrus Center at USC know, they are trying to preserve the self-esteem, the dignity, and the happiness of men and women in the second half of life, in a social environment traditionally hostile to old people, or indifferent at the very least. It's different in Japan, in China, England, and Central Asia. America's shame is its blindness to its elderly.

For reasons of time, I have omitted a large part of this address about my own heroes in the gerontological Hall of Fame: friends who helped me see old age as something not to be feared, but to be looked forward to as a goal achieved—as guru, artist, bon vivant, saint, veteran of many wars, all in one. I think of my debt to Pierre Van Paassen, Emily Balch, Thomas Mann, Harry Emerson Fosdick, Anna Louise Strong (who ended her years in China and, I think, was probably responsible for our invitation), to mention only a few dear friends I knew, provocative, creative people to be cherished and loved. Then there is the inspiration of the power of men and women who influenced me greatly one, two, or twenty steps removed, people I never knew in person because I am not quite that old: Bertrand Russell, Mark Twain, Ralph Waldo Emerson, John Lilburne, [George] Bernard Shaw, and, if you will permit me, Shakespeare and Beethoven; people who were very productive to the end, who used their powers of imagination and love of humanity with a passionate intensity. They helped me to be a happier old man.

But the trouble with such a catalog of heroes is that they are so individualistic. Whereas, I am pleading this morning that you see in every man and woman—plain, poor, handicapped, of a despised minority, another faith or nation—a human being who deserves to live to be one hundred and twenty, if the medical lads and lasses can help them do it. Or, as in Peru, leave them alone so they can do it on their own. This is not a plug for doctors, much as I love them, but for people everywhere being allowed to have agendas of worth and joy, and the means to live without needless disease and poverty and ignorance. The real target is to advance the humanity of our species as well as its longevity. It won't happen overnight, but if we don't blow ourselves to ashes meanwhile, it can come to pass. I am not at all certain that it will be started in my native land, not yet at least.

Ralph Waldo Emerson reminded us in one of his essays that "age has weathered the perilous capes and shoals in the sea wherein we sail, and the chief evil is taken away in removing the grounds of fear." Emerson's comment, "The essence of age is intellect," refers, I think, to the fact that the person who has developed his mind and feelings to be a source of pleasure and satisfaction finds much of old age a period of great reward and pleasure.

Arteries will harden, muscles stiffen, metabolism slow down, glands reduce their energy, but compensations will accrue, so that one can say in all sincerity with Jonathan Swift, "No wise man ever wishes to be younger."

I wish today to pay tribute to those exemplars, past and present, who have taught us who would listen the prime necessity of not running away from life and reality in old age, but rather of enjoying its accumulated rewards. What used to be singular examples are now becoming a mass demonstration of preserving creative strength in older years. We benefit from the inspiration and power of men and women who influence us. Those I have mentioned, and many more, have helped me be a happier person, and I thank them wherever they are. A true human being knows no age: he communicates his humanity as a young man of twenty or a sage of eighty. My hope is that we Americans will not respect our youth less, but learn to appreciate our older members more.

I hope the day will come soon when we still cease grading every American as a high or low achiever, cease having a cash nexus mentality toward what we do in our old age. Let some settle for a one-room shack in the desert far from a single neon sign. Others will be miserable without two swimming pools and golf links with pink petunias. The main goal is that age be not a terror, but a joy; that there will be books on orchid growing as well as the total technology and satisfaction of sex from cradle to grave; and above all, that we learn some of the wisdom of those who advocate contemplation as well as winning gold medals in the Olympics.

Lewis Mumford wrote: "No historic religion has yet sought to sustain life in its fullness and wholeness. It has been too preoccupied with life after death." It is a terrible truth that most religions still concentrate on life after death, and as a result place a secondary value on life on this planet in childhood or old age or any other time. Well, here stands one parson this morning who says, "Live it up now!" To those people who are not sure they have a ticket to the other world: have fun, be happy, and share a lot more love now!

In old age it is not important to be the guy who finishes first: the important thing is to be the guy who finishes *last!*

Part Five

Biographical Sketches

Schweitzer, Gandhi, and the Common Man
February 8, 1948

When this sermon was announced, there was no expectation in the minds of any of us that Gandhi would so soon perish at the hands of one of his own faith. This morning, I intend to proceed as though his death had not taken place, to comment on his leadership and that of the great Christian doctor of Lambarene, the Alsatian Dr. Albert Schweitzer, and to make some appraisal, for us who are of the liberal persuasion, regarding this part in modern thought and life.

Unitarians have been interested in Albert Schweitzer for several years, giving funds to some of his work in his hospital in Central Africa. Our own denominational press has issued in recent months a splendid anthology of Schweitzer's writings edited by Dr. Charles R. Joy. Few would quarrel with the dictum that aside from heads of states, Gandhi and Schweitzer have been the two major figures of influence over scores of millions of men and women in this generation. Schweitzer, a very individualistic Christian, and Gandhi, a very individualistic Hindu, have set ideas to work in our time which millions of men have accepted and employed in their personal and social living.

We are not, this morning, saying that Gandhi and Schweitzer are Unitarians, because they are not. But what they say and what they are doing in the world are often things which we, in our household of faith, have long preached and practiced. Both are men of revolutionary idealism and practice, both men are offering an almost savage criticism of Western industrial society, making sharper judgments than the average Unitarian would think of making. Both have contempt for the acquisition of personal property and for those class distinctions that private wealth produces. Both are men of complete simplicity of life and manner,

327

rude, undiplomatic, and, at some points, one could almost say "mad" for their departure from the accepted norms of our society. Yet these men in whom the acquisitive instinct is dormant or atrophied are shaping tomorrow's world probably more than any other two persons of our time. They need to be understood, and we need, I think, to learn from them, and select that which seems of help in our American society. As a religious people who welcome creative leadership from all religious traditions, natural and so-called revealed, we Unitarians should especially welcome an understanding of Schweitzer and Gandhi.

Schweitzer, today, lives in the heart of Africa at Lambarene [in Gabon] as a doctor in a hospital, serving the native people with unremitting devotion. He was born and bred in Alsace, a product of French and German culture. His biography is one of incredible fascination; he is a modern Leonardo da Vinci in versatility of talent, a Doctor of Philosophy, a Doctor of Theology, a Doctor of Music, a Doctor of Medicine, all of them earned. Schweitzer is famed for the most original and important religious study of this century, *The Quest of the Historical Jesus*; famed for a very gifted interpretation of the organ music of Johann Sebastian Bach; famed for the application of modern medical discoveries to the needs of people in Africa; and most of all, famed for the development of an ethical and philosophic world view welcomed by men on every continent and of all religious heritages. It is indeed an amazing life that he has lived. He emerges in the history of our time as a giant surpassing Gandhi from the viewpoint of intellectual understanding, and certainly he is his equal in personal and sacrificial service to the disinherited plain people of the earth, the people who, unhappily, are termed "the common man," but who are the people for whom all service should be given.

In his autobiography, *Out of My Life and Thought*, Schweitzer tells us that at the age of twenty-one he awakened one morning to the song of birds, and the thought came to him that he must not accept this happiness as a matter of course, that he must do something to show his thankfulness, and pondering over the matter at that early age he calmly determined to give himself to science and to art and to learning until he was thirty, and then devote himself from that time on to the direct service of humanity. And he did precisely that. He followed out the plan with a thoroughness exceedingly rare in history. He made a plan at twenty-one and he is still proceeding on it! It is a planned life of immense proportions and gives one pause as to whether there is not some argument for planning our lives far more than most of us do.

We Unitarians should be especially conscious of Schweitzer's monumental contribution to the study of the historical Jesus. It is ammunition for our liberal arsenal. He is an orthodox Christian in many ways, but what he has to say is what Arius, Channing, and all the great Unitarian thinkers in theology have said. The book, *Out of My Life and Thought,* divests Jesus of the supernatural nimbus which has for centuries accompanied him and still does for most Christians. Schweitzer showed that Jesus had a human consciousness, that he was capable of erring, and he named some of the errors. The chief error was the expectation of an early end of the world. Schweitzer in his theology, of course, supported the Unitarian minority on the view of Arius, as opposed to Athanasius and historic trinitarianism. It was Schweitzer who exposed the false "two natures in one" theory of Jesus that was set up at the Council of Calcedon in the fifth century, the idea that Jesus was both divine and human at the same time. As one writer has said, "Schweitzer removed the Lazarus-like grave clothes from the doctrine of Jesus and revealed a human being in history." But he did not simply perform a negative operation on the metaphysical Jesus. He revealed the absolute ethic of love as taught by Jesus. Whether we accept it or not, whether we think it is workable or not, it is the part of the contribution that Jesus made to history that certainly should survive rather than the theological accretions that later times have put upon his ministry. To Schweitzer, Jesus is no theological conundrum. He is a spirit alive and in the world in terms of influence and power, working through an absolute ethic of love.

It is necessary to say, and certainly I think true, that Schweitzer is much more a mystic than most Unitarians. Jesus, says Schweitzer, spoke the words "Follow me" to men and they followed him, and still today his spirit commands. "He reveals himself in the toils and sufferings and conflicts of people today." Schweitzer is closer to George Fox, to the Quakers, and to a great part of the Pietistic tradition of orthodox Christianity than to our Unitarian viewpoint. He has taken Jesus out of the political and social struggle of men and has made him a personal presence and spirit rather than a prophet of an equalitarian religion.

The motive that prompted Schweitzer to take himself to Africa was not, according to him, essentially heroic in intent. He says in his book, *On the Edge of the Primeval Forest,* "There was a long series of injustices and cruelties that the colored races of mankind suffered at the hands of Europeans, the primitive at the hands of the so-called civilized. We in our civilization are burdened with a great debt and anything we give these men of the colored races is not benevolence but atonement." And it is not for any of us, who accept the fruits of colossal exploitation in our Western society, to call Schweitzer an escapist. If white men had not stolen diamonds, gold, and other wealth from enslaved Africa, and if we Americans had not brought black people to our eastern shores for sale, Schweitzer would not have felt impelled to spend over half of his life ministering to the minds and bodies of the dark continent's peoples.

Schweitzer supports much of our Unitarian approach to religion. This fact will not be stressed in Congregational, Baptist, or Methodist churches, which properly honor him. If we read our Schweitzer, we will find out why the Beacon Press chose to publish him. He is profoundly disinterested in and skeptical of metaphysics in religion. To him an ethical view of life is the central matter for man to grasp. Reverence for life and the will to live are the heart of religion to Albert Schweitzer. These together can awaken our sense of responsibility and ennoble our social and political life. Theological systems are absolutely out in all of the works of Schweitzer. In the preface to his *Civilization and Ethics*, he writes, "A new Renaissance must come and a much greater one than that which stepped out of the Middle Ages, a great Renaissance in which mankind discovers that the ethical is the highest truth and the highest practicality. I would be a humble pioneer of this Renaissance and throw the belief in a new humanity like a torch out into the world. I make bold to do this because I believe I have given the disposition to humanity a firm foundation in a world view that can be intelligible to everyone." And Schweitzer has given it a firm foundation. With great skill, scholarship, and imagination, he reaches into every great humanistic and ethical tradition and brings forth that goal which will be useful to a world view today. He goes back to Socrates, who shattered skepticism with a mighty earnestness by saying, "What is moral can be determined by thought." That is not being said in most churches today! He goes back to Epicurus. He says he is guided solely by the effort at veracity that is the beginning of wisdom. In fact, it is most interesting to see how a Christian thinker like Schweitzer goes to the Stoics for inspiration. In my study of religion, I have long noticed how our theological schools and churches avoid the Stoics as though they were the plague. The Stoics belong to humanism; they belong to liberal Christianity, and Schweitzer knows it. He says of them: "In the Stoics the ideal of humanity has come into view. Marcus Aurelius, Seneca, Epictetus, all Stoics, teach us to renounce the self-regarding spirit and develop an ethic of universal brotherhood." We are urged to possess the spirit of sincerity, to be more inward, to find a sense of responsibility.

Schweitzer then pays tribute to the men of the Age of Reason in the eighteenth century whom we in the Unitarian Church have so long recognized as part of our fellowship of rational religion:

> The first task of the state is to insure to every human being a human value with an inviolable measure of freedom of which he must not be robbed. The proclamation of the rights of men by the states of North America and by the French Revolution give sanction to what time has done. These men were masters of the facts of life to an extent which we are unable and do not realize. The greatness of the philosophy of the 18th century rationalism is that its hands were blistered.

That is a phrase worth remembering. Few philosophers have had blistered hands.

We Unitarians find Schweitzer strengthening our best insight that the only knowledge is that which one experiences himself as "ethical will." That is not the definition of traditional theology. In fact, it would flunk out of almost any seminary in the country if he said, "God is ethical will." No more deeply religious spirit has marked our generation than Albert Schweitzer. Yet we should note the understatement of the man in talking about God, his modesty and reserve and humility in not claiming too much. There is no such arrogance as marks most mystics in Christianity about Schweitzer. Let me quote, "It has been my principle never to express my philosophy more than I have experienced as a result of logical reflection. That is why I never speak in philosophy of God, but only the universal will to live which I realize in my consciousness in a two-fold way as creative will outside myself and as an ethical will within me." If every Unitarian in America could catch this spirit and avoid the arrant dogmatism of any atheist and many a humanist, the spirit of truth and of good will would be greatly advanced.

One is reminded of James Freeman Clark and of Jabez Sunderland in Schweitzer's compass of religious inspiration coming from many fountains: Hinduism, Confucianism, Judaism, Christianity, and the rational philosophers. One of his best books, *Indian Thought and Development*, was used by Gandhi. No ethics can be won by a knowledge of the universe, says Schweitzer. Man must steer his independent course across an uncharted sea. It sounds like the skepticism of Oliver Wendell Holmes, of an Emerson or a Parker, rather than a devout Christian pietist. We Americans think so particularly of progress in terms of Edison's lamp, Bell's telephone, Wright's plane, and Ford's automobile that it is important for us to stop and listen to a voice like Schweitzer's in Lambarene reminding us that these magnificent tools are engines of the devil unless they are related to an ethical purpose. It is interesting that both Schweitzer and Gandhi have gone into backward areas of the world where there are very few Fords, very few electric lights, and very few other modern inventions. The difference is, however, that Schweitzer wants them in Africa, hopes they will come, while Gandhi resolutely took the position that these were evil things. "Ethics," says Schweitzer, "is responsibility with our limits to all that live, animal and human." "Ethics consists in experiencing the compulsion to show to all creatures the same reverence that I do to myself." "It is good to support life and it is bad to destroy or obstruct it," says Schweitzer. "The right to the soil, the right to freedom of labor, the right to justice, the right to live within a natural organization, the right to education—these are basic to a good society." Many will find in these words of Schweitzer a bridge between his individual ethic and the so-called collectivism of governments which realize that these rights must be fulfilled in practical terms for modern peoples in every continent.

Regarding Gandhi, whom Nehru called the architect of India's destiny for twenty years, I would remind you simply that he was born in 1869, that his father had been a prime minister of his local state, that his parents were people of privilege and opportunity, that his mother was a very devout Hindu. He went to England at an early age to finish a legal education. He was an unsuccessful attorney in India. A case then took him to South Africa, and he stayed there to help the depressed people of India living in South Africa. He was admitted to the bar and became extremely successful, financially and in prestige. He then ran across Tolstoy's teachings of the moral ideal of the Sermon on the Mount. It gripped him tremendously and he became an advocate of the life of poverty and nonviolence, to which he gave himself for the rest of his life. He linked the New Testament teaching with the Hindu ethical teachings, which is, I think, one of the few times in history when it has been done with any workable success. He did not become a Christian and rejected a great deal of Christian teaching. In 1915 he returned to India and in 1920 came his break with the British government.

His first fast was in 1924 to stop the riots between the Moslems and the Hindus, and it worked, just as his fast worked in the last few days of his life to stop tremendous loss of life. The struggle for Indian freedom continued through the remainder of his life as his absorbing responsibility. Some have asked if he were not quixotic in his fasting in order to get political action. It was not a new or unique thing. Mr. Joseph Martin or Senator Taft probably do not plan to fast in order to change the Marshall Plan, but in American history we have had fasting that affected politics. In the days of Jefferson when the British threatened to close the port of Boston June 1, 1774, it was recommended that the people have a fast day of protest, and Jefferson wrote:

> We, under necessity of arousing our people from the lethargy into which they have fallen, feel a day of fasting and prayer would be most likely to call an alarm to their attention. The people did meet generally with anxiety and alarm in their countenance and the effect of the entire day throughout the colony was a shock of electricity, arousing every man and placing him solidly in the center.

And I would remind you, of course, of the hunger strike effecting legislation in Ireland in the recent days of struggle for Irish independence. I think it was the Lord Mayor of Cork who died fasting, and whose death notably succeeded in affecting public opinion.

We have not the time to summarize Gandhi's teachings. You know of his vow of truth, that we should never say "no" when we mean "yes," or "yes" when we mean "no." His doctrine of nonkilling and of nonviolence, of returning good for evil he borrowed directly from the Sermon on the Mount. His repudiation of untouchability, his vow of kadar (using homespun cloth), his use of simple tools in the home and in the community, and his opposition to the factory system probably are the most controversial of all his teachings. If you believe the factory is here to stay and that mass production is here to stay, I urge you to recognize that he was talking about a colonial people who were not enjoying the fruits of modern industrial production.

One major point of difference between Gandhi and Schweitzer is the religious use of politics. Schweitzer has almost entirely withdrawn from the struggle of men for political action. Gandhi gave a lifetime of evidence to the thesis that politics is essential to building a good world. Gandhi was not encumbered, as was Jesus, with the idea that the end of the world was about to take place. He taught his millions of followers that we must learn to live in this world and build institutions in it. That is a permanent contribution of Gandhi. Also he taught that inward principles of an ethical character must be tested in the field of action. "By their fruits shall ye know them," was his favorite text from the New Testament. He taught the technique of politics as well as ideals. We may differ with some of his techniques, but that there are necessary techniques is a fundamental lesson to be learned. He never made the mistake that many Christians make of exalting "spirituality," implying that religion is in the clouds, that religion is simply an attitude, that religion is goodness in the abstract. Gandhi was an extraordinarily acute political realist as well as a religious teacher of the first order.

That he opposed doctors, scientists, and manufacturers as evil men is not at the moment the point. We may think that those are rather quixotic positions. But he realized the need for all people to learn a pattern of practical living. That social insight of democracy relates him to William Lloyd Garrison, Dorothea Dix, Starr King, and many other muscular Unitarians of our tradition. The test of real leadership is whether the leader serves the needs of the great masses of living men, rather than those of special groups, however good those groups may be. The reason for the great appeal of Schweitzer and Gandhi in the world today is that they are men who have seen the impoverished, the ill, and the needy as having a first claim on the conscience of mankind! These must be the people a real leader serves first. To them, the most must be given. There is no selfish motivation in either of these, Schweitzer or Gandhi. We realize that these two world leaders are like Jesus and St. Francis, that is, they are men with a contempt for the things that motivate much political and religious leadership today.

The test of profound twentieth-century leadership is the ability to move men toward a universal religion as well as toward a universal society. Gandhi and Schweitzer have done more than any other two men of our time to break down the barriers of revealed religions, to break down the wicked and evil separation of men by creeds. Both of them have shown our common ground in religion. Schweitzer is a humanist and a lover of Christianity, of the Greek ethic, and of Hinduism. His books breathe a universalism that Emerson and Parker would understand. Gandhi lived and died in a colossal effort to bring two great religions into mutual tolerance, Mohammedanism and Hinduism, religions larger in number than all of Christianity put together. We should not underestimate how much influence Gandhi has had in bringing together the Hindu and the Moslem to end the communal struggle, which must be ended or neutralized before democracy and social progress will come to India.

Others will follow in India, in Africa, in the United States, and elsewhere who will carry the universal and humanistic ideals of these two men into new social, religious, and political patterns of brotherhood. In our lifetime we will live to see these two men honored for what they have most truly given, a spirit of modern humanistic equality and integrity to both politics and religion.

The Paralysis of the Liberal
An Address Celebrating the
206th Birthday of Thomas Jefferson
April 10, 1949

There could be no better day to discuss the role of the authentic liberal than today as we approach the 206th birthday of the greatest Unitarian America has yet produced: Thomas Jefferson.

These are days of sharpening distinctions, of taking sides, of making decisions, of recognizing issues, and the liberal who mistakes liberalism for suspension of judgment, or withdrawal from participation, or sheer toleration for its own sake is hard put to it.

I should like to discuss the concept of liberalism with the figure of Jefferson close behind us in our discussion. His concept has much still to commend itself to our present age. He was, with his immense humanity, a bulwark of our democratic heritage.

I need hardly remind you of this congregation that there are devastating forces trying daily to destroy this liberal heritage. There are those who resent bitterly any spiritual communication and fellowship among men of various persuasions, left and right, orthodox and heterodox, conservative and radical. This church with its honest respect for variety of conscience is resented deeply by extremists who consider it impertinent for Republicans, Democrats, Socialists, and Communists to ever speak to one another, to seek to understand one another's minds even under the roof of a church that teaches goodwill. But if a liberal church cannot prove this communion of minds and people possible, how can we talk of "one world" and mean it? I am sure that I reflect the sentiments of many of you in deeply resenting the impertinence of those who seek by direct or devious means to surrender the liberalism upon which our Unitarian religion is founded.

There are men of great power in American public life today who would dynamite liberalism's bridge of toleration. They have nothing but contempt for the temper of mind that seeks to avoid an *either or* approach to truth. The bridge of liberalism has borne much traffic in the making of this country and of other nations of the earth. The men who think in terms of *either or* are the real totalitarians. The men who cry *either or* have no conception of the saving power of what Jefferson meant by the liberal spirit. Nor do they realize what ruin they call on their own heads.

Jefferson, may I add, gave his entire life to the practice of a positive and creative liberalism, and suffered many years of merciless attack for it. The calumny heaped upon him by President Dwight of Yale, by the New York and Philadelphia papers, resembles in an astonishing fashion the abuse leveled today at men and women who insist upon the process of reason, of social reform, of a healthy toleration of variety. Those of you who saw Sidney Kingsley's *The Patriots*, a play based on the life of Jefferson, will remember the loneliness and isolation of the man who never surrendered his faith in the people or in the power of popular education. Here the liberal temper came to supreme flower in a man who won the highest office of the land because he never compromised his faith in the liberal principle of understanding and respecting the rival opinion and insisting upon ideas bearing fruit for man.

This is no time for the liberal to take a sick leave. The greatness of Jefferson's liberalism was that when gigantic issues were being debated on every farm, in every shop and office, he spoke his mind with great clarity. He wrote a statute on religious freedom when the state church was seeking an ever tighter law on conformity, he favored universities for the people and founded a great institute of learning, he supported universal suffrage when the Tories sought to restrict the ballot with property qualifications, he saw the role of profit-making in the newspaper industry as a drag on responsible journalism and wrote, "The newspapers of the country by their abandoned spirit of falsehood have more effectively destroyed the utility of the press than all the shackles devised by Bonaparte." He criticized American policy or institutions for the only reason any man should criticize his own land, because he loves it deeply and suffers to see it fail at a point where it needs to succeed. For example, we who are liberal resent slanders on our loyalty. America is my homeland where my own ancestors have worked for two hundred years as citizens. Like any average American, I can write, without a chemist's trace of chauvinism, a patriot's lyric about the glory of my country—especially if I may include the coast of Maine, the mountains of the Southwest, and the camaraderie of our people who made a culture and a nation from a new continent and who never bent a knee to any monarch on our soil. I know the pride in America Samuel Adams and Walt

Whitman felt, for, without their talent, I feel the same emotions of inordinate pride in this magnificent assembly of resources, races, gifts of mind and hand that adds up to a country and a nation.

One reason I grow weary and sometimes indignant and find my patience grow thin with men who would lynch liberals with labels is that they cast their innuendos at all who maintain a power of self-criticism in their patriotism. Too many liberals are paralyzed today, immobilized by fear of being called names, or being bracketed with Communists because they stand for some of the elementary decencies of mankind that Communists advocate along with other men. Jefferson was called a Jacobin, a label awarded in his day for French radicals. This because his patriotism as an American did not exonerate him from seeing good in another nation or real limitations in his own from time to time. We need liberals to read this lesson from Jefferson today. Here was a man who gave his life prodigally for America, who helped write its laws, shape its institutions, invent its tools, raise its schools, and prove beyond a shadow of a doubt his affection and loyalty to the land of his birth. It should be the same for each of us in our more modest way. We rejoice in America as did he. We add as fully as time and our gifts permit to the wealth of our nation. We repair what seems amiss and like a loving parent chide what seems wrong with our habits, both our neighbors' and our own.

In all of his activities Jefferson demonstrated with magnificent prodigality the creative energy of true liberalism. Too often we have allowed it to decay into a feeble and false criticism of all sides, a platform for crying "a plague on both your houses" with fine impartiality. Jefferson loved life and people far too much to play so mean a role.

The liberal asks for the give and take of sincere discussion, but he also knows that moments come for bold decision, for taking action, for building the dam, for planting the crop, for establishing the school system, for placing the scientist at the disposal of the people's welfare. He moves from discussion to legislation, from debate to appropriations. These things are as much the role of liberalism as the preliminary step of listening to all viewpoints. No president ever proposed more new projects than Thomas Jefferson. Let us remember that the liberal is not, by definition, a man of indecision.

Let me suggest somewhat more fully what I mean by the liberal spirit. Then we can face together the peril of the tired liberal's paralysis today. There is no hope of victory for the free men if we who are liberals fail to exercise our daily franchise of thought and responsibility.

There are many points of departure for defining the liberal, but let us use Jefferson's own words: "Opinion, and the just maintenance of it, shall never be a crime in my view, nor bring injury to the individual." Supreme Court Justice Oliver Wendell Holmes, a later Unitarian, in a famous dissent stated the same idea when he wrote, "Congress cannot forbid all effort to change the mind of the country." The liberal emphasizes the *process of change!*

The liberal is a man marked with a clear-eyed human sweetness of temper. He respects gentleness in human relations and seeks a balance between the feminine element of compassion and the masculine element of firmness. He honors nobility in character wherever it is found, and his God, if he pays homage to a God, is one of benignant toleration.

The liberal abjures the customary piety, he is suspicious of conventional religion, he rejects self-satisfied morality and sees only impertinence to man's dignity in the bigotry of the creed makers.

The liberal in religion and society is constantly seeking to create a certain kind of atmosphere, where growth of mind can take place, where the process of sharing truth and ethical judgment can take place. Upon the creation of such an atmosphere depends our personal and collective salvation. If I did not believe it both desirable and possible, I would close my Jefferson and desert the pulpit, neither of which I have any intention of doing.

Liberalism does not equate itself with acceptance of complacency or stupidity, nor does it fear the operation of the imagination. It does not resent idealism, but insists upon seeing its good works.

The liberal knows that we re-win our liberty every day and has discovered that a rusting liberty is a feeble weapon with which to combat the tyrant.

I sometimes regret that the founding fathers deleted so much of Jefferson's writing in the Declaration of Independence. One deleted sentence I especially regret being blue-pencilled:

> King George I, has waged cruel wars against human nature itself, violating the most sacred rights of life and liberty in the persons of distant peoples who never offended him.

The passage, of course, refers to African slavery, but can represent far more. There are still the cruel wars against human nature itself with which we should be most concerned as liberals today. We are in firm opposition to the man who seeks to close the door on truth, who says it is not dynamic, that it has been discovered once and for all.

I have had recent occasion to talk with two men who in their politics are Republican and in religion, Protestant in one case and Jewish in the other. Both were men eminently liberal, both men of extraordinary success and achievement, both deeply concerned at the cloud of intolerance obscuring the vision of Americans today, both resolutely resisting the effort to legislate conformity of opinion. This they are doing as good Americans, as fairly conservative Americans, but as men who feel their principles can survive encounter in the open with rival ideas, and they resent as profoundly un-American the stifling of opinion by gag or padlock or deportation or prison cell for the nonconformist.

A few weeks ago I gave you a Spring reading list. It included books by liberals of various philosophies. May I add another to that list: Barbara Ward's *The West at Bay*. And from it I should like to offer one quotation:

> One thing at least the Communists may accomplish for a Western union, and perhaps the men of the West will one day be grateful to them just as, in their daily lives, they are sometimes grateful for the pains and sorrows that have given them strength. So long as Communism, with its apocalyptic appeal, its vision of a classless society, its cry of brotherhood, its claim to offer a society based, not upon exploitation, but justice, stands on the frontiers of the West, there can be *no respite from its challenge*. The West is offered the choice of fulfilling the promise inherent within it of creating a free, good and just society, or it will fail all the more speedily because of the chasm between its pretensions and its practice. These are the stakes.

Miss Ward, an outspoken non-Communist, an editor of the London *Economist*, is a liberal who believes in a Western association of nations. She makes the case as intelligently as I have yet seen done, and every man who calls himself a liberal would do well to read the book.

Here is where the liberal is so often paralyzed. He must find the spiritual fortitude, in days of colossal intimidation, to say that a moral substitute for communism and its program must be offered in good faith by those who reject its program. The liberal who picks up the anti-Communist banner today so often finds himself winning the plaudits of the very men he most despises: the men who would rearm Germany a third time, and forget the days when fascist arms came very close to victory; who would welcome Salazaar and Franco into the United Nations; the men who would silence the dissenters with loyalty purges and padlocked halls at home. The liberal on Jefferson's birthday rejects the paralysis of inaction and insists it is not too late to play the role of liberal. The Unitarian Church should, for example, be a place in a free America, where a man like Prof. William Stapleton, the British philosopher, could say, as he recently did in New York, that "the commercial licentiousness and ruthlessness of America are proverbial," and go on to say, as he did, that the ruthlessness of the removal of the kulaks in Russia at the beginning of the revolution was undeniable. "It may be," he adds, "that the original temper of that revolution has been seriously perverted. We well know that power inevitably corrupts."

I happen to agree with Dr. Stapleton when he adds: "There is a lack of clear religious consciousness on both sides. . . . In the West there is far more religious doctrine than religious perception."

One reason I regret that the foreign delegates to the New York peace conference were not permitted by our State Department to come to Los Angeles was that I felt a liberal and fair criticism of some Russian policy by a disinterested English philosopher would be a good thing. Here was a man who in one speech, unnoticed by the press hungry for political scandal, stated what he considered wholesome truths. "The West, under a cloak of freedom, violates its professed ideals by indulging in licentious commercial exploitation of its workers and economically backward peoples," and also, in a further paragraph, added, "The Russians have damaged the precious tradition of spiritual integrity, of personal gentleness and honest dealing and without a widespread acceptance of this moral standard as obligatory for all personal beings there can be no mutual trust or decent society."

Professor Stapleton observes that the Communists believe the war fever is being whipped up in America in order to mobilize the country's strength for breaking the one society that has wholly rejected capitalism. This does not minimize one iota his sharp criticism of Russian moral failure, but it surely does not excuse the West for its unwillingness to let a tremendous economic experiment take place without thirty-two years of constant attack. Justice Holmes said: "The community has the right to try experiments."

I feel that the liberal is a man who believes that experiments have a right to be tried *under favorable circumstances*. Those who place obstacles in the way of an experiment are not coming into court with clean hands in protesting the immorality of the experimenters who resist vigorously the external obstruction.

We should be able to see the role of criticism in the liberal way of life as it applies to us and to others. I am at times somewhat annoyed with friends of the Soviet Union who can see no possible error in that country's calling Anna Louise Strong a spy with no supporting evidence, or no error in withdrawing from the World Health Organization and other United Nations agencies.

We are pleading today for the legitimate role of the liberal in the world. There are men and women who say it is an impossible position, but this church, and hundreds of Unitarian churches like it, are for continuing the four-century experiment. It assumes not paralysis by liberals, but accelerated participation. It does not require a nonpartisan mentality, but a broad and generous hospitality to rival ideas. It assumes agreement will often be made, but that disagreement will not frighten us into immobility.

No system of religion, government, or education can survive that allows no place for self-criticism. This applies to America, France, Holland, or Russia. Chancellor Robert Hutchins of the University of Chicago spoke at Spokane, Washington, on Thursday and said: "America's use of the atom bomb on Japan was a gross mistake, a military and moral mistake." He said it the same day that President Truman threatened to use it again. Dr. Hutchins is a good American and a good liberal and I want to see America always large enough to welcome such severe criticism. It is the guarantee of our liberties and sound health.

I am one who believes peace is a number-one priority today. I believe it is not too late to avoid the annihilating catastrophe of another war. I believe a *modus vivendi* with Russia can be found. This does not mean excusing her mistakes when they occur nor rejecting her overtures when they are made.

The bridge of friendship with other nations must be built at *both ends*. We need men of good will at both ends. We need participation at both ends. The spectator critic with no mental muscles being used constructively is a real liability.

In the past twenty-four hours I heard a speaker from the Conference on Peace held recently in New York. The eminent journalist Mr. I. F. Stone stressed a point I wish many liberals would grasp. He said: "There was repeatedly expressed in New York the need for self-respect in world relations between left and right, capitalist and Socialist, East and West. Peace does not rest upon a faith in Soviet perfections." I would add that those in America who feel Russia can do no wrong, nor any right are both injuring the peace.

The liberal today is to be found in many places, and we Unitarians have no monopoly upon the precious ore. In a day of hushed voices, tongues are being used that should cause us to reestimate who is liberal and who is not. I, for one, measure liberals by the relevance of the subject matter of their statements, as well as the vigor of their words.

Here are the Methodists, 8.5 million strong, our largest American Protestant church, saying in their latest quadrennial conference: "Peace in the immediate future depends primarily upon the establishment of better relationships between the Soviet Union and the United States. When nations depend primarily upon military force, both the spiritual and economic foundations of peace are undermined. The militarization of the public mind reduces the possibility of the free play of ideas." That is a *liberal* statement, which Jefferson would have honored.

Listen to the recent statements of the General Synod of the Reformed Church in America: "Our people should not tolerate any complacency about war, they should combat a mood of hysteria and blind hatred; they should press for positive programs of peace and justice, especially for greater use of the processes of international conversation and negotiation."

That is liberalism and would have been understood in Jefferson's Monticello.

Listen to the Northern Baptist Convention at its latest conference: "We are resolved to work with other religious bodies in starting an immediate world peace movement to save the world from destruction. Every possible avenue of diplomatic interchange between the United States and Russia should be kept open and used." This is liberalism at work.

A liberal is a man who resists the closing of shutters on human intercourse and the reliance on brute power. The liberal is not afraid to take sides. He is not afraid of partisanship, but he takes the side of the generous program for mankind, not the defense of privilege and personal aggrandizement, and the dead hands of the past holding the living generation from its work of change and advance.

The liberal is rightfully frightened at the breakdown of human relations anywhere, the withdrawal of mind from mind, whether in Washington or Moscow, whether in the university or the courts or the church or the diplomat's chambers. There can be no hope for men who dismiss the media of humanity, the media of honest measurement and judgment, the media of planning for all men's welfare and not that of a few.

I am personally very proud of the role of millions of church people today. They are expressing themselves with passionate vigor and liberal responsibility.

Peace is not subversive; honest debate and inquiry are not subversive; planning for the material, spiritual, economic, and intellectual necessities of our people is not subversive. The only thing that can be subversive to a liberal is surrender to intolerance, to lynching with labels, to sealing the tomb of the thinker, and seeking, like the villains in Verdi's *Aida*, to end with a living death the operation of the human spirit.

The paralysis of the liberal can be ended only when the temper of Thomas Jefferson can become the possession of free men. Remember Jefferson's words:

> Lay aside all prejudices on both sides, and neither believe nor reject anything because any other persons have rejected or believed it. Your own reason is the only oracle given you by heaven, and you are answerable, not for the rightness, but uprightness of the decision.

Let us offer a Unitarian prayer of thanks for the testimony of so clear a witness to the indomitable integrity of the human spirit.

The Rediscovery of Thomas Jefferson on His 219th Birthday
April 15, 1962

It has been thirteen years since your minister addressed you on a Sunday morning on the subject of Thomas Jefferson. Before I close this morning, I trust that it will be quite clear why another commentary on this extraordinary American seemed appropriate; in fact, why the temptation was irresistible to remind myself and all of you of his untarnished character, his glorious humanity, his pertinence in our present situation.

If the inner light which my Quaker ancestors bequeathed me still burns in my Unitarian soul, I can attribute it to my compulsion to share with you a continuing enthusiasm for the greatest of the Founding Fathers, a man far more alive at this hour for many of us than many men and women now walking the streets of our cities.

I am really no evangelist or missionary, but simply a witness to greatness and courage that I meet as the years pass, an advocate of human goodness wherever it appears. Happily, you provide a platform where this advocacy may be heard, if perchance you choose to eavesdrop on my discoveries. Whether you elect to come, to listen, or accept a portion of my witness is entirely a private matter. There is no compulsion, no coercion, and, I trust, no fragment of guilt on your part if you elect to find other evidence more persuasive.

If there be a modicum of virtue in my labors, any profit in my words, it is due in no mean degree to the power that this heroic American has exercised over me during the past forty years. Though few of you may know it, Jefferson has rebuked me a thousand times with his example, opened my all too rigid mind to new truth, and set my emotions aflame with love for those who are my chance and my chosen companions.

Thomas Jefferson's stature is increasing with the years, and as crisis deepens in our public life, his significance becomes even more apparent. By vocation and avocation he was a practicing farmer and active politician. His livelihood was derived from his large plantation in Virginia and from the many public offices that he occupied for forty years. Let us remember that he was a member of the Virginia legislature and the Continental Congress, governor of his state, minister to France, United States secretary of state, vice-president, and twice-elected president of the United States.

After retirement from the White House in 1809, he spent seventeen years farming his acres, building and organizing the University of Virginia, and maintaining an enormous correspondence with thousands of persons who flooded Monticello with letters. He arose with the sun, worked methodically throughout the day and far into the night.

It is not, however, with his amazing activity that we should be primarily concerned this morning, but rather with the basic commitments of his mind and conscience, his concept of man, including man the citizen in a free nation so recently hammered out by himself and his fellow revolutionaries. If there were to be a Jeffersonian text today it would be this: "No vice is so mean as the want of truth."

The life of Thomas Jefferson is a monument to the idea that the free mind at work is the most indispensable attribute of our humanity. "Freedom," he wrote in one letter, "is the most sacred cause that man has ever engaged in; without the precious blessing of liberty, life has no sense and no dignity."

In the presidential campaign of 1800, bigoted men tried vigorously to stir public opinion against Jefferson for his unorthodox religious views. And little wonder, for this man was indeed a religious revolutionist from youth to old age. To Horatio Spafford he had written:

> In every country and in every age, the priest has been hostile to liberty. They have perverted the purest religion ever preached to man into a mystery and jargon unintelligible to all mankind. I have sworn upon the altar of God eternal hostility to every form of tyranny over the mind of man. I am not amongst those who fear the people. Educate and inform the mass of the people. Enlighten the people generally and tyranny and oppression of the body and mind will vanish like evil spirits at the dawn of day. The people are the origin of all just power.

As today we find it increasingly difficult to maintain a lively and effective sense of the people at work shaping policy and structure of their institutions, this fundamental confidence of Jefferson's acquires fresh importance. How are the people to grasp the handle of self-government?

Before we recall some of the specific issues that absorbed this great American for a lifetime, let us remember the character of his liberal mind, which could not be beaten down, perverted, or silenced. In his day he was called a Jacobin because of his sympathy for the French Revolution, a term equivalent to "Communist" of our time, a term of opprobrium and contempt as used by conservatives. Jefferson was not paralyzed by this name-calling, which dogged him throughout his long career. He had risked the King's gallows in 1776, in his early thirties, for his leadership in achieving our independence. He insisted upon an examination of alternatives, even those foreign to our tradition or novel in their proposals.

It was essential, Jefferson felt, to exercise the franchise of thought if we are to maintain it. No president ever offered so many proposals for reform and progressive advances in our nation. They flowed like a torrent from the study in the White House, concerned with agriculture, trade, science, education, foreign affairs. He insisted that there be debate, and that it end after time had been allowed for free and full consideration of issues, and that action be undertaken. "Opinion and just maintenance of it shall never be a crime," he declared at one time. "It will never bring injury to a single individual." There was none of the hesitancy characteristic today in public debate. I cannot conceive of Jefferson's saying, "A plague on both your houses!" and equating the proposals of the left and the right as both automatically untenable, with virtue always presumed to be found neatly in the middle of the road.

I was reminded of this a few days ago when a Unitarian newsletter reached my desk with the sermon title announced as "The Peril of the Middle Way," the point being, I gathered, that avoiding extremes is not necessarily the surest way of finding the correct path for action. The middle may be a defensive equilibrium, a static surrender to habit, a deliberate refusal to look beyond self-interest and present advantage. It may not be a road but a shelter, safe, it is hoped, from small arms fire or long-range missiles. It is often hard for people, eager to avoid controversy or a revoked clearance rating, to understand the total absence of such concern in a Thomas Jefferson. The dialogue of progress for mankind was his meat and drink.

So able a spokesman of the non-Communist world as the British economist, Barbara Ward, recognized this in her statement, which in these times takes so little courage: "One thing the Communists may accomplish for the West. So long as Communism, with its apocalyptic appeal, its vision of a classless society, its cry of brotherhood, its claim to offer a society based not on exploitation but justice, stands on the frontiers of the West, there can be no respite from its challenge."

Since Barbara Ward is a British citizen, she cannot run the risk of the marshals with subpoenas in their hands from the Committee on Un-American Activities now roaming our city. I have read enough of Barbara Ward to know full well that she never equates the fears of the ultra-right with the proposals of the ultra-left. Many of us who attended the Shrine Auditorium Town Meeting for Democracy last Thursday night heard Miss Marsha Hunt declaim with eloquence that the real subjects for our wrath, if we would be good Americans, are "the irresponsible monopolies, racial segregation, illiteracy, slums, unemployment." Jefferson would have cheered her to the rafters, as did those present in the great audience of five thousand.

Thomas Jefferson believed in experimentation and believed we must make room for the advocates of change, asking them to speak without being judged in advance because of party, sect, or origin. For half a century he insisted on a real consideration of issues by the people themselves.

Those of you who were present in this auditorium on last Friday night, when our Public Forum presented a panel on the ultra-right, will recall Mr. Phil Kerby's deeply moving words about the absence of authentic political dialogue in America at this time. Because the energetic and well-nourished campaigns of the House and Senate investigative committees under administrations of both parties have cut off all serious debate from the left, there is an absence of true democratic discussion of the actualities confronting our people.

President Kennedy, Mr. Kerby told us, recently complained with some irritation to Marquis Childs that he hears too little from the liberals and the left. His mail is from the right! Thomas Jefferson's ghost could have told him why. The left has been treated with isolation, unemployment, and obloquy for at least thirty years. With loyalty checks, FBI harassments, black lists, imprisonment, and even personal violence, the American people have sought to drive Communists, many Socialists, and other critics of conservative policies into the wilderness, and then they wonder why there is so little support or comment from the left!

As one who has known something of the wrath of the inquisitors, I can agree with Mr. Kerby and Mr. Jefferson that there must be unpenalized debate of all grievances and proposals—authentic, intelligent, sincere debate. Viable alternatives from all directions must have sober, responsible consideration, or we make a dumb show of freedom, a mockery of popular government.

Without debate one has the silence of the tomb or the cackling of joys in meaningless nonsense, such as we hear now from the irresponsible right and from most of the center. This is the certain path to dictatorship or revolution unless it is replaced with free speech, without reprisals, for all men and women, including the left.

Whether or not one likes the conversation of a Communist, it must be heard if we are really to proceed as Americans to fulfill the early promise of our Madisons, our Jeffersons, and our Paines. Even if every solution proposed by the Communists and other advocates of the left were wrong, it would be better to have it said, without threat of subpoena, prison, or excommunication at the paymaster's office, than to have the banal imitation of debate and dialogue now going on in our country. Until we attain such genuine discussion, we are in very great danger.

Jefferson's advice, given in the midst of one great struggle, remains germane today: "Lay aside all prejudices on both sides, and neither believe nor reject anything because other persons have rejected or believed it. Your own reason is the only oracle given you by heaven, and you are answerable, not for the rightness, but the uprightness of the decision." Would that such a declaration could be lettered in gold at the entrance of every American public school today! Then teachers could speak with freedom and pupils discuss without fear in the classroom.

Having decided that a democracy could be built out of the thirteen colonies and the yet unsettled territories to the West, Jefferson proceeded to a program rich in conception, experimental in design. Let us, on this 219th anniversary of his birth, mention five areas of that program:

First, there must be widespread suffrage. "Every man, and every body of men on earth, possess the right of self government. They receive it with their being from the hand of nature." "My opinion has always been in favor of universal suffrage." We have made progress in 175 years with the extension of suffrage to women, and without property qualifications for the ballot, but millions of Americans, white and colored, still are deprived of the ballot by state legislation, by poll taxes, by residence requirements, and other barriers. And great segments of our population tremble as suffrage is won in South America, in Algeria, in China, and [in] Africa.

Second, said Jefferson, there must be popular education and it must be with unfrightened teachers and equal opportunities for rich and poor alike. He not only presented legislation far in advance of his time for tax-supported schools, but also for the selection of talented students to be given advance education at federal expense, something still to be achieved in a large way in 1962. He was a pre-Fulbright scholarship man, and would have such aid widespread and available from a generous and eager government. He was proudest, above all else, of having fathered the University of Virginia, and hoped to see a great national university established before his death, which, of course, we do not yet possess. He gave his magnificent library to the government to initiate what later became the Library of Congress. Yet today, 150 years later, many a Negro child is forbidden entrance to the local public library in several of our states for no reason other than the color of his skin.

Third, Jefferson was a militant advocate of a free press, and let us not confuse this with a commercial press, interlarded with advertising, privately owned in most cities by individuals with an eye on profit sheets rather than coverage of all of the news coming to them from the four corners of the earth. He believed, with Tom Paine, that the people must own, write, and distribute the news themselves without interference. He had no illusions about a kept press used against the masses of the people. During his two administrations, Jefferson watched the editors of the Federalist newspapers assault him without mercy, and declared: "The newspapers of the country by their abandoned spirit of falsehood have more effectively destroyed the utility of the press than all of the shackles devised by Napoleon Bonaparte."

With the McCarran Act at this hour being used to silence the left wing press, already reduced to virtual impotence, the relevance of Jefferson's words need no extended commentary from this pulpit. Jefferson would be appalled today at the newspapers of our land, with rare exceptions so bereft of ethical standards that even the most unsophisticated citizen believes only a small fraction of what he reads in his daily editions of sifted information.

Fourth, Jefferson was a devoted advocate of free science in the service of peace and democracy. He was himself an inventor, an agriculturist, an engineer, and an architect. A free people must have, he repeatedly emphasized, the tools for their own progress. One can easily imagine what Jefferson would say about planned obsolescence, shoddy materials, short-weight merchandise, adulterated drugs, suppressed inventions! Science was for life, not death; for progress, not profit; for human happiness, not private advantage.

The enormous expansion of the practical sciences in the socialist nations today is something Jefferson, like Lenin, would applaud to the skies. There is no crime greater against the heritage of Jefferson than the prostitution of science in our own time and our own nation. If anyone seeks evidence, visit Mexico today. It is still bereft of the fruits of science in the twentieth century because of American trade practices and price tags.

"Science," Jefferson stated on one occasion, "is more important in a republican than in any other government. I am not afraid of new inventions or improvements, nor bigoted in the practices of our forefathers. It is bigotry" (he wrote Robert Fulton of steamboat fame) "that still keeps Connecticut in the practice of their forefathers." His emphasis was on the utility of science for the welfare of the people.

Fifth, Jefferson gave the primary attention of his life to the shaping of a democratic strategy and an imaginative foreign policy, in a time before the airplane, the ocean liner, the radio, and [the] telegraph. It was Jefferson who worked practically for strategies that could move a new nation forward in progress and security. We do not often remember his genius in making a single nation out of frontiersmen, planters, mechanics, and merchants. In a time when Europe was ruled by aristocrats and kings, he shunned entangling alliances, yet it was Jefferson who urged

President Monroe to accept a British alliance in order to defend the young Latin American republics from monarchs in Europe seeking to capture them. Of the recent betrayal of the spirit of this policy I shall not speak today.

Jefferson's respect for multiple patterns of government in the world was prophetic. Listen to his words: "We surely cannot deny to any nation the right whereon our own government is founded . . . that every one may govern itself according to its own will, and that it may transact its business through whatever organ it thinks proper, whether kings, conventions, assemblies, presidents, or anything else it may choose." Could this be bettered today as we labor to make the United Nations an effective instrument in our world? It would certainly get the United States out of Viet Nam, South Korea, the Formosa Straits, and Cuba, if we took it seriously!

Why is Thomas Jefferson so significant in this second half of the twentieth century? Because he was far more interested in the future than in the past, because he cared for all of the people and not only a favored elite, because he had confidence in an educated people to manage their own affairs, because he despised war and cared magnificently for the opportunities of peace.

Jefferson actively resisted every obstacle to man's exercise of his powers, in church or government, in custom or trade. He believed that man is an intelligent creature who must explore his world, who must pursue his curiosity, who must fortify himself with knowledge to use his power. He must depart from the cave and the forest and settle the uplands where the sun shines and the rivers run freely. He must discover and reserve an ethic of truth, lying neither to himself nor his fellows. He dare not forfeit his vision or compromise his dream.

Truth is uniquely his treasure as man and it must be the core of his philosophy. Jefferson declared that man is responsible for the consequences of his choices, but he must be allowed to make them. All of the charlatanism of church and state, mass media and corrupted schooling must be swept away if man is to come into his inheritance. His loves and joys, hopes and sorrows are precious to him. No invention, no Congress, no liturgy, nothing whatsoever must circumvent man's march to freedom. "A little rebellion," he said on one occasion, "is a good thing, and as necessary in the political world as storms in the physical."

We need to reflect on these sharp words from the great statesman of Monticello as we walk through a murky atmosphere of hate and suspicion today. Above all else we need his humanity, his courage, and his respect for the human mind freely at work. In a social context Jefferson honored the ethic of the individual: his dignity, his potentiality, his integrity. One can only imagine his contempt, were he here now, for every force that squeezes the juice of independence out of a man today, the frightful burden of conformity so many men and women carry about on their shoulders. He never claimed that there was some mysterious superiority in the state that gave it the privilege of riding over its citizens booted and spurred. Individual men must have a Bill of Rights to insure their liberty from the temptations of any state to play the tyrant.

He felt that the earth is our home, our only certain frame of reference. If this planet is even to approach the aspects of a paradise, it must be by man's own untiring efforts. No threats must cripple man's energies nor darken his mind nor paralyze his will.

Jefferson did not shout jeremiads against the moral decadence of his time (though there was plenty of it), but concentrated on the liberation of each man's genius, aiding him with the tools of government to find himself. He believed in altruism and love of man for man. No cynicism clouded his thousands of speeches and letters, though anger at the stiff-necked and the predatory man flashed like lightning when occasion called for it. The mentality of the munitions laboratory never seduced him. The efforts of a congressional committee to march millions of citizens into straitjackets of docility and silence would have outraged his conscience, as his victory over the Alien and Sedition Acts makes transparent to every student of history who bothers to look. The mind of man and the conscience of man are the only possessions deserving the name sacred.

No supernatural power can aid us, no gods await our adulation or our fear. We possess the keys to heaven, a heaven bounded by two poles, spinning in a galaxy immense and glorious. We can enter into our heritage at this moment, and none can stay us but ourselves. Let us salute in love and with clear minds this exemplar of all our liberties, that all men and women of every land and clime may share his gifts, no less avilable because his voice is silent and his heart grown cold.

Happy birthday, Tom!

George Bernard Shaw
An Appreciation
January 28, 1951

In the preface to *Three Plays for Puritans* George Bernard Shaw wrote:

> It does not follow that the right to criticize Shakespeare involves the power of writing better plays. The contempt of the academic pedant for the original artist is often founded on a genuine superiority of technical knowledge and aptitude; he is sometimes a better anatomical draftsman than Raphael, a better hand at triple counterpoint than Beethoven, a better versifier than Byron. If technical facility were the secret of greatness in art, Mr. Swinburne would be greater than Browning and Byron rolled into one, Stevenson greater than Scott or Dickens, Mendelssohn than Wagner.

Today we are honoring an original artist. Let me say that I am not offering a technical discussion of Shaw as a dramatist and playwright partly because I am not competent to do so. I happen to feel that he was a very great playwright, that his talent for the drama was of a very high order, but it is not of these matters in the field of play construction, dialogue, characterization, and motivation that I wish to speak today. Such subjects will for years absorb students and craftsmen of the theater, including our own playwriting group and our Theatre Lab. My concern is with George Bernard Shaw as a dynamic, intellectual, and moral force in our century in a culture and society undergoing shocks and catastrophes beyond the imagination of our grandfathers to conceive of. Neither am I exploring his orthodoxy or heterodoxy as a political analyst. Lenin once said Shaw was a good man fallen among Fabians, and writers on the left are now debating with heated words whether to bless or curse the Irish playwright of Ayot St. Lawrence. With this debate, I am not today concerned.

Probably no man of this century angered more ecclesiastics and conventional church-goers than George Bernard Shaw with his merciless satires, his cold-blooded summaries of theological absurdities, and his exposés of the church's alliances with the powers of this world over the years. Relatively few clergymen will probably admit it, but the long preface to *Androcles and the Lion*, published in 1915, was one of the clearest and most readable discussions of Christian teaching and New Testament criticism produced by anyone of this generation, ordained or otherwise. I know many fellow Unitarian ministers who first discovered the chemical astringency of liberal religion reading the seventy-seven pages of the preface to *Androcles and the Lion*. You could not do much better than to read the paragraphs on "Salvation a Class Privilege," "The Alternative to Barabbas," "Redistribution," [and] "The Limits of Free Will" to discover some of the basic tenets of twentieth-century Unitarianism.

These literary, political, and religious limitations of my subject this morning bring me to one major observation: The world around us has sought to dismiss George Bernard Shaw as a charlatan and a clown, as the modern king's jester, as a wit toying with politics and with the sacred institutions of love and marriage. Let no one be deluded by this abracadabra of the high priests of education, politics, and religion. They know much better. The Civil Liberties Union of southern California reports this week that several school libraries have removed Shaw and Mark Twain from their shelves in recent days. One does not purge library shelves of jesters and clowns unless they are taken seriously beyond the bounds of comedy. H. N. Brailsford, the distinguished British journalist, in his extremely thoughtful tribute in the *Nation*, November 25, comments upon the factors in Shaw's early life, which made him pose as a paragon of vanity. He tells us of the drunken father, the bawdy uncle, the middle-class snobbishness of the Dublin Shaws with their pretension at nobility and their proximity to some of the worst slums in the world. Above all, Mr. Brailsford reminds us of the humiliating failure of Bernard Shaw's first years in London, his nine years of hard work that netted the young critic exactly six pounds. "In order to convince himself that he was not an ignoramus he adopted the manner of a bragging Cyrano. It became part of the Shaw legend and he kept it up. It amused his readers more than it irritated them." But thousands of humorless people have been terribly deceived into thinking they were dealing with a boasting fool, a brash literary bull in a china shop. And they were dreadfully mistaken. No one was more in earnest about our unfinished world than George Bernard Shaw.

Today my chief concern is to present one man's appreciation of a fighting idealist, a prophet without clerical frocking, a man of genius who brought the first-line issues of our society onto the stage for more than gentle treatment. In a decade like our own, when Frederic March and

Arthur Miller's revival of Ibsen's *An Enemy of the People* lasts two weeks on Broadway, and only the most exceptional *Death of a Salesman* redeems the theater from froth, mysticism, and scandal as dramatic fare, it is salutary to remember that Shaw made his reputation making good theater out of such subjects as slum housing, prostitution, war and peace, the revolutionary message of Christianity, and the merits of Darwinian evolution. One has only to read Tennessee Williams's *Streetcar Named Desire* to see how far down the ladder playwriting has descended since 1915 to appreciate the courage and the responsibility of citizenship that motivated George Bernard Shaw.

Some of you may have read Sean O'Casey's tribute to Shaw in the *New York Times* November 12. In that statement Mr. O'Casey wrote:

> Possibly the venerable figure of Bernard Shaw may some day appear in a panel of glass in an equally venerable cathedral as the lively saint of the machine age and the social revolution. Maybe he was in a glass panel in some big church nigh a hundred years ago as a young red-headed warrior saint who had died in battle, becoming a reincarnation of one impatient at the sleepiness of the church in whose window he stood, angrily watching those who came and went, listening to them chant praises, not to god but to their own self-righteous respectability.
>
> It is well to remember that Shaw as a child wandered through the corroding streets grouped around St. Patrick's Cathedral where white washed hovels gave a dangerous shelter to many of Dublin's hard pressed workers and their women. It was a panorama of dirt and drabness, an enigma which Dubliners call the will o'God.
>
> But to George Bernard Shaw it was not the will o'God. He was a born fighter . . . he was a man of tenacious courage. He threw aside a safe, secure job in Dublin and went to London where there was no security or success for many, many years. He had a divine call more than many a minister . . . to preach a sensible gospel to yearning and ignorant people, even those groomed in the universities of Oxford and Cambridge.

Carlyle was still talking when Shaw was born. Darwin punctured the pride of our species while Shaw was a school boy. Marx's *Das Kapital* and Ibsen's plays crossed his path before he was thirty. Freud soon followed. Later came Lenin's revolution and the waves of German, Italian, and Spanish fascism. In this world—social, scientific, intellectual—Shaw came with youth and ardor, never losing his zest or curiosity or courage. He shouted, he invented startling exaggerations, he turned truth upside down to draw men's attention to it. He put Humpty Dumpty together again for the duration of a play's performance and, like William Lloyd Garrison, he insisted upon being heard.

He did not toy with art for art's sake. He was possessed of the high seriousness of a Sophocles, even when his weapon was an epigram. With astonishing craftsmanship, he gave two hemispheres plays that entertained, but also frankly taught a moral one generation in advance of the time. He was more of a preacher than a house of bishops, more of a moralist and more of a prophet than a dozen Niebuhrs. He refused to be worried or diverted from his main task, which was to make the earth a fairer place to live in. Whether he exaggerated the great man idea of Carlyle or not, whether he wanted all the world to be patterned after the British middle class, whether he expected capitalists to vote in socialism in a sudden paroxysm of goodwill or not, he hammered away year after year, and in play after play, on the necessity for justice and the end forever of poverty. Very few preachers of religion ever were possessed of such tenacity regarding their basic gospel.

He fought with all of his courage and intellect against poverty, which offended him from early childhood both esthetically and morally, and later politically. Poverty was ugly, poverty was stupid, and it offended a deep sense of righteousness in his bones. In Shaw's preface to *Androcles and the Lion*, you will remember, he says:

> It needs no Christ to convince anybody today that our system of distribution is wildly and monstrously wrong. We have million dollar babies side by side with paupers worn out by a long life of unremitting drudgery. One person in every five dies in a workhouse, a public hospital or a madhouse. Naturally so outrageous a distribution has to be enforced by violence pure and simple. Iniquity can go no further. The need for drastic redistribution of income in all civilized countries is now as obvious and as generally admitted as the need for sanitation.

Before some people dismiss this kind of statement as the vaporous mutterings of the king's jester, or others dismiss it as a commonplace, let us ask what dramatist is saying it on Broadway or in Hollywood today. Shaw was, for all of his fun, not unlike his character Ferrovius in *Androcles and the Lion*, of whom Metullus says: "There are men who are a sort of walking conscience. He makes us all feel uncomfortable." Most dramatists have portrayed Christ with unctuous sentimentality. Shaw, in speaking of Jesus, gives us fresh evidence of his sensitive, alerted conscience:

> You may doubt whether Jesus ever existed, you may reject Christianity; and the iconoclasters, placidly contemptuous, will classify you as a free thinker or a heathen. But if you venture to wonder how Christ would have looked had he shaved, or had his hair cut, or whether he laughed over the repartees by which he baffled the priests when they tried to entrap him into sedition or blasphemy, you will produce an extraordinary dismay and horror among the iconoclasters . . . you will have made the story real, the figure to come out of the frame.

Shaw then points out that most of the people expressing an interest in religion are only passionately affirming the established religion or passionately attacking it. "You never have," he writes, "a nation of millions of Wesleys and one Paine. You have millions of Worldly Wisemans, one Wesley with his small congregation, and one Tom Paine with his smaller congregation. The people hunger and thirst, not for righteousness, but for rich feeling and comfort and social position. If Savanarola only tells the ladies of Florence that they ought to tear off their rich jewelry and finery and sacrifice them to God, they offer him a cardinal's hat and praise him as a saint, but if he induces them to actually do it, they burn him as a public nuisance." This is a clearer reading of the gospels than one will find to this day in ninety-nine pulpits out of one hundred. George Bernard Shaw and Harry Ward were not far apart.

The bridge between religion and economics is a short one. The same man that wrote *Androcles and the Lion* and *Three Plays for Puritans* also wrote *Major Barbara*. His thesis in all of his writing on this subject—pamphlets, dramas, and prefaces—can be given a text out of his own writing: "Poverty does not produce unhappiness, it produces degradation: that is why it is dangerous to society. Its evils are infectious, and cannot be avoided by any possible isolation of the rich. We cannot afford to have the poor always with us." From Godwin, from Shelley, from Marx, from Spencer, [and] from Henry George Shaw learned the lessons of equality and the need for material security by the masses of men. He stated his ideal sometimes as a democracy of supermen and gave it the mythology of the Methuselah legend, stating that we create ourselves by willing. After the depression that set in men's minds following the findings of Darwin and Huxley, Shaw brought back rationality, the role of thinking, the possibility of human freedom within conditions set by nature. His universe included, in his words, "Justice, mercy and humility." I am sure many of us would rejoice if this trinity of virtues were the goal of the men who sit around the horseshoe table at Lake Success, or the trinity sought by our neighbors on our street, or that its advocacy in a school room would not lead to a subpoena for the teacher.

As Mr. Alec West has indicated in his new critique of Shaw as a Fabian, there will long be debate as to whether Shaw lacked faith in the power of the working class to act in its own interest. I think he believed in the power of exploited people to shed their illusions that wealth and leisure are just around the corner for them if they only guess the right tune on the radio quiz program, or pull the right lever at the exact moment in Las Vegas. This address today is an appreciation and not a fluoroscopic photograph of his political structure as a thinker. This I do know, and ask all of you to note: Shaw expected people to do something about the evils of life after having a conviction of sin, after discovering their guilt and responsibility. This is more than I ever received from seeing a play by Mr. Saroyan or Mary Chase. Shaw lived in no ivory tower.

He knew the baptism of fire involved in speaking at political street meetings, of asking questions of a speaker in a hostile hall, of working into the late hours on committees of the Fabians. In the preface to *Widowers' Houses* he says, "this play is deliberately intended to induce people to vote on the progressive side in the next County Council elections." To him, drama was a form of art which makes an audience into a group, united in a common desire to gain refreshment and strength from expressive action. Shaw brought the facts of England's economic society onto the stage for the first time in his generation and expected people to leave and do something about it. Theater was not mere entertainment after a dinner of roast beef and Yorkshire pudding. He wrote a book called *An Intelligent Woman's Guide to Socialism* as a handbook for those who wished one thousand pages of information of what he thought they should do. He studied countries attempting to establish socialism: the Scandinavian countries, the Soviet Union, and, later, England itself. He was never guilty of dilettantism. He made millions of enemies by expressing his loyalties and beliefs on unpopular subjects with gifted clarity. He again and again criticized the temptation of the Fabians in England to live in the cumulus clouds of an academic rationalism. He insisted that the common emotions of united people, workers and middle class, can become the creative power in life to change the world.

Widowers' Houses is not a mere tract, it is a play with a disturbing power to show people as they are, members of a society based upon exploitation of man by man. Its theme is the slums of London and the means by which the owners of the houses fatten themselves on the rents that come from hovels reeking of disease and misery. I would like to think this play is out-of-date, but I know Los Angeles too well.

Later, after the play was produced, Shaw wrote:

I had better written a beautiful play like *Twelfth Night*, but frankly I was not able to: modern commercialism is a bad art school, and it can not, with all its robberies, murders and prostitutions, move us in the grand manner to pity and terror as Aristotle suggested. It is squalid, futile, blundering, mean, ridiculous, forever uneasily pretending to be wide-minded, humane, enterprising. It is not. My life has been passed mostly in large towns, where my sense of beauty has been starved whilst my intellect has been gorged with problems like that of the slums in this play, until at last I have come, in a horrible sort of way, to relish them enough to make them the subjects of my essays as an artist.

Much in *Widowers' Houses* may already seem archaic, and many may prefer the Shaw of *St. Joan,* but this last week the headlines on the defeats suffered by our housing authority, the victories of the Sartoriuses of today should make us stay our tongues from too premature a dismissal of this play. Since the end of the living newspaper plays of the 1930s, and such musicales as *The Cradle Will Rock* and *No For An Answer,* I have seen nothing that even tried to attack similar evils with such bold strokes.

Shaw wrote Ellen Terry in 1897, speaking of his play *Mrs. Warren's Profession,* "It is much my best play, but it makes my blood run cold. Ah, when I wrote it, I had some nerve." It was based on the theme of prostitution. This was no eighteenth-century comedy of manner. Vivie Warren's mother operates a brothel. The daughter has a great sense of detachment from society. She has no idea of her mother's means of livelihood. The reader discovers in this play that no one can forever remain detached from the struggle of the rich and the poor, that one cannot always deny the bonds between oneself and one's fellows. Vivie's inhuman self-detachment and hollow rationalism are exposed with sharp strokes as the play proceeds. It dramatizes, in the relations between Vivie and her mother, the relation of the individual to modern capitalist society. No wonder members of our school system who read books have run to the library to remove Mr. Shaw's plays from the shelves. One might indeed see the parallels here to the Old Testament prophets crying, "Woe unto them that lay field to field—that take a man's cloak as a pledge."

There is much in the play that may in a few years make *Mrs. Warren's Profession* seem dated and irrelevant, but Shaw, through the theater in this case, proclaimed powerfully the truth that the individual is not self-sufficient, that he owes his existence to others and his survival to others. Mrs. Warren is eloquent in her denunciation of those, like her daughter, who consider themselves "self-made." Hundreds of luncheon clubs—Rotarian, Kiwanian, Lions, and Lambs—could read this play to their profit. The Horatio Alger myth is dealt a telling blow.

Time forbids the discussion of the Shaw plays one by one. That is not the purpose of this appreciation today. But I certainly urge you all during 1951 to reread Shaw plays, prefaces, and other prose work, including *An Intelligent Woman's Guide to Socialism.* Such a reading of Shaw will hurt none of you, and immensely strengthen many. Shaw, like all of us who want a better world for man, has moments of discouragement, despair, sadness, bitterness, and resignation. One finds it in *Captain Brassbound's Conversion,* in *You Never Can Tell,* in *Candida,* in *The Perfect Wagnerite,* in the play *Immaturity.* As Mr. West has noted, *The Devil's Disciple* is a play with a setting of the American Revolution in which Dick Dudgeon's most real trait is not the intellectual audacity to challenge the accepted value, but his loneliness and compassion. Even at the end of the play, when the townspeople hoist him to their shoulders cheering him, he is not one of them; he is still a lonely Christ who suffers the little children to come unto him.

The same mood of the tormented idealist is found in *John Bull's Other Island*, a savage satire on British imperialism, on the inhuman discipline of the army, on the corruption of a military caste, on the atrocities committed against subject peoples and the rationalizations of a government in defending them. To be sure, the alternative to imperialism in this play is not made explicit, but while the dreamer makes compromises that Shaw later recognized as self-defeating, here was a play on the stage in London that discussed the greatest issue of the twentieth century for the British, and helped to open eyes to understand what later transpired in India and China and the West Indies. For all of its limitations, this play better presented the evils of imperialism than the majority of delegates at the United Nations seem capable of doing.

Probably the play that made a greater impact on contemporary England than any other in his lifetime was *Major Barbara*. In the preface to this play (which was one of three made into films) Shaw wrote:"All institutions have been thrown out of date by the industrial revolution." This play says the people must have power. He himself in the play does not trace the growth of people's power in trade union movements, in cooperatives, in new parties of workers. There is much missing in *Major Barbara* that in the light of forty-five years of history seems to us should have been present, but this morning we can say that here was an immensely sensitive and eloquent playwright admitting on the British and American stage what is rarely admitted even by indirection by other dramatists: that there is a working class, that it is exploited, that its redemption from its degradation lies in its own hands.

To Shaw, the strong men were the capitalists like Undershaft in *Major Barbara*, like Sartorius in *Widowers' Houses*. One reason Shaw did not portray strong, militant, effective leadership on the side of labor was that he saw no such leadership around him in England. He saw a Ramsey MacDonald surrendering to wealth and a knighthood. He saw labor leaders yield to bribe after bribe. His heroes of the people against the exploiters he found outside of England, and outside of his own Ireland. In the forty-five years since this play was written, we, too, in America have seen leaders, not only of business, but of trade unions wickedly corrupted, bought and sold, by money at times and by power and position more frequently. *Major Barbara* portrays one of the facts of our modern world that few playwrights dared report: the power of a capitalist society to buy everything, including men, even men elected by workers. Whether new forms of society can end the lust for personal power and control the drives toward exploitation of man by man, and bring a greater measure of equality and security, our children will report in years to come. But that yet to be written chapter does not for one instant alter the problem that is ours—as it was Shaw's—of describing the brutal realities of what we see about us and changing them for the better. One need not yield to any dithyramb of praise for any new society in process of building to protest the visible evils waiting to be purged in the one we now inhabit.

More important than any of his plays, or any message in any play, is for us to recognize today the role George Bernard Shaw played in the first half of this century. He brought thousands of people who never saw one of his plays on a stage out of the darkness of this world's orthodoxies, secular and religious. He was a prophet of reality and not of mysticism. He helped men and women on several continents to clear their minds of cant and nonsense. He challenged the authorities by which millions of Englishmen and Americans lived complacently. He shook and worried the prejudices of those who took their churches and parties and economic systems for granted. He was a dedicated revolutionary who set the world ablaze. Even in his final months he made statements about Gandhi and Stalin that upset the academic and journalistic fraternity who had Shaw catalogued as a learned comic, a carpenter of good plays who, by their scattered records, had stopped saying anything since Edward of Wales met Mrs. Simpson. He insisted on the right of private judgment on his holy wafer.

In one of the Undershaft speeches to Major Barbara he says: "You have learnt something. That always feels at first as though you had lost something." Shaw never issued a brighter epigram. We Unitarians, especially those of us nourished in our youth on traditional faiths, know how true Undershaft's remark can be. Whether one dismisses great areas of Shaw's work as nonsense, or outdated, or inconsistent, the electric fact remains: it was Shaw who brought many of us to boil. He exploded a neat and trim world with high fences behind which lurked much that we now discuss. He made sex, morality, religion, evolution, business practices, imperialism, [and] war matters of open conversation. In his *Caesar and Cleopatra*, Theodotus reproaches Caesar for the burning of the library at Alexandria, and asks wildly, "Will you destroy the past?" and Caesar replies, "Aye, and build the future with its ruins."

I am not advocating a burning of the books. I am recognizing his emphasis in uprooting some of the past. His work as a playwright was partly destructive. But he added a cubit to the stature of many a living man and woman. He had a passionate love of life, his life force was contagious, and many were wakened to whole continents of thought and sympathy by his trenchant pen, his searing wit, his holy compassion, his brutal laying on of the sword when need be. He was not impressed with the fears of death or the promises of immortality. He urged, in *Back to Methuselah*, that men learn to live a hundred years or more since in three-score years they just begin to get over an addiction to cigars, champagne, and the lust of exploitation, and just begin to learn the meaning of ideas and civilization.

Here was an essentially healthy mind. He rarely spoke of his own approaching death, but on one occasion when he did speak of it he wrote: "I want to be thoroughly used up when I die. For the harder I work the more I live. I rejoice in life for its own sake. Life is no brief candle to me. It is sort of a splendid torch, which I have got hold of for a moment . . . and I want to make it burn as brightly as possible before handing it on to future generations." This is a great epitaph for a courageous spirit, a man who had the rare gift of admitting when he was wrong, who loved his fellowmen and opened doors for them to pass through, who shared his talent with prodigal enthusiasm and never suffered from a lack of self-respect, seasoned with humility. He cared nothing for the baubles and trinkets given by kings and college faculties. When asked whether he would accept the royal Order of Merit, he replied briskly, "No, I gave it to myself years ago." Such a spirit needs a reproduction a thousand-fold in the decade of the intimidated man.

A Forgotten American
Eugene V. Debs
March 22, 1953

A few weeks ago we spoke of a forgotten American, Jack London. Today we shall speak of Eugene V. Debs. For the benefit of visitors or members not present at the earlier address, permit me to say that this is not a seminar on American history. But this is a church that, like many other Unitarian churches, believes that no revelation is ever closed, that whatever in human nature had the stamp of divinity upon it in ancient times can have a similar divinity today. We look for exemplars in the days of Moses and Jesus, but also in the days of John Brown and Eugene Debs.

In recent months I have emphasized the need for our discovery, or rediscovery, of some of our giants in America, in churches, in the labor movement, in the colleges, in reform movements like woman suffrage and abolition of chattel slavery. We have met here, in several series of addresses, dedicated and heroic leaders of the people: Susan B. Anthony, Samuel Adams, Ralph Waldo Emerson, and Robert Ingersoll, to name but a few. It is good in these disturbing days to feel the warm companionship of these fearless Americans. Certainly I am not minimizing the importance of recognizing our vigorous citizens on today's ramparts— the Bishop Oxnams and the Norman Cousinses and the Owen Lattimores. But it is very important to know our past! It is a great past and a pillar of strength to those who sometimes feel alone.

The words "courage" and "justice" and "brotherhood" ring with a hollow echo through our halls and homes unless we see them embodied in fellow citizens recent and immediate—not effigies in marble in a hall of fame, but flesh and blood, whose risks were as real as our own, whose decisions were as unpredictable in outcome as those we make each day, but whom history vindicated for their insight and humanity. The calendar of saints for a Unitarian may begin with Iknaton or Asoka, but it ends with today's newspaper telling us of Dr. Schweitzer or Pablo Neruda or Mme Pandit doing their work with uncompromising devotion.

It is especially necessary today that this American heritage of bold radicalism be appropriately studied by all of us. We have had great conservatives serve us well, and forthright liberals. But too often the more radical citizen who made a great contribution is omitted from the record for reasons of prudence or concession. Certainly the Unitarian tradition has no excuse for such censorship. We seek to honor without prejudice all who serve our country and the commonwealth of man. This is a necessary task if truth is to prevail over passion. Washington and Edison, Henry Ford and Alexander Hamilton are secure; no histories will leave them out. But the Londons and Debses and Lincoln Steffenses need to be summoned from the less familiar halls of fame. That is why we are speaking of them in these days when our children need the full story of our past. We have had radical movements in America since Shay's Rebellion in eighteenth-century Massachusetts. In the contemporary United States one sometimes loses sight of this fact. Many schoolbooks have been abandoned that told the simple facts of the Populist movement, the local collective experiments at Brook Farm and New Harmony, the Shakers at Harvard and Lebanon, the Mormons in Utah, and countless others.

These experiments at solving the bread, butter, and cultural problems of rank-and-file Americans are as proud a part of our history as the rise of vast industries at River Rouge or Chicago, and should be taught along with the building of the railroads, the settlement of the farm belt, the gold rush of '49. I share Chet Huntley's bristling temper last Friday night at those who dismiss serious and thinking men as "egg heads, long hairs and do-gooders." Eugene Debs was all three at least parabolically. When we allow scorn to creep into our teaching tones at school when the name of a bold agitator is mentioned, we are subverting the very democracy we claim to love. If our editors and professors, parents and film makers were truly about their job, a Unitarian pulpit would not be needed to speak of a political leader like Gene Debs.

In even so brief a study as this today I should still like to share with you a thumbnail sketch of the life of Eugene Debs. It is unwise to assume that we all learned it in school if we were not old enough to learn it firsthand from the newspapers.

He was born November 5, 1855, as one of ten children born to parents who came from Alsace to this country. He left school at fifteen years to start work in the railroad shops of the Terre Haute and Indiana Railway. In 1870 he became a fireman on the railroad and clerked in a wholesale grocery store. In 1875 he organized a lodge of the Broth-

erhood of Locomotive Firemen, his first labor achievement in a long
and incredible career of serving the industrial workers of the country.
In 1878 he was made associate editor of the *Fireman's Magazine,* and
two years later elected national secretary-treasurer of the Brotherhood
of Locomotive Firemen. In 1879 he was elected city clerk. For some
years he was working night and day as editor, city clerk, and grocery
clerk at the same time. In 1885 he married Katherine Metzel of Pittsburgh and was elected to the Indiana legislature.

In June 1893, following his deep conviction that American labor
must come to industry-wide union organization, he formed and was
elected president of the American Railway Union, winning almost
immediately several contests with management, including the eighteen-
day strike for higher wages from the Great Northern Railway in 1894.
That year came the famous Pullman strike. The Pullman Palace Car
makers were not in the Debs union, but at a convention of the America Railway Union it was voted to support the striking car makers
with a sympathetic boycott. Debs felt it inexpedient in so new a union
as his to take on so dangerous an undertaking, but when it was voted
by his members, he threw himself vehemently into the campaign. It
was a year of panic and frightening depression. Debs warned his comrades of the slogan of the early pioneers of 1877, the Knights of Labor, that "an injury to one is an injury to all." It was this idea that
consolidated the car workers and railroad workers in the face of the
injunction. Locomotive fires were dumped in the yards and freight cars
stood miles long on the sidings. Against the advice of a progressive
governor of Illinois, John Peter Altgeld, President Grover Cleveland
ordered Federal troops into Chicago. Judges Grosscup and Woods issued sweeping injunctions against the unions.

A nation still in a horse-and-buggy stage, without automobiles or
trucks or airplanes, faced economic paralysis. The strength of labor became a shocking reality to men in power, unaccustomed to resistance
from any quarter. Debs brought American labor to maturity and taught
it the elementary lessons of solidarity. Bankers and traders and investors,
accustomed to organization into national associations to protect their
interests, found a young Terre Haute idealist had copied their formula
for the benefit of hard-muscled firemen and miserably underpaid car
builders. The gospel of wealth, buttressed by Supreme Court injunctions,
threw the power of the federal government against the trade union
movement. Debs was jailed—but labor became a new force for future
decades to reckon with. Henry George, Edward Bellamy, Lester Ward,
and the Christian socialists were dismissed as fanatic dreamers, but tough-
minded farmers, stockyard-workers, railroad engineers, and low-paid
teachers or ministers did not forget these intellectual pioneers of American reform, these advocates of a planned welfare state. Least of all did

they forget Debs, the eloquent and persuasive platform campaigner. His integrity, courage, logic, and example swept America. Justice Brewer defined the power of the federal troops to break strikes injurious to interstate commerce, but Eugene Debs defined the power of united workers conscious of what the new American science and industry could bring to all toilers who would make government their tool and not their master.

Although later many trade union leaders opposed Debs for his break with our present capitalist philosophy of business, it must never be forgotten that it was he who helped labor to mature so that strikes could be won, usually without violence (which he abhorred), but won with a real increase in the living standards, self-respect, and civic participation of workers. Every American trade unionist lives off the spiritual capital of Debs, even if his name is mentioned only with a footnote in our present school books.

On July 10, 1894, Debs was brought before a federal grand jury and charged with conspiracy to obstruct the mails. He and three others were arrested. On February 12, 1895, Debs and six others were sentenced to six months in the Woodstock jail for contempt, which has a familiar ring in our own time. Eugene Debs, as head of the American Railway Union, was sent to jail for disobeying a sweeping injunction that forbade any union activity in the Pullman strike crisis. The assumption was made that spoken or written words might induce some unknown person to commit murder. As in the case of the Homestead strike two years before, suppression of labor leaders was justified in the minds of the courts and the White House on the grounds of possible, though unproven, relationships between speech and violent action. Robert G. Ingersoll, William Dean Howells, and Samuel Gompers had protested in vain against the execution of the Haymarket prisoners on these grounds. Debs and the Haymarket martyrs knew the passion that could be aroused when property rights were threatened by a growing labor movement, even one far from socialist in its rank and file support. The Ludlow, Herrin, and Chicago massacres of workers remind us how difficult it is for workers to practice free speech in our country when such speech is aimed at revision of our laws and economic institutions.

But the alternative to such revision, as Debs well knew, is violent and prolonged struggle between workers and owners, marked by an intensity unsurpassed anywhere in the world. Beard and Laski, in their histories of the United States, dispel any illusion that sections of big business will not use the National Guard, private police, or armed vigilantes for the employers' interest. The LaFollette Committee investigations a few years ago gave volumes of documentation to the willingness of industry to crush organized and insistent workers with violence. The New Deal sought to give legal methods and peaceful development to the American labor movement, and to an impressive degree succeeded.

The Wagner Act, the Norris-LaGuardia Act, and other legislation substituted commissions and boards for tear gas and bloodshed. Debs did not live to see his hopes fulfilled to this degree. But millions of his admirers gained from him a fresh confidence that America can move toward a classless society of brothers, with order and law prevailing, if enough people have an opportunity to think and act without penalty.

One can wonder whether the judge would have given Debs a prison term in 1895 if he could have forseen how it would be used. Here Debs read and wrote, like St. Paul, Bunyan, Fox, Biddle, and John Brown before him. He came out a convinced socialist. He returned to Chicago and was given one of the greatest demonstrations in the history of that city.

In 1896 he campaigned for William Jennings Bryan for the presidency, but after that campaign he worked to transform the remnants of the American Railway Union into the Socialist Democratic Party. In 1899 this party fused with the Socialist Labor Party to run Debs for the presidency. He secured 96,000 votes in 1900. Later that year the two groups merged and formed the Socialist Party, and in 1904 as candidate for president Debs polled 402,000 votes. In 1905 he aided in the founding of the International Workers of the World. From this he withdrew later over disagreements on policies and program. Under the Socialist Party banner he ran for president in 1908 and again in 1912. In that latter year he was running against Theodore Roosevelt and Woodrow Wilson, both seeking liberal votes, yet Debs won the sensational number of 901,000 votes, 6 percent of the total.

In 1917 at the St. Louis Convention, the party denounced the war in Europe, and two months after America entered that war Debs made a speech at Canton, Ohio, assailing the prosecution of persons charged with sedition for opposing the war. Four days later he was indicted by a grand jury for violation of the Espionage Act, and after a four-day trial was sentenced to a term of ten years. He was sent first to Moundsville, and later to Atlanta Penitentiary. While still a prisoner in 1920, he was nominated for president again by the Socialists and received his largest vote: 919,799. This is one of the most significant figures in American political history, and was a comment upon the state of public thought and of the poverty of the major parties in regard to leadership. Debs, a man of no "creeping" socialist views, but an advocate of militant, forthright socialism, won nearly a million votes, while Warren Gamaliel Harding, an untalented country editor with an uninspiring record as senator, entered the White House only to leave it to die in San Francisco, a broken man, enmeshed in one of the worst scandals of the nation's history. It was one of the few memorable acts of Harding's administration that he gave Debs a pardon on Christmas Day, 1921. Debs's return home was one of the stirring episodes of this great man's life. Friends and citizens of all parties welcomed him with unashamed tears of gratitude. The contrast between the man who had lost the election and the man who had won it and given the pardon dramatized the plight of a nation on the march so few could miss it. But Debs was broken in health. He entered a sanitarium in 1922, and while he came out to edit the *American Appeal* and assist LaFollette in his presidential campaign in 1924, he left for Bermuda to find strength in 1926. He returned to his home that year to die on October 26.

He was mourned for his dedicated leadership of people who welcomed sincerity, passion, and devotion to the cause of a better world. His influence surpassed party lines, as did Franklin Roosevelt's after him. A California assemblyman of a few years ago, who is joining our church on Easter-Passover Sunday, wrote me last week of his memory of Debs, which I should like to share with you today:

> I first met Eugene Debs in the summer of 1904. He spoke at Lake Madison, Chautauqua, but a few miles from where we lived. He had a tall, rather slim, straight, agile body with an extremely expressive face. His words, facial expression and gestures were very revealing. His logic and love carried conviction that few could escape. His enthusiasm was so intense, his words were so eloquent, and his aim was so ideal and practical that he would turn the opinions of men as a strong wind would turn a weather vane.
>
> I was secretary of the Madison Socialist Local and in this capacity I came in direct contact with Debs, a privilege I shall never forget. He was like a doctor who has a sure cure for a devastating scourge. His was a rare soul and a brilliant mind. We invited him to our home, he ate at our table (an event in my life I highly prize, never to be forgotten). He was all that the poet James Whitcomb Riley said of him:
>
> > An' there's Gene Debs, a man that stands
> > An' jest holds out in his two hands,
> > As warm a heart as ever beat
> > 'Twixt here and the judgment seat.

I am reminded of Clarence Darrow's comment: "There may have lived somewhere, some time, a kindlier, gentler, more generous man than Gene Debs, but I have never known him."

Let us note today that Debs was no academic theoretician of a democratic and socialist America. He was a popular leader of hard-pressed workers and farmers who knew the hunger and sickness that come from cyclical paralysis of business, depressions that not only plunge the stocks downward but bring unemployment, bitterness, and unrest to millions. It was the Pullman strike and the Haymarket tragedy that educated Debs far more than his formal studies of Marx or Henry George, Edward Bellamy or Henry Demarest Lloyd. He always was suspicious of Victor

Berger, a fellow socialist with a library filled with European political writers: Engels, Liebknecht, Kautsky. Debs was more impressed by the bald fact of 80 percent of our citizens being impoverished and dispossessed in the year 1885, by the abject servility of our high courts to industrial leaders than he was by the labor theory of value delineated by a German scholar named Marx.

It is sufficient now to emphasize that Debs contributed a healthy American pragmatism to the labor movement in America. His experiences as a railway worker had taught him early the great unlikelihood that a capitalist society would bring a concern for workers to a higher level than concern for profit and property. His idealism and integrity advanced the cause of militant labor across the nation. He spoke not only to workers in factories, in transportation, and on farms, but to hundreds of thousands of teachers, ministers, editors, and small businessmen. He was a teacher of the people, as clearly American as the Appalachians, as authentic a product of our traditions as Lincoln or Jackson, and of the same clay. He helped make the words "comrade" and "radical" good, indigenous terms for people in Kansas and Ohio and California. John Steinbeck has recently written in the *Christian Science Monitor* urging a return of these words to our American vocabulary. I am all for it, and see nothing but fear to stop him or anyone else from recovering them.

While the newspapers and radio and the *Congressional Record* explode daily over developments in China or Russia, it becomes increasingly clear to me that 99 percent of our task as Americans is a domestic one: catching up with ourselves. Here is where the heritage of a forgotten man named Debs is so valuable. We cannot—and should not —seek to be isolated from our world neighbors; the thinking through of our United Nations' duties is fundamental to our future; but still most of us day in and day out have a lot to learn from the man from Terre Haute, Indiana, who knew that we have a Constitution and Bill of Rights and a physical plant of arms and factories adequate to bring lasting security and happiness to the people of this nation. The obstacles to this fulfillment of the prophetic promise, learned from Old and New Testaments read in white clapboard churches, are basically domestic obstacles: a thin, dry individualism that denies responsibility for others' welfare, a superficial and inadequate education in home and school regarding our American institutions and their potentiality for bringing in a full democracy, a tragic willingness to leave leadership to professionals instead of pitching in to play our part as active citizens in an unfinished job of clearing the wilderness. I am not interested in Debs as a Socialist Party leader nearly as much as I am interested in his legacy of responsibility for human welfare, not for one group but for all the people. He would be opposed now as he was in 1917 to the suicidal character of world wars, but his great emphasis was on building a just and prosperous America for the working people in overalls or at desks with white collars or anywhere else doing useful jobs. There was a religious quality about his dedication to this cause. He had short shrift for exploiting robber barons or well-nourished editor-critics unwilling to help fulfill the American democratic dream.

This forgotten American, Eugene Debs, was tender in compassion, yet unsparing in his militant defense of the working class in its organization and its resistance to a brutally hostile profit-centered economy. He grappled intellectually with the socialist ideas of English, German, and Russian thinkers, but gave to us an American philosophy of progress that was unmistakably native and indigenous. He knew the American people very well, as a worker, as a son of the farm land, as a child of the so-called Bible belt. He knew we were not an anticlerical culture, not a country with a record of wide-scale pogroms, not a society of prince and peasant, but rather a new nation with a growing middle class. He knew his medium, he knew his fellow citizens, he knew his oligarchs of wealth, his Colorado miners' families, his farmers unprotected from dust storms and droughts. I am stressing today—even with intentional repetition—that Debs worked in the medium of the American people, with American traditions and habits, not self-consciously or as an intellectual, for he was not an intellectual, but rather as a passionate campaigner.

He lived through the period of the Russian Revolution, though he was in prison during its formative years and had limited materials for study in making his conclusions. (So, I might add, did many of us on the outside of prison walls in those days.) This seems like an appropriate place to make a brief digression on the matter of an American's relationship to revolutionary struggles outside our country. Debs was a socialist, a militant one, and yet he never hesitated to express forthrightly his concern about aspects of the Soviet civil war. He expressed his strong support of the new Soviet state in 1922 in words that leave no room for ambiguity. These words have often been forgotten, or never known to many American Socialists. He firmly opposed efforts to rally American labor against the workers' new government in Russia. Yet he felt the execution of the Czar to be a needless cruelty, and cabled Lenin to protest the threatened execution of twenty-two socialist revolutionaries on trial in Moscow. However, unlike so many folks today, as he spoke his criticisms, he expressed his sympathy with the government as a whole, writing: "The Russian Revolution was the greatest and most luminous and far reaching achievement in the entire sweep of human history. The Soviet government is the beginning of self-government throughout the world."

I think Debs's example has meaning for us today. Candor, honest criticism, praise, and understanding regarding the USSR, all are possible, as they are possible regarding the United States. Today, as Americans who look forward to a classless nation, we gain nothing by being blind to the costliness of Soviet socialism. Dr. Corliss Lamont writes that he, who has visited the USSR and is as objective and just an observer as one could find, is repelled by dictatorial and repressive aspects of the regime. To be sure, he refuses to join, as do I, in the thirty-six-year-old campaign of wholesale condemnation, but he is not, nor should we be, unaware of the Soviet Union's real failures and limitations. On principle we should be no less critical of the Soviets than we are properly critical of ourselves.

One does not have to share the average newspaper reader's inculcated belief that the USSR is a bottomless pit of grinding poverty and gruelling dictatorship and human misery to recognize factors we have not had in a large scale in America to date: A one-party press, limits to free speech, large-scale treason trials, counterrevolutionary violence, biased and harsh justice to political prisoners, secret police, imprisonment of thousands of persons in periodic party purges. I have studied in their context the evidence of these grim aspects of Soviet life in the past thirty-six years, studied them in the context of history's largest successful revolution, and wish I could persuade all sober Americans to do the same. I wish, for example, that during these years of the cold war hundreds of us would read Frederick Schuman's *Soviet Politics*, Richard Lauterbach's *These Are the Russians*, Sidney and Beatrice Webb's *Soviet Communism*, Edgar Snow's *The Pattern of Soviet Power*, E. H. Carr's *Soviet Impact on the Western World*, [and] Corliss Lamont's *Soviet Civilization*. It is safe to conclude from the inner and outer evidence of these books that none of the authors are Communists. But neither are they hate-Russia propagandists. They do not dismiss these facts of repression or injustice they find, but they do insist on seeing them in the full context of Soviet life in the world and in history. There is no excuse and there is real peril in our tolerating illiteracy about the Soviet Union today and tomorrow.

I have made this long aside in a talk on Eugene Debs because I believe America is not the Soviet Union, that there are real historical factors in our life here that can save us, if we are vigilant, from some of these costly liabilities of Soviet experience since 1917. A socialist planned society, a free and democratic welfare state, such as Debs envisioned, is possible in this century in America because of our advanced industrial resources, or history of civil liberties, our relative success in bridging class chasms. I protested three weeks ago in this pulpit the overswift execution of the death sentences of the Czech political prisoners, and spoke of our long practice of granting appeal after appeal in our courts to those found guilty of major crimes. These traditions of civil toleration for the accused have worked well during our Revolution, our Civil War, and during two world wars. My hope is that they can be maintained in the rigorous political struggles ahead for a new pattern of socialism in America, which will be in important ways unlike any pattern yet established in the world. As China's new society differs from Russia's, so will ours differ from both of these, not because we are proudly different or a better people, for we are not, but because we have had many social experiences neither of these great nations have had. I am thinking of experiences under Jefferson, Lincoln, and Roosevelt, which helped us to see how social progress can be made if we will use our schools, our press, our courts, our Congress, and our great industrial and agricultural plant as they are capable of being used, for the benefit of the many and not the few. These resources and tools of peaceful men and women can and should be used rather than those of force and violence. Management and labor both need to learn this lesson. Nothing should be above the sovereign will of the people themselves, the ultimate authority of a democracy expressed through secret ballot available to all, without exception. It will be a great half-century ahead, and those who protest rightly the violent purge, the concentration camp, the swift death penalty will have much to do to prove the possibility of a real transformation of society here without such harsh methods. The arson attacks against mine unions in New Mexico recently, the revelations about high officials in New York conniving with murderous racketeers on the Jersey waterfront, the bludgeoning assaults by Reps. Richard Velde and Donald Jackson upon college and church leaders make it apparent that we too easily use here the very devices we properly condemn in other countries. If the spirit of tolerating free agitation that motivated President Harding in pardoning Debs and President Roosevelt in pardoning Browder can operate in the White House today, several dozen radical leaders, imprisoned under the Smith Act, will be pardoned in the months to come by President Eisenhower, and we shall then know that America does not intend to purge by imprisonment its advocates of a socialist society. Debs believed in the free play of political opinion, and so do I. Whatever frustrates such free play points in the direction of violence and cruel civil struggle in the future, for nowhere on earth will people long remain docile before inequity or accept needless suffering when a remedy is within their grasp. If the story of Jewish suffering under the pharaohs means anything in this Passover season, it means that Moses gave an oppressed people faith in their own strength. If the story of the trial and death of Jesus means anything this Easter season, it means that He gave lowly hardworking folk under Roman occupation a bold courage to throw off a yoke of bondage and walk in freedom of soul and body. We should see parables for our own time in these ancient celebrations of militancy by the Jewish people. No one accepts indefinitely a status of inferiority when equality and security are possible for him.

It was apparent to Debs and others after the Haymarket Massacre and the Pullman strike in the late 1890s that hatred and fear and violence (on both sides of the struggle) would be inevitable under a profit-centered economy. With fortunes at stake, millionaires will not be indifferent to the possibility of a lost fortune. Even small investors, retired teachers and dentists and preachers will find it easy to resent labor's demands for a larger share of profits when this brings down to a trickle the quarterly dividend in the mailbox. So are the middle class and working class set against each other. People are far better than the system, insisted Debs. They are not wolves and jackals at heart. But fear and division keep them at their worst. A planned society without worry about old age will make no millionaries, but it will make children without rickets and parents without neuroses. This was the faith of Debs.

All I feel we can do today is to see the domestic character, the homespun American thinking and action of this greatest of our nation's socialist citizens. While he believed firmly in the class struggle, he refused to use the Marxist term "dictatorship of the proletariat" for the leadership of labor in the new society he worked for. He was utterly opposed to war, preferring prison to defense of World War I. He saw the relationship of war to the international search for profits—a competition between jackals for the common prey. He believed that a world of working-class nations would end war forever. While not associating himself actively after his release from prison with socialist party or trade union struggles because of his lost health, he supported Foster against Gompers in the battle over industrial organization of labor rather than craft organization. His idea of industrial unions formed the core of the Congress of Industrial Organizations. The names of Murray, Lewis, Hillman, and Bridges came to replace those of Debs and Haywood. For all of the new problems and issues raised for labor during the Franklin Roosevelt administration, the long shadow of Debs fell benevolently over the trade union tables of America. His deeds were many.

Debs opposed the open shop, agitated for an eight-hour-day, fought vigorously against child labor in factories and fields. He saw the peril of Billy Sunday's evangelistic furor against militant labor unions and denounced him with biblical fervor. He aided in the fight for women's suffrage. He was forthright in defense of the Negro people and their rights, and stood up with high courage to the Ku Klux Klan; he agitated for workman's compensation laws, for popular election of U.S. Senators. He believed (to use his own words): "Men and women can walk the highlands and enjoy the vision of a land rejuvenated and resplendent in the triumph of freedom and civilization."

Citizens of all parties, people of all races and creeds, have seen in

Eugene Debs a leader of unquestioned idealism, but typically practical in the implementation of his ideals. It was this combination that won him his millions of friends and his implacable foes. His vision has not been lost in this generation of the hucksters and the generals. It is more than likely that the hall of fame at New York University in the Bronx will someday see the bust of Eugene Debs grace its amphitheater, to stand beside Emerson, Tom Paine, Lincoln, Booker T. Washington, and Susan B. Anthony. Our forgotten Americans have a way of someday being remembered, though the mills of gods grind slowly. The lean Indiana fireman will come into his own, when the Harding who defeated him for the White House chair will be generously forgotten by our children's children.

Michael Servetus
Advocate of Liberty
October 25, 1953

Today and on Tuesday next throughout the entire world, many thousands of men and women will pay tribute to a giant of liberty, a son of Aragon in ancient Spain: Michael Servetus.

Four hundred years ago, on October 27, this apostle of freedom died at the stake near Geneva in the country now called Switzerland. Most of the observances will emphasize his brave martyrdom for religious liberty. It is my deep conviction that our two programs, the one this morning and the larger one tonight, will make transparently clear that Servetus was even more a liberator of the total human spirit. This fact is true, as I hope to make clear in my brief tribute this morning. Tonight the appearance of Professor D. O'Malley from Stanford University in Palo Alto will underscore our debt to Michael Servetus, the man of science, while the greatest scholar of early Unitarianism, Earl Morse Wilbur, will discuss our religious heritage from Servetus.

I cannot too strongly emphasize the importance of this observance, nor too urgently press upon you the importance of these two services, this one and the one tonight, sponsored by the Council of Liberal Ministers of Southern California and Arizona. The world immediately around us should take cognizance of our honor to this first Protestant martyr and the meaning of his life for all freedom-loving citizens today. We, as Unitarians, have few historical events that we celebrate, but the life of Servetus should give us reason for noble pride. It is my fervent prayer that no member of this church, no regular friend, no church school teacher, no pupil in the upper school be ignorant of the stature and significance of Michael Servetus from this day on. He is our St. Peter; he is our Abraham. If Unitarians kept a year of Jubilee, this would be it. We date our history as Unitarians from this date: October 27, 1553.

Michael Servetus was possible because of the new day in which he lived. The medieval regions of Heaven, Purgatory, Hell—where Dante had wandered—had dissolved forever into infinite space with the publication in 1543 of Copernicus's *Revolution of the Heavenly Bodies*, and Vesalius's *Structure of the Human Body*. In a new-world arena man now stood free. In the center of this new arena, marking the end of the Middle Ages, the triumph of the Renaissance, stood Michael Servetus. In the emancipated mind of this great Spaniard we have the union of the scientific spirit of the Renaissance and the skepticism of the Protestant Reformation—so soon to shape new fetters for the religious man. He was the only figure of that turbulent century who was burned by the Catholics in effigy and the Protestants in actuality.

In this day of contemporary intolerance, of clerical persecution abroad and incipient religious persecution at home, when a Methodist bishop is denied a church auditorium to speak on the Bill of Rights, the commanding presence of Michael Servetus has useful meaning for religious liberals and other democratic citizens in our own century.

Let us remember that Michael Servetus was a disciple of the secular Renaissance academy of the neo-platonists in Florence, Italy, and was also a disciple of that militant sect of Protestants, the Anabaptists, whose zeal for reform entered into their religious creeds, their political organizations, and their advanced ideas of economic justice. Let us not forget that it was a proletarian movement of workers that welcomed a professional man, a scientist, a doctor, a geographer, like Servetus—for he was all of these things—in addition to being a theologian. He was a universal man of the Renaissance. In him the diverse tendencies of the Reformation and the Renaissance blended, as they did not blend in Martin Luther or John Calvin, in Zwingli or in Melancthon.

We shall note briefly today the life story of Servetus, but I would call attention to a splendid new biography, *Haunted Heretic* by Dr. Roland Bainton, which comes off the press this month. I sat up most of a night recently reading the entire book in galley proofs. I trust that you will purchase it soon. Happily it is under four dollars—and worth every penny of it.

Michael Servetus was born at Villanueva in Aragon, Spain, in 1511. Well-born and of generous talents, he was educated for the law, philosophy, science, and literature. He traveled widely, to Italy, Germany, Switzerland, and France, and lived in Paris, Lyons, and Vienne. He distinguished himself as a doctor of medicine, and gained fame for his speculations regarding the circulation of blood a century and a half before Harvey. The merit of these speculations is fully discussed by Dr. O'Malley in this evening's address.

Servetus gave of himself unstintingly in the time of an epidemic in Vienne, a deed remembered by thousands when later he was tried for heresy and burned. I like to think of him as a premature member of a Unitarian Service Committee Medical Mission, going far beyond the call of duty to bring relief to the suffering, a man of genius washing the wounds of the peasant at his doorstep with unaffected simplicity.

While in France he published an edition of the Bible, explaining rationally the prophecies of the Old Testament as applying, not to Jesus but to Hebrew history. He wrote another book, his most famous one, *The Errors of the Trinity*, in which he maintained that Jesus was not the eternal son of God, but the son of the Eternal God. As one friend pointed out a day before his death, he could have saved his life if only he would move an adjective by three words in a simple sentence. Thus always do we find the rationalizer seeking to destroy the man of principle.

Servetus had a correspondence with the great Presbyterian reformer John Calvin, who ruled as virtual dictator of Geneva. Servetus, perhaps fearful of his fate in France in 1546, wrote to him, asking if he might go through Geneva without being troubled. Calvin wrote a friend, "If he comes here, and I have any authority, he shall never go out alive."

In 1553 Servetus published one thousand copies of a book, *The Restitution of Christianity*, in which he denied the doctrine of the Trinity, the divinity of Jesus—and came out as a Unitarian. The book was privately printed, and the author's name, the writer's name, and the place of publication were all concealed. However, a copy came into the hands of John Calvin, and he immediately had Servetus denounced to the Catholic inquisitor in Lyons, France, where the book had been published. The bales of this edition were burned in savage thoroughness so that only three copies exist today. Servetus was arrested and imprisoned, and would surely have died at the hands of the Catholics had not friends among the common folk of Vienne, at risk of life itself, aided in his night-time escape.

Calvin had sent to the Catholic inquisitors letters privately received from Servetus sixteen years earlier to help insure a severe sentence. It is well to note that the clerical informer is no new creation of our twentieth-century world. He also sent the inquisitors a manuscript of a new theological book by Servetus, once loaned to him, and which he refused to return.

On Sunday, August 12, 1553, Michael Servetus rode on horseback into a village on the French border near Geneva. He sold his horse and walked into the city and tried to get a boat across the lake in an attempt to seek safety in eastern Europe where the radical sects were strong enough to give him friendly asylum. But he made the great mistake of arriving on Sunday, as no boats could be rented, and if he were not in church he would be picked up and questioned, since compulsory church attendance was the inflexible rule in that Puritan city-state.

He was recognized in church and arrested as the man who had published *The Restitution of Christianity*, forbidden copies of which were selling
well in Frankford and Lyons, working class centers in Catholic France.
So again, Protestant Calvin sought to finish the job that Catholic Inquisition had bungled. The Council of Geneva held a trial and sentenced
Servetus to death. Calvin weakened only far enough to ask for beheading instead of burning at the stake, which was denied.

Servetus was forbidden counsel, a clean cell, or any of the rights
even then allowed to common criminals. Calvin traveled from city to
city during the trial, whipping up enmity against his captured prize.
Although the council in Geneva was of the anti-Calvinist party, they
did not dare to cross the mounting sentiment of the Calvinist clergy
from the towns and villages, crying with but one exception for the blood
of the Spanish Unitarian. That one dissenting village minister of incredible courage and integrity had to flee the country to save his life.

A hard theology had eaten the heart out of the council and the church
officials. They led Servetus to the stake on the morning of October 27,
and by noon he was dead, his book *The Errors of the Trinity* and his
flesh both burned to ashes together. The foremost man of the sixteenth
century Christendom had paid completely for his free inquiry into the
Bible, into the creed, into the power apparatus of organized Christianity
—Catholic and Protestant alike.

One hundred years ago today in Boston Theodore Parker delivered
a great sermon on Michael Servetus. I should like to share with you
a portion of that valiant prophet's address:

> All that was left was a pile of black and smoking cinders . . . there
> was a spot in the Christian world which all the waters of the Rhone
> and Lake Geneva can never wash away. Since then what fires have
> burned, what inquisitions and what massacres there have been. The
> fire of the green oak faggots shone in many a dark place, and woke
> up great men. But even now we do not, in 1853, understand the value
> of spiritual freedom. It is not established, even yet.

I dare not imagine what might be the words of Parker if he were
to be alive and speak tonight at our observance here. The very walls
would tremble!

It is worth our noting on this occasion that on the 350th anniversary
—in 1903—certain lineal descendants and spiritual disciples of John Calvin, realizing the dreadful blot upon the record of his life, and desiring to
atone so far as possible for the intolerance of his deed, erected to the memory of Servetus an expiatory monument at the foot of the hill of execution
called Champel. In a small triangular plot of ground stands a huge stone
boulder with tablets of bronze on either side. On one tablet can be read:

Sons, respectful and grateful of Calvin our great reformer, but condemning an error which was that of his age, and firmly attached to the liberty of conscience according to the true principles of the Reformation and the Gospel, have raised this expiatory monument on October 27, 1903.

But the work of expiation is not only for the Calvinists of the early years of this twentieth century. We are this weekend paying tribute to Michael Servetus because at this very hour we need to do deeds of expiation. We should not be thinking primarily of our past sins against the religious conscience in Salem, Massachusetts, or to the Quakers in New York; or to Baptists, or Mormons, or Jews in colonial America.

We should be thinking of our own snuffing out of the free mind and conscience at this very hour across our continent. Our people are on every side being led down the pathways of bigotry, fear, suspicion, and intolerance. Hatred is made easier than thought. Yesterday a Catholic cardinal from New York explained the necessity for a purging of nonconformists to his co-religionists in Belgium. My friend, Professor Herbert Phillips of Washington State, who spoke in this church, is to be imprisoned for three years because as a simple witness in a Seattle trial he refused to inform on innocent men and women. My friend, Professor Barrows Dunham, author of *Men Against Myth*, is dismissed from his chair of philosophy at Temple University for the crime of silence before the new inquisitors. My honored Unitarian colleague, Reverend Donald Lothrop of Boston, is deprived of John Hancock Hall for religious services because his forums, like ours, invite men of independent mind to speak their hearts and minds freely.

Indeed, the lesson of Servetus is written in very contemporary terms. Rev. Duncan Howlett of the First Church Unitarian in Boston recognized this when he wrote in the *Christian Register* this month, reviewing the Bainton life of Servetus:

> What does a man do when he finds himself thinking what the rulers of society regard as "dangerous thought"? If he believes in his heart that the expression of his thoughts will make the world a better place, can he remain silent? Michael Servetus, prosperous and respected, was not able to remain silent. Shall we bury the truth that is in us for safety's sake?

From Boston to San Francisco, Unitarian pulpits are today speaking in this tone.

Servetus was a radical scientist in the sixteenth century, when in the days of Charles V, the emperor and other potentates valued mathematics and astronomy as aids to navigation and war; they wanted the services of the great physicians when they were ill. But Servetus, like many a contemporary atomic physicist, wanted to examine the larger implications of his discoveries. And for this he was to be mortally punished, for heresy was scientific as well as theological—then and now.

As few books will tell you, Servetus was a political revolutionist as well as a religious one. Geneva was a city of cloth-making. The textile manufacturers supported the ministers in martialling the workers in groups of ten to swear allegiance to God and his elect, for that oath implicitly bound them to make no protest concerning wages or conditions of labor. Calvinism increased the prosperity of Geneva's upper class, as later it made rich the China traders of Salem, the slave and rum dealers of Newburyport, and the mill owners of the Merrimac River estuary.

Servetus was arrested in Geneva as he was trying to reach eastern Europe. Calvin knew that if that heretic arrived in Bohemia, he would make common cause with the radical Moravian brethren whose economic doctrines could easily add to the protests already coming from the weavers of Geneva.

The anger and resentment of the Peasant's War had not been entirely smothered by Martin Luther and the nobility of the German states. New and dangerous doctrines of equality were infecting thought across all Europe. The Anabaptist doctrines, shared by Servetus and later to be a part of Unitarianism, taught a seditious brotherhood of man, a distribution of property to the poor, inspired by the fourth chapter of the Book of Acts in the New Testament. The merchants and manufacturers of Geneva were unable to predict what would happen if these disorders grew amongst the people now gaining ground in Bohemia and Poland.

Servetus was articulate. He was a rationalist. He displayed a scientific objectivity that could in the end destroy the frozen dogmas of Calvin's Christian institutions and, even worse, destroy the rigid class structure of this city-state in the Alps. Calvin was the last great figure of the Middle Ages who sought to marshal God himself against the coming storm of mankind—the storm of which Servetus was so glorious a symbol down the centuries that followed.

In closing these comments this morning—and they are but a prelude to our gathering here tonight with friends from many churches—I would share with you a few words written by a far later Unitarian of courage, Henry David Thoreau. At the time of the death of John Brown of Harper's Ferry fame, the sage of Walden wrote:

> When we heard at first that he was dead, one of my townsmen observed that "he died as the fool dieth"; which, pardon me, for an instant suggested a likeness in him dying to my neighbor living. Others, craven

hearted, said disparagingly that "he threw his life away," because he resisted the government. Which way have they thrown their lives, pray? . . . Can you dry up the fountains of thought? High treason, when it is resistance to tyranny here below, has its origin in the power that makes and forever recreates man. When you have caught and hung all these rebels you have accomplished nothing but your own guilt, for you have not struck at the fountain head.

As it was true of John Brown, so also is it true of Michael Servetus. In paying our tribute this morning, we are not retreating into the sixteenth century for a sentimental indulgence in religious retrospection. We are focusing our eyes on a man of courage and intelligence who stood to his death against the same black evils that beset us now in this mid-twentieth century: the forces that order conformity, that steal the soul from out of the human breast, that reduce men to units of consumption, to abject and sodden listeners to electronic jingles, to narcotic commercials, and the ceaseless torrent from television tube, movie screen, and radio speaker.

In Servetus we see a rebel against the forces of eternal slavery: kings, popes, merchant princes, purchased artists, mindless teachers, conscienceless salesmen, and all other destroyers of human freedom in whatever coats of many colors they may be attired—ordained, invested, appointed, confirmed. Against this entire conspiracy of serfdom Servetus stands alive today, calling men to the liberty that echoed from the lips of Isaiah; from the teaching of Jesus, the people's carpenter; from Pelagius, the lover of mankind; from all the sects and schools of Christianity in the hills of Transylvania that stood against imperial papal Rome in the heyday of her power.

This is our heritage—more precious than the wealth of Croesus, more life-giving than the wheat fields of the western plains. The Spanish heretic still stands today against a host of men intent on cosmic decimation of the human race. And he will be the victor when the final words are written, for he breathed the deathless air of liberty against which there is no law, no death, no ending, while the stars continue and the planets roll.

Eulogy to Dr. Albert Einstein
April 24, 1955

This morning we memorialize the seventy-six years of Dr. Albert Einstein who died Monday morning, April 18, in Princeton, New Jersey. We memorialize a man whose genius and its fruit shall very probably place his name in history beside those of Archimedes, Galileo, and Newton.

Beyond his contributions to science, millions mourn his death this week because of his uncompromised dedication to human welfare, and most especially to the cause of intellectual freedom. To Einstein the words of Lessing had peculiar significance: "The search for truth is more precious than its possession."

We are honoring today not only the exponent of the theory of relativity, not only the scientist whose name is so closely associated with atomic research and electronics, but even more the man who taught humble citizens the grandeur of an unbribed conscience, the glory of an independent opinion. He was committed to truth, to patience, to simplicity, but beyond these to human brotherhood undivided, unexploited, free.

Let us remember Einstein's own words:

Man is here for the sake of other men. My inner and outer life are built upon the labors of other men, living and dead. Possessions, outward success, publicity, luxury, to me these are contemptible. My political ideal is democracy. Everyone should be respected as an individual, but no one idolized. Distinctions separating social classes are false. Degeneracy follows every autocratic system of violence. I cannot imagine a God who rewards and punishes the objects of his creation, whose purposes are modelled after our own, a God in short, who is but a reflection of human frailty.

We have learned to fly, to send messages and news without difficulty over the entire world through electric waves. But the production and distribution of commodities is entirely unorganized, so that everyone must live in fear of being eliminated. The economic anarchy of capitalist society as it exists today is, in my opinion, the real source of the evil. The representatives of the people do not sufficiently protect the interests of the underprivileged sections of the population.

Dr. Einstein is not only a great physicist and mathematician, not only a man whose ideas have reshaped our conception of the universe, but he is a man who has spoken for the living people in that universe. He has insisted upon a discussion of their poverty, their persecution, their fears, their stolen freedoms of mind and conscience. He was never halted by slanders from men of power and authority. No American was ever less impressed with the panoply of special privilege and material success. He shared his compassion with Jewish refugees, Spanish Republicans in exile, dismissed teachers in American schools, and any and all who felt the whiplash of man's inhumanity to man.

Dr. Einstein is only relatively our fellow citizen. Far more does he belong to all nations, to all ages, to all lovers of truth. His unflinching heroism of spirit, his innocence of our current delusions, his astonishing insight into the secrets of the mysterious universe around us, all are reasons for rejoicing that his life came into being seventy-six years ago to bless a civilization in desperate need of such examples. We are stronger for his having lived, and for that reason we say farewell with gratitude and pride.

Clarence Darrow
Citizen Extraordinary
A Memorial Tribute
May 23, 1958

March 13 of this year marked the 101st birthday of Clarence Darrow. During that week Prisoner 9306-D at Stateville Penitentiary in Illinois walked out of a prison world he had occupied for thirty-three years. Nathan Leopold, Jr. was paroled from a life sentence to take a lab technician's job in a Puerto Rican hospital. His words at the prison gate were words Clarence Darrow, his defense attorney, now dead twenty years, would have rejoiced to hear. "I beseech you to give me a gift almost as precious as freedom itself—the gift of privacy." Darrow's moving appeal to the judge thirty-three years before had borne its prophetic fruits. A man who had been very close to execution had been reclaimed. One of the deepest convictions of Clarence Darrow had been justified. Society can pass from vengeance to reconstruction in its handling of its lawbreakers, even the worst.

But this is not a tribute today to an attorney, important as his profession was to the fulfillment of the man. I wish to speak of one of our great Americans of all time. We need to pause in our daily round from time to time to study the life of giants who walk amongst us. Clarence Darrow was no distant hero, no aristocrat who walked like a Roman patrician through the masses below him. There is a grandeur in the man that comes in part from his humble origins, his familiar virtue, his undeniable weaknesses. I often share with you from this pulpit the story of monumental figures from the past—Voltaire and Socrates, Jefferson and Milton—and so I shall do in days to come, for we need such company if our spirits are not to flag and our best efforts to die stillborn. But this morning my tribute is to a fellow son of Ohio, born a few miles from my own birthplace. His heroic proportions and astonishing successes have given me great courage in the years past and for my unfinished years. And he can do the same for all of us gathered here. I may be prejudiced and you may allow for it if you will. I remember he once wrote: "The best jurors for the defense are Catholics, Unitarians, Congregationalists, Universalists, Jews and agnostics!" That is good company indeed. My prejudice may also be reflected in my admiration for the last words he ever wrote, words found after his death on his desk scribbled in a composition book: "The fact that my father was a heretic always put him on the defensive and we children always thought it only right and loyal that we should defend his cause." This man was a warrior—and we need them desperately in this world of sanctioned privilege and incorporated plunder.

At sixteen Clarence Darrow of Kinsman, Ohio, was a poor school teacher, at twenty-one a lawyer. When he died at eighty-one he was acknowledged to be America's greatest trial lawyer; but far more, he was enshrined in the minds and affections of millions of Americans as the kind of human being they really would like to be: compassionate, courageous, intellectually curious and well-informed, generous and dedicated to the progress of the race from pole to pole. He had burned out of himself, better than most of us succeed in doing, the self-interest, the self-indulgence, and the self-justification that paralyze us year after year. He had no illusions and he nourished no Utopias.

If we Americans are to transcend our present age of conformity, our preoccupation with pleasure-seeking, our indolence of mind, it will be by the production of more sons and daughters of Darrow's stripe and timbre. His credo can be our credo if we choose to adopt it and practice it, as men in an earlier age subscribed to the Sermon on the Mount. "I speak," said Clarence Darrow, "for the poor, for the weak, for the weary who in darkness and despair have borne the labors of the human race." He was in all his seriousness a man of the people and close to them.

Like all truly great men and women Darrow was possessed of a sense of humor that can belong only to those who have cast fear out of their hearts and can see life in true perspective. I mention this because even a memorial tribute must not be solemn; for while this was a dedicated man, terribly earnest, he was not a saint, nor a divinity, or one who took himself too seriously, except when girt for battle.

When he was a budding lawyer in his early twenties, he found himself in the courtroom facing a veteran attorney who several times referred to him as a "beardless youth." At length Darrow's temper had endured enough, and he rejoined:

My opponent seems to condemn me for not having a beard. The King
of Spain once dispatched a youthful nobleman to the court of a
neighboring king who received the visitor with the outraged complaint:
"Does the King of Spain lack men that he sends me a beardless boy?"
To which the young nobleman replied: "Sir, if my King had supposed
you imputed wisdom to a beard, he would have sent you a goat."

Darrow won the case!

I should like to make it clear this morning that Clarence Darrow
was more than an attorney, great as that profession is. Lincoln Steffens
was right: Darrow was a philosopher. He was no example of Edmund
Burke's dictim, "The Law sharpens the mind by narrowing it." It is the
breadth, the compass of this man's genius for humanity that makes him
live in our memories this morning. This breadth is the reason why the
Player's Ring Gallery this week will doubtless play to capacity houses
with that moving drama, Inherit the Wind, which presents Darrow and
Bryan at the Scopes Trial in Tennessee in all its passionate context of
science challenging bigotry.

I am speaking of Darrow today because we Americans need to
rediscover the American pattern of democracy at its best—all of us, and
our children with us. We are entering very difficult years, I do believe,
and we have titanic forces to resist. If there be skills and oracles, we
need to find them for our own immortal salvation as a people.

Let me speak of a few of the many facets of this extraordinary man.
He came from a home of plain living and hard thinking. His father was
a man who loved books and often bought them instead of bread. In
his teens Clarence Darrow devoured night after night (when required
lessons were done) the poetry of Walt Whitman, the novels of Flaubert
and Zola, the social theory of Henry George, the penology of John Peter
Altgeld. He went, in his early Chicago years, to the Sunset Club, where
men debated for hours—noisily, bitterly, and joyously—Carlyle, Burns,
Voltaire, Tom Paine. In the years that followed, in the apartments Darrow lived in, people came regularly for discussions of socialism, anarchism, pacifism, and all the issues of the day. Out of that reading, which
he began so early, came a wealth of knowledge and experience from
past ages that illuminated many a controversy and opened the way to
fresh and bold answers. Darrow read for his work, not just for pleasure;
but he loved ideas, he enjoyed books from all viewpoints.

It was John P. Altgeld's Live Questions on Our Penal Machinery and
Its Victims that first convinced Darrow that in sending a man to prison
we are usually just revenging ourselves on him, not reforming him. It
was Altgeld who claimed that man had made a society where the many
are poor and the few are rich, yet the laws are the same for both. He
pointed out to Darrow, the young lawyer fresh from Ashtabula, Ohio,

that poverty and slums and lack of education drove men to commit crimes. The law should get at the root of the criminal's troubles, and not hide the victims of society's own folly away in prisons where they are quietly forgotten.

I hope many of you today will secure one or both of the biographies of Darrow listed [*Clarence Darrow for the Defense* by Irving Stone and *Clarence Darrow: Defense Attorney* by Iris Noble] for I cannot now tell you the full story of this magnificent man. I hope you will read the account of his first leap into the public eye at a mass meeting at which Henry George was the chief speaker. His attack that night on the city administration in Chicago eventuated in his being appointed by the new reform mayor, DeWitt Creiger, to the office of assessment attorney. In a few months he was corporation counsel for the city. His career was in orbit.

None of us should be ignorant of the great cases in the life of Darrow. They are not events of interest to attorneys only. They are chapters in American social history. We cannot afford to be unarmed with the munitions of thought and actual history they contain. It was Eugene V. Debs who dealt the first shattering blow to Darrow by asking him to leave a highly profitable position with the Chicago and Northwestern Railway to be his defense attorney and later attorney for the American Railway Union. This case changed Darrow's life and set its direction for the next sixty years. Here the philosophy of his career found its first expression. To the jury he declared: "This is a historic case which will count much for liberty or against liberty. Conspiracy, from the days of tyranny in England, has been the favorite weapon of every tyrant. It is an effort to punish the crime of thought."

Darrow knew whereof he spoke. He had read books and pamphlets on socialism and anarchism and capitalism, on unions and trade associations and employer's organizations, and debated them endlessly in the Sunset Club, with friends in his home, at union halls, in lawyers' offices. He knew what we have too often forgotten: that thought and speech, even radical, even silly speech, is not conspiracy. It is the blood and muscle of a free people's society. Darrow's life flourished on controversy, on the sharp clashing of ideas, on debate, on heresy.

Years later, during the Palmer Raids of the early twenties, Darrow took the case of twelve members of the Communist Labor Party indicted in Rockford, Illinois. He wanted to do more than save twelve unpopular persons from jail. He wanted to strike at the un-American philosophy of the Overthrow Act, then recently passed by Congress—the Smith Act of that period. He spoke not so much to the jury as to the Attorney General and the U.S. Supreme Court. Listen to his words: "I know the humblest and meanest man who lives should have his say. I know he ought to speak his mind. I know the Constitution is a delusion and a snare if the weakest and humblest in the land cannot be defended in his right to speak and his right to think, as much as the greatest and strongest in the land." This speech was water thrown on a growing fire of intolerance and hatred against radicals. The Palmer Raids died out in shame. The governor of Illinois pardoned all the Communist leaders. Darrow's name became associated with intellectual and political freedom for millions of Americans from that day on.

But Darrow was not defending only the right to think and speak. He was defending the rights of working people to join unions, to strike against intolerable conditions, to shape their own social destiny by their control of the economic and political machinery of their country. The case of Debs and the railway workers had shown this, but it came out even more eloquently and with great clarification for future years in the case of the woodworkers of Oshkosh, Wisconsin, on strike against George M. Paine's lumber company. It was a company that paid sixteen hundred workers an average of ninety-six cents for a ten-hour day of work, and children even less. Paine broke child labor laws to hire boys and girls from ten years up at sixty-five cents a day. Women were paid eighty cents a day. The union leaders were jailed for conspiracy and Darrow took the case.

I hope we Americans will never forget the words of Clarence Darrow in that trial. They belong with the words of Amos and Lincoln and John Brown:

> George Paine is a liar. He does not believe these clients are guilty of conspiracy against the laws of this land. He believes them guilty of conspiring against him. He believes himself a god, with the right of life and death, life and starvation, over his workers. He believes he may destroy what little is left of that spirit of independence and manhood which he has slowly been crushing from the breasts of those who toil for him.

Then turning to the jury he added:

> I appeal to you for those men and women who rise in the morning before daylight and go home after the light has faded from the sky, and give their lives, their toil and strength, to make others rich and great.

Darrow was not a joiner. He joined but one organization for reform in his life: the NAACP. But he attended and he listened and he argued and he pleaded with men and women who did join all sorts of organizations. He knew they had to associate and advocate together if the conscience of America was to be awakened. He took unpopular cases, large and small, from rich and poor. He was a university in himself, a labor union in himself, a church in himself, and in one great and celebrated case a psychiatric clinic in himself.

In many ways the Loeb-Leopold case was the most important in his career. In one sense it was the Chessman case of 1924. It also has parallels to the Thomas Cordrey case this year in Palo Alto. A terrible crime had been committed. The families of the two teenage murderers were rich and prominent. It was a case that had shocked the nation, and the cry for vengeance deafened all other thoughts that might be expressed. Eventually Darrow was able to talk great wisdom to the judge (there was no jury). He could speak of what happens to boys with much money but no love in their lives. He was able to show that brilliance of mind without sympathy, tenderness, or affection can transform a youth into a monster. He was able to show the relationship of an acquisitive and morally delinquent society to youthful crime.

The shrill voices of fanatics, the cry of blood lust, the primitive emotions of thousands screaming at Darrow on the street and into his telephone have now faded. We have the perspective of thirty-three years to judge a few of his words to the judge in Chicago in the afternoon of his closing appeal. They are words worthy of repetition now.

> Do I need to argue to Your Honor that cruelty only breeds cruelty; that hatred only causes hatred; that if there is any way to soften this human heart, which is hard enough at its best, if there is any way to kill evil and hatred and all that goes with it, it is not through evil and hatred and cruelty? It is through charity, love and understanding. How often do people need to be told this? Look back at the world. There is not a philosopher, not a religious leader, not a creed, that has not taught it.
>
> I am not pleading so much for these boys as I am for the infinite number of others to follow, those who perhaps cannot be as well defended as these have been, those who may go down in the tempest without aid. It is of them I am thinking and for them I am begging of this court not to turn backward toward the barbarous and cruel past.
>
> . . . I know Your Honor stands between the future and the past. I know the future is with me and what I stand for here; not merely for the lives of these two unfortunate lads, but for all boys and all girls, all of the young, and, as far as possible, for all of the old. I am pleading for life, understanding, charity, kindness and the infinite mercy that considers all. I am pleading that we overcome cruelty with kindness and hatred with love. I know the future is on my side. You may hang these boys; you may hang them by the neck until they are dead. But in doing it you will turn your face toward the past. In doing it you are making it harder for every other boy who in ignorance and darkness must grope his way through the mazes which only childhood knows.

Last Thursday night Mrs. Fritchman and I saw one of the most moving and searching films of this decade, *Twelve Angry Men*. That film, which for script and acting should win Academy Awards, reflected the influence of Clarence Darrow's eloquence and compassion in the Loeb-Leopold case. A step along the highway to abolition of capital punishment was taken in 1925 in a Cook County courtroom. Man's primitive impulses were bypassed to let the rationality of which he is capable take over.

I shall say little today of Darrow's religion. He claimed to have none. Many Unitarians have made the same claim. We must judge by his actions and the totality of his words over the eighty years of his life. Frankly, at all of the great trials in which he participated, he showed a profound religious insight and commitment. The dignity, anger, sacrifice, and courage of the man combined to give us a prophet of high religion, without benefit of surplice or ordination. Let us remember that Jeremiah and Amos and Isaiah never wore clerical collars and were never ordained either. Was there not something deeply religious in his words at Dayton, Tennessee, at the beginning of the Scopes trial when he declared: "Scopes is not on trial. Civilization is on trial. The prosecution is opening the doors for a reign of bigotry equal to anything in the Middle Ages. No man's belief will be safe, if they win."

The trial on evolution and the Bible in Dayton affected American thought for decades to follow. A wedge had been driven between private religious training and public education. It may well be that in this country the wedge thus driven will make it impossible ever for a state or a nation to impose one religious doctrine on the children of that state. The ignorance of Bryan as exposed in examination of the famed politician fundamentalist opened the eyes of millions to the quicksand foundation of much popular religion. The task was not completed in 1925, but it was well started, and neither Billy Graham nor Oral Roberts nor Bishop Sheen can restore foundations shaken in Tennessee that year. Religious freedom had gained millions of friends throughout the land because this reverent agnostic, this advocate of inquiry, even in the house of the Lord, had entered into combat with the champion of the Bible folk and proven him but a man, unread, uncritical, intolerant. John Scopes by action of the Supreme Court of Tennessee went free.

Clarence Darrow would have loved the fight we are waging here in California for religious freedom and all that it symbolizes. Just as he had battled for the rights of anarchists and socialists to think and advocate their ideas, just as he had labored in court to preserve the right of Negro-Americans to live in houses of their own choosing, just as he had risked reputation and fortune for the basic right of labor to choose its terms of toiling, so in the greatest right, that of mental and immoral independence, this champion of humanity left us a heritage of flaming power for the living present.

The words that Darrow delivered at the funeral of Governor Peter Altgeld could well be spoken of himself: "In the great flood of human life that is spawned upon the earth it is not often that a man is born. Altgeld was a soldier in the everlasting struggle of the human race for liberty and justice. He gave his life to liberty's immortal cause."

Darrow belongs with Paine and Ingersoll, Voltaire and Debs, men who, in their hierarchy of values, placed freedom first. He knew men must eat bread, he knew that men cherished love and comradeship, but he knew these cannot survive for long without the touchstone of an unfettered mind. He was a rebel who stepped down into the arena of life and risked everything he possessed for men of every color and creed, of every political persuasion and economic state. Fear never entered his veins. Power and egotism never corrupted his soul. In our era of the intimidated man, his figure stands like an archangel and sears our consciences with his example of a decent, bold, and compassionate advocate. I cannot agree with John Haynes Holmes that Darrow was an "unbeliever." He was an agnostic regarding the heavenly ramparts and the countenance of the Almighty, but his belief in man and his vast powers outshone the sun in glory. His faith in humanity put timid beliefs of little men to everlasting shame. Of such spirits will tomorrow's commonwealth be composed until the planet cools and the race dissolves.

John Milton
Advocate of Freedom
A Tribute on His 250th Birthday
June 21, 1959

In the magazine *The Reporter* for June 11 there is an interview with the novelist Nelson Algren by David Ray, a witty and incisive bit of conversation. It has much to say about complacency, about the absence of compassion and the growth of mediocrity in American life today. He discusses beatniks and what he terms "Norman Vincent Pealniks." Both of these rare blooms are given special and loving care by Time, Inc., says Mr. Algren, because they debase the concept of artist from one who historically is interested in the condition of man to one who simply entertains. The interview at times is razor-edged, and not a moment too soon. I firmly agree that this entire preoccupation with transforming the writer or artist into a gin-struck eccentric, detached from our common life, has gone far enough. With savage irony Mr. Algren says of contemporary America: "In gaining an affluence so great, we are at last able to support infantilism as a trade, one followed by professional infants; we have scored another first."

I mention all of this in an address dedicated to John Milton because our encircling infantilism has sought to absorb the clergy of all faiths. The combined press assault on the mere possibility of the Methodists of this area speaking out on recognition of China at their annual conference this week is a case in point! We are told that it is fine for Methodists to discuss theology or plan new churches, but we must make sure that they do not propose acknowledgment of half a billion Chinese as members of the world family or renew last year's resolution against all nuclear testing. The Methodists folded under the attack. Infantilism prevailed, at least in Southern California; in Connecticut, the Methodists passed their resolution on China.

So much for an introduction. Understanding John Milton of the seventeenth century is essential, in my opinion, to understanding the role of a Unitarian or anyone else claiming adult status in 1959, 351 years after the birth of this giant poet-citizen of Cromwellian England. To this congregation I do not need to defend biographical preaching. You know my views on it.

I had planned this address for December 9, 1958, but events prevented its preparation, so this is a tardy but nonetheless heartfelt birthday tribute to John Milton, a few months late. Since many, even in our own Unitarian fold, do not know him as more than the author of *Lycidas* and *Paradise Lost* (which they have never read or only in their youth for a cursory few hours), I feel no compunction in speaking of him on this June Sunday. We need this man, whom Percy Shelley referred to as "this sacred Milton, republican and bold inquirer into morals and religion." In seventeenth-century England, republican was a very radical word. Unless your education was far more fortunate than mine, you learned little of Milton's advanced views in religion or politics from your teachers. The Milton I speak of this morning was discovered in my private studies long after my degrees were finished and filed.

I am not speaking of John Milton because of a special fascination with research into history for its own sake, but because this valiant and many-talented genius wrestled with many of the crucial problems we face at this hour in our Sputnik and Univac civilization: separation of church and state; achievement of equality for women with the right of divorce fully understood; abolition of censorship over books, art, and all forms of cultural expression; the struggle for popular government in contrast to royal tyranny (or its equivalents in a bourgeois democracy); the rejection of scholastic education, and the full use of science and humanistic disciplines for man's rational control of his life and environment. As we think of the hundred and more subpoenaed California teachers this morning, let us remember John Milton, a reformer of education, a militant advocate of the inquiring mind, a partisan leader of a revolutionary movement, a religious independent in a day when it nearly cost him his head to oppose the English Protestant hierarchy. John Milton is far more a citizen of the twentieth-century adult world than Liberace, Bing Crosby, or Admiral Lewis Strauss.

Let us refresh our memories about John Milton, and as we so often do we start with a father; in this case, a grandfather. Milton's father was disinherited by his father, a wealthy Catholic yeoman of Oxfordshire in Elizabethan England, for being a premature Protestant, that is, for embracing Protestantism too eagerly and too soon. John Milton, Sr., father of the poet, came to London and became, in time, a successful scrivener, a combination of notary, law writer, investment counsellor, and debt collector. On December 9, 1608, his son was born and the parents soon discovered they had given birth to a genius of rare abilities. The father was, by avocation, a musician and composer. He was an accomplished organist, and his hymns won recognition even as far away as Poland, where a prince struck off a medal to honor some of his hymn tunes. John Milton, Sr. encouraged his son's gifts in music and poetry and saw to it that he received an excellent education at Cambridge University, having provided him earlier with tutors in French, Italian, music, and the classics.

Of the medieval patterns of the curriculum, I wish we could say more than we can today. Milton began his lifelong rebellion against the weight of tradition when it opposed progress by his advocacy of education reform at Cambridge. He was a Baconian who shared that Elizabethan's conviction that knowledge should be "enlarging the bounds of human empire, to the effecting of all things possible." Suffice this morning to read one passage from his essay *Against the Scholastic Philosophy*:

> Besides all this, it not infrequently happens that those who have entirely devoted and dedicated themselves to this blight of disputation lamentably display their ignorance and absurd childishness when faced with a new situation outside their usual idiotic occupation. Finally, the supreme result of all this earnest labour is to make you a more finished fool and cleverer contriver of conceits, and to endow you with a more expert ignorance; and no wonder, since all these problems at which you have been working in such torment and anxiety have no existence in reality at all, but like unreal ghosts and phantoms without substance obsess minds already disordered and empty of all true wisdom.

In days like ours, when Robert Hutchins and others urge us to a more humanistic and less traditional concept of education, it is profitable to remember Milton's classic comment on the great emancipating role of learning. It is still a bold and prophetic statement of the task of education:

> When universal learning has once completed its cycle, the spirit of man, no longer confined within this dark prison house, will reach out far and wide, until it fills the whole world and the space far beyond with the expansion of its divine greatness. . . . Man will seem then to be one whose rule and dominion the stars obey, to whose command earth and sea hearken, and whom winds and tempests serve; to whom, lastly, Mother Nature herself has surrendered, as if indeed some god had abdicated the throne of the world and entrusted its rights, laws, and administration to him as governor.

This almost seems written with Sputnik or nuclear power in mind!

As in many an American college in our own time, so in Milton's day, the wealthy young men cared far more for wenching and drinking than for study and creative writing, or other intellectual initiatives. The second greatest English poet of all time used his pen to express his contempt for this inverted sense of values, and, if the Puritans of Burbank and Glendale who are trying to dry up sin in our local bookstores really knew their business of censorship, they would quit worrying about Henry Miller and D. H. Lawrence and go after John Milton.

Milton proved to be one of the greatest Latinists of all English history in both prose and poetry, and it was his linguistic talent that later opened the door to him into the highest echelons of Cromwell's government as Latin Secretary for Foreign Affairs. He began writing brilliant Latin paraphrases of the Psalms at the age of sixteen and proceeded eventually to write—in Latin, of course, as the international language of diplomacy in those days—the most devastating attack on the royalist theory of government composed during the years of the Commonwealth; it was called *Pro Populo Anglicano Defensio* and was published in 1651. It was an annihilating reply to Salmasius of Leyden, Holland, who had written, at the request of the exiled family of the beheaded Charles I, a defense of the late king. The brilliance of the polemic and the perfection of the Latin invective gave a continental prestige to the Cromwellian cause that it needed, and had lacked before.

It should be remembered that John Milton, like his father, had shown premature enthusiasm. The first Englishman out of Parliament after Charles I was executed in 1649 to attach himself openly to the new republic was John Milton in a pamphlet *On Tenure of Kings and Magistrates*, a now classic statement of the people's right to regicide under proper provocation. Since Milton's name is today often associated with the concept of complete toleration of all positions, with no limits of free speech, it might be well to speak of historical realities. Milton advocated sharp debate, true controversy, popular expression of thought, but he certainly opposed freedom of speech and publication for Papists and royalists. He drew lines and limits to freedom, as did Thomas Jefferson and James Madison, leaders of a later bourgeois and religious revolution.

Milton was no absolutist or purist in this matter of intellectual or political freedom. He expected youth to be educated in the ideas and responsibilities of government (so unlike our own education today in America where such matters are sources of suspicion by parents, administrators, and congressional committees). Milton felt that pupils should study "the beginning, the end and reasons of political societies, that they may not be, in a dangerous fit of the commonwealth, such poor, shaken, uncertain reeds, of such tottering conscience, as many of our great counsellors have lately shown themselves, but steadfast pillars of the state."

John Milton found himself in the Commonwealth struggle with many diverse reformers of England. He believed, as an antimonarchist, that all sovereign power derives from the people by some form of social contract. If a king waxes tyrannical or prevents the exercise of men's religion, he should be resisted. If the king is stubborn after efforts are made to correct him, then he should be deposed and, if necessary, slain. In France such doctrine was taught by the Huguenot, Beza; by the Catholic, Louis d'Orleans; in Scotland by John Knox; in Holland by Grotius. These were not theoreticians alone; they led men to action. In 1581 the States-General of Holland deposed Philip II of Spain, in 1566 the Scotch Parliament deposed Mary Stuart, and in England Harrington and Cromwell beheaded Charles I.

We Americans should know this Unitarian revolutionary John Milton better than we do. His *Essay on the Tenure of Kings and Magistrates* was pored over by our founding fathers many, many times. Listen to Milton's words:

> It being manifest, that the power of kings and magistrates is nothing else but what is only derivative, transferred, and committed to them in trust from the people to the common good of them all, in whom the power yet remains fundamentally, and cannot be taken from them without a violation of their natural birthright . . . it follows from necessary causes that the titles of sovereign lord, natural lord, and the like are either arrogancies or flatteries. . . . unless the people be thought to be created all for him, he not for them, and they all in one body inferior to him single; which were a kind of treason against the dignity of mankind to affirm. . . . It follows, lastly, that since the king or magistrate holds his authority of the people both originally and naturally for their good, in the first place, and not his own, then may the people, as oft as they shall judge it for the best, either choose him or reject him, retain him or depose him.

This is a gospel taught by a great scholar, a man of the middle class, yet colleague with leaders of the workers and shopkeepers who made up Cromwell's remarkable people's army, the same kind of people that rallied to the American cause at Lexington and Concord a century later.

After the victory of the Cromwellian army, when the new government took power, the independent farmers, small merchants, some shipowners, and craftsmen influenced by John Lilburne looked for really progressive reforms. They stood for strong individual liberty, legal equality, and the abolition of vested interests. They were called the Levellers. They expected free trade and lowered taxes. The large bourgeois interests, however, dominated Cromwell's parliament and determined that the revolution had gone far enough. To the left of John Lilburne and his group were others who were even more discontented by the new order of Cromwell. They were the poor workers and farmers known as Diggers, under the leadership of Gerrard Winstanley. They were basically communist in their thinking: men who felt that all citizens should live by their own personal efforts; they were agrarians who opposed land lying fallow while people starved, a quaint notion indeed that the Cromwellians soon began to punish vigorously. You couldn't have men like Winstanley asking: "What stock is provided for the people, for the poor, the fatherless, the widows and impoverished? What encouragement for the laboring and industrious as to take off their burthens?"

The only task John Milton as Secretary for Foreign Tongues in the new government did not accept was writing an answer to John Lilburne's *New Chains for Old*, which attacked Cromwell for many parliamentary abuses (of which Milton was also critical at many points), although his class background was different from Lilburne's. Milton knew the need for a broad coalition of forces in the Commonwealth, but he did not defend publicly actions he personally condemned. It is well for us to remember that while Milton accepted as expedient for survival of the government Cromwell's dissolving of Parliament in 1653 and assuming the title of Lord Protector, he was very critical of the action in print and in personal controversy with Cromwell. Milton disliked dictatorship. Listen to his words in his unfinished *History of Britain*: "The votes and ordinances which should have contained the repealing of bad laws and the immediate constitution of better, resounded with nothing else but new impositions, taxes, excises, not to mention the offices, gifts, and preferments bestowed and shared among themselves." That is strong language!

His *Defensio Secundo* warns Cromwell of the dangers of dictatorship and an appeal to maintain England's liberty. We can read it as a pre-cold-war masterpiece.

> War had made many great whom peace makes small. If after being released from the toils of war, you neglect the arts of peace, if your peace and your liberty be a state of warfare; if war be your only virtue, the summit of your praise, you will, believe me, soon find a peace adverse to your interests. Your peace will be only a more distressing war; and that which you imagined liberty will prove the worst of slavery.
>
> If you think that it is a more grand, a more beautiful, or a more wise policy, to invent subtle expedients for increasing the revenue, to multiply our naval and military force, to rival in craft the ambassadors of foreign states, to form skillful treaties and allegiances, than to administer unpolluted justice to the people, to redress the injured, and to succour the distressed, and speedily to restore to everyone his own, you are involved in a cloud of error.

Milton also found himself in sharp disagreement with Cromwell over religious freedom, specifically over disestablishing the state religion. He had in *Defensio Secundo* courageously warned Cromwell against self-will, overlegislation, and overpolicing of the people. But his strongest words were over religion. Milton wanted to abolish a state-paid clergy and tax-supported churches. He felt, as a liberal Christian, that the trouble with Christianity since Constantine in the fourth century had been state control and aid to religion, everything from tax exemption to tax support. The propagation of the Christian message in all its moral power, said Milton, called for real separation of the church from the state. Cromwell did not agree, and this fact must have been Milton's deepest disappointment with the Commonwealth.

In September 1658 Cromwell died and his son, Richard, was made Protector. In October Milton published one of his most important pamphlets (certainly for its effect on American history later), the *Treatise of Civil Power in Ecclesiastical Causes showing that it is not lawful to compel in matters of religion*, in which he advocated separation of church and state. It hasn't happened yet in England. I thought of John Milton on May 17 when I stood in Theophilus Lindsay's Unitarian pulpit in London, for it was Lindsay who inspired Franklin, Jefferson, and Priestley a century after Milton to carry on the struggle for a free and liberal church, and who did succeed! I do not know how well you were taught English history, but I did not know until a few weeks ago about the vigorous and bold role of Milton in trying to stave off and prevent the restoration of the throne in England. Even in so brief an address as is mine today, I should mention his two pamphlets in the final tragic period: first, *A Free Commonwealth and the Excellence thereof compared with the inconveniences and dangers of re-admitting Kingship to this Nation*, and secondly, *Ready and Easy Way*, a violent denunciation of the royal family and a prophecy of disaster if it was returned.

On April 25, 1660, the Convention Parliament convened and on May 1 voted to restore the throne. On May 29, Charles II made a triumphal entry into London. How Milton escaped the scaffold after the Restoration is still a mystery. He was the most eloquent and vehement and unremitting of the Cromwellian voices, even though blind. Andrew Marvell, the poet and friend of Milton's for many years, probably interceded in his behalf. All copies of *Defensio Primo* and *Eikonoklastes* were burned by the hangman, but not the living body of the learned and unrepenting author. So he lived to retire and dictate to his daughter the most famous poem in our language, *Paradise Lost*. (I did not say the most read, but the most famous. If you have not read a few hundred lines aloud recently, I recommend it as a pleasant way to forget the prose style of the *Los Angeles Times* editorial page or the gritty paragraphs of Henry Luce's several rubbings.)

Many who know of Milton as a powerful advocate of individual liberty and of a popular commonwealth do not think of him as a religious liberal, or specifically as a Unitarian. He held to the humanist's faith in reason, but his greatest poems, *Paradise Lost* and *Paradise Regained*, employ the mythology and vocabulary of the Christian faith more magnificently than from any other pen in history. As John Morris wrote in the *Unitarian Register* last December, Milton's *Paradise Lost* may stand beside Homer and Dante in grandeur of epic expression, but one does not think of it as a declaration of liberal religion. The English critic, Walter Raleigh, called it a "monument to dead ideas." Samuel Johnson, T. S. Eliot, and Ezra Pound have assailed both its theology and its poetry. To us of a twentieth-century Unitarian culture, its liberalism may seem muted indeed, but measured by seventeenth-century historical conditions it is very liberal. The Calvinist concept of God, then so dominant, which made a puppet out of man, is replaced with the concept of man, a child of freedom. Man is not overruled by fate. Adam had a real choice between good and evil, not a fictitious one. The religion of Eden in Milton's poem is without creeds and rituals and formal prayers, and no hierarchy stood between man and his God. Milton rejected the concept of the Trinity completely, a very bold idea indeed in the mid-seventeenth century, and still, may I remind you, a heresy in twentieth-century Christianity, three centuries later in the United States. Christ in *Paradise Regained* is a perfect man, not a god. No other Unitarian in seventeenth-century England took so radical a theological view.

This was no late-in-life afterthought by a retired revolutionary. In his vigorous days under Cromwell, having written *Areopagitica* on the evils of censorship, Milton insisted upon allowing the publication of the forbidden Socinian catechism, the Unitarian question-and-answer book used by ministers and laymen all over Europe, but never before allowed in England. When criticized for giving the stamp of approval to this heretical book, he simply replied that he did not approve of prohibiting the publication of books. Cromwell thought of himself as very advanced to favor a multiple establishment, namely government support to several religious faiths, though not of course to Catholics, Jews, or Unitarians. Milton argued fiercely with Cromwell against the entire proposal.

Milton's most radical religious views, found in his book *Christian Doctrine*, were not printed until 1825, 150 years after his death. Whether correct in strategy or not, he doubtless concluded that publication of such advanced ideas during the days of the Commonwealth would have brought its cause into further disrepute and jeopardized its very existence. Again we have evidence of a man who believed in expediency, as well as a large margin of controversy.

It is interesting that William Ellery Channing in the early nineteenth century was ambivalent regarding Milton. He welcomed the Unitarians

Milton, Locke, and Hume as valiant allies in the case of rational religion, but could not forgive Milton for leaning heavily on the Bible. This will strike many of you as strange, since to most Unitarians of this generation Channing seems disturbingly Bible-centered himself. Of course, Channing's real quarrel with Milton was his shock at an English Unitarian supporting divorce, and, even worse, polygamy even on biblical grounds. But Channing, nevertheless, was glad this great man of letters and Cromwellian democrat read Servetus, studied the Polish Socinian catechism, and admired Castillio, the great humanist defender of Servetus.

We, a century after Channing, can also salute Milton for his advanced and progressive views on marriage, divorce, and the woman question. He was married three times; his first wife left him a few weeks after the marriage, possibly for political reasons rather than marital, she being a royalist. Milton's recognition of the intellectual equality of women and his confession of their superiority in some cases was heresy, indeed, both under Charles I and Cromwell. He ought to be given a posthumous invitation to address our new Unitarian women's club with its proven interest in such matters.

Probably Milton's most famous single sentence is this: "Give me the liberty to know, to utter and to argue freely according to conscience, above all other liberties." Milton's *Areopagitica* and John Locke's *Letter Concerning Toleration* are two of the great English documents of history on behalf of human freedom. Both drew limits, possibly not the same limits as you think you would have drawn under similar conditions; this depends on whether you would have sided with Lilburne or with Charles I (both doubtless thought Milton a pious compromiser). But the important fact to me is that since Milton, English education, popular democracy, rational religious thought, and separation of church and state had an easier time of it. He opened many a door and held it open under devastating onslaughts to which he refused to bow, including blindness and the imminent danger of death by the hangman for subversion against the royal house of Stuart. We should be exceedingly proud of this Puritan Unitarian who was without much humor and without much patience with the slow of mind. He was a giant intellect and could have followed patrician ways without discomfort. He chose to be a warrior all his life on behalf of the people, as he understood their cause. He endured a royalist brother who hated his every thought; he survived thousands of enemies in England who felt their privileges threatened and their status shaken, . . . and so they were, for the sword of Milton was a sharp blade indeed.

I should like to close with words, not from the seventeenth century, but from the twentieth century. Dr. Brock Chisholm, in his charming little book, *Can People Learn?*, writes:

Fortunately there are many and increasing numbers of heretics throughout the world now. Many are fighting lone battles, largely with their own early taught desire to conform, but many others have really freed themselves and are on the way to fearless living. They may be identified as Humanists, free thinkers, rationalists, Unitarians or by many other names. What they have in common is the fact that they have not nailed any flag to any fixed mast, but remain free to grow. They are concerned with taking man the next step, freeing him from his anchors to old absolutes, helping wherever possible in progress toward a rational, free and satisfying world.

So we come from Milton to Brock Chisholm. The first helped to make the second possible. Milton can help each of us also if we will let him. He is no messiah, no savior, no perfect man. I think I would have liked him personally, but I might not have liked him; it is of no importance. He gave you and me a passport to a better world both of the mind and of the body, a world where the people shape their destiny with their own hands. For this I shall be eternally grateful.

Let us close with Milton's line from *Comus*:

> Mortals that would follow me,
> Love virtue, she alone is free.

The Hammer and the Forge
Theodore Parker
A Centenary Sermon
May 8, 1960

On May 10 the Unitarians of the world, and many other liberal religionists, including not a few unregenerated agnostics and atheists, honored the memory of Theodore Parker of Boston who died on that day in 1860, and was buried in the Protestant cemetery outside the Pinto gate of Florence, Italy. It seems appropriate this morning that we collectively invoke the spirit of that giant reformer, possibly the greatest of the Unitarians produced to date on this soil of ours.

On this centenary of Parker's death every Unitarian minister will probably seek to array himself in the cloak of this latter-day Elijah, and hope, by some miracle, to ride in his flaming chariot of fire that Scripture tells us carried the earlier prophet to his just reward. And obviously I am not totally exempt from the temptation. I can imagine no exercise more profitable in early May, 1960, than for several hundred preachers of the free faith to look and sound as much like Theodore Parker as they possibly can. I only regret that the novelty of the effort may startle some of their congregations, and I fear that the exertion of the occasion may, for some at least, result in a fatigue from which they will find it embarrassing to recover.

This morning we can launch ourselves with one of the more celebrated passages of Theodore Parker, even if the fuel does not hold out for a permanent orbiting for the remainder of the sermon. Listen to Theodore Parker in his sermon on *Speculative Atheism*, one of my long-time favorites:

> I never despair of truth, of justice, of love, of piety. I know that man
> will triumph over matter, the people over tyrants, right over wrong,

love over hate. Let the world have peace for 500 years. The aristocracy of blood will have gone, the aristocracy of gold will have gone also. The aristocracy of talent will have come. Then shall come the aristocracy of goodness which is the democracy of man, the government of all by all.

Theodore Parker was indeed the hammer striking the anvil in the forge of nineteenth-century America. This morning I shall not attempt the sweeping survey of Parker's life and thought that the anniversary deserves. For that I urge your reading Prof. Henry Steele Commager's classic biography, *Theodore Parker: Yankee Crusader*. And for a special study of the hammer of Boston, I urge a reading of Truman Nelson's *The Sin of the Prophet*, a novel about the Anthony Burns period in Parker's life.

A Freudian analyst would probably trace a portion of my admiration for this great Unitarian to the fact that his very appearance gives one courage. Many of us less-favored Unitarian ministers have rejoiced in his plain appearance, his unmusical voice, his awkward stance. Parker had few physical gifts to enhance his professional labors. He counted on reasoning, not fashionable rhetoric; on presentation of irrefutable facts, not sentiment and emotion; hard work, not prestige of a profession. The true genius of this man can be measured, in part, by the fact that the religious views he advocated and which so disturbed his contemporaries have become the characteristics of their descendents. If we can do half as well, we shall be the most fortunate of men and women in this twentieth century.

Theodore Parker was indeed the hammer of his generation. Many of his contemporaries wished he had never been born. One preacher in Park Street Church, Calvinist to the core, prayed before his congregation one morning, "Lord, place a hook in this man's jaw that he may be silenced." Parker often wrote sermons with a loaded pistol on his desk. He made up agendas for his expected days in prison. In Boston's Public Library recently, I saw the original edition of his own legal defense for his trial in the fugitive slave case, a trial never held because the charges were dropped.

In his early years he used a pseudonym so that he might publish his bold heresies without reprisals being immediately taken by his clerical enemies. In fact, I was tempted to announce today's address as the *Legacy of Levi Blodgett* just to see how curious you might be to know who Levi Blodgett really was. Parker used the quaint alias to first present his theological conviction that man has an intuitive religious faculty that makes all external props like miracles quite needless. He later openly advocated this opinion at length in his famous *South Boston Sermon*, now one of the classics of Unitarianism.

Many of his friends fled the ministry in the days of Unitarian "orthodoxy" in the 1830s and 1840s, Ralph Waldo Emerson most notably. But Parker remained until hemorrhages condemned him to his sickbed and consumption destroyed him at the age of fifty. He enjoyed the controversies and tensions of his profession. He reached out for its most arduous assignments, serving on a secret committee to aid John Brown's foray into the mountains of Virginia, writing ninety-eight lectures a year to be delivered in lyceum halls across the nation, organizing abolitionist societies and peace movements, hiding fugitive slaves [such as] William and Ellen Craft, and attempting unsuccessfully to secure the freedom of Thomas Sims and Anthony Burns. He felt a divine compulsinn to cry aloud and awaken the slumbering conscience of his generation.

While his words were read across the nation on Monday mornings (unlike any other minister of his age), he was still the pastor of his congregation in Boston's drafty Music Hall. He counselled the despairing, labored with the discouraged, buried the dead. He preached a fifty-minute sermon at Music Hall at 11 o'clock on Sunday morning and then drove out to Watertown and repeated it on Sunday evening. He would often write forty long-hand letters a day. His zeal for action and reform and education was boundless. In the Boston Public Library collection I saw his diaries, his committee files, his memoranda, and notebooks. He was a geyser of creative energy, a perpetual fountain of ideas and proposals, a firebrand in the night. His achievements shame us of today's pulpit—so often barren and so often empty echoes of voices long since dead.

He was a father image for tens of thousands. His mind and conscience fortified a generation of men and women who needed strength to face the whirlwind that they knew was certain soon to sweep across the land —the bloodiest in the history of warfare, the unparalleled fratricide of four millennia, which our bland professors glibly dismiss as "the war between the states."

There may be elements of the fiery temperament of Theodore Parker that leave one unmoved, or even freshly hostile to so restless a mind, so inexhaustible a dynamo. One of my colleagues has sought to dismiss him as a man of paranoid compulsions, a troubler of the peace better forgotten in a time so clearly improved over Parker's turbulent day. I never cease to marvel at the ecclesiastical ability of some men to flee the noontime sun.

It is my theory that we gather here on Sunday mornings primarily to recover our sense of authentic values, to associate with our best thoughts, and to find companionship with our friends who hold to some of our first principles. The emotional costliness of the age of the cold war is something a minister has occasion to witness every hour of his working day. Never, in my own experience, have so many sincere and ethnically conscientious people found so great difficulty in maintainng themselves spiritually as now. Irrespective of philosophical or political or religious differences, I have an increased compassion for the torment of many I meet, and who is not among them, who need far more strength and courage and affection and self-confidence than they are now finding within themselves, or from their friends. The more one feels he has of moral capital in reserve, the less he wishes to see it bartered in compromise, or lost by erosion, or stolen by those with eyes blind to human values. We need a sympathy and tolerance for all persons of goodwill who are seeking, according to their existing lights, to live with honor, reason, and responsibility. And they are many. These are days of monumental disillusionment for countless folk.

Theodore Parker can be a friend of incalculable assistance in times such as these. He is a prototype of the mature Unitarian. For all his faults, and they were several, he fulfilled much in his life that remains in most of us but formless aspiration or a First-of-January resolution. While psychology was still in its prescientific swaddling clothes, he taught men the peril of too much straining for perfection in the mind while failing to take the first steps with the feet. He had a robust appreciation of man's physical resources for happiness and never let himself become too sophisticated to enjoy the basic pleasures of life. An outstanding intellectual of his age, he never became so bogged down in ideas that he forgot the people who have little time for books, but whose valiant efforts keep the world running. He had a lively consciousness of those who toil, a fact which his more effete clerical comrades in Boston Unitarianism never forgave him, and for which they held him more guilty than his skepticism about the gospel miracles.

In my reading of various histories of the United States I find that no Unitarian, aside from Jefferson, appears more frequently as a pervasive force in shaping the currents of thought and action than this grandson of Captain Parker of Lexington, the intrepid leader of the Minute Men. From Lincoln in the White House to the blacksmith at the forge, the words and the spirit of Theodore Parker played a direct influence —they were bread and wine to a hungry people taming a continent. Aside from yielding to some of the less disastrous occupational hazards of the ministry, Parker kept himself close to the American people in a way that is the inspiration and despair of thousands after him.

Theodore Parker above all else was in love with life and its possibilities for all men. Before the dwarfing forces of modern industrialism, which we know so well had done their work, before war and preparation for war became the consuming economic enterprise of our nation, Parker saw organized religion as the primary source of belittling man. And it infuriated him. Man was not made for dread alone.

Parker had a great respect for intellectual freedom as a fruit of natural religion and its postulates about man. He was quite possibly the best read man in America, even though the busiest reformer on the continent. He took for granted, as he did air and water and bread, the privilege of thought, unhampered, far-reaching, fertilized by the centuries and by the nations of living men. Out of this freedom he made a Unitarian religion that has been a lifting inspiration for over a hundred years. The First Amendment guarantees of free thought and association were as axiomatic as the multiplication tables.

His formulations in theology are not ours—and he would not want them to be. He despised the custodians of metaphysics who swept the altar stairs and shielded the candles of orthodoxy in his time. The professors at Harvard and the clergy on Beacon Street equally resented Parker's call for a renaissance of naturalistic religion, a clearing of the atmosphere so that the sun could shine once more—the blazing sun of human intelligence.

His hymns were rich in feeling, dedicated to the dignity of man, yet cast in a theological dress we cannot don today with comfort. Theodore Parker in his day taught thousands that religion is not orthodox theology, not miracles and ritual, not the sacerdotal and ecclesiastical, but a fresh, creative energy of the soul. He burst out in a consuming wrath against the ethical blindspots of the Calvinist conscience. He spoke for man, free and alive for other's freedom. One hundred years later he would shout again at the dismal formality and moral emptiness of our revival of religion. The churches again need such a hurricane to blow.

Theodore Parker was a pre-Marxian socialist, a pragmatic reformer who believed in the collective concept for man's economic and social living. His sermons on society must be read in the perspective of the times.

In our day of multimillionaire industrialists and multibillion dollar budgets for national armaments, it is hard for us to remember the Americans who have proceeded along fraternal lines of communal sharing: the Dunkards and Quakers, Mennonites and Moravians, the Transcendentalists of Brook Farm and Fruitlands, and the prophets who built them, not least of them, Theodore Parker. As one writer has observed:

> He warned against the materialism that might later destroy the individual by destroying social equality. The American builders of cooperative communities (most of them deeply religious) were trying to sidestep the danger of a struggle between classes. Parker saw clearly, though he was a preacher and not a social scientist, the psychological peril of a class that had nothing to sell but its labor power.

This social and economic theorizing was but the beginning. For decades Parker threw himself into a program of action that consumed his days and nights until his body collapsed in fatigue.

His sermons on the *Dangerous and Perishing Classes* were devastating sociological studies, documented with census bureau statistics and reports from the city hall on delinquency and crime, prostitution, housing shortages, and, above all, poverty. "Society, not the individual is at fault, nine-tenths of all prisoners come from the impoverished. Seventeen-twentieths of all crimes are against property." His documentary sermons on illiteracy and school shortages were unequalled for their accuracy, for society was no abstraction in the Parker lexicon.

"Society," he pointed out, "consists of men who pay low wages and high dividends, who collect exorbitant rents for wretched slums. Society must be responsible for its own shortcomings." His reforms were many and he proposed them in season and out: the end of slavery, peace and disarmament, the abolishing of capital punishment. The handling of juvenile delinquency must be altered, labor must take political office. Women must have real equality. The prudery about sex must be ended.

Parker was on every significant committee of his day which advocated an assault on corporate evil. He worked fifty hours a week outside of parish duties and sermon writing. He rallied the leaders of his day behind peace, abolition of slavery, education, prison reform. Emerson, Garrison, Phillips, Thoreau, Sumner, Alcott, Howe, scores of the giants of his generation responded to the sound of his trumpet. They met in committees, they wrote handbills, they hid fugitive slaves, they entertained outcasts in their home, men like John Brown and Frederick Douglass. All of this and much more grew naturally out of his tenet that "man comes first": "If we begin by taking care of the rights of man, it seems easy to take care of the rights of capital and labor."

As several biographers have observed, one reason Parker succeeded where so many reformers fail, was the quality of his dedication. His bitterest enemies knew there was not a trace of self-seeking in the man. Venality and greed corrupted no molecule of his body. Channing had said earlier: "No man should take on the office of reformer whose zeal is not tempered by extensive sympathies and universal love." Of Parker's deep affection for his fellowman no honest observer had a doubt. He did not fear the honest emotion and people knew it. The dry rot of mid-nineteenth-century Unitarian intellectualism was not infecting him as it was Orestes Brownson and others of his circle.

Our duty today is to see the movement of a polarized conscience, the actions of a man with a transforming gospel with a reasoned philosophy in a changing world. Darwin, Marx, Freud had not yet given their explosive thoughts to the world. But Parker was incredibly prescient about their contributions. One feels in his letters and sermons, in the reports of his labors a man superlatively sensitive to the harassed citizen of our own day and the need for his release from shackles, inner and outer.

Much has changed since 1860; much remains as it was then. The number and power of the engines of destruction have increased; the merchants of fabulous wealth have captured the centers of public and private power which Parker never dreamed of. On the other hand, vast strides have been taken by hundreds of millions across the face of the earth on every continent. To be sure, this has been at a terrible cost in life and suffering, of imprisonment and cruelty to mind and body. Great areas of our planet have learned the wisdom of Parker's first principle about human solidarity.

There is no easy optimism possible in sensitive hearts at this hour, as public moral standards have been revealed as more corrupt than millions of us had dreamed. The tarnished American principles of diplomacy, so righteously held to be above those of our international neighbors, have been exposed to public view and national humiliation. The justified and rationalized lie has been discovered not only in a Charles Van Doren, but now in a Christian Herter with full knowledge of the president. Yet for all this the dawn may be nearer than we know. The strife of the earth's peoples that tortures our waking hours grows out of a new confidence in man's possible victory over his oldest enemies at home and abroad. Parker shared this faith when the hopeful evidence was far less impressive. Nature is now tamed at many points of crucial significance: engineering, physics, chemistry, medicine, and psychiatry await our bidding as no slave people ever knew them to be in Greece, Rome, or ancient Egypt. Our industrial society is in process of being matured at fearful cost, but this generation has more reason than any before in history to expect it to be completed if manmade desolation does not intervene. The dream of the Lexington prodigy who gave his strength to the cleansing of his church and his state seems to be substance and not fancy. The words he gave to Lincoln echo in even our darkest days: "Government of the people, by the people and for the people will not perish from the earth."

In closing let me say that I have a very strong conviction that Theodore Parker would by now be restless, were he present here. I can hear his dry New England voice protest:

> Enough of the tributes, my good friend; on to the tasks of the hour. Are you going to stand idly by while Forest Lawn refuses the ashes of Caryl Chessman because he was an unrepentant agnostic? Are you now forgetting the seven men and one woman in the California death row at San Quentin awaiting the governmental cyanide and sulphuric acid?
>
> What are you doing about the omnibus bill of Senator Eastland, calculated to unravel the work of ten years by the U.S. Supreme Court and restoring the Smith Act to its original fury, cancelling the right to travel of all dissenters to the Victorian economic orthodoxies of President McKinley?

Are you standing idle as the nuclear bombs are loaded into dug-outs in two hemispheres and alerts are called at every American base?

Have your feet blisters on them from walking for peace and against biological warfare?

How are you supporting the students of South Korea, Japan, and Turkey, of Alabama and Louisiana as they take action their parents have so long been too paralyzed to take?

Where, person, is your tongue? This is no hour for chanting my victories in Boston on the eve of a civil war. This is no time to praise and repeat my Music Hall sermons on the goodness of God. I would draft them differently today. You have had an Einstein and a Huxley to correct my metaphysics. Speak up! Give man a better chance than did we of the transcendental generation. Get a new hammer. There is a new anvil and a new forge to work upon. Don't spend the power of your blows on centenary eulogies of me. I am dead. You are alive. Organize, my friend, organize."

*   *   *

The above sermon at the suggestion of Dr. John Haynes Holmes was sent to the Theodore Parker Memorial Committee to be added to the Centenary collection being gathered by it.

Remarks at a Dinner Honoring
Dr. Linus Pauling
and Ava Helen Pauling
March 6, 1976

Since tonight's celebration opens the first door for the 1977 centenary of the founding of the First Unitarian Church of Los Angeles by Caroline Severance and her friends, we may appropriately indulge in a little sectarian pride and comment on the participation of our honored guests as members of this society of heretics since 1962. Mrs. Pauling, besides speaking from our pulpit and in the Severance Room, was a member of the steering committee of our Unitarian Public Forum in its most vibrant years, along with Janet Stevenson, David Clavner, Elmer Mahoney, Madeline Borough, Gene Stone, and Martin Hall. They all deserve laurels for the energy dedicated to making the Unitarian Church a center known across the nation where speakers appeared when no lecture agency would handle them. Our Forum was a dissenter's holy campground, a glorious center for prophets and pariahs. Ava Helen spoke on women's liberation around the world, as she also bore constant witness to the primacy of peace, civil liberties, and civil rights. Here tonight we salute her leadership on these and other concerns, as manifested at our Eighth Street citadel in those rugged days when subpoena-servers lurked around every corner of what Art Seidenbaum has called "our hot-bed of nonviolence."

In one of his columns in the *New York Herald Tribune*, the infamous witch-hunter Herbert Philbrick apologized for merely "excerpting" from Dr. Pauling's multitudinous subversive activities: among them he noted his sponsorship in 1949 of the Waldorf Astoria Arts, Sciences and Professions Conference in New York; his being a "bulwark of Fritchman's church"; his opposing the Korean War; objecting vehemently to the McCarran Act; and protesting the deportation of Hans Eissler. In his book, *No More War*, Dr. Pauling unwittingly (if he ever does anything unwittingly) on one single page (page 170) alludes to three Unitarians involved in scientific work of one kind or another: Albert Schweitzer, Benjamin Franklin, and Joseph Priestley. Certainly we can be proud that the Paulings joined our Unitarian family because we were a religious group that honest scientists could join without compromise. Our freethinkers' church, organized by that theologian and medical researcher, Michael Servetus, has helped us all, over four centuries, to learn that the most deadly errors arise from obsolete assumptions.

On May 15, 1957 Dr. Pauling wrote and issued the now famous *Scientists' Appeal to Stop the Testing of Nuclear Bombs*, following a lecture at Washington University in St. Louis. In a week he had twenty-six signatures; ten days later two thousand American scientists had already signed it. Shortly thereafter, he and Ava Helen sent out from their Pasadena home, helped by a voluntary task force some of whom were such sister Unitarians as Mary Clarke and Janet Stevenson, letters asking for signatures from scientists all over the world. Seventy-five hundred scientists sent their signatures, including thirty-seven Nobel Laureates. Fulton Lewis, Jr. surmised in his syndicated column that some sinister organizations must have invested at least $100,000 in this vast achievement. Actually, Dr. Pauling noted in *No More War*, the cost was $600, and that from his own purse. On January 13, 1958, eight months after this first appeal, Linus and Ava Helen Pauling in person presented the petition to United Nations Secretary-General Dag Hammarskjold in New York. By that day the total number of signatures was 11,021.

Many of us in Los Angeles remember the marches and demonstrations for peace led by the Paulings, in which many local Unitarians walked with vast pride. Some gatherings were large; some were small. I remember one cool morning in a Los Angeles park when weather and poor publicity by a student group resulted in only a few dozen young people huddled under trees in Griffith Park, but the world-renowned scientist and militant for peace spoke and answered questions as long as the students wanted him to stay. That is the kind of man Linus Pauling is.

Then there was the peace march in Los Angeles, the first of any where Angelenos saw a sight familiar to peace lovers all over the world: the Paulings, side by side, leading the parade. People had said it could not be done: no one in Los Angeles could walk a block, let alone several miles; very few people would dare to demonstrate for peace. But the authentic magic of the Pauling name prevailed. It was a great day and a historic march.

Those of us who were members of First Church during the "dreadful fifties," when advocacy of peace and nuclear disarmament was both necessary and hazardous, remember gratefully that Linus Pauling *never* declined a request to speak at our church, however busy he was. His presence invariably filled the church. Ava Helen, of course, was equally generous, and gave us needed courage with first-hand news of the growing peace forces around the world.

There are some subjects most of us bypass in honoring these two cherished members of our church. We do not go into detail about the structure of crystals, the nature of the chemical bond, and the structure of molecules. We do not find ourselves explaining the Pauling resonance theory of chemical valence, or the construction of the first model of a benzine molecule, the brilliant scientific breakthrough which won him a Nobel Laureate in chemistry.

This is not a Unitarian revival meeting tonight, though no new membership applications will be rejected if you send them in; but remember that joining does not guarantee that you will get to heaven, or, more importantly, get a Nobel prize. But you can emulate Dr. Pauling in many ways. We can remember that he called from our Los Angeles pulpit for the impeachment of President Lyndon B. Johnson because of his massive betrayal of his campaign pledges to bring peace to Vietnam. It was a moment those of us who were present will never forget. *Anyone* with a hatred of war and oppression, and a love of truth, can emulate the Paulings, and many of you have.

With great respect, we Unitarians and our friends can honor a citizen-scientist even if we are without his unique genius and have not shared his explorations of what goes on within the atom or far away in the stellar universe. Many of us can understand the harassment he endured from the passport division of the State Department, which sought to keep him locked within his own land even when the British Royal Society asked him to lecture in London on the structure of proteins. Dr. Pauling managed to open the lock with the golden key of a Nobel Laureate (as Cedric Belfrage so well phrased it) and, with an invitation to Oslo, received the prize from the King of Sweden.

Linus Pauling taught many of us how to stand firm before inquisitorial committees of the state and federal thought police. It is pleasant to recall his statement to a committee in Washington, which wanted to be reassured one more time that he was not part of a sinister organization exercising thought control. In refusing to repeat his denial, Linus finally declared: "Nobody tells me what to think except Mrs. Pauling." A later inquisitor, Senator Thomas Dodd of the Senate Internal Security Subcommittee, saw to it that the media listed Dr. Pauling's heresies, but omitted his most cogent observation: "The nuclear war age is so lacking in logic that it's hard to say anything logical about it." Senator Dodd, fearing boomerang publicity about himself, did not further press charges for a contempt of congress citation.

There is so much we can all understand about Linus Pauling: his immense courage, his willingness to join in necessary confrontations, his decades of teaching students how to study and think for themselves in and out of the college classroom, his sense of social responsibility to his fellow men and women. Whenever I think of these two people, this joyous partnership of man and wife, I recall Hezekiah Williams' words: "Any knowledge held exclusively by the oppressor is a threat to the oppressed. Let the oppressors own the realm of science and in your ignorance you are owned." Ava Helen and Linus have helped us at the First Unitarian Church of Los Angeles and many others in this catastrophic era to escape this oppression, a deliverance for which, above all, we welcome them tonight. It is also true that we love you deeply and wish you long life and happiness and as many more Nobel prizes as you both want.

Books by Stephen H. Fritchman

Beyond Dogma: A Unitarian Story of Man's Faith in Man. With Henry Leland Clarke, John K. Findly, Harold Koppelman, and Frank Weymouth. Los Angeles: The Hodgin Press, 1956.

The Heretic: A Partisan Autobiography. Boston: Beacon Press, 1977.

Men of Liberty: Ten Unitarian Pioneers. Boston: Beacon Press, 1944; Port Washington, N.Y.: Kennikut Press, 1968.

Prayers of the Free Spirit [Editor]. New York: Women's Press, 1945.

Religious Education Committee in the Local Church. Boston: American Unitarian Association, n.d.

Shall I Be a Unitarian Minister? Boston: American Unitarian Association, n.d.

Teaching Function of the Liberal Church. Boston: American Unitarian Association, n.d.

Together We Advance [Editor]. Boston: Beacon Press, 1946, 1947.

Unitarianism in Transition. Boston: Unitarian Church of the Larger Fellowship, 1960.

Unitarianism Today. Boston: American Unitarian Association, 1950.

Young People in a Liberal Church. Boston: Beacon Press, 1941.

Addresses by Stephen H. Fritchman

*(All addresses are listed in chronological order. The symbol
* indicates that the address is included in this volume.)*

Jan 55   Interview with Dr. Harry F. Ward by SHF on KABC Radio
2 Jan 55   Could We Have Done Better?: A Survey of 1954 ("Religion and Modern Life"—KABC Radio)
16 Jan 55   *The Church and Anticommunism
Feb 55   Challenge of Africa to the Conscience of the World
20 Feb 55   Is Agnosticism the First Step to Mature Religion? ("Religion and Modern Life"—KABC Radio)
27 Feb 55   Church and the Loyalty Oath
Mar 55   *Are We Accepting a Cult of Violence?
27 Mar 55   Opportunity for a Liberal Faith
28 Mar 55   Man and His Survival—Easter 1955
3 Apr 55   How Unitarians Think of Jesus
24 Apr 55   *Eulogy to Dr. Albert Einstein
May 55   *Thou Shalt Not Bear False Witness: The Informer in Contemporary America
1 May 55   *The Indian in America Today
18 May 55   Letter to a Prisoner (a young Unitarian conscientious objector)
June 55   Is There Something Unique in Religion?
26 June 55 Gospel of Univac
Sept 55   Axioms of Freedom: Three Addresses on Unitarianism (printed by Hodgin Press, Los Angeles)
Sept 55   Faith or Skepticism in a Day of Magic
25 Sept 55 Is It Only Now Beginning (on Wesley's Judgment of Julius and Ethel Rosenberg)
Oct 55   City We Live In: How Successful Is Racial Integration in L.A.?
23 Oct 55   Some Peace Perspectives of the United Nations (given in L.A. and San Jose)
Nov 55   Renewal of Life
Dec 55   Children of Divorce
25 Dec 55   Common Cause with Love: A Christmas Message
1956   Beyond Dogma: A Unitarian Story of Man's Faith in Man (SHF and four other authors, Hodgin Press, L.A.)
Jan 56   Signs of a Good Unitarian
1 Jan 56   Year of Decision: A Survey of 1955
22 Jan 56   Canopy of Death: Must L.A. Citizens Live and Die Under Smog?
Feb 56   New Opiates for Old: Religion as a Narcotic Is Still Being Marketed
Mar 56   Challenge of Integration: A Sermon for White Americans (Negro History Week)
11 Mar 56   Message to Montgomery, Alabama (pulpit editorial)
Apr 56   Enduring Graces

July 66   Black Power: Mildred Walter, SHF, Rev. Robert E. Lacey
               (four talks)
24 July 66   Leisure Time: Who Needs It?
31 July 66   Maybe It Is Time for a New Unitarian Rebellion
30 Oct 66   Fine Art of Being a Convincing Hypocrite
Nov 66   White Power: Emergence of Neo-Nazism in the U.S.
6 Nov 66   Of Cabbages and Kings (pulpit editorial)
10 Nov 66   Post Mortem on an Election: Of Governor Ronald Reagan
18 Dec 66   That Great Flying Saucer: The Star of Bethlehem
14 Jan 67   Beginnings and Becoming: Story of the Chalice of Blood
15 Jan 67   School Is a School Is a School
12 Feb 67   Mankind in Shock: Review of Jacques Ellul's Book
17 Feb 62   Vietnam War Teach-In at Cal State Fullerton
19 Feb 67   Exploring the Tribal Village of Marshall McLuhan
5 Mar 65   Joining a Church Is Not Traumatic
19 Mar 67   *The Curse of Vietnam: Brutalization of the American Soul
               (at the University of Victoria [Canada] International Viet-
               nam Seminar)
21 May 67   *The Colossus of the North: The U.S. in Latin America
               Today
21 May 67   *Reply to Doctoral Degree Award Presented by the Starr
               King School for the Ministry in San Rafael, California
4 June 67   Ordination of Roy A. Ockert in Oakland, California
Sept 67   Don't Steal the Mask I Wear
10 Sept 67   Caesar Is Vulnerable: How the American Establishment
               Looks from English Shores
24 Sept 67   Struggle in Greece Is Our Concern
8 Oct 67   *Toward Sanity in the Israeli-Arab Struggle: What Have We
               Learned in the Past Four Months?
26 Nov 67   Credibility Gap and the Unitarians of America
10 Dec 67   First Fifty Years of Soviet Socialism (on visit to USSR in
               November 1967)
17 Dec 67   Can an Over-Thirty Square Comprehend the Hippie
               Rebellion?
4 Feb 68   How Sadistic Are You?
10 Mar 68   Conflict Not Consensus: An Election Sermon
24 Mar 68   Parable of the Sticks: Obligation of the Unitarian Congre-
               gation (given at Santa Barbara Unitarian Church)
31 Mar 68   Unitarianism's Magna Carta: The Diet of Torda; also: Is
               Optimism Dishonest and Irresponsible Today?
5 May 68   Celebration of Cinco de Mayo (Molina); Protest from the
               Barrios (SHF); Cry from the Barrio (Martinez)
9 June 68   Turn Toward Violence in U.S. (memorial for Sen. Robert
               F. Kennedy)

FRITCHMAN, STEPHEN

FOR THE SAKE OF
CLARITY